PERFORMANCE MANAGEMENT

PERFORMANCE MANAGEMENT

FOURTH EDITION

Herman Aguinis
School of Business
George Washington University

CHICAGO
BUSINESS PRESS

CHICAGO
BUSINESS PRESS

© 2019 CHICAGO BUSINESS PRESS

PERFORMANCE MANAGEMENT, FOURTH EDITION

For product information or assistance, visit www.chicagobusinesspress.com

Print Edition ISBN-13: 978-0-9988140-8-7
eBook ISBN-13: 978-0-9988140-9-4

BRIEF CONTENTS

DEDICATION

···

To my daughters Hannah Miriam and Naomi Rebecca, and my wife Heidi, whom I love and admire and are my superb coaches on how to become a better father and husband

CONTENTS

Part IV REWARD SYSTEMS, LEGAL ISSUES, AND TEAM PERFORMANCE MANAGEMENT *299*

PREFACE AND INTRODUCTION

In today's globalized world, it is relatively easy to gain access to the competition's technology and products. Thanks to the Internet and the accompanying high speed of communications, technological and product differentiation is no longer a key competitive advantage in most industries. For example, most banks offer the same types of products (e.g., different types of savings accounts and investment opportunities). If a particular bank decides to offer a new product or service, such as an improved mobile phone app, it will not be long until the competitors offer precisely the same product. As noted by James Kelley, former performance management project leader at Idaho Power, "Technology is a facilitator, but not a guarantor, of effectiveness or efficiency of a company's workforce."[1]

So, what makes some businesses more successful than others? What is today's key competitive advantage? The answer is: people. Organizations with engaged and talented employees offering outstanding service to customers pull ahead of the competition, even if the products offered are similar to those offered by the competitors. This is a key organizational resource that many label "human capital" or "talent" and gives organizations an advantage over the competition.[2] Customers want to get the right answer at the right time and they want to receive their products or services promptly and accurately. Having the right human capital can make these things happen. Only human capital can produce a sustainable competitive advantage. And performance management systems are the key tools that can be used to transform people's talent and motivation into a strategic business advantage.

Unfortunately, performance management is not living up to its promise in terms of turning human capital into a source of competitive advantage. For example, consider Mercer's 2013 Global Performance Management Survey, which gathered data from more than 1,050 performance management leaders representing 53 countries. These organizations varied in size from about 1,000 to more than 10,000, and represented several types of industries (e.g., for-profit, nonprofit, government). A very troubling result was that only 3 percent reported that their performance management system delivers exceptional value. Also, many aspects of organizations' performance management approach were evaluated as ineffective.[3] So, there is big disconnect between the *potential* that performance

---

[1]Generating buzz: Idaho Power takes on performance management to prepare for workforce aging. (2006, June). *Power Engineering*. Retrieved January 3, 2018, from http://www.powergenworldwide.com/index/display/articledisplay/258477/articles/power-engineering/volume-110/issue-6/features/generating-buzz-idaho-power-takes-on-performance-management-to-prepare-for-workforce-aging.html

[2]Cascio, W. F., & Aguinis, H. (2019). *Applied psychology in talent management* (8th ed.). Thousand Oaks, CA: Sage.

[3]*2013 Global Performance Management Survey*. Mercer. Retrieved January 3, 2018, from https://www.mercer.com/content/dam/mercer/attachments/global/Talent/Assess-BrochurePerfMgmt.pdf

management has in terms of turning human capital into an organization's source of competitive advantage and the actual role of performance management in most organizations. As noted in Mercer's report, "Establishing an effective employee performance management system is a major challenge for most organizations, making performance management a perennial hot topic . . . companies around the world are regularly in search of best practices and new solutions for this core process." And hence, the need for this book.

I am delighted to offer this fourth edition in partnership with Chicago Business Press. You will find this edition much updated and improved in terms of content, as well as easier to read because of its improved and more user-friendly layout and design. This fourth edition includes the following ten important changes. More detailed information on each of these issues is provided in the section titled "Improvements in this Fourth Edition."

- Each of the chapters includes updated content and material, new sources, and new sections (but the book is similarly concise as the previous edition).
- This edition highlights the role of context within which performance management takes place.
- This fourth edition describes the key "strategic partner" and "internal consultant" role played by the HR function in the design and implementation of the performance management system.
- There is an emphasis on the changing nature of work and organizations, including globalization, technology and Big Data, team work, and demographics (e.g., generational differences), and how these changes affect the design and implementation of performance management systems.
- This fourth edition emphasizes that knowledge generated regarding performance management is essentially multidisciplinary.
- This edition emphasizes the important interplay between science and practice.
- This edition describes the technical aspects of implementing a performance management system in detail, and, in addition, emphasizes the key role that interpersonal and social dynamics play in the process.
- This edition includes new "Company Spotlights" boxes in each chapter featuring The Gap, Sears, Yahoo, Adobe, United States Department of Defense, Discover, Google, Airbnb, Sprint, Xerox, Deloitte, GE, and many others.
- This fourth edition includes two new hands-on "Exercises" at the end of each chapter—for a total of 22.
- This new edition also includes two case studies at the end of each chapter, also for a total of 22.

SOME UNIQUE FEATURES OF THIS BOOK

Performance management is a continuous process of identifying, measuring, and developing the performance of individuals and teams and aligning their performance with the strategic goals of the organization. Performance management is critical to small and large, for-profit and not-for-profit, and domestic and global organizations, and to all industries. In fact, the performance management model and processes described in this book have been used to create systems to manage the performance of students in colleges and universities[4] and employees in small and medium enterprises (SMEs).[5] After all, the performance of an organization depends on the performance of its people, regardless of the organization's size, purpose, and other characteristics. As noted by former Siemens CEO Heinrich von Pierer, "Whether a company measures its workforce in hundreds or hundreds of thousands, its success relies solely on individual performance." As an example in the not-for-profit sector, Youth Villages, a private child welfare provider operating in 12 states and the District of Columbia, has gained national recognition for its evidence-based performance management system. By tracking performance data on children and families, both during and after leaving care, Youth Villages is able to better understand its program outcomes and effectiveness in delivering social value to the community. The information collected from the performance management system is also used to manage employee performance, assess the achievement of strategic goals, and upper-management decision making. The performance management system provides a detailed description of practices to help guide implementation, the metrics used to quantify performance, and how employees are scored on whether they adhere to those metrics.[6]

Unfortunately, few organizations use their existing performance management systems in effective ways. Performance management is usually vilified as an "HR department requirement." In many organizations, performance management means that managers must comply with their HR department's request and fill out tedious, and often useless, evaluation forms. These evaluation forms are often completed only because it is required by the "HR cops." Unfortunately, the only tangible consequence of the evaluation process is that managers have to spend time away from their "real" job duties.

In the latest wave of criticisms of performance management, performance ratings are now the target. Also, there is quite a bit of popular media and business press hype about the "demise" of performance evaluation, performance measurement, and performance reviews. Currently, many companies, including GE, Microsoft, Google, Yahoo, Adobe, and Accenture, are going through a similar process of transitioning from a performance appraisal (i.e., dreaded once-a-year evaluation and review) to a performance management system (i.e., ongoing evaluation and feedback). However, contrary to the way this trend is usually described in business publications and the media with such headlines as "Performance Evaluation is Dead" and "The End of Performance Reviews," the evaluation of performance is not going away. In fact, performance assessment and review are becoming a normal, routine, built-in, and ever-present aspect of work in twenty-first-century organizations. As described in this text since its first edition published in 2008, performance management systems play a critical role and serve important purposes.

[4]Gillespie, T. L., & Parry, R. O. (2009). Students as employees: Applying performance management principles in the management classroom. *Journal of Management Education, 33,* 553–576.
[5]Na-Nan, K., Chaiprasit, K., & Pukkeeree, P. (2017). Performance management in SME high-growth sectors and high-impact sectors in Thailand: Mixed method research. *International Journal of Engineering Business Management, 9,* 1–8.
[6]Kamensky, J. M. (2016). Tennessee child-services provider's performance-management system offers balanced scorecard of metrics. *Government Technology.* Retrieved January 3, 2018, from http://www.govtech.com/opinion/Tennesee-Child-Services-Providers-Performance-Management-System-Offers-Balanced-Scorecard-of-Metrics.html

So, it is not the case that companies are abandoning ratings and performance measurement and evaluation. They are actually implementing performance systems more clearly aligned with best practices, as described in this text, that involve a *constant and ongoing evaluation of performance*! The companies mentioned above and many others in all industries, including government, such as the United States National Security Agency (NSA), have eliminated the labels "performance evaluation," "performance review," and even "performance management." Instead, they use labels such as "performance achievement," "talent evaluation and advancement," "check-ins," and "employee development." But they still implement performance management, but use new, more fashionable, and perhaps less threatening labels. It has been extremely gratifying to see the transition of so many companies from performance appraisal to performance management, as has been described since the first edition of this text more than 10 years ago. To sum this up by paraphrasing Mark Twain, we can say with certainty that the death of performance management has been vastly exaggerated.

This book is about the design and implementation of effective and successful performance management systems. In other words, it focuses on research-based findings and up-to-date applications that help increase an organization's talent pool. Performance management is ongoing and cyclical; however, for pedagogical reasons, the book needs to follow a linear structure. Because performance observation, evaluation, and improvement are ongoing processes, some concepts and practices may be introduced early in a cursory manner, but receive more detailed treatment in later sections. In addition, many issues such as training of raters and employee development will be discussed in multiple chapters. So, you will see that several chapters may refer to similar issues. When this happens, content included in more than one chapter will be cross-referenced.

Finally, this book focuses on best practices and describes the necessary steps to create a top-notch performance management system. As a result of practical constraints and lack of knowledge about system design and implementation, many organizations cut corners and do not have systems that follow best practices. Environmental and political issues (e.g., goals of raters may not be aligned with goals of the organization) also play a role. Because the way in which systems are implemented in practice is often not close to the ideal system, the book includes numerous examples from actual organizations to illustrate how systems are implemented, given actual situational constraints.

IMPROVEMENTS IN THIS FOURTH EDITION

As mentioned earlier, this edition includes ten important changes throughout the book. First, this edition includes important updates and additional information. In preparation for revising and updating this book, I gathered more than 2,000 potentially relevant articles and books. More than 250 of those sources are now included in this edition. These sources have been published since the third edition of the book went into production. This vast literature demonstrates an increased interest in performance management on the part of both academics and practitioners.

Second, there is an emphasis on the role of the context within which performance management takes place. Performance management does not operate in a vacuum. Rather, it takes place within a particular organizational context, and organizations have a particular history, and unwritten norms about what is valued and what is not (i.e., an organization's culture). Also, they have unwritten norms about communication, trust, interpersonal relations, and many other factors that influence daily activities. Thus, for example, implementing an upward feedback system may be effective in some organizations, but not in others (Chapter 8). As a second illustration, some organizations may have a culture that emphasizes results more than behaviors which, in turn, would dictate that the performance management system also emphasize results; instead, other organizations may place an emphasis on long-term goals, which would dictate that performance be measured by emphasizing employee behaviors, rather than results (Chapter 4). Also, we need to understand the contextual reasons why, sometimes, performance ratings may not be accurate—particularly if there is no accountability for raters to provide valid assessments (Chapter 6). As yet another example, cultural factors affect what sources are used for performance information. In a country such as Jordan, whose culture determines more hierarchical organizational structures, the almost exclusive source of performance information is supervisors, whereas employees and their peers almost have no input; this situation is different in countries with less hierarchical cultures in which not only performance information is collected from peers, but also supervisors are rated by their direct reports (Chapter 6). To emphasize the role of national culture, this edition describes examples and research conducted in organizations in the United States and Canada, but also Jordan, Japan, China, Turkey, Eritrea, Germany, Spain, South Korea, Mexico, Australia, the United Kingdom, Brazil, India, and others.

Third, this edition describes two key roles played by the HR function: strategic partner and internal consultant. Regarding the first role, the HR function is unfortunately often vilified as being merely operational and not able to think or act strategically. Well, over the past two decades or so, an entire new field of research has emerged called "strategic human resource management." Strategic human resource management is about planning and implementing HR policies and activities with the goal of enabling an organization to achieve its strategic goals.[7] Performance management is an ideal vehicle to demonstrate the strategic role of the HR function because it allows for explicit and clear linkages between an organization's mission, vision, and objectives, and individual and team performance. By helping implement a successful performance management system, the HR function can get a "seat at the table" of the top management team. In fact, the few CEOs with HR background, including Samuel R. Allen at John Deere, James C. Smith at Thomson Reuters, Steven L. Newman at Transocean, and Mary Barra at General Motors have been able to serve as strategic partners, which is, in large part, what propelled their trajectory from an HR role to the very top of their organizations. Second, the HR function serves as an internal consultant for all organizational members participating in the performance management system. For example, it offers advice on how to measure performance, resources in the form of training opportunities, and can also lead the strategic planning process. So, although the HR function is certainly not the "owner" of the performance management system, it adds value by playing a key role in its design and implementation.

[7]Wright, P. M., & Ulrich, M. D. (2017). A road well traveled: The past, present, and future journey of strategic human resource management. *Annual Review of Organizational Behavior and Organizational Psychology, 4*, 45–65.

Fourth, this edition highlights important changes in the nature of work and organizations and how these changes have a direct impact on the design and implementation of performance management systems. These changes involve issues about globalization, technology, and demographics. Regarding globalization, consider the example of a firm that is based in the United States, does its software programming in Sri Lanka, its engineering in Germany, its manufacturing in China, and has a call center in Brazil. How do we design a successful performance management system that takes into account the fact that employees work together across time zones on a daily basis without having ever met in person—although they have regular interactions using Skype? Regarding technology, companies are now able to gather employee data that was simply unimaginable just a few years ago—what is usually called "Big Data." For example, the use of GPS allows companies to track the location of its sales force real-time 24/7. Also, Web and mobile access allows employees to provide and receive feedback on an ongoing basis from anywhere and at any time. The availability of data offers almost unlimited opportunities to measure different facets of performance, but also creates challenges and the need to understand the different between "Big Data" and "Smart Data." Third, regarding team work, there is hardly any job that is done without working with others. These changes highlight the importance and pervasiveness of teams, and the need for a performance management system to include a formal team management component—as well as consider different types of teams such as virtual teams. Fourth, regarding demographic changes, because baby boomers are retiring in large numbers, members of Generation X, Generation Y or Millennials, and Generation Z or Post-Millennials are now entering the workforce in large number. Gen X and Gen Y employees are "digital natives" and are used to immediate feedback—just like when receiving a grade immediately after completing a Web-based exam in high school and college. A successful performance management system must consider generational differences to be successful.

Fifth, this edition emphasizes that knowledge generated regarding performance management is essentially multidisciplinary. Accordingly, the sources used to support best-practice recommendations offered in this book come from a very diverse set of fields of study, ranging from micro-level fields focusing on the study of individual and teams (e.g., organizational behavior, human resource management) to macro-level fields focusing on the study of organizations as a whole (e.g., strategic management, accounting, information systems, engineering). This is consistent with a general movement toward multidisciplinary and integrative research in the field of management.[8] For example, best-practice recommendations regarding performance management analytics originate primarily from industrial and organizational psychology (Chapter 5). On the other hand, best-practice recommendations regarding the relation between performance management and strategic planning were derived primarily from theories and research from strategic management studies (Chapter 3). In addition, much of the best-practice recommendations regarding team performance management originated from the field of organizational behavior (Chapter 11).

Sixth, this edition emphasizes the important interplay between science and practice. Unfortunately, there is a great divide in management and related fields

[8]Aguinis, H., Boyd, B. K., Pierce, C. A., & Short, J. C. (2011). Walking new avenues in management research methods and theories: Bridging micro and macro domains. *Journal of Management, 37*, 395–403.

between scholars and practitioners. From the perspective of scholars, much of the work conducted by practitioners is seen as relevant, but not rigorous. Conversely, from the perspective of practitioners, the work done by scholars is seen as rigorous, but mostly not relevant. This "science-practice divide" has been documented by a content analysis of highly prestigious scholarly journals, which regularly publish research results that do not seem directly relevant to the needs of managers and organizations.[9] This edition attempts to bridge this divide by discussing best-practice recommendations based on sound theory and research, and at the same time, discussing the realities of organizations and how some of these practices have been implemented in actual organizations.[10]

Seventh, this edition, as its predecessor, describes the technical aspects of implementing a performance management system in detail. In addition, this edition emphasizes the key role that interpersonal dynamics play in the process.[11] Traditionally, much of the performance appraisal literature has focused almost exclusively on ratings and the measurement of performance—for example, whether it is better to use 5-point versus 7-point scales. However, more recent research suggests that issues such as trust, politics, leadership, negotiation, mentorship, communication, and other topics related to interpersonal dynamics are just as important in determining the success of a performance management system. Accordingly, this edition discusses the need to establish a helping and trusting relationship between supervisors and employees (Chapter 9), the role of an organization's top management in determining the success of a system (Chapter 3), and the motivation of supervisors to provide accurate performance ratings (Chapter 6), among many other related issues throughout the book.

Eighth, this edition includes "company spotlight" boxes in every chapter. The addition of these application boxes is important because they serve the purpose of illustrating the concepts described in each chapter using contemporary examples. Also, these boxes will allow you to see how performance management is done in real organizations as well as allow you to think about some thorny, and, in some cases, unresolved issues. Some of the organizations featured in this fourth edition include The Gap, Sears, Yahoo, Adobe, United States Department of Defense, Discover, Google, Airbnb, Sprint, Dollar General, Xerox, Intermex, BT Global Services, Accenture, Deloitte, GE, and many others—including several less-known SMEs.

Ninth, this fourth edition includes new hands-on "Exercises" at the end of each chapter. These hands-one exercises will make learning the material more fun, and also enhance the pedagogical experience of your course—particularly for graduate- and executive-level courses. In total, this edition includes 22 exercises (i.e., two per chapter).

Finally, this new edition includes two case studies in each chapter, also for a total of 22. In addition, the instructor's manual includes approximately several more cases per chapter, for a total of about 40 additional ones. Thus, depending on an instructor's preference, a course based on this new edition could be

[9]Cascio, W. F., & Aguinis, H. (2008). Research in industrial and organizational psychology from 1963 to 2007: Changes, choices, and trends. *Journal of Applied Psychology, 93*, 1062–1081.
[10]Levy, P. E., Tseng, S. T., Rosen, C. C., & Lueke, S. B. (2017). Performance management: A marriage between practice and science—Just say "I do." *Research in Personnel and Human Resources Management, 35*, 155–213.
[11]Aguinis, H., & Pierce, C. A. (2008). Enhancing the relevance of organizational behavior by embracing performance management research. *Journal of Organizational Behavior, 29*, 139–145.

taught entirely following a case format, experiential format, a lecture format, or a combination of the three.

In addition to the aforementioned changes that permeate the entire book, each chapter includes new sections. As illustrations, consider the following chapter-by-chapter nonexhaustive additions:

- Chapter 1: Expanded material on the contributions of performance management, expanded material on dangers of poorly implemented performance management systems, discussion of the elimination of performance ratings, impact of technological advancements, Big Data, and demographic changes on performance management.
- Chapter 2: Expansion of job to work analysis, introduction of carelessness bias, expanded description of O*NET, new material regarding "check-ins," and new discussion of steps for conducting productive performance reviews.
- Chapter 3: Why and how the HR function plays the role of strategic partner, discussion of the balanced scorecard and the strategy map, the critical role of the HR function in the strategic planning process, and expanded discussion of SWOT and gap analysis.
- Chapter 4: Definition of performance as both behaviors and results, expanded discussion of determinants of performance including abilities and other traits (including personality), knowledge and skills, and context (e.g., HR policies, organizational and national culture, resources and opportunity to perform), expanded discussion of counterproductive performance; and new material on adaptive performance.
- Chapter 5: Expanded discussion of management by objectives (MBO) and goal setting, the transition of many companies from a performance appraisal (i.e., dreaded once-a-year evaluation and review) to a performance management system (i.e., ongoing evaluation and feedback), the evolution of forced distribution systems, the apparent abandonment of performance ratings, and new material on the nature of the performance distribution and star performers.
- Chapter 6: Emphasis on performance analytics, discussion of performance management systems "without ratings," expanded discussion on how to make appraisal forms more useful, expanded discussion on the nature of and number of formal review meetings, advantages and disadvantages of collecting performance data from different performance "touchpoints" (e.g., supervisors, peers, direct reports, customers), and new material on employee performance monitoring and big data.
- Chapter 7: How to address cognitive biases and resistance to change when rolling out the performance management system, and training programs for minimizing unintentional rating errors.
- Chapter 8: The development of career competencies, expanded discussion of developmental activities, the role of the direct supervisor in the creation and completion of the employee's development plan, and multisource feedback systems.
- Chapter 9: New emphasis on performance management leadership, evidence of the benefits of coaching, expanded discussion on how to give praise and constructive (i.e., "negative") feedback and using a strengths-based approach to giving feedback, generational and individual differences regarding feedback reactions and preferences, making tough

calls such as disciplinary process and organizational exit, and expanded material on coaching, development, and performance review meetings.

- Chapter 10: Expanded material on work–life focus and relational (i.e., intangible, nonfinancial) returns, expanded discussion on problems resulting from contingent pay plans, how to turn recognition and other nonfinancial incentives into rewards, discussion of the latest legal developments regarding performance management, performance management legal issues faced by organizations operating across national borders, discussion of more recent cases regarding major legal principles (e.g., negligence, defamation, illegal discrimination), and laws affecting performance management in the United States, Canada, Australia, Germany, and Spain.

- Chapter 11: Discussion of team-based organization design, new material on performance management for virtual teams, characteristics of effective team charters, skills needed for team leaders to turn teams with B-players into winning teams, and knowledge, skills, and abilities needed to be an effective team member.

ORGANIZATION OF THE BOOK

Part I, which includes Chapters 1 through 3, addresses general as well as strategic considerations regarding performance management. Chapter 1 discusses the advantages of implementing a successful performance management system, as well as the negative outcomes associated with deficient systems, including lowered employee motivation and perceptions of unfairness. This chapter also includes the features of an ideal system. Chapter 2 describes the performance management process, starting with what should be done before a system is implemented and ending with the performance review stage. Chapter 3 links performance management systems with an organization's strategic plan. This chapter makes it clear that a good performance management system is a critical component of the successful implementation of an organization's strategy.

Part II, including Chapters 4 through 7, addresses the details of system implementation. This discussion is sufficiently general, yet detailed enough so that all managers, not just HR managers, will benefit from this material. Chapters 4 and 5 describe some of the technical aspects associated with the assessment of performance and how to identify and measure both behaviors and results. Chapter 6 discusses performance analytics and discusses the advantages and disadvantages of using various sources of performance information (e.g., supervisor, peers, and customers). Finally, Chapter 7 describes the steps involved in rolling out the new performance management system or changes in an existing system, including a communication plan and pilot testing of the system before it is implemented.

Part III, including Chapters 8 and 9, addresses employee and leadership development issues. Chapter 8 includes a description of employee development plans and the advantages of using multisource feedback systems for developmental purposes. Chapter 9 addresses the skills needed by supervisors to become true "performance management leaders."

Part IV, including Chapters 10 and 11, concerns the relationship among performance management, rewards, the law, and teams. Chapter 10 includes a discussion of different types of rewards (including relational or intangible rewards), traditional and contingent pay plans, and their links to performance management. In addition, this chapter provides a discussion of legal issues to consider when implementing a performance management system. Finally, Chapter 11 addresses the timely topic of how to design and implement performance management systems dealing specifically with team performance.

FACULTY AND STUDENT RESOURCES

Each of the chapters includes a list of its actionable learning objectives at the beginning as well as summary points at the end, two hands-on exercises, and two case studies for discussion. I hope this material will allow students to have an enjoyable and productive learning experience that will enhance your own individual human capital. Also, there are additional resources available for instructors, including PowerPoint slides, exam questions and answers (multiple choice and essay-type), and additional case studies that can be used for in-class discussions or also as examination materials or take-home homework or examinations. These materials will allow instructors to prepare for teaching this course quicker, and also make teaching this course a more enjoyable and interactive experience. These faculty resources can be requested by visiting www.chicagobusinesspress.com.

ACKNOWLEDGMENTS

I would like to thank several individuals who were extremely instrumental in allowing me to write the first, second, third, and current fourth edition of this book. I am indebted to Graeme Martin for encouraging me to start this project more than a decade ago. Nawaf Alabduljader and Ravi S. Ramani helped me gather the numerous examples and illustrations that I have used throughout in the fourth edition. Wendy O'Connell, Jon Dale, and Barbara Stephens helped me update many of these examples in the previous editions. Christine Henle allowed me to use her extremely useful lecture notes in previous editions. Nawaf Alabduljader and Ravi S. Ramani also assisted me in writing the Instructor's Manual for this fourth edition. Teaching and giving lectures and workshops on performance management at the Instituto de Empresa (Madrid, Spain), Université Jean Moulin Lyon 3 (Lyon, France), University of Johannesburg (South Africa), University of Salamanca (Spain), and University of Melbourne (Australia) allowed me to pilot test and improve various sections of the book. Also, I would like to thank my publisher, Paul Ducham of Chicago Business Press, for his outstanding professionalism. I am delighted to have Paul as my partner for this fourth edition. Finally, this fourth edition benefited greatly from the feedback provided by the following individuals who have used the third edition to teach courses at universities throughout the United States and Canada, and were kind enough to offer their suggestions for improvements and additions:

Stan Arnold, *Humber College*
Christine R. Day, *Eastern Michigan University*
Eric Ecklund, *Saint Francis University*
Douglas Flint, *University of New Brunswick*
David Garic, *Tulane University*
Kathleen Gosser, *University of Louisville*
Alan P. Huston, *Portland State University*
Denise Kestner, *Franklin University*
Kenneth S. Shultz, *California State University, San Bernardino*
Therese A. Sprinkle, *Quinnipiac University*
Thomas Timmerman, *Tennessee Technological University*
Bruce E. Winston, *Regent University*
Colette M. Young, *Washtenaw Community College*

I thank each of you for your time and intellectual investment in this project. Your coaching and feedback certainly helped me improve my performance!

Herman Aguinis
Washington, D.C.

ABOUT THE AUTHOR

Dr. Herman Aguinis is the Avram Tucker Distinguished Scholar and Professor of Management at George Washington University School of Business. Previously, he was the John F. Mee Chair of Management and the Founding and Managing Director of the Institute for Global Organizational Effectiveness in the Kelley School of Business, Indiana University. He has been a visiting scholar at universities in the People's Republic of China (Beijing and Hong Kong), Malaysia, Singapore, Argentina, France, Spain, Puerto Rico, Australia, and South Africa. His research, teaching, and consulting activities focus on the acquisition, development, and deployment of talent in organizations. Dr. Aguinis has written and edited five books, including *Applied Psychology in Talent Management* (with Wayne F. Cascio, 8th ed., 2019, Sage) and *Regression Analysis for Categorical Moderators* (2004, Guilford). In addition, he has written about 150 refereed journal articles in *Academy of Management Journal, Academy of Management Review, Strategic Management Journal, Journal of Applied Psychology*, and elsewhere. Dr. Aguinis has been elected to serve as President of the Academy of Management (AOM), and is a Fellow of AOM, the American Psychological Association, the Society for Industrial and Organizational Psychology, and the Association for Psychological Science. He has served as President of the Iberoamerican Academy of Management, Division Chair for the Research Methods Division of the Academy of Management, and editor-in-chief for the journal *Organizational Research Methods*. He has delivered about 250 presentations and keynote addresses at professional conferences, delivered more than 120 invited presentations in all seven continents except for Antarctica, raised about $5MM for his research and teaching endeavors from private foundations and federal sources (e.g., National Science Foundation), and consulted with numerous organizations in the United States, Europe, and Latin America. Among the many awards he has received are the 2017 Losey Award by the Society for Human Resource Management Foundation for lifetime achievement in human resource research, the Academy of Management Practice Theme Committee Scholar Practice Impact Award recognizing an outstanding scholar who has had an impact on policymaking and managerial and organizational practices, Academy of Management Research Methods Division Distinguished Career Award for lifetime contributions; Academy of Management Entrepreneurship Division IDEA Thought Leader Award, and Best Article of Year Awards from five refereed journals. His research has been featured by *The Economist, Forbes, BusinessWeek, National Public Radio, USA Today, Univision*, Mujer Actual (Spain), and La Nación (Argentina), among many other outlets. For more information, please visit http://www.hermanaguinis.com

part one

Strategic and General Considerations

1

Performance Management in Context

People think they're too busy for performance management. That's your number one job

–Jack Welch

Learning Objectives

By the end of this chapter, you will be able to do the following:

1. Compare and contrast the concepts of performance management and performance appraisal.

2. Appraise strategic, administrative, informational, developmental, organizational maintenance, and documentation purposes of performance management.

3. Create a presentation providing persuasive arguments to argue for the business case and benefits for employees, managers, and organizations of implementing a well-designed performance management system.

4. Assess the multiple negative consequences that can arise from the poor design and implementation of a performance management system.

5. Judge the extent to which dysfunctional performance ratings may be signs that the performance management system is broken.

6. Prepare a list of the key features of an ideal performance management system.

7. Propose relationships and links between performance management and other human resources functions, including recruitment and selection, training and development, workforce planning, and compensation.

8. Assess the impact of globalization and technological and demographic changes on the design and implementation of performance management systems.

1-1 DEFINITION OF PERFORMANCE MANAGEMENT

Consider the following scenario:

> Sally is a sales manager at a pharmaceutical company. The fiscal year will end in one week. She is overwhelmed with end-of-the-year tasks, including reviewing the budget she is likely to be allocated for the following year, responding to customers' phone calls, dealing with vendors, and supervising a group of 10 salespeople. It's a very hectic time, probably the most hectic time of the year. She receives a phone call from the human resources (HR) department: "Sally, we have not received your performance reviews for your 10 direct reports; they are due by the end of the fiscal year." Sally thinks, "Oh, again, those performance reviews . . . . What a waste of my time!" From Sally's point of view, there is no value in filling out those seemingly meaningless forms. She does not see her direct reports in action because they are in the field, visiting customers most of the time. All that she knows about their performance is based on sales figures, which depend more on the products offered and geographic territory covered than the individual effort and motivation of each salesperson. And based on her own experience, she thinks that little will happen in terms of compensation and rewards, regardless of her ratings. These are lean times in her organization, and salary adjustments are based on seniority rather than on merit. She has less than three days to turn in her forms. What will she do? In the end, she decides to follow the path of least resistance: to please her employees and give everyone the maximum possible rating. In this way, Sally believes the employees will be happy with their ratings and she will not have to deal with complaints or follow-up meetings. Sally fills out the forms in less than 15 minutes and gets back to her "real job."

There is something very wrong with this picture, which unfortunately happens all too frequently in many organizations and across industries. Although Sally's HR department calls this process "performance management," it is not.

Performance management is a *continuous process of identifying, measuring, and developing the performance of individuals and teams and aligning performance with the strategic goals of the organization.* Let's consider each of the definition's two main components in more detail:

1. *Continuous process.* Performance management is ongoing. It involves an ongoing process of setting goals and objectives, observing performance, talking about performance, and giving and receiving ongoing coaching and feedback.[1]

2. *Alignment with strategic goals.* Performance management requires that managers ensure that employees' activities and outputs are congruent with the organization's goals, and consequently, help the organization gain a competitive advantage.[2] Performance management therefore creates a direct link between employee and team performance and organizational goals, and makes the employees' contribution to the organization explicit.

Just like in the case of Sally, many organizations have what is labeled a "performance management" system. However, we must distinguish between performance management and performance appraisal. A system that involves employee evaluations once a year without an ongoing effort to provide feedback and coaching so that performance can be improved is not a true performance management system. Instead, this is only a performance appraisal system. Performance appraisal is the measurement and description of an employee's strengths and weaknesses. Thus, performance appraisal is an important component of performance management, but it is just a part of a bigger whole because performance management is much more than just performance measurement.[3]

As an illustration, consider how Bank of America Merrill Lynch has transitioned from a performance appraisal system to a performance management system. Merrill Lynch was acquired by Bank of America in 2009, and then, merged into Bank of America Corporation in October 2013, creating Bank of America Merrill Lynch, which is one of the world's leading financial management and advisory companies. Specifically, it employs more than 15,000 financial advisors in offices in about 35 countries and manages private client assets of approximately US$2.2 trillion. As an investment bank, it is a leading global underwriter of debt and equity securities and strategic advisor to corporations, governments, institutions, and individuals worldwide. Bank of America Merrill Lynch started the transition from giving employees one performance appraisal per year to focusing on one of the important principles of performance management: the conversation between managers and employees in which feedback is exchanged and coaching is given, if needed. In January, employees and managers set employee objectives. Mid-year reviews assess what progress has been made toward the goals and how personal development plans are faring. Finally, the end-of-the-year review incorporates feedback from several sources, evaluates progress toward objectives, and identifies areas that need improvement. Managers also get extensive training on how to set objectives and conduct reviews. In addition, there is a website that managers can access with information on all aspects of the performance management system. In sharp contrast to their old performance appraisal system, Bank of America Merrill Lynch's goal for its newly implemented performance management program is worded as follows: "This is what is expected of you, this is how we're going to help you in your development, and this is how you'll be judged relative to compensation."[4]

As a second example, consider the performance management system for managers at Germany-based Siemens, which used to focus on mobile phones, computer networks, and wireless technology. Siemens' current areas are electrification, automation, and digitalization. It is the largest industrial manufacturing company in Europe and employs more than 350,000 people in 190 countries. One of the world's largest producers of energy-efficient, resource-saving technologies, Siemens is a leading supplier of systems for power generation and transmission as well as medical diagnosis, and in 2015, its global revenue totaled around €75.6 billion. At Siemens, the performance management system is based on three pillars: setting clear and measurable goals, implementing concrete actions, and imposing rigorous consequences. The performance management at Siemens has helped change people's mind-set, and the organization is now truly performance-oriented. Every manager understands that performance is a critical aspect of working at Siemens, and this guiding philosophy is communicated in many ways throughout the organization.[5]

Much like those that focus on performance appraisal only, performance management systems that do not make explicit the employee contribution to the organizational goals are not true performance management systems. Making an explicit link between employee and team performance objectives and the organizational goals also serves the purpose of establishing a shared understanding about what is to be achieved and how it is to be achieved. This is painfully clear in Sally's case described earlier: from her point of view, the performance review forms did not provide any useful information regarding the contribution of each of her direct reports to the organization. Sally's case is, unfortunately, more common than we would like. For example, a survey of 13,000 employees worldwide conducted by the Corporate Executive Board (CEB) found that about 95% of managers are not satisfied with their organization's performance management system. Moreover, 66% of employees say that the performance review process not only does not help, but actually *interferes* with their productivity![6]

Our discussion thus far makes it clear that performance management systems serve multiple purposes. The information collected by a performance management system is most frequently used for salary administration, performance feedback, and the identification of employee strengths and weaknesses. In general, however, performance management systems can serve the following six purposes: strategic, administrative, informational, developmental, organizational maintenance, and documentation purposes.[7] Let's consider each of these purposes next.

1-2 PURPOSES OF PERFORMANCE MANAGEMENT SYSTEMS

1-2-1 Strategic Purpose

The first purpose of performance management systems is to help top management achieve strategic business objectives. By linking the organization's goals with individual and team goals, the performance management system reinforces behaviors consistent with the attainment of organizational goals. Moreover, even if, for some reason, individual goals are not achieved, linking individual and team goals with organizational goals serves as a way to communicate the most crucial business strategic initiatives. As an example of how this is accomplished at Sears, see Box 1-1.

A second strategic purpose of performance management systems is that they play an important role in the *onboarding* process.[8] Onboarding refers to the processes that lead new employees to transition from being organizational outsiders to organizational insiders. Performance management serves as a catalyst for onboarding because it allows new employees to understand the types of behaviors and results that are valued and rewarded, which, in turn, lead to an understanding of the organization's culture and its values.

1-2-2 Administrative Purpose

A second function of performance management systems is to furnish valid and useful information for making administrative decisions about employees. Such administrative decisions include salary adjustments, promotions, employee retention or termination, recognition of superior individual performance, identification of high-potential employees, identification of poor performers, layoffs, and merit increases. Therefore, the implementation of reward systems based on information provided by the performance management system falls within the administrative purpose. For example, the government in Turkey mandates

Box 1-1

Company Spotlight: How Sears Uses Performance Management to Focus on Strategic Business Priorities

The top management team at Sears is utilizing performance management practices and principles to align human resources with business strategy. Headquartered in Hoffman Estates, Illinois, Sears is the 18th largest retailing company in the United States. And it is the fifth largest American department store company by sales, (behind Walmart, Target, Best Buy, and The Home Depot), and the third largest broadline retailer in the United States, with approximately US$22.14 billion in annual revenues and approximately 651 retail stores. Sears is a home appliance retailer and offers tools, lawn and garden products, home electronics, and automotive repair and maintenance. Following the merger with Kmart Corp. and Sears, Roebuck & Co., Aylwin B. Lewis was promoted to chief executive and tasked with a strategic culture change initiative in hopes of reinvigorating the struggling retail company. A strategic objective is to move from an inward focus to a customer service approach. A second key objective is to bring about an entrepreneurial spirit, where store managers strive for financial literacy and are challenged to identify opportunities for greater profits. Several aspects of the performance management system are being utilized to achieve these strategic objectives. For example, employee duties and objectives are being revised so that employees will spend less time in back rooms and more time interacting with customers to facilitate purchases and understand customer needs. In addition, leadership communication with employees and face-to-face interaction are being encouraged. Lewis, who is now CEO of Potbelly, used to spend three days per week in stores with employees and frequently quizzed managers on their knowledge, such as asking about profit margins for a given department. The greatest compliment employees receive is to be referred to as "commercial" or someone who can identify opportunities for profits. All Sears headquarters employees are also required to spend a day working in a store, which many had never done before. Executive management has identified 500 employees who are considered potential leaders who are given training and development opportunities specifically aimed at cultural and strategic changes. In sum, the performance management system at Sears is used as a strategic tool to change Sears' culture because senior management views encouraging key desired behaviors as critical to the company's success in the marketplace.[9]

performance management systems in all public organizations in that country with the aim to prevent favoritism, corruption, and bribery, and also, to emphasize the importance of impartiality and merit in administrative decisions.[10]

1-2-3 Informational Purpose

Performance management systems serve as an important communication device. First, they inform employees about how they are doing and provide them with information on specific areas that may need improvement. Second, related to the strategic purpose, they provide information regarding expectations of peers, supervisors, customers, and the organization, and what aspects of work are most important.

1-2-4 Developmental Purpose

As noted earlier, feedback is an important component of a well-implemented performance management system. This feedback should be used in a developmental manner. Specifically, managers can use feedback to coach employees and improve performance on an ongoing basis. This feedback allows for the identification of strengths and weaknesses of employees as well as the causes for performance deficiencies (which could be due to individual, team, or contextual factors). Of course, feedback is useful only to the extent that remedial action is taken and concrete steps are implemented to remedy any deficiencies. Feedback is useful only when employees are willing to receive it. Organizations should strive to create a "feedback culture" that reflects support for feedback, including feedback that is nonthreatening and is focused on behaviors and coaching to help interpret the feedback provided.[11]

Another aspect of the developmental purpose is that employees receive information about themselves that can help them individualize their career paths. For example, by learning about their strengths, they are better able to chart a more successful path for their future. Thus, the developmental purpose refers to both short-term and long-term aspects of development.

1-2-5 Organizational Maintenance Purpose

A fifth purpose of performance management systems is to provide information to be used in workforce planning. Workforce planning comprises a set of systems that allows organizations to anticipate and respond to needs emerging within and outside the organization, to determine priorities, and to allocate human resources where they can do the most good.[12] An important component of any workforce planning effort is understanding the *talent inventory*, which is information on current resources (e.g., skills, abilities, promotional potential, and assignment histories of current employees). Buying talent is extremely expensive and top performers know their worth in the market through social media and career sites. In the case of executives, the stock market is a good metric of perceived worth.[13] For example, when Kasper Rosted left his position of CEO at packaged-goods company Henkel to become CEO of Adidas, Adidas gained US$1 billion. Performance management systems are the primary means through which accurate talent inventories can be assembled. Moreover, as we will describe later, talent inventories are critical in terms of keeping track of high-potential employees.[14]

Other organizational maintenance purposes served by performance management systems include assessing future training needs, evaluating performance achievements at the organizational level, and evaluating the effectiveness of HR interventions. For example, accurate data on employee performance can be used to evaluate whether employees perform at higher levels after participating in a training program. These activities aimed at assessing the effects of HR and other interventions on performance cannot be conducted effectively in the absence of a good performance management system.

1-2-6 Documentation Purpose

Finally, performance management systems allow organizations to collect useful information that can be used for several necessary—and sometimes, legally mandated (as described in Chapter 10)—documentation purposes. First, performance data can be used to validate newly proposed selection instruments. For example, a newly developed test of computer literacy can be administered to all administrative personnel. Scores on the test can then be paired with scores collected through the performance management system. If scores on the test and on the performance measure are correlated, then the test can be used with future applicants as predictors of performance for the administrative positions. Second, performance management systems allow for the documentation of important administrative decisions, such as terminations and promotions. This information can be especially useful in the case of litigation.

Several companies implement performance management systems that allow them to accomplish the multiple objectives described earlier. For an example of one such company, consider the case of SELCO Credit Union in Eugene, Oregon, a not-for-profit consumer cooperative that was established in 1936.[15] SELCO serves more than 127,000 members. In 2016, SELCO closed with a record US$1.4 billion in assets, US$1.1 billion in loans, and US$1.3 billion in deposits. SELCO offers many of the same services offered by other banks, including personal checking and savings accounts, loans, and credit cards. Being members of the credit union, however, allows individual members a say in how the credit union is run, something a traditional bank does not permit. Recently, SELCO scrapped an old performance appraisal system and replaced it with a new multipurpose and more effective performance management system. First, the timing of the new system is now aligned with the business cycle, instead of the employee's date of hire, to ensure that business needs are aligned with individual goals. This alignment serves both strategic and informational purposes. Second, managers are given a pool of money that they can work with to award bonuses and raises as needed, which is more effective than the complex set of matrices that had been in place to calculate bonuses. This improved the way in which the system is used for allocating rewards, and therefore, serves an administrative purpose. Third, managers are required to sit down and have regular conversations with their employees about their performance and make note of any problems that arise. This gives the employees a clear sense of areas in which they need improvement and also provides documentation if disciplinary action is needed. This component serves both informational and documentation purposes. Finally, the time that was previously spent filling out complicated matrices and forms is now spent talking with the employees about how they can improve their performance, allowing for progress on an ongoing basis. This serves a developmental purpose.

Although multiple purposes are desirable, 62% of HR executives from Fortune 500 companies say that their performance management system serves mostly administrative (e.g., salary decisions) and developmental (e.g., to identify employees' weaknesses and strengths) purposes.[16] As will be discussed in Chapter 9, these purposes place conflicting demands on those providing ratings because they must be both judges (i.e., make salary decisions) and coaches (i.e., provide useful feedback for performance improvement) at the same time.

Now, think about the performance management system implemented in your organization or the last organization for which you worked. Table 1-1 summarizes the various purposes served by a performance management system. Which of these purposes are being served by the system you are considering? Which are not? What are some of the barriers that prevent achieving all six purposes?

Subsequent chapters describe best practices on how to design and implement performance management systems. For now, however, let us say that well-designed and implemented performance management systems achieve all six purposes, and also, make substantial contributions to the organization. This is why a survey of almost 1,000 HR management professionals in Australia revealed that 96% of Australian companies currently implement some type of performance management system.[17] Similarly, results of a survey of 278 organizations, about

TABLE 1-1
Purposes Served by a Performance Management System

1. *Strategic:* To help top management achieve strategic business objectives
2. *Administrative:* To furnish valid and useful information for making administrative decisions about employees
3. *Informational:* To inform employees about how they are doing and about the organization's, customers', and supervisors' expectations
4. *Developmental:* To allow managers and peers to provide coaching to their employees
5. *Organizational maintenance:* To create a talent inventory and provide information to be used in workplace planning and allocation of human resources
6. *Documentation:* To collect useful information that can be used for various purposes (e.g., test development, administrative decisions)

two-thirds of which are multinational corporations from 15 different countries, indicated that about 91% of organizations implement a formal performance management system.[18] Moreover, organizations with formal and systematic performance management systems are 51% more likely to perform better than the other organizations in the sample regarding financial outcomes, and 41% more likely to perform better than the other organizations in the sample regarding other outcomes, including customer satisfaction, employee retention, and other important metrics. In fact, a study conducted by Development Dimensions International (DDI), a global human resources consulting firm specializing in leadership and selection, found that performance management systems are a key tool that organizations use to translate business strategy into business results. Specifically, performance management systems influence "financial performance, productivity, product or service quality, customer satisfaction, and employee job satisfaction." In addition, 79% of the CEOs surveyed say that the performance management system implemented in their organizations drives the "cultural strategies that maximize human assets."[19] Based on these results, it is not surprising that senior executives of companies listed in the *Sunday Times* list of best employers in the United Kingdom believe that performance management is one of the top two most important HR management priorities in their organizations.[20] Let us describe these performance management contributions in detail.

1-3 THE PERFORMANCE MANAGEMENT CONTRIBUTION

There are many advantages associated with the implementation of a performance management system.[21] A performance management system can make the following important contributions for employees, managers, the HR function, and the entire organization[22]:

1. *Self-insight and development are enhanced.* The participants in the system are likely to develop a better understanding of themselves and of the kind of development activities that are of value to them as they progress through the organization. Participants in the system also gain a better understanding of their particular strengths and weaknesses, which can help them better define future career paths.

2. *Self-esteem is increased.* Receiving feedback about one's performance fulfills a basic human need to be recognized and valued at work. This, in turn, is likely to increase employees' self-esteem.

3. *Motivation to perform is increased.* Receiving feedback about one's performance increases the motivation for future performance. Knowledge about how one is doing and recognition about one's past successes provide the fuel for future accomplishments.

4. *Employee engagement is enhanced.* A good performance management system leads to enhanced employee engagement. Employees who are engaged feel involved, committed, passionate, and empowered. Moreover, these attitudes and feelings result in behaviors that are innovative, and overall, demonstrate good organizational citizenship and active participation in support of the organization. Employee engagement is an important predictor of organizational performance and success, and consequently, engagement is an important contribution of good performance management systems.[23]

5. *Employees become more competent.* An obvious contribution is that employee performance is improved. In addition, there is a solid foundation for helping employees become more successful by establishing developmental plans.

6. *Voice behavior is encouraged.* A well-implemented performance management system allows employees to engage in voice behavior that can lead to improved organizational processes. Voice behavior involves making suggestions for changes and improvements that are innovative, challenge the status quo, are intended to be constructive, and are offered even when others disagree.[24] For example, the performance review meeting can lead to a conversation during which the employee provides suggestions on how to reduce cost or speed up a specific process.

7. *The definitions of job and criteria are clarified.* The job of the person being appraised may be clarified and defined more clearly. In other words, employees gain a better understanding of the behaviors and results required of their specific position. Employees also gain a better understanding of what it takes to be a successful performer (i.e., what are the specific criteria that define job success).

8. *Employee misconduct is minimized.*[25] Employee misconduct is an increasingly pervasive phenomenon that has received widespread media coverage. Such misconduct includes accounting irregularities, churning customer accounts, abusing overtime policies, giving inappropriate gifts to clients and potential clients, hoping to secure their business, and using company resources for personal use. Although some individuals are more likely to engage in misconduct compared to others, based on individual differences in personality and other attributes, having a good performance management in place provides the appropriate context so that misconduct is clearly defined and labeled as such and also identified early on before it leads to sometimes irreversible negative consequences.

9. *Declines in performance can be addressed early on.* Because good performance management systems include ongoing performance measurement, declines in performance can be noticed, which allows for immediate feedback and continuous coaching. When such declines are observed, remedial action can be taken immediately and before the problem becomes so entrenched that it cannot be easily remedied.

10. *Motivation, commitment, and intentions to stay in the organization are enhanced.* When employees are satisfied with their organization's performance management system, they are more likely to be motivated

to perform well, be committed to their organization, and not try to leave the organization.[26] For example, satisfaction with the performance management system is likely to make employees feel that the organization has a great deal of personal meaning for them. In terms of turnover intentions, satisfaction with the performance management system leads employees to report that they will probably not look for a new job in the next year and that they do not often think about quitting their present job. As an illustration of this point, results of a study including 93 professors at a university in South Africa suggested that the implementation of a good performance management system would be useful in preventing them from leaving their university jobs.[27]

11. *Managers gain insight about direct reports.* Direct supervisors and other managers in charge of the appraisal gain new insights into the person being appraised. Gaining new insights into a person's performance and personality will help the manager build a better relationship with that person. Also, supervisors gain a better understanding of each individual's contribution to the organization. This can be useful for direct supervisors, as well as for supervisors once removed.

12. *There is better and more timely differentiation between good and poor performers.* Performance management systems allow for a quicker identification of good and poor performers. This includes identifying star performers—those who produce at levels much higher than the rest. For example, without a good performance management system, it is not easy to know which particular programmers are producing more and better code.[28] Also, this includes identifying high-potential employees who can be identified as future leaders—also called "HiPos." For example, PepsiCo's performance management system includes what they call Leadership Assessment and Development (LeAD). A unique aspect of this system is the emphasis on identifying HiPos by measuring specific job and leadership requirement in the future.[29]

13. *Supervisors' views of performance are communicated more clearly.* Performance management systems allow managers to communicate to their direct reports their assessments regarding performance. Thus, there is greater accountability in how managers discuss performance expectations and provide feedback. When managers possess these competencies, direct reports receive useful information about how their performance is seen by their supervisor.

14. *Administrative actions are more fair and appropriate.* Performance management systems provide valid information about performance that can be used for administrative actions, such as merit increases, promotions, and transfers, as well as terminations. In general, a performance management system helps ensure that rewards are distributed on a fair and credible basis. In turn, such decisions based on a sound performance management system lead to improved interpersonal relationships and enhanced supervisor–direct report trust.[30] For example, a good performance management system can help mitigate explicit or implicit emphasis on age as a basis for decisions. This is particularly important, given the aging working population in the United States, Europe, and many other countries around the world.[31]

15. *Organizational goals are made clear.* The goals of the unit and the organization are made clear, and the employee understands the link

between what she does and organizational success. This is a contribution to the communication of what the unit and the organization are all about, and how organizational goals cascade down to the unit and the individual employee. Performance management systems can help improve employee acceptance of these wider goals (i.e., unit and organizational levels).

16. *There is better protection from lawsuits.* Data collected through performance management systems can help document compliance with regulations (e.g., equal treatment of all employees, regardless of sex or ethnic background). When performance management systems are not in place, arbitrary performance evaluations are more likely, resulting in an increased exposure to litigation for the organization.

17. *Organizational change is facilitated.* Performance management systems can be a useful tool to drive organizational change. For example, assume an organization decides to change its culture to give top priority to product quality and customer service. Once this new organizational direction is established, performance management is used to align goals and objectives of the organization with those of individuals to make change possible. Employees are provided training in the necessary skills and are also rewarded for improved performance so that they have both the knowledge and motivation to improve product quality and customer service. This is precisely what IBM did in the 1980s, when it wanted to switch focus to customer satisfaction: the performance evaluation of every member in the organization was based, to some extent, on customer satisfaction ratings, regardless of function (i.e., accounting, programming, manufacturing, etc.).[32] For IBM, as well as numerous other organizations, performance management provides tools and motivation for individuals to change, which, in turn, helps drive organizational change. In short, performance management systems are likely to produce changes in the culture of the organization, and therefore, the consequences of such cultural changes should be considered carefully before implementing the system.[33] As noted by Randy Pennington, president of Pennington Performance Group, "The truth is that the culture change is driven by a change in performance. An organization's culture cannot be installed. It can be guided and influenced by policies, practices, skills, and procedures that are implemented and reinforced. The only way to change the culture is to change the way individuals perform on a daily basis."[34]

Table 1-2 lists the 17 contributions made by performance management systems. Recall Sally's situation earlier in the chapter. Which of the contributions included in Table 1-2 result from the system implemented at Sally's organization? For example, are Sally's employees more motivated to perform as a consequence of implementing their "performance management" system? Is their self-esteem increased? What about Sally's insight and understanding of her employees' contributions to the organization? Is Sally's organization now better protected in the face of potential litigation? Unfortunately, the system implemented at Sally's organization is not a true performance management system, but simply an administrative nuisance. Consequently, many, if not most, of the potential contributions of the performance management system are not realized. In fact, poorly implemented systems, as in the case of Sally's organization, not only do not make positive contributions, but instead can be very dangerous because of their several negative outcomes. Let us consider those next.

TABLE 1-2
Contributions of
Performance Management
Systems

Self-insight and development are enhanced.
Self-esteem is increased.
Motivation to perform is increased.
Employee engagement is enhanced.
Employees become more competent.
Voice behavior is encouraged.
The definitions of job and criteria are clarified.
Employee misconduct is minimized.
Declines in performance can be addressed early on.
Motivation, commitment, and intentions to stay in the organization are enhanced.
Managers gain insight about direct reports.
There is better and more timely differentiation between good and poor performers.
Supervisors' views of performance are communicated more clearly.
Administrative actions are more fair and appropriate.
Organizational goals are made clear.
There is better protection from lawsuits.
Organizational change is facilitated.

1-4 WHEN PERFORMANCE MANAGEMENT BREAKS DOWN: DANGERS OF POORLY IMPLEMENTED SYSTEMS

What happens when performance management systems do not work as intended, as in the case of Sally's organization? What are some of the negative consequences associated with low-quality and poorly implemented systems? Some of these disadvantages are simply the opposite of the contributions discussed in the previous section because, in many ways, these consequences are symptoms that the performance management system is broken and something needs to be done about it. Consider the following list:

1. *Lowered self-esteem.* Self-esteem may be lowered if feedback is provided in an inappropriate and inaccurate way. This, in turn, can create employee resentment.
2. *Increased turnover.* If the process is not seen as fair, employees may become upset and leave the organization. They can leave physically (i.e., quit) or withdraw psychologically (i.e., minimize their effort and engage in cyberloafing until they are able to find a job elsewhere). This is particularly a problem for star performers, who are attracted to organizations that recognize individual contributions.[35]
3. *Damaged relationships.* As a consequence of a deficient system, the relationship among the individuals involved may be damaged, often permanently.
4. *Decreased motivation to perform.* Motivation may be lowered for many reasons, including the feeling that superior performance is not translated into meaningful tangible (e.g., pay increase) or intangible (e.g., personal recognition) rewards.
5. *Employee burnout and job dissatisfaction.* When the performance assessment instrument is not seen as valid and the system is not perceived as fair, employees are likely to feel increased levels of job burnout and

job dissatisfaction. As a consequence, employees are likely to become increasingly irritated.[36]

6. *Use of misleading information.* If a standardized system is not in place, there are multiple opportunities for fabricating information about an employee's performance.

7. *Wasted time and money.* Performance management systems cost money and quite a bit of time. These resources are wasted when systems are poorly designed and implemented.

8. *Emerging biases.* Personal values, biases, and relationships are likely to replace organizational standards.

9. *Unclear ratings system.* Because of poor communication, employees may not know how their ratings are generated and how the ratings are translated into rewards.

10. *Varying and unfair standards and ratings.* Both standards and individual ratings may vary across and within units and also be unfair.

11. *Unjustified demands on managers' and employees' resources.* Poorly implemented systems do not provide the benefits provided by well-implemented systems, yet they take up managers' and employees' time. Such systems will be resisted because of competing obligations and allocation of resources (e.g., time). What is sometimes worse, managers may simply choose to avoid the system altogether, and employees may feel increased levels of overload.[39]

12. *Increased risk of litigation.* Expensive lawsuits may be filed by individuals who feel they have been appraised unfairly. As an example, see the case of Yahoo in Box 1-2.

Box 1-2

Company Spotlight: What Happens When Performance Management Is Implemented Poorly?

One recent example of a performance management that may have been implemented poorly involves a lawsuit and the company Yahoo. Gregory Anderson said he received a promotion, a pay raise, and praise for the work he had done. But in November 2014, he was told he was in the bottom 5% of Yahoo's employees, based on quarterly performance reviews, and was fired. Anderson was Yahoo's editorial director in charge of autos, shopping, homes, travel, and small-business sites and had been employed for four years. In its defense, Yahoo issued a statement saying that its performance management system allows employees to "develop and do their best work" and "the performance review process was developed to allow employees at all levels of the company to receive meaningful, regular, and actionable feedback from others." Moreover, Yahoo said that "Our performance review process also allows for high performers to engage in increasingly larger opportunities at our company, as well as for low performers to be transitioned out." Anderson's case is unique because he argued that Yahoo manipulated the performance management system that led to his termination.

The lawsuit says managers were required to rank employees so that a specific percentage would be placed in each rank even if all the employees were performing well or at the same level. Then, higher-level management who often does not interact with the employees are allowed to modify those scores. The lawsuit argues that "The performance management system was opaque and the employees did not know who was making the final decisions, what numbers were being assigned by whom along the way, or why those numbers were being changed." Also, the lawsuit argues that changes in scores were due, in many cases, to gender discrimination. In a separate lawsuit, Scott Ard, a media executive who worked for Yahoo for about three and a half years until he was fired in January 2015, alleged that Yahoo's CEO Mayer, one of the highest paid and most prominent female executives in the United States, "encouraged and fostered the use of the performance management system to accommodate management's subjective biases and personal opinions, to the detriment of Yahoo's male employees."[37] Anderson's lawsuit seeks damages, pay back, and benefits.[38]

1-4-1 Performance Ratings: The Canary in the Coal Mine

Table 1-3 summarizes the list of negative consequences resulting from the careless design and implementation of a performance management system. As you can see from this list, many of the negative consequences are directly related to the issue of performance ratings. For example, ratings are biased, unjustified, inaccurate, a waste of time and resources, and their use leads to the departure of star performers, and even litigation.

But performance ratings are the canary in the coal mine, rather than the problem per se. Before modern methods were available, coal miners in the early twentieth century used to carry a caged canary with them down into the mine tunnels. In the presence of toxic gases such as carbon monoxide, the canary would faint, or even die, quickly alerting the miners of imminent danger. So, the canary was not the problem, but a sign of the presence of unobserved toxic gases. Similarly, what are the *unseen reasons* why performance ratings are biased, impractical, and cause more harm than good? What are the "toxic gases" that may be producing problems in the ratings? Consider just three of many possibilities. First, ratings may be not be directly related to an organization's strategic goals. Second, they may not refer to performance dimensions under the control of the employee. Third, it may take too long for supervisors to fill out complicated and convoluted evaluation forms.

Given problems noticed with performance ratings, in the past few years, several organizations such as Eli Lilly, Adobe, Microsoft, Accenture, Goldman Sachs, IBM, Morgan Stanley, New York Life, Medtronic, Juniper Networks, and Gap announced that they were going to seriously curtail or even discontinue their use. In fact, survey results by WorldatWork and Willis Towers Watson Talent Management indicate that between 8% and 14% of large corporations in North America have eliminated performance ratings since 2014.[40]

But, although the elimination of ratings seems to be the latest and newest innovation, performance management without ratings was implemented by GE in the 1960s. In addition to no summary ratings, this system at GE included frequent discussions of performance and an emphasis on mutual goal planning and problem-solving.[41] But, years later, GE not only brought ratings back, but became famous for the use of former CEO Jack Welch's "vitality curve" in which employees were ranked in the top 20%, middle 70%, or bottom 10% of

TABLE 1-3
Negative Consequences of Poorly Implemented Performance Management Systems

Lowered self-esteem
Increased turnover
Damaged relationships
Decreased motivation to perform
Employee job burnout and job dissatisfaction
Use of false or misleading information
Wasted time and money
Emerging biases
Unclear ratings system
Varying and unfair standards and ratings
Unjustified demands on managers' and employees' resources
Increased risk of litigation

the performance distribution. Going full circle, GE is now one of the companies reevaluating their use of the annual reviews.

So, despite widespread media coverage and hype about many companies "abandoning performance reviews and ratings,"[42] many of these companies quickly realized that even if performance ratings are abolished, supervisors evaluate the performance of their direct reports implicitly—and so do peers—even if evaluations forms and ratings are not used. Also, without performance ratings, how are we going to identify, reward, and retain top performers? How will organizations make fair compensation and promotion decisions and deal with possible discrimination lawsuits? The answer is that performance ratings—*good-quality* performance ratings—are needed.[43] This is why companies such as Deloitte and many others that tried to eliminate performance ratings are now using ratings again—but they are using more than one system and emphasize developmental feedback.[44] For example, see the case of Adobe described in Box 1-3. Clearly, measuring performance is not easy. However, this is not a good excuse to abandon ratings, given the large body of research that has accumulated over decades and resulted in clear implications for practice.[45] So, Part II in this book addresses how to implement state-of-the-science performance management systems, including how to define and measure performance using different types of rating systems.

Now, once again, consider Sally's organization. What are some of the negative consequences of the system implemented by her company? Let us consider each of the consequences listed in Table 1-3. For example, is it likely that the performance information used is false and misleading? How about the risk of litigation? How about the time and money invested in collecting, compiling, and reporting the data? Unfortunately, an analysis of Sally's situation, taken with the positive and negative consequences listed in Tables 1-2 and 1-3, leads to the conclusion that this particular system is likely to do more harm than good. Now, think about the system implemented at your current organization, or at the organization you have worked for most recently. Take a look at Tables 1-2 and 1-3. Where does the system fit best? Is the system more closely aligned with some of the positive consequences listed in Table 1-2 or more closely aligned with some of the negative consequences listed in Table 1-3? Returning to the canary analogy, are ratings healthy or not? If not, what are the unseen "toxic gases" that may be the underlying reasons why ratings are "unhealthy"?

Box 1-3

Company Spotlight: Good Performance Management Implementation Pays Off at Adobe

In 2012, Adobe Systems, one of the largest computer software companies in the world, decided to scrap their obsolete annual performance appraisal in favor of a continuous performance management approach. The new approach allowed employees to proactively, rather than retroactively, get feedback on their current roles in the company, future career goals, and information on the knowledge, skills, and abilities needed to improve their performance. In the first year alone, Adobe estimated it saved 80,000 manager hours, the equivalent of 40 full-time employees, which would have been required by the old process. Two years later, Adobe found that morale had increased, turnover decreased by 30%, and involuntary departure increased by 50%.[46]

Thus far, we have defined performance management and its purposes, spelled out its contributions, and discussed benefits of good systems as well as dangers or bad ones. So, it is time to summarize what decades of research has concluded about what an ideal performance management system looks like. These characteristics can have slight variations across contexts. But overall, they are considered fairly universal.[47]

1-5 CHARACTERISTICS OF AN IDEAL PERFORMANCE MANAGEMENT SYSTEM

The following characteristics are likely to allow a performance management system to be successful. Clearly, practical constraints may not allow for the implementation of all these features. The reality is that performance management systems are seldom implemented in an ideal way.[48] For example, there may not be sufficient funds to deliver training to all people involved, supervisors may have biases in how they provide performance ratings, or people may be just too busy to pay attention to a performance management system that seems to require too much time and attention. Also, there may be organizational or even country-level constraints that prevent the implementation of a good performance management system. For example, consider the case of Korea, which is a country that espouses collectivist values over individual performance, and is a society that is male-dominated and also dominated by political and administrative leaders, and where these sociocultural norms have a clear influence on organizational decision making and practices.[49] These institutional constraints that are so pervasive in Korea and many other emerging market countries must be taken into consideration in terms of what type of performance management system it would be possible to implement as well as the effectiveness of such a system. However, regardless of the societal, institutional, and practical constraints, we should strive to place a check mark next to each of these characteristics: the more features that are checked, the more likely it will be that the system will live up to its promise and deliver the benefits listed in Table 1-2.

- *Strategic congruence.* The system should be congruent with the unit and organization's strategy. In other words, individual goals must be aligned with unit and organizational goals.
- *Context congruence.* The system should be congruent with the organization's culture as well as the broader cultural context of the region or country. The importance of context in implementing highly effective performance management systems is emphasized throughout the book. However, for now, consider the example of an organization that has a culture in which communication is not fluid and hierarchies are rigid. In such organizations, an upward feedback system, in which individuals receive comments on their performance from their direct reports, would be resisted and likely not very effective. Regarding broader cultural issues, consider that performance management research published in scholarly journals has been conducted in about 40 countries around the world.[50] Taken together, this body of work suggests that

culture plays an important role in the effectiveness of a performance management system. For example, in countries such as Japan, there is an emphasis on the measurement of both behaviors (i.e., how people do the work) and results (i.e., the results of people's work), whereas in the United States, results are typically preferred over behaviors. Thus, implementing a results-only system in Japan is not likely to be effective. Specifically, although performance is measured similarly around the world (see standardization criterion below), the interpersonal aspects of the system are adapted and customized to the local culture. For example, performance management systems in the subsidiaries are more likely to differ from those in the headquarters as power distance differences (i.e., degree to which a society accepts hierarchical differences) increase between countries.

- *Thoroughness.* The system should be thorough regarding four dimensions. First, all employees should be evaluated (including managers). Second, all major job responsibilities should be evaluated (including behaviors and results; a detailed discussion of this topic is presented in Chapter 5). Third, the evaluation should include performance spanning the entire review period, not just the few weeks or months before the review. Finally, feedback should be given on positive performance aspects as well as those that are in need of improvement.

- *Practicality.* Systems that are too expensive, time-consuming, and convoluted will obviously not be effective. Good, easy-to-use systems (e.g., performance data are entered via user-friendly Web and mobile apps) are available for managers to help them make decisions. Finally, the benefits of using the system (e.g., increased performance and job satisfaction) must be seen as outweighing the costs (e.g., time, effort, expense).

- *Meaningfulness.* The system must be meaningful in several ways. First, the standards and evaluations conducted for each job function must be considered important and relevant. Second, performance assessment must emphasize only those functions that are under the control of the employee. For example, there is no point in letting an employee know she needs to increase the speed of service delivery when the supplier does not get the product to her on time. Third, evaluations must take place at regular intervals and at appropriate moments. Because one formal evaluation per year is usually not sufficient, frequent informal reviews are recommended. Fourth, the system should provide for the continuing skill development of evaluators. Finally, the results should be used for important administrative decisions. People will not pay attention to a performance system that has no consequences in terms of outcomes that they value. For example, a study compared performance management systems in the former East versus former West Germany. Results showed that in former West German companies, there was a stronger link between the performance management system and administrative decisions such as promotions. This relationship was weaker in former East German companies, and this difference is probably due to the socialist political system in the former German Democratic Republic, which has had a long-lasting effect.[51]

- *Specificity.* A good system should be specific: it should provide detailed and concrete guidance to employees about what is expected of them and how they can meet these expectations.
- *Identification of effective and ineffective performance.* The performance management system should provide information that allows for the identification of effective and ineffective performance. That is, the system should allow for distinguishing between effective and ineffective behaviors and results, thereby also allowing for the identification of employees displaying various levels of performance effectiveness. In terms of administrative decisions, a system that ranks all levels of performance, and all employees, similarly is useless.
- *Reliability.* A good system should include measures of performance that are consistent and free of error. For example, if two supervisors provided ratings of the same employee and performance dimensions, ratings should be similar.
- *Validity.* The measures of performance should also be valid. In this context, validity refers to the fact that the measures include all relevant performance facets and do not include irrelevant information. In other words, measures are relevant (i.e., include all critical performance facets), not deficient (i.e., do not leave any important aspects out), and are not contaminated (i.e., do not include factors outside of the control of the employee or factors unrelated to performance). In short, measures include what is important and do not assess what is not important and outside of the control of the employee. For example, the *gondolieri* in the city of Venice (Italy) have had a performance management system for about 1,000 years. Among other relevant performance dimensions, older versions of the performance management system required *gondolieri* to demonstrate their level of rowing skills and their ability to transport people and goods safely. These are clearly relevant performance dimensions. However, the system was contaminated because it included the following requirement which is unrelated to performance: "Every brother [sic] shall be obliged to confess twice a year, or at least once and if after a warning, he remains impenitent, he shall be expelled . . . [from the *gondolieri* guild]."[52]
- *Acceptability and fairness.* A good system is acceptable and is perceived as fair by all participants. Perceptions of fairness are subjective and the only way to know if a system is seen as fair is to ask the participants about the system. Such perceptions include four distinct components. First, we can ask about *distributive justice*, which includes perceptions of the performance evaluation received relative to the work performed, and perceptions of the rewards received relative to the evaluation received, particularly when the system is implemented across countries. For example, differences in perceptions may be found in comparing employees from more individualistic (e.g., United States) to more collectivistic (e.g., Korea) cultures.[53] If a discrepancy is perceived between work and evaluation or between evaluation and rewards, then the system is likely to be seen as unfair.[54] Second, we can ask about *procedural justice*, which includes perceptions of the procedures used to determine the ratings as well as the procedures used to link ratings with rewards. Third, we can assess perceptions regarding *interpersonal justice*, which

refers to the quality of the design and implementation of the performance management system. For example, what are employees' perceptions regarding how they are treated by their supervisors during the performance review meeting? Do they feel that supervisors are empathic and helpful? Finally, *informational justice* refers to fairness perceptions about performance expectations and goals, feedback received, and the information given to justify administrative decisions. For example, are explanations perceived to be honest, sincere, and logical? Because a good system is inherently discriminatory, some employees will receive ratings that are lower than those received by other employees. However, we should strive to develop systems that are regarded as fair from the distributive, procedural, interpersonal, and informational perspectives because each type of justice perception leads to different outcomes.[55] For example, a perception that the system is not fair from a distributive point of view is likely to lead to a poor relationship between employee and supervisor and lowered satisfaction of the employee with the supervisor. On the contrary, a perception that the system is unfair from a procedural point of view is likely to lead to decreased employee commitment toward the organization and increased intentions to leave.[56] One way to improve all four justice dimensions is to set clear rules that are applied consistently by all supervisors.

- *Inclusiveness.* Good systems include input from multiple sources on an ongoing basis. First, the evaluation process must represent the concerns of all the people who will be affected by the outcome. Consequently, employees must participate in the process of creating the system by providing input regarding what behaviors or results will be measured and how. This is particularly important in today's diverse and global organizations, which include individuals from different cultural backgrounds, which may lead to different views regarding what is performance and how it should be measured.[57] Second, input about employee performance should be gathered from the employees themselves before the performance review meeting.[58] In short, all participants must be given a voice in the process of designing and implementing the system. Such inclusive systems are likely to lead to more successful systems, including less employee resistance, improved performance, and fewer legal challenges.[59]

- *Openness.* Good systems have no secrets. First, performance is evaluated frequently and performance feedback is provided on an ongoing basis. Therefore, employees are continually informed of the quality of their performance. Second, the review meeting consists of a two-way communication process during which information is exchanged, not delivered from the supervisor to the employee without his or her input. Third, standards should be clear and communicated on an ongoing basis. Finally, communications are factual, open, and honest.

- *Correctability.* The process of assigning ratings should minimize subjective aspects; however, it is virtually impossible to create a system that is completely objective because human judgment is an important component of the evaluation process. When employees perceive an error has been made, there should be a mechanism through which this error can be corrected. Establishing an appeals process, through which employees can challenge what may be unjust decisions, is an important aspect of a good performance management system.

- *Standardization.* As noted earlier, good systems are standardized. This means that performance is evaluated consistently across people and time. To achieve this goal, the ongoing training of the individuals in charge of appraisals, usually managers, is a must.
- *Ethicality.* Good systems comply with ethical standards. This means that the supervisor suppresses his or her personal self-interest in providing evaluations. In addition, the supervisor evaluates only performance dimensions for which she has sufficient information, and the privacy of the employee is respected.[60]

Table 1-4 lists the characteristics of an ideal performance management system. Implementing a performance management system that includes the characteristics just described will pay off. A study conducted for Mercer, a global diversified consulting company, revealed that the 1,200 workers surveyed stated that they could improve their productivity by an average of 26% if they were not held back by a lack of "direction, support, training, and equipment." Successfully implementing a performance management system can give workers the direction and support that they need to improve their productivity.

Now, think about the performance management system implemented in your organization or the last organization for which you worked. Which of the features listed in Table 1-4 are included in the system you are considering? How far is your system from the ideal?

TABLE 1-4
Characteristics of an Ideal Performance Management System

Strategic congruence
Context congruence
Thoroughness
Practicality
Meaningfulness
Specificity
Identification of effective and ineffective performance
Reliability
Validity
Acceptability and fairness
Inclusiveness
Openness
Correctability
Standardization
Ethicality

1-6 INTEGRATION WITH OTHER HUMAN RESOURCES AND DEVELOPMENT ACTIVITIES

Performance management systems serve as important "feeders" to other human resources and development activities. For example, consider the relationship between performance management and *training*. Performance management provides information on developmental needs for employees. In the absence of a good performance management system, it is not clear that organizations will use their training resources in the most efficient way (i.e., to train those who most need it in the most critical areas). One organization that is able to link its performance management system to training initiatives is General Electric (GE). GE's performance management system includes over 180,000 salaried employees spread across almost 180 countries. Recently, GE updated their performance management practices, moving from a formal "once-a-year" performance review to an app-based system that allows managers to provide more immediate feedback and coaching to their employees. The app accepts voice and text inputs, attached documents, and even handwritten notes. Managers can use the app's categories such as "priorities," "touch points," "summary," and "insights," to send short messages (up to 500 characters) to individual team members or groups. For example, a manager can use the app to provide suggestions to employees on areas of developmental needs and where employees may benefit from additional training. Based on this data, the manager, employee, and the human resources department can work together to schedule training classes and off-site training opportunities. GE is already seeing the benefits of this partnership between performance management and training, with some divisions reporting a fivefold increase in employee productivity.[61]

Unfortunately, despite the successful GE example, most organizations do not use performance management systems to determine training content and waste an opportunity to use the performance management system as the needs assessment phase of their training efforts.[62] Specifically, a survey including 218 HR leaders at companies with at least 2,500 employees revealed that there is tight integration between performance management and learning/development activities in only 15.3% of the organizations surveyed.[63]

Performance management also provides key information for *workforce planning*. As noted earlier, an organization's talent inventory is based on information collected through the performance management system. Development plans provide information on what skills will be acquired in the near future. This information is also used in making *recruitment and hiring* decisions. Knowledge of an organization's current and future talent is important when deciding what types of skills need to be acquired externally and what types of skills can be found within the organization.

Finally, there is an obvious relationship between performance management and compensation systems. Compensation and reward decisions are likely to be arbitrary in the absence of a good performance management system, which is an issue described in detail in Chapter 10.

In short, performance management is a key component of talent management in organizations. It allows for assessing the current talent and making predictions about future needs both at the individual and organizational levels. Implementing a successful performance management system is a requirement for the successful implementation of other HR functions, including training, workforce planning, recruitment and selection, and compensation.

1-7 THE FUTURE IS NOW: PERFORMANCE MANAGEMENT AND THE NATURE OF WORK AND ORGANIZATIONS TODAY

We know that performance management is pervasive across industries and around the world today. But, performance management has a long history and is actually not something new. In fact, the Wei dynasty (魏朝) in China, which was a Han dynasty that was in power between years 206 BCE and 220 CE, implemented a performance management system for government employees. An important component was something called the nine-rank system, by which workers were rated based on their performance. A low ranking meant the worker would be fired. Fast forward to nineteenth-century England. The performance of officers in the Royal Navy was routinely rated by their peers. At approximately the same time, Robert Owen, a Welsh industrialist, set up a large cotton mill in New Lanark (Scotland), which can still be visited today. He mounted a block of wood on each machine with four sides painted, based on a performance rating system: white was best, then yellow, then blue and the worst, which was black. At the end of each workday, the marks were recorded and each worker was evaluated by turning the block to the appropriate side, which would face the aisle. Owen would walk the mill floor daily to see the block color on each machine. It is safe to say that performance management is one of the oldest topics in talent management in the history of human kind.

But the nature of work and organizations today is quite different from those in China about 2,000 years ago and England and Scotland in the nineteenth century. Due to technological advancements, globalization, and demographic changes, we are now witnessing nothing less than a new industrial revolution. Technological changes have occurred on an ongoing basis in the past two centuries. But, the Internet and cloud computing have fundamentally changed the way people work.[64] These advancements give everyone in the organization, at any level and in every functional area, amazing access to information—instantaneously from anywhere. Vast amount of data, what is often referred to as "Big Data," are collected on an ongoing basis: what employees are doing, what they are producing, with whom they are interacting, and where they are doing what they are doing. What does this mean for performance management? The old days of paper-and-pencil performance evaluations are mostly gone. So are the old days of static in-house enterprise technology platforms. Instead, performance management can be implemented using dynamic online systems accessed via Web and mobile apps.[65]

The use of cloud computing for performance management is much more than a mere translation of paper evaluation forms to digital format. Cloud computing technology allows supervisors and peers to provide performance evaluations on an ongoing basis and in real time. It allows employees to receive feedback also on an ongoing basis and in real time. Related to the strategic and informational purposes of performance management, it allows organizations to update goals and priorities and communicate them also real-time to all organizational members, thereby allowing them to also update their team and individual goals and priorities. So, the cascading of goals, which we will discuss in Chapter 2, can be implemented successfully across thousands of employees in just a few weeks. Also, cloud computing allows for a clearer understanding of the role of managers in the performance management process. For example, how often are they communicating with direct reports about their performance? How often do "check-ins" take place? Companies such as Zalando, an e-retailer delivering merchandise to about 15 European countries, are already implementing these advancements. Specifically, Zalando put in place an online app that crowdsources performance feedback from meetings, problem-solving sessions, completed projects, launches, and campaigns.[66] Zalando employees can request feedback from their supervisors, peers, and internal customers that lets people provide both positive and more critical comments about each other in a playful and engaging way. An important innovation is that the system then weighs responses by how much exposure the rater has to the ratee. Every time an employee requests feedback, the online app prompts a list of questions that can be answered by moving a slider on the touchscreen of a smart phone or tablet. This is a good example of "constant feedback" (Chapter 9 addresses issues about feedback in more detail). Clearly, this is very different from a traditional annual performance appraisal, which is currently the target of sharp criticism.

The availability of Big Data is also changing performance management in important ways. Specifically, about 80% of organizations use some type of electronic performance monitoring (EPM).[67] In its early days, EPM included surveillance camera systems and computer and phone monitoring systems. But, today EPM includes wearable technologies and smartphones, including Fitbits and mobile GPS tracking applications. Indeed, in the contemporary workplace, every email, instant message, phone call, and mouse-click leaves a digital footprint, all of which can be used as part of a performance management system. But we should not be enamored by the presence of Big Data, and instead, should think about "Smart Data." Beginning with Chapter 4, we will discuss how to define, measure, and gather data that are useful and accurate.

Technological advancements and the Internet have also served as catalysts for globalization. Consider the example of a firm that is based in the United States, does its software programming in Sri Lanka, its engineering in Germany, its manufacturing in China, and has a call center in Brazil. All of this is possible due to improved Web-based communications and flow of information. And full-time, part-time, contract employees, and consultants all work together across time zones on a daily basis without having ever met in person—although they may have regular interactions using Skype. Performance management is a global phenomenon and organizations all over the world are implementing various types of performance management systems. But as discussed earlier, context matters. The availability of online tools allows for the customization of performance management systems such that every step of the performance management system, as discussed in the next chapter, can be customized and tailored to local contexts. For example, consider the case of providing feedback. People from more individualistic cultures, such as the United States, expect to receive feedback and many performance management systems include training for supervisors on how to provide one-on-one feedback in the most effective way.[68] However, in collectivistic cultures, such as China and Guatemala, open discussions about an individual's performance clash with cultural norms about harmony and the direct report may perceive negative feedback as an embarrassing loss of face. This is why successful performance management systems need to consider local norms—including societal and organizational cultural issues. Chapter 7 addresses several issues about how to implement successful performance management systems.

Finally, another important change relates to demographic trends. In the United States and many other Western countries, baby boomers (i.e., born approximately between 1946 and 1964) are retiring in large numbers, members of Generation X (i.e., born approximately between 1965 and 1976) and Generation Y or Millennials (i.e., born approximately between 1977 and 1995) are now entering the workforce in large numbers. Gen X and Gen Y employees are "digital natives." Also, they are used to immediate feedback—just like when receiving a grade immediately after completing a Web-based exam in high school and college. A performance management system must consider generational differences to be successful. For example, it is important to include "check-in" mechanisms to give managers and direct reports the opportunity to discuss performance issues on an ongoing and real-time basis. These issues will be addressed in Chapter 9 and elsewhere.

In closing, to be successful and produce the benefits for employees, managers, the HR function, and organizations listed in Table 1-2, performance management must evolve from a dreaded and painful once-a-year "soul-crushing" exercise to an agile and dynamic performance enabler. But as the saying goes, the devil is in the details. The remainder of the book will delve deep into strategic and operational steps to design and implement state-of-the science performance management systems.

SUMMARY POINTS

- Performance management is a continuous process of identifying, measuring, and developing the performance of individuals and teams and aligning performance with the strategic goals of the organization.
- Although many organizations have systems labeled "performance management," they usually are only performance *appraisal* systems. Performance appraisal emphasizes the assessment of an employee's strengths and weaknesses and does not include strategic business considerations. Also, performance appraisal systems usually do not include extensive and ongoing feedback that an employee can use to improve her performance in the future. Finally, performance appraisal is usually a once-a-year event that is driven by the HR department, whereas performance management is a year-round way of managing business that is driven by managers.
- Performance management systems serve multiple purposes. First, they serve a strategic purpose because they help link employee and team activities with the organization's mission and goals; they identify results and behaviors needed to carry out strategy; and they maximize the extent to which employees exhibit the desired behaviors and produce the desired results. Second, they serve an administrative purpose in that they produce information used by the reward system and other HR decision making (e.g., promotions, termination, disciplinary actions). Third, they serve

an informational purpose because they enable employees to learn about their performance in relation to the organization's expectations. Fourth, they serve a developmental purpose in that performance feedback allows individuals to learn about their strengths and weaknesses, to identify training needs, and to make better decisions regarding job assignments. Fifth, performance management systems serve an organizational maintenance purpose because they provide useful information for workforce planning and for evaluating the effectiveness of other HR systems (e.g., comparing performance before and after an expensive training program to determine whether training made a difference). Finally, performance management systems also serve a documentation purpose; for example, they support HR decisions and help meet legal requirements.

- Implementing a well-designed performance management system has many advantages. From the perspective of employees, a good system enhances self-insight and development, increases self-esteem and motivation, helps improve performance, clarifies job tasks and duties, and clarifies the definitions of job and criteria. From the perspective of managers, good systems allow them to gain insight into employees' activities and goals, allow for more fair and appropriate administrative actions, allow them to communicate organizational goals more clearly, let them differentiate good and poor performers, help drive organizational change, encourage voice behavior, and improve employee engagement. Finally, from the perspective of the HR function and the organization, a good system provides protection from litigation and can also help minimize employee misconduct, which can have so many negative consequences for the organization.

- Poorly designed and implemented performance management systems can have disastrous consequences for all involved. For example, star employees may quit; those who stay may be less motivated; and relationships (e.g., supervisor–direct report) can suffer irreparable damage. Also, poorly designed systems can be biased, resulting in costly lawsuits and wasted time and resources. In the end, low-quality or poorly implemented systems can be a source of enormous frustration and cynicism for all involved. Many of the negative consequences associated with poor performance management systems are related to dysfunctional performance ratings. But performance ratings are the canary in the coal mine, rather than the problem per se. In other words, bad ratings serve as signals that the performance management system is broken.

- Ideal performance management systems are rare. Such ideal systems are:
  - congruent with strategy (i.e., there is a clear link among individual, unit, and organizational goals)
  - congruent with context (i.e., the system is consistent with norms based on the culture of the organization and the region and country in which the organization is located)
  - thorough (i.e., all employees are evaluated, they include all relevant performance dimensions)
  - practical (i.e., they do not require excessive time and resources)
  - meaningful (i.e., they have important consequences)
  - specific (i.e., they provide a concrete employee improvement agenda)

- able to identify effective and ineffective performance (i.e., they help distinguish employees at different performance levels)
- reliable (i.e., the measurement of performance is consistent)
- valid (i.e., the measures of performance are not contaminated or deficient)
- acceptable and fair (i.e., people participating in the system believe the processes and outcomes are just)
- inclusive (i.e., they include input from multiple sources on an ongoing basis)
- open (i.e., they are transparent and there are no secrets)
- correctable (i.e., they include mechanisms so that errors can be corrected)
- standardized (i.e., performance is evaluated consistently across people and time)
- ethical (i.e., they comply with ethical standards)

- Many trade-offs take place in the real-world implementation of performance management systems. However, the closer the system is to the ideal characteristics, the greater the return will be for the employees, managers, the HR function, the organization as a whole.

- A performance management system is the key factor used in determining whether an organization can manage its human resources and talent effectively and has important linkages with other HR systems. For example, performance management provides information on who should be trained and in what areas, which employees should be rewarded, and what type of skills are lacking at the organization or unit level. Therefore, performance management also provides information on the type of employees that should be hired. When implemented well, performance management systems provide critical information that allows organizations to make sound decisions regarding their people resources.

- Performance management is adapting to the current nature of work and organizations involving technological and demographic changes and globalization. First, the Internet and cloud computing have fundamentally changed the way people work. Accordingly, performance management can be implemented using dynamic online systems accessed via Web and mobile apps that give everyone in the organization, at any level and in every functional area, amazing access to information—instantaneously from anywhere and at any time. Second, performance management is a global phenomenon and organizations are implementing various types of performance management systems worldwide. Thus, the availability of online tools allows for the customization of performance management systems, and every step of the performance management system, as discussed in subsequent chapters, can be customized and tailored to local and cultural contexts. Third, Millennials are now entering the workforce in large numbers and they are "digital natives." To maximize its contributions, a successful performance management system must consider generational differences.

As should be evident by now, implementing an ideal performance management system requires a substantial amount of work, expertise, and effort. So, in a way, performance management *is* rocket science. The process of implementing a performance management system does not start when the system is put into place. The process starts much earlier because unless specific conditions are present before the system is implemented, the system will not achieve its multiple purposes. Chapter 2 provides a description of the entire performance management process.

EXERCISE 1-1 IDEAL VERSUS ACTUAL PERFORMANCE MANAGEMENT SYSTEM

The table below summarizes the key characteristics of an ideal performance management system, as discussed in this chapter. Think about a performance management system you know. This could be the one implemented at your current (or most recent) job. If you do not have information about such a system, talk to a friend or acquaintance who is currently working and gather information about the system used in his or her organization. Use the Y/N column in the table to indicate whether each of the features is present (Y: yes) or not (N: no) in the system you are considering. In some cases, some elements may be present to a matter of degree and may require that you include some additional information in the Comments column.

Next, prepare a brief report addressing the following issues:

1. How many of the 15 characteristics of an ideal system are present in the system you are evaluating?

2. Identify two characteristics that are not present at all, or barely present, in your system. Discuss the implications that the lack of these characteristics has on the effectiveness of the system.

3. Identify one characteristic that is clearly present in your system. Discuss the implications of the presence of this characteristic on the effectiveness of the system.

4. Identify the characteristic in your system that is furthest from the ideal. What can be done to produce a better alignment between your system and the ideal? Who should be responsible for doing what so that your system becomes "ideal" regarding this characteristic?

Characteristics	Y/N	Definition	Comments
Strategic congruence		Individual goals are aligned with unit and organizational goals.	
Context congruence		The system is congruent with norms based on the organization's culture.	
		The system is congruent with norms based on the culture of the region and country where the organization is located.	
Thoroughness		All employees are evaluated.	
		All major job responsibilities are evaluated.	
		Evaluations include performance spanning the entire review period.	
		Feedback is provided on both positive and negative performance.	

(Continued)

Characteristics	Y/N	Definition	Comments
Practicality		It is readily available for use.	
		It is easy to use.	
		It is not too expensive or time-consuming.	
		It is acceptable to those who use it for decisions.	
		Benefits of the system outweigh the costs.	
Meaningfulness		Standards and evaluations for each job function are important and relevant.	
		Only the functions that are under the control of the employee are measured.	
		Evaluations take place at regular intervals and at appropriate moments.	
		System provides for continuing skill development of evaluators.	
		Results are used for important administrative decisions.	
Specificity		Detailed guidance is provided to employees about what is expected of them and how they can meet these expectations.	
Identification of effective and ineffective performance		The system distinguishes between effective and ineffective behaviors and results, thereby also identifying employees displaying various levels of performance effectiveness.	
Reliability		Measures of performance are consistent.	
		Measures of performance are free of error.	
Validity		Measures include all critical performance facets.	
		Measures do not leave out any important performance facets.	
		Measures do not include factors outside employee control or unrelated to performance.	
Acceptability and fairness		Employees perceive the performance evaluation and rewards received relative to the work performed as fair (distributive justice).	
		Employees perceive the procedures used to determine the ratings and subsequent rewards as fair (procedural justice).	
		Employees perceive the way they are treated in the course of designing and implementing the system as fair (interpersonal justice).	
		Employees perceive the information and explanations they receive as part of the performance management system as fair (informational justice).	
		Set clear rules that are applied consistently by all supervisors.	

Characteristics	Y/N	Definition	Comments
Inclusiveness		Employee input about their performance is gathered from the employees before the appraisal meeting.	
		Employees participate in the process of creating the system by providing input on what behaviors and results will be measured and how performance should be measured.	
		Multiple sources of information (e.g., peers, supervisors, direct reports) are used to evaluate performance	
Openness		Performance is evaluated frequently and feedback is provided on an ongoing basis.	
		Appraisal meeting is a two-way communication process and not one-way communication delivered from the supervisor to the employee.	
		Standards are clear and communicated on an ongoing basis.	
		Communications are factual, open, and honest.	
Correctability		There is an appeals process, through which employees can challenge unjust or incorrect decisions.	
Standardization		Performance is evaluated consistently across people and time.	
		Ongoing training of the individuals in charge of appraisals increases consistency.	
Ethicality		Supervisors suppress their personal self-interest in providing evaluations.	
		Supervisors evaluate performance dimensions only for which they have sufficient information.	
		Employee privacy is respected.	

EXERCISE 1-2   DISTINGUISHING PERFORMANCE MANAGEMENT SYSTEMS FROM PERFORMANCE APPRAISAL SYSTEMS

What are the differences between a performance appraisal system and a performance management system? How are the two systems related to each other? After answering these questions, consider the following 11 criticisms. Which of the following criticisms pertain to performance appraisal systems, but not to performance management systems? Which criticisms pertain to both performance appraisal and performance management systems? Use Xs on the table below to denote answers. Then, provide an explanation for categorizing the 11 criticisms in the way you did.

Criticism 1: "[There can be] inconsistency between comments and scores on an employee's evaluation."

Criticism 2: "The annual performance review is a bad management tool. To start with, it is not timely. If your direct report is deficient in some ways, you wait 11 months to say something about it. How does that help next week's performance?"

Criticism 3: "The evaluation is usually a hit-and-run exercise. It rarely takes the form of a dialogue between the supervisor and direct report and, instead it is an isolated event and not part of performance/career management more generally."

Criticism 4: "A number of years ago, the U.S. Equal Employment Opportunity Commission (EEOC) created a 'Like Me' task force. Its general conclusion—there was a human tendency to favor employees who are like the managers making the employment assessment."

Criticism 5: "Few managers jump with glee at appraisal time. When they triage workplace demands, many times appraisals end up at the bottom. As a result, late appraisals are often the norm and not the exception."

Criticism 6: "Because performance is ultimately measured on a nonstop, continuous basis, managers may become overwhelmed with cognitive load, paperwork, and generally more work to do."

Criticism 7: "What's left is the more important strategic role of raising the reputational and intellectual capital of the company—but HR is, it turns out, uniquely unsuited for that."

Criticism 8: "Goal-setting, when done wrong, gives the employee the wrong goals—those, for instance, which are not aligned with the organization's strategic orientation."

Criticism 9: "Often, an employee with substandard performance is evaluated as meeting expectations or even better, and the average employee receives an above-average evaluation."

Criticism 10: "[The process does not involve helping or making employees] set goals for the future."

Criticism 11: "Coaching can be tricky. When done wrong, it can be devastating. For example, a coach's feedback can have detrimental effects if it focuses on the employee as a whole, as opposed to specific work behaviors at work."

Criticisms	Pertains to Performance Appraisal Systems only	Pertains to Performance Management Systems only	Pertains to Both Performance Appraisal and Management Systems
1			
2			
3			
4			
5			
6			
7			
8			
9			
10			
11			

Source: Some of these criticisms were derived from the following sources: (a) Aguinis, H., Joo, H., & Gottfredson, R. K. (2011). Why we hate performance management—And why we should love it. *Business Horizons, 54,* 503–507; (b) Adler, S., Campion, M., Colquitt, A., Grubb, A., Murphy, K., Ollander-Krane, R., & Pulakos, E. (2016). Getting rid of performance ratings: Genius or folly? A debate. *Industrial and Organizational Psychology, 9,* 219–252; (c) Ryan, L. (2009, June 30). CEOs should skip performance reviews in 2009. *Bloomberg Businessweek.* Retrieved from http://www.businessweek.com/managing/content/jun2009/ca20090630_736385 .htm; (d) Segal, J. A. (2011, January 14). The dirty dozen performance appraisal errors. *Bloomberg Businessweek.* Retrieved from http://www.businessweek.com/managing/content/jan2011/ca20110114_156455.htm; and (e) Hammonds, K. H. (2005, August 1). Why we hate HR. *Fast Company.* Retrieved from http://www .fastcompany.com/magazine/97/open_hr.html?page=0%2C0

Performance Management at Network Solutions, Inc.

Network Solutions, Inc.,[69] is a worldwide leader in hardware, software, and services essential to computer networking. Until recently, Network Solutions, Inc., used more than 50 different systems to measure performance within the company—many employees did not receive a review; fewer than 5% of all employees received the lowest category of rating; and there was no recognition program in place to reward high achievers. Overall, it was recognized that performance problems were not being addressed, and tough pressure from competitors was increasing the costs of managing human performance ineffectively. In addition, quality initiatives were driving change in several areas of the business, and Network Solutions decided that these initiatives should also apply to "people quality." Finally, Network Solutions wanted to improve its ability to meet its organizational goals and realized that one way of doing this would be to ensure that they were linked to each employee's goals.

Given this situation, Network Solutions' CEO announced that he wanted to implement a forced distribution performance management system in which a set percentage of employees were classified in each of several categories (e.g., a rating of 1 to the top 20% of performers; a rating of 2 to the middle 70% of performers; and a rating of 3 to the bottom 10% of performers). A global cross-divisional HR team was put in place to design and implement the new system. The first task for the design team was to build a business case for the new system by showing that if organizational strategy was carried down to team contributions and team contributions were translated into individual goals, then business goals would be met. Initially, the program was rolled out as a year-round people management system that would raise the bar on performance management at Network Solutions by aligning individual performance objectives with organizational goals by focusing on the development of all employees.

The desired outcomes of the new system included raising the performance level of all employees, identifying and retaining top talent, and identifying low performers and improving their performance. Network Solutions also wanted the performance expectations for all employees to be clear.

Before implementing the program, the design team received the support of senior leadership by communicating that the performance management system was the future of Network Solutions and by encouraging all senior leaders to ensure that those reporting directly to them understood the process and also accepted it. In addition, they encouraged senior leaders to use the system with all of their direct reports and to demand and utilize output from the new system. Next, the design team encouraged the senior leaders to stop the development and use of any other performance management system, and explained the need for standardization of performance management across all divisions. Finally, the team asked senior leaders to promote the new program by involving employees in the training of talent management and by assessing any needs in their divisions that would not be addressed by the new system. The Network Solutions global performance management cycle consisted of the following process:

1. Goal cascading and team building
2. Performance planning
3. Development planning
4. Ongoing discussions and updates between managers and employees
5. Annual performance summary

Training resources were made available on Network Solutions' intranet for managers and individual contributors, including access to all necessary forms. In addition to the training available on the intranet, one- to two-hour conference calls took place before each phase of the program was begun.

Today, part of the training associated with the performance management system revolves around the idea that the development planning phase of the system is the joint year-round responsibility of managers and employees. Managers are responsible for scheduling meetings, guiding employees on preparing for meetings, and finalizing all development plans. Individual contributors are responsible for documenting the developmental plans. Both managers and employees are responsible for preparing for the meeting, filling out the development planning preparation forms, and attending the meeting.

With forced distribution systems, there is a set number of employees that have to fall into set rating classifications. As noted, in the Network Solutions system, employees are given a rating of 1, 2, or 3. Individual ratings are determined by the execution of annual objectives and job requirements as well as by a comparison rating of others at a similar level at Network Solutions. Employees receiving a 3, the lowest rating, have a specified time period to improve their performance. If their performance does improve, then they are released from the plan, but they are not eligible for stock options or salary increases. If performance does not improve, they can take a severance package and leave the company or they can start on a performance improvement plan, which has more rigorous expectations and timelines than did the original action plan. If performance does not improve after the second period, they are terminated without a severance package. Individuals with a rating of 2 receive average-to-high salary increases, stock options, and bonuses. Individuals receiving the highest rating of 1 receive the highest salary increases, stock options, and bonuses. These individuals are also treated as "high potential" employees are given extra development opportunities by their managers. The company also makes significant efforts to retain all individuals who receive a rating of 1.

Looking to the future, Network Solutions plans to continue reinforcing the needed cultural change to support forced distribution ratings. HR Centers of Expertise of Network Solutions continue to educate employees about the system to ensure that they understand that Network Solutions still rewards good performance; they are just measuring it in a different way than in the past. There is also a plan to monitor for and correct any unproductive practices and implement correcting policies and practices. To do this, Network Solutions plans on continued checks with all stakeholders to ensure that the performance management system is serving its intended purpose.

Consider Network Solutions' performance management system in light of what we discussed as an ideal system. Then, answer the following questions:

1. Overall, what is the overlap between Network Solutions' system and an ideal system?

2. What are the features of the system implemented at Network Solutions that correspond to the features described in the chapter as ideal characteristics? Which of the ideal characteristics are missing? For which of the ideal characteristics do we need additional information to evaluate whether they are part of the system at Network Solutions?

3. Based on the description of the system at Network Solutions, what do you anticipate will be some advantages and positive outcomes resulting from the implementation of the system?

4. Based on the description of the system at Network Solutions, what do you anticipate will be some disadvantages and negative outcomes resulting from the implementation of the system?

Performance Management at CRB, Inc.

Car Restoration Business (CRB, Inc.) is interviewing you for a position as its human resources manager on a part-time basis, working 20 hours per week, while you complete your degree. You would be the first HR manager they have ever been able to afford to hire, and the husband and wife owners (Al and Mary Brown) have been operating the small business for 10 years. In addition to you, they recently hired a part-time janitor. This brought the paid staff to six full-time employees: a foreman who is responsible for scheduling and overseeing the work, two auto body repair workers, a person who disassembles and reassembles cars, a painter, and a detail person who assists the painter with getting the car ready to paint and sanding and waxing it afterward. Al Brown handles sales and estimating prices, runs errands and chases down parts, and envisions the future. Mary has been doing the bookkeeping and general paperwork. The owners and employees are very proud of CRB's reputation for doing high-quality work in the restoration of old cars made as far back as the 1930s.

CRB pays its employees based on "flagged hours," which are the number of paid hours that were estimated to complete the work (e.g., the estimate may say that it will take three hours to straighten a fender and prepare it for painting. When the auto body repair worker has completed straightening the fender, he would "flag" completion of three hours, whether it took him two or six hours to actually complete the work. It is to his benefit to be very fast and very good at what he does).

CRB pays the workers 40% of what it charges the customer for the flagged hours; the other funds are used to pay the employer's share of the taxes and overhead, with a small margin for profit. The foreman, who does some "flagged hours" auto body repair himself, is also paid a 5% commission on all the labor hours of the other employees, after the car is accepted as complete by the customer and the customer pays for the completed work.

Employees are given feedback by Al, the foreman, and by customers on an infrequent basis. Right now, everything is going well and the employees are working as a team. In the past, the situation was less certain and some employees had to be fired for poor work. When an employee filed for government-paid unemployment compensation saying that he was out of work through no fault of his own, CRB challenged the filing, and was able to prove that Al had given a memo to the employee requesting improvements in quality or quantity of work. There has never been a formal planning or appraisal process at CRB.

Mary Brown is reading about performance management and is wondering whether CRB should implement such a system. Please answer Mary's questions based on your understanding of this small business:

1. Would a performance management system work for our small business?
2. Discuss benefits that such a system would provide for us as owners and for our employees.
3. Explain any dangers our company faces if we do not have a performance management system. What could be a problem if we go with a poorly implemented system?
4. What 10 characteristics, at a minimum, should we include in a performance management system? Explain your answer with one to three sentences for each characteristic you recommend.
5. Explain how we could tie our current reward system to a performance management system.

ENDNOTES

1. DeNisi, A. S., & Kluger, A. N. (2000). Feedback effectiveness: Can 360-degree appraisals be improved? *Academy of Management Executive, 14*, 129–139.
2. Aguinis, H., Gottfredson, R. K., & Joo, H. (2012). Using performance management to win the talent war. *Business Horizons, 55*, 609–616.
3. Halachmi, A. (2005). Performance measurement is only one way of managing performance. *International Journal of Productivity and Performance Management, 54*, 502–516.
4. Fandray, D. (2001, May). Managing performance the Merrill Lynch way. *Workforce Online.* Retrieved January 2, 2018, from http://www.workforce.com/archive/feature/22/28/68/223512.php
5. Bisoux, T. (2004). Man, one business. *BizEd, 3*(4), 18–25.
6. Meinert, D. (2015). Reinventing reviews. *HR Magazine, 60*(3), 36–42.
7. Cleveland, J. N., & Murphy, R. E. (1989). Multiple uses of performance appraisal: Prevalence and correlates. *Journal of Applied Psychology, 74*, 130–135.
8. Allen, T. D., Eby, L. T., Chao, G. T., & Bauer, T. N. (2017). Taking stock of two relational aspects of organizational life: Tracing the history and shaping the future of socialization and mentoring research. *Journal of Applied Psychology, 102*, 324–337.
9. Berner, R. (2005, October 31). At Sears, a great communicator. *Business Week.* Retrieved January 2, 2018, from http://www.businessweek.com/magazine/content/05_44/b3957103.htm
10. Bilgin, K. U. (2007). Performance management for public personnel: Multi-analysis approach toward personnel. *Public Personnel Management, 36*, 93–113.
11. Adil, S. (2014). Building a culture of feedback. *Human Capital*, 32–34. Retrieved January 2, 2018, from Business Source Complete, EBSCOhost.
12. Cascio, W. F., & Aguinis, H. (2017). *Applied psychology in human resources management.* 7th ed. Thousand Oaks, CA: Sage.
13. Colvin, G. (2016). Developing an internal market for talent. *Fortune.* Retrieved January 2, 2018, from http://fortune.com/2016/03/11/acquisition-hires-recruiting-talent/
14. Finkelstein, L. M., Costanza, D. P., & Goodwin, G. F. (2017). Do your high potentials have potential? The impact of individual differences and designation on leader success. *Personnel Psychology, 71*(1), 3–22. doi:10.1111/peps.12225
15. Fandray, D. (2001, May). The new thinking in performance appraisals. *Workforce Online.* Retrieved January 2, 2018, from http://www.workforce.com/archive/feature/22/28/68/index.php?ht=selco%20selco
16. Gorman, C. A., Meriac, J. P., Roch, S. G., Ray, J. L., & Gamble, J. S. (2017). An exploratory study of current performance management practices: Human resource executives' perspectives. *International Journal of Selection and Assessment, 25*, 193–202.
17. Nankervis, A. R., & Compton, R. (2006). Performance management: Theory in practice? *Asia Pacific Journal of Human Resources, 44*, 83–101.
18. Cascio, W. F. (2011). The puzzle of performance management in the multinational enterprise. *Industrial and Organizational Psychology, 4*, 190–193.
19. Sumlin, R. (2011). Performance management: Impacts and trends. *DDI White Paper.* Retrieved January 2, 2018, from http://www.exinfm.com/pdffiles/pm.pdf
20. Maxwell, G., & Farquharson, L. (2008). Senior managers' perceptions of the practice of human resource management. *Employee Relations, 30*, 304–322.
21. Aguinis, H., Joo, H., & Gottfredson, R. K. (2011). Why we hate performance management—And why we should love it. *Business Horizons, 54*, 503–507.
22. Thomas, S. L., & Bretz, R. D. (1994). Research and practice in performance appraisal: Evaluating employee performance in America's largest companies. *SAM Advanced Management Journal, 59*(2), 28–34.
23. Mone, E. M., & London, M. (2010). *Employee engagement through effective performance management.* New York: Routledge.
24. Andiyasari, A., Riantoputra, C. D., & Matindas, R. W. (2017). Voice behavior: The role of perceived support and psychological ownership. *South East Asian Journal of Management, 11*, 1–24.

25. Hochstein, B. W., Lilly, B., & Stanley, S. M. (2017). Incorporating a counterproductive work behavior perspective into the salesperson deviance literature: Intentionally harmful acts and motivations for sales deviance. *Journal of Marketing Theory & Practice, 25*, 86–103.

26. Kuvaas, B. (2006). Performance appraisal satisfaction and employee outcomes: Mediating and moderating roles of work motivation. *International Journal of Human Resource Management, 17*, 504–522.

27. Pienaar, C., & Bester, C. (2009). Addressing career obstacles within a changing higher education work environment: Perspectives of academics. *South African Journal of Psychology, 39*, 376–385.

28. Aguinis, H., & O'Boyle, E. (2014). Star performers in twenty-first-century organizations. *Personnel Psychology, 67*, 313–350.

29. Silzer, R., Church, A., Rotolo, C., & Scott, J. (2016). I-O practice in action: Solving the leadership potential identification challenge in organizations. *Industrial and Organizational Psychology, 9*, 814–830.

30. Keeping, L. M., & Levy, P. E. (2000). Performance appraisal reactions: Measurement, modeling, and method bias. *Journal of Applied Psychology, 85*, 708–723.

31. Kulik, C. T., Ryan, S., Harper, S., & George, G. (2014). Aging populations and management. *Academy of Management Journal, 57*, 929–935.

32. Peters, T. (1987). *The new masters of excellence*. Niles, IL: Nightingale Conant Corp.

33. Bititci, U. S., Memdibil, K., Nudurupati, S., Turner, T., & Garengo, P. (2004). The interplay between performance measurement, organizational culture and management styles. *Measuring Business Excellence, 8*, 28–41.

34. Pennington, R. G. (2003). Change performance to change the culture. *Industrial and Commercial Training, 35*, 251.

35. Menefee, J., & Murphy, R. (2004). Rewarding and retaining the best: Compensation strategies for top performers. *Benefits Quarterly, 20*, 13–20.

36. Gabris, G. T., & Ihrke, D. M. (2001). Does performance appraisal contribute to heightened levels of employee burnout? The results of one study. *Public Personnel Management, 30*, 157–172.

37. Yahoo faces gender discrimination lawsuits from two men. (2016). *San Francisco Chronicle*. Retrieved from http://www.sfchronicle.com/business/article/Yahoo-faces-gender-discrimination-lawsuits-from-9972811.php; http://www.cnbc.com/2016/10/07/lawsuit-yahoo-ceo-tried-to-get-rid-of-male-employees.html

38. Yahoo ex-employee sues, alleging manipulation of performance reviews and gender bias. (2016). *Los Angeles Times*. Retrieved from http://www.latimes.com/business/technology/la-fi-tn-yahoo-lawsuit-20160202-story.html

39. Brown, M., & Benson, J. (2005). Managing to overload? Work overload and performance appraisal processes. *Group & Organization Management, 30*, 99–124.

40. Giancola, F. (2017). Getting perspective on the latest attempt to replace the most disliked HR practice. *Employee Benefit Plan Review, 71*(9), 5–8.

41. Meyer, H. H., Kay, E., & French, J. R. P. (1965). Assessing performance: Split roles in performance appraisal. *Harvard Business Review*. Retrieved from https://hbr.org/1965/01/split-roles-in-performance-appraisal

42. Cunningham, L. (2015). In big move, Accenture will get rid of annual performance reviews and rankings. *The Washington Post*. Retrieved from https://www.washingtonpost.com/news/on-leadership/wp/2015/07/21/in-big-move-accenture-will-get-rid-of-annual-performance-reviews-and-rankings/?utm_term=.bf3b8b986285

43. Adler, S., Campion, M., Colquitt, A., Grubb, A., Murphy, K., Ollander-Krane, R., & Pulakos, E. (2016). Getting rid of performance ratings: Genius or folly? A debate. *Industrial and Organizational Psychology, 9*, 219–252.

44. Cappelli, P., & Tavis, A. (2016, October). The performance management revolution. *Harvard Business Review*, 58–67.

45. DeNisi, A. S., & Murphy, K. R. (2017). Performance appraisal and performance management: 100 years of progress? *Journal of Applied Psychology, 102*, 421–433.

46. Burkus, D. (2016, June 1). How Adobe scrapped its performance review system and why it worked. *Forbes*. Retrieved January 2, 2018, from https://www.forbes.com/sites/davidburkus/2016/06/01/how-adobe-scrapped-its-performance-review-system-and-why-it-worked/#753a008755e8

47. Aguinis, H., Joo, H., & Gottfredson, R. K. (2012). Performance management universals: Think globally and act locally. *Business Horizons, 55*, 385–392.
48. McAdam, R., Hazlett, S., & Casey, C. (2005). Performance management in the UK public sector: Addressing multiple stakeholder complexity. *International Journal of Public Sector Management, 18*, 256–273.
49. Kim, Y. (2016). Introduction to contemporary practice of performance management and measurement systems in Korea. *Public Performance and Management Review, 39*, 273–278.
50. Claus, L., & Briscoe, D. (2009). Employee performance management across borders: A review of relevant academic literature. *International Journal of Management Reviews, 11*, 175–196.
51. Grund, C., & Sliwka, D. (2009). The anatomy of performance appraisals in Germany. *International Journal of Human Resource Management, 20*, 2049–2065.
52. Johnston, J. (2005). Performance measurement uncertainty on the Grand Canal: Ethical and productivity conflicts between social and economic agency? *International Journal of Productivity and Performance Management, 54*, 595–612.
53. Chang, E., & Hahn, J. (2006). Does pay-for-performance enhance perceived distributive justice for collectivistic employees? *Personnel Review, 35*, 397–412.
54. Taylor, M. S., Masterson, S. S., Renard, M. K., & Tracy, K. B. (1998). Managers' reactions to procedurally just performance management systems. *Academy of Management Journal, 41*, 568–579.
55. Thurston, P. W., Jr., & McNall, L. (2010). Justice perceptions of performance appraisal practices. *Journal of Managerial Psychology, 25*, 201–228.
56. Erdogan, B. (2002). Antecedents and consequences of justice perceptions in performance appraisals. *Human Resource Management Review, 12*, 555–578.
57. Taormina, R. J., & Gao, J. H. (2009). Identifying acceptable performance appraisal criteria: An international perspective. *Asia Pacific Journal of Human Resources, 47*, 102–125.
58. Cawley, B. D., Keeping, L. M., & Levy, P. E. (1998). Participation in the performance appraisal process and employee reactions: A meta-analytic review of field investigations. *Journal of Applied Psychology, 83*, 615–633.
59. Elicker, J. D., Levy, P. E., & Hall, R. J. (2006). The role of leader-member exchange in the performance appraisal process. *Journal of Management, 32*, 531–551.
60. Eddy, E. R., Stone, D. L., & Stone-Romero, E. F. (1999). The effects of information management policies on reactions to human resource information systems: An integration of privacy and procedural justice perspectives. *Personnel Psychology, 52*, 335–358.
61. Baldassarre, L., & Finken, L. (2015, August 12). GE's real-time performance development. *Harvard Business Review*. Retrieved January 2, 2018, from https://hbr.org/2015/08/ges-real-time-performance-development
62. Kirkpatrick, D. L. (2006). Training and performance appraisal—Are they related? *T&D, 60*(9), 44–45.
63. Ruiz, G. (2006). Performance management underperforms. *Workforce Management, 85*(12), 47–49.
64. Cascio, W. F., & Aguinis, H. (2008). Staffing twenty-first-century organizations. *Academy of Management Annals, 2*, 133–165.
65. Hunt, S. T. (2011). Technology is transforming the nature of performance management. *Industrial and Organizational Psychology, 4*, 188–189.
66. Ewenstein, B., Hancock, B., & Komm, A. (2016). Ahead of the curve: The future of performance management. *Mckinsey Quarterly, 2*, 64–73.
67. Tomczak, D. L., Lanzo, L. A., & Aguinis, H. (2018). Evidence-based recommendations for employee performance monitoring. *Business Horizons, 61*, 251–259.
68. Cascio, W. (2011). The puzzle of performance management in the multinational enterprise. *Industrial and Organizational Psychology, 4*, 190–193.
69. This case study is based, in part, on actual information. Network Solutions, Inc., is a pseudonym which is being used to protect the identity of the actual company in question.

2

Performance Management Process

*One bad day from one member of my staff doesn't mean they are not really good
at their jobs the rest of the time. I play a long game in terms of management.*

—Helen McCabe

Learning Objectives

By the end of this chapter, you will be able to do the following:

1. Articulate that performance management is an ongoing and circular process that includes the interrelated components of prerequisites, performance planning, performance execution, performance assessment, and performance review.

2. Argue that the poor implementation of any of the performance management process components has a negative impact on the system as a whole and that a dysfunctional or disrupted link between any two of the components also has a negative impact on the entire system.

3. Assemble important prerequisites needed before a performance management system is implemented, including knowledge of the organization's mission and strategic goals through strategic planning and knowledge of the job in question through work analysis.

4. Conduct work analysis to determine the tasks; knowledge, technology and other skills, and abilities (KSAs); work

activities, work context and working conditions of a particular job; and produce a job description that incorporates the KSAs of the job and information on the organization and unit mission and strategic goals.

5. Distinguish results from behaviors and understand the need to consider both as well as development plans in the performance planning stage of performance management.

6. Critique the employee's role in performance execution and distinguish areas over which the employee has primary responsibility from areas over which the manager has primary responsibility.

7. Recommend the employee's and the manager's responsibility in the performance assessment phase.

8. Be prepared to participate in appraisal meetings that involve the past, the present, and the future.

As described in Chapter 1, performance management is an ongoing process. It certainly does not take place just once a year. Also, performance management is a continuous process and includes several components.[1] Moreover, performance management is not "owned" by the HR function. Clearly, the HR function plays a critical role in terms of offering support and resources such as in-person and online training opportunities and online tools that can be used to measure performance and share feedback. But performance management must be owned and managed by each unit, and supervisors play a critical role. After all, the principal responsibility of managers is to manage, right?

The components of a performance management system are closely related to each other and the poor implementation of any of them has a negative impact on the performance management system as a whole. The components in the performance management process are shown in Figure 2-1. But here is an important clarification about this chapter: It is a sort of preview because it provides an overview and brief description of each of these components. So, when appropriate, the various sections in this chapter refer to which subsequent chapters include more detailed information on various topics. Let us start with the prerequisites.

FIGURE 2-1

Overview of Performance
Management Process and its
Components

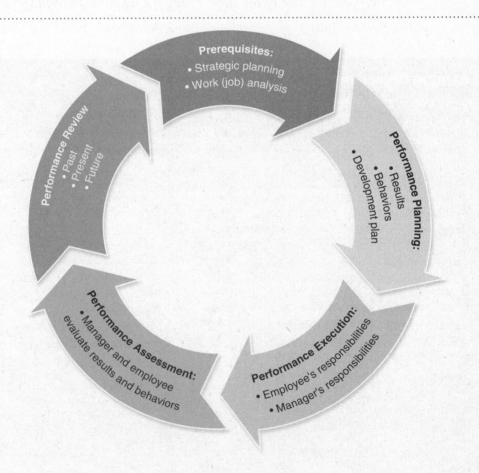

2-1 PREREQUISITES

There are two important prerequisites that are required before a performance management system is implemented. First, knowledge of the organization's mission and strategic goals. Second, knowledge of the job in question.[2]

2-1-1 Strategic Planning

Chapter 3 will address the strategic planning process in detail. For now, please consider that knowledge of the organization's mission and strategic goals is a result of strategic planning. Also, as will be discussed in detail in Chapter 3, the strategic planning process may actually take place *after* the mission and vision statements are created. In other words, there is a constant back and forth between mission and vision and strategic planning.

Strategic planning allows an organization to clearly define its purpose and reasons for existing, where it wants to be in the future, the goals it wants to achieve, and the strategies it will use to attain these goals. Once the goals for the entire organization have been established, similar goals cascade downward, with units setting objectives to support the organization's overall mission and objectives. The cascading continues downward until each employee has a set of goals compatible with those of the entire organization. The same process applies to large, small, and medium-size organizations.

Unfortunately, it is often the case that many organizational units are not in tune with the organization's strategic direction. However, there seems to be a trend in the positive direction. For example, a study including public sector organizations in Queensland, Australia, showed a fairly high level of strategic integration of the human resources (HR) function. Specifically, approximately 80% of the organizations that participated in the study were categorized as having achieved the highest level of strategic integration. This level is characterized by a dynamic and multifaceted linkage based on an "integrative relationship between people management and strategic management process."[3] Recall that an important objective of any performance management system is to enhance each employee's contribution to the goals of the organization. If there is a lack of clarity regarding where the organization wants to go, or if the relationship between the organization's mission and strategies and the unit's mission and strategies is not clear, there will be a lack of clarity regarding what each employee needs to do and achieve to help the organization get there.

2-1-2 Work (Job) Analysis

The second important prerequisite before a performance management system is implemented is to understand the job in question. Although, traditionally, the literature has used the term "job," the use of "work" is more appropriate today because job seems to convey the notion that there is a static, constant, and even rigid set of tasks and responsibilities.[4] In fact, given changes in the nature of work and organizations (as discussed in Chapter 1), jobs are anything but static. Because people are asked to work on new projects, participate in different teams, and use new apps and technologies on an ongoing basis, jobs also change on an ongoing basis. So, because new tasks and responsibilities are created all the time, new "jobs" are also created all the time and old ones are redesigned on an ongoing basis.[5] From this point onward, we will still use the term "job," but make sure you keep in mind this dynamic point of view.

Understanding employees' tasks and responsibilities is done through work analysis. Work analysis is a process of determining the key components of a particular job, including activities, tasks, products, services, and processes. A work analysis is a fundamental prerequisite of any performance management system because without a work analysis, it is difficult to understand what constitutes the required duties for a particular position. If we do not know what an employee is supposed to do on the job, we will not know what needs to be evaluated and how to do so.

As a result of a work analysis, we obtain information regarding the tasks to be carried out and the knowledge, skills, and abilities (KSAs) required of a particular job. Knowledge includes having the information needed to perform the work, but not necessarily having done it earlier. Skills refer to required attributes that are usually acquired by having done the work in the past. Ability refers to having the physical, emotional, intellectual, and psychological aptitude to perform the work, though neither having done the job nor having been trained to do the work is required.[6]

The tasks and KSAs needed for the various jobs are typically presented in the form of a job description, which summarizes the job duties, required KSAs, and working conditions for a particular position. As an illustration, see Figure 2-2. This job description includes information about what tasks are performed (e.g., operation of a specific type of truck). It also includes information about the required knowledge (e.g., manifests, bills of lading), skills (e.g., keeping truck and trailer under control, particularly in difficult weather conditions), and abilities (e.g., physical and spatial abilities needed to turn narrow corners).

Work Analysis Methods   Work analysis can be conducted using observation, off-the-shelf questionnaires, or interviews.[7] Data are collected from job incumbents (i.e., those doing the job at present) and their supervisors. Alternatively, if the job is yet to be created, data can be gathered from the individual(s) responsible for creating the new position and those who will supervise individuals in the new position. Observation methods include job analysts watching incumbents do the job, or even trying to do the work themselves, and then, producing a description of what they have observed. This method can be subject to biases because job analysts may not be able to distinguish important from unimportant tasks. Such analysis may not be suitable for many jobs. For example, a job analyst could not do the work of a police officer for safety reasons, or the work of a software programmer for lack of knowledge and skills to do the work. Off-the-shelf methods involve distributing questionnaires, including a common list of tasks or KSAs, and asking individuals to fill them out, indicating the extent to which each task or KSA is required for a particular job in question. These generic off-the-shelf tools can be practical, but they might not capture the nuances and idiosyncrasies of jobs out of the mainstream or jobs that involve novel technologies.

FIGURE 2-2

Job Description for Trailer Truck Driver: Civilian Personnel Management Service, U.S. Department of Defense

Operates gasoline- or diesel-powered truck or truck tractor equipped with two or more driving wheels and with four or more forward speed transmissions, which may include two or more gear ranges. These vehicles are coupled to a trailer or semitrailer by use of a turntable (fifth wheel) or pintle (pivot) hook. Drives over public roads to transport materials, merchandise, or equipment. Performs difficult driving tasks such as backing truck to loading platform, turning narrow corners, negotiating narrow passageways, and keeping truck and trailer under control, particularly on wet or icy highways. May assist in loading and unloading truck. May also handle manifest, bills of lading, expense accounts, and other papers pertinent to the shipment.

Interviews are a very popular work analysis method. During a work analysis interview, the job analyst asks the interviewee to describe what he or she does (or what individuals in the position do) during a typical day at the job from start to finish (i.e., in chronological order). Alternatively, the job analyst can ask the interviewee to describe the major duties involved in the job, and then, ask him or her to break down these duties into specific tasks. Once a list of tasks has been compiled, all incumbents should have an opportunity to review the information and rate each task in terms of frequency and criticality. The frequency and criticality scales may be the following[8]:

Frequency	Criticality
0: not performed	0: not critical
1: every few months to yearly	1: low level of criticality
2: every few weeks to monthly	2: below average level of criticality
3: every few days to weekly	3: average level of criticality
4: every few hours to daily	4: above average level of criticality
5: hourly to many times each hour	5: extremely critical

Rating both frequency and criticality is necessary because some tasks may be performed regularly (e.g., making coffee several times a day), but may not be very critical. The job analyst can then multiply the frequency scores by the criticality scores to obtain an overall score for each task. So, if making coffee receives a frequency score of 4 (i.e., "every few hours to daily") and a criticality score of 0 (i.e., "not critical"), the overall score would be $4 \times 0 = 0$. Considering frequency scores alone would have given us the wrong impression that making coffee is a task that deserved a prominent role in the job description. Overall scores for all tasks can be ranked from highest to lowest to obtain a final list of tasks.

Numerous work analysis questionnaires are available online. These questionnaires, which can be administered online, with a paper survey, or in interview format, can be used for a variety of positions. For example, the state of Delaware uses a work analysis questionnaire available at http://www.delawarepersonnel.com/class/forms/jaq/jaq.shtml. This questionnaire includes 18 multiple choice job content questions. Job content information is assessed through three factors (1) knowledge and skills, (2) problem solving, and (3) accountability and end results. For example, consider the following question about problem solving:

Which one statement most accurately describes your freedom to consider alternatives when addressing issues or problems? Select only one choice below.

- I follow detailed task lists or instructions from my supervisor or lead worker to get my work done. I refer problems immediately to my supervisor or others.
- I follow detailed standard procedures or instructions from my supervisor to get my work done. Occasionally, I change the work procedures or the order of the tasks (for example, filing records, sorting mail, cleaning floors).
- I follow standard work routines and well-understood tasks. Problems are alike from day-to-day. When problems arise, I can often respond by changing the order in which tasks are done (for example, typing, record

keeping, supply delivery, telephone console operation, technical assistance on a survey crew).

- Due to changing work situations, I solve problems by considering different options with the guidance of my supervisor or within well-defined principles and procedures. I often consider the most appropriate procedure or example to follow (for example, deciding the layout of bridge designs, counseling clients on social services options, or investigating and interpreting State and Federal laws in response to a complaint, and recommending an appropriate course of action).

- I solve problems by considering many different principles, procedures, and standards. Because of changing priorities and work situations, I may consider which among several procedures to follow, and in what order to achieve the proper results (for example, administering State support services, considering family counseling or foster care options for a family in crisis, or how to organize health screening clinics).

- I solve problems by considering courses of action within the framework of existing policies, principles, and standards. I know what needs to be accomplished, but must decide how to accomplish it. I may consider whether new methods need to be developed to achieve the proper results (for example, reengineering the way work is done and organized to improve the delivery of State services).

- I solve problems by considering courses of action within broad State or Department policies and immediate objectives. I may determine that new Department policies are needed. Although general goals are in place, I must set the plan and determine the priorities and processes to achieve State or Department objectives (for example, considering efficient organization of the largest Divisions in the State; developing new principles and practices affecting services to citizens).

As a second example, consider the following question about "external contacts:"

Which one statement best describes the degree that your job is accountable for establishing or maintaining relationships with external contacts? (External contacts may include the Federal Government, the legislature, the media, community service and action groups, vendors, contractors, other government Departments, the general public, etc.). Select only one choice below.

- Most job contacts are with other Department employees; external contacts sometimes occur (for example, food service and laundry work, or custodial work).

- Collecting or exchanging information, making or responding to inquiries (for example, clerical work, laboratory work, collecting tolls or groundskeeping).

- Providing Department or State services requiring explanation of somewhat complicated but standard procedures (for example, explaining how to get a State permit or license.)

- Ensuring or controlling the delivery of complex and somewhat controversial Department or State services to the public (for example, explaining child support payment schedules to a non-custodial parent, explaining environmental conservation laws).

- Persuading or influencing others within the framework of existing Department or State policies and practices and/or Federal law (for example, problem resolution in an environmental crisis or negotiating right-of-way for the State).
- Initiating new leads and contacts, building and improving external contact networks for the primary purpose of establishing new and substantial long-term strategic relationships and alliances for the Department or the State (for example, developing collaborative efforts with the Federal Government, negotiating union contracts).

Conducting a Google search for the phrase "job analysis questionnaire template" leads to several other instruments offered free of charge by the following organizations, among many others:

- Society for Human Resources Management
- University of Houston
- University of Toledo
- WorldatWork

Be aware that some of these instruments may have been created for specific types of positions and industries (e.g., service jobs, nonsupervisory jobs). Make sure you check the suitability of the instrument before using it in a different organizational and industry context. Combining items and formats from various instruments already available may be the most effective way to proceed.

An important component of a good work analysis is rater training. Such training helps mitigate several biases that can affect the accuracy of the information provided by individuals regarding KSAs needed for a job.[9] Consider the following biasing factors:

1. *Self-serving bias*. This bias leads people to report that *their own* behaviors and personality traits are more needed for successful job performance compared to behaviors and personality traits of others. This is because people tend to attribute success to themselves and failure to external causes (i.e., factors outside of their control).

2. *Social projection and false consensus bias*. Social projection bias leads people to believe that others behave similarly to themselves, and hence to think about themselves when reporting KSAs for their job, instead of people in general. False consensus bias is similar in that it leads people to believe that others share the same beliefs and attitudes as themselves.

3. *Carelessness bias*. Participants in job analysis differ in how carefully they attend to the job analysis rating task.[10] For example, they differ regarding how closely they read items, how appropriately they answer a specific question, and the extent to which they make needed distinctions between items. This bias is related to how people process information. Specifically, people rely on automatic (i.e., fast, effortless) and controlled (i.e., slow, effortful) information processing modes. So, they represent a potential trade-off between accuracy and quality (controlled processing) versus speed and efficiency (automatic processing). Careless bias results from the use of automatic versus controlled processes.

Taken together, self-serving, social projection, false consensus, and carelessness biases affect work analysis ratings because they lead people to believe that their own KSAs are those driving success on their jobs. So, these lead to an exaggerated view regarding the KSAs needed—and this exaggeration is based on precisely the KSAs that job incumbents have.

How do we address these biases? An experimental study involving two independent samples of 96 administrative support assistants and 95 supervisors working for a large city government implemented a successful Web-based training program that was able to mitigate some of these biases.[11] Specifically, across the five job characteristics rated in that study, individuals who did not participate in the Web-based training program were 62% (administrative support assistants) and 68% (supervisors) more likely to provide a higher rating than if the same individual provided the work analysis ratings after participating in the training program. The Web-based training program, which takes about 15 minutes to administer, provides a common frame of reference for all raters, and includes the following five steps:

1. provides raters with a definition of each rating dimension
2. defines the scale anchors
3. describes what behaviors were indicative of each dimension
4. allows raters to practice their rating skills, and
5. provides feedback on the practice

Job Descriptions The information obtained from a work analysis is used for writing a job description. Writing a job description may seem like a daunting task; however, it does not have to be difficult. Generic job descriptions can be obtained online from the Occupational Informational Network (O*NET), (https://www.onetonline.org). O*NET is a comprehensive database of worker attributes and job characteristics that provides a common language for defining and describing occupations. The information available via O*NET can serve as a foundation for a job description. For each job, O*NET provides information on tasks, knowledge, technology skills, abilities, work activities, work context, job zone, education, interests, work styles, work values, and credentials. Specifically:

- Personal requirements: the skills and knowledge required to perform the work
- Personal characteristics: the abilities, interests, and values needed to perform the work
- Experience requirements: the training and level of licensing and experience needed for the work
- Job requirements: the work activities and context, including the physical, social, and organizational factors involved in the work
- Labor market: the occupational outlook and the pay scale for the work

O*NET descriptions can be easily adapted and changed to accommodate specific local characteristics of a given organization. For example, see O*NET's description for truck drivers in Figure 2-3. This figure includes only some of the categories, and only the top five topics (you can see the full information online). First, the summary description can be checked for accuracy and relevance by supervisors. Then, the list of KSAs provided by O*NET can be readily rated by incumbents (and additional KSAs may be added, if needed). Clearly, this is a more detailed and useful job description compared to the generic description of truck driver in Figure 2-2.

FIGURE 2-3

Summary Report for Heavy and Tractor-trailer Truck Drivers (from O*NET)[a]

DESCRIPTION

- Drive a tractor-trailer combination or a truck with a capacity of at least 26,000 pounds Gross Vehicle Weight (GVW). May be required to unload truck. Requires commercial drivers' license.
- TASKS
- Check vehicles to ensure that mechanical, safety, and emergency equipment is in good working order.
- Follow appropriate safety procedures for transporting dangerous goods.
- Inspect loads to ensure that cargo is secure.
- Maintain logs of working hours or of vehicle service or repair status, following applicable State and Federal regulations.
- Secure cargo for transport, using ropes, blocks, chain, binders, or covers.

TECHNOLOGY SKILLS

- Database user interface and query software—ddlsoftware.com drivers daily log program DDL; Easy Trucking Software; Fog Line Software Truckn2004; TruckersHelper
- Office suite software—Microsoft Office
- Operating system software—Microsoft Windows
- Route navigation software—ALK Technologies PC Miler; MarcoSoft Quo Vadis
- Spreadsheet software—Microsoft Excel Hot technology.

KNOWLEDGE

- Transportation—Knowledge of principles and methods for moving people or goods by air, rail, sea, or road, including the relative costs and benefits.
- Public Safety and Security—Knowledge of relevant equipment, policies, procedures, and strategies to promote effective local, state, or national security operations for the protection of people, data, property, and institutions.
- Customer and Personal Service—Knowledge of principles and processes for providing customer and personal services. This includes customer needs assessment, meeting quality standards for services, and evaluation of customer satisfaction.
- English Language—Knowledge of the structure and content of the English language, including the meaning and spelling of words, rules of composition, and grammar.
- Mechanical—Knowledge of machines and tools, including their designs, uses, repair, and maintenance.

SKILLS

- Operation and Control—Controlling operations of equipment or systems.
- Operation Monitoring—Watching gauges, dials, or other indicators to make sure a machine is working properly.
- Time Management—Managing one's own time and the time of others.
- Critical Thinking—Using logic and reasoning to identify the strengths and weaknesses of alternative solutions, conclusions, or approaches to problems.
- Monitoring—Monitoring/Assessing performance of yourself, other individuals, or organizations to make improvements or take corrective action.

ABILITIES

- Control Precision—The ability to quickly and repeatedly adjust the controls of a machine or a vehicle to exact positions.
- Far Vision—The ability to see details at a distance.
- Multilimb Coordination—The ability to coordinate two or more limbs (for example, two arms, two legs, or one leg and one arm) while sitting, standing, or lying down. It does not involve performing the activities while the whole body is in motion.
- Near Vision—The ability to see details at close range (within a few feet of the observer).
- Reaction Time—The ability to quickly respond (with the hand, finger, or foot) to a signal (sound, light, picture) when it appears.

(Continued)

FIGURE 2-3

Summary Report for Heavy and Tractor-trailer Truck Drivers (from O*NET)[a] (*Continued*)

WORK ACTIVITIES
- Operating Vehicles, Mechanized Devices, or Equipment—Running, maneuvering, navigating, or driving vehicles or mechanized equipment, such as forklifts, passenger vehicles, aircraft, or water craft.
- Inspecting Equipment, Structures, or Material—Inspecting equipment, structures, or materials to identify the cause of errors or other problems or defects.
- Getting Information—Observing, receiving, and otherwise obtaining information from all relevant sources.
- Identifying Objects, Actions, and Events—Identifying information by categorizing, estimating, recognizing differences or similarities, and detecting changes in circumstances or events.
- Controlling Machines and Processes—Using either control mechanisms or direct physical activity to operate machines or processes (not including computers or vehicles).

DETAILED WORK ACTIVITIES
- Inspect motor vehicles.
- Follow safety procedures for vehicle operation.
- Inspect cargo to ensure it is properly loaded or secured.
- Record operational or production data.
- Record service or repair activities.

WORK CONTEXT
- In an Enclosed Vehicle or Equipment—88% responded "Every day."
- Duration of Typical Work Week—84% responded "More than 40 hours."
- Outdoors, Exposed to Weather—76% responded "Every day."
- Time Pressure—69% responded "Every day."
- Very Hot or Cold Temperatures—60% responded "Every day."

EDUCATION
- High school diploma or equivalent (56% of respondents)
- Less than high school diploma (19% of respondents)
- Post-secondary certificate (15% of respondents)

WORK STYLES
- Dependability—Job requires being reliable, responsible, and dependable, and fulfilling obligations.
- Self-control—Job requires maintaining composure, keeping emotions in check, controlling anger, and avoiding aggressive behavior, even in very difficult situations.
- Attention to Detail—Job requires being careful about detail and thorough in completing work tasks.
- Integrity—Job requires being honest and ethical.
- Stress Tolerance—Job requires accepting criticism and dealing calmly and effectively with high-stress situations.

WORK VALUES
- Support—Occupations that satisfy this work value offer supportive management that stands behind employees. Corresponding needs are Company Policies, Supervision: Human Relations, and Supervision: Technical.
- Independence—Occupations that satisfy this work value allow employees to work on their own and make decisions. Corresponding needs are Creativity, Responsibility, and Autonomy.
- Working Conditions—Occupations that satisfy this work value offer job security and good working conditions. Corresponding needs are Activity, Compensation, Independence, Security, Variety and Working Conditions.

[a]This description includes the top five in each category only.

O*NET is a particularly useful resource for small businesses because for most of them, conducting a work analysis may not be feasible simply because there are not sufficient numbers of people in any particular position from whom to collect data. In addition, O*NET can be used when organizations expand and new positions are created. Again, one thing needs to be clear, however: jobs change. Thus, job descriptions must be checked for accuracy and updated on an ongoing basis.

Job descriptions are a key prerequisite for any performance management system because they provide the criteria (i.e., yardsticks) that will be used in measuring performance. Such criteria may concern behaviors (i.e., how to perform) or results (i.e., what outcomes should result from performance). In our truck driver example, a behavioral criterion could involve the skill "equipment maintenance." For example, a supervisor may rate the extent to which the employee "performs routine maintenance on equipment and determines when and what kind of maintenance is needed." Regarding results, these criteria usually fall into one of the following categories (1) quality, (2) quantity, (3) cost-effectiveness, and (4) timeliness.[12] In the truck driver example, results-oriented criteria can include number of accidents (i.e., quality) and amount of load transported over a specific period of time (i.e., quantity).

Some organizations are becoming aware of the importance of considering prerequisites before implementing a performance management system. Take the case of AllianceHealth Deaconess Hospital in Oklahoma City, Oklahoma, which includes a workforce of more than 500 healthcare professionals, who maintain a 291-bed facility offering cancer care, cardiac care, orthopedic care, and wound care and rehabilitation. AllianceHealth Deaconess Hospital has been able to effectively integrate employees' job descriptions within their performance management system. The need for this integration was reinforced by results from an employee survey revealing that employees did not know what they were being evaluated on. Therefore, with the input of employees, the hospital updated each of the 260 job descriptions. At present, each employee's job description is part of the performance review form. The new forms incorporate task performance standards as well as behaviors specific to individual jobs. For example, a nurse may be evaluated on "how well he or she safely, timely, and respectfully administers patient medication and on his or her planning and organization skills." In addition, Deaconess Hospital has been able to link each employee's performance to the strategic goals of the organization. Specifically, all employees are rated on the following core behaviors considered to be of top strategic importance: (1) adaptability, (2) building customer loyalty, (3) building trust, and (4) contributing to team success.[13]

In summary, there are two important prerequisites that must exist before the implementation of a successful performance management system. First, there is a need to have good knowledge of the organization's mission and strategic goals. This knowledge, combined with knowledge regarding the mission and strategic goals of their unit, allows employees to make contributions that will have a positive impact on the unit and on the organization as a whole. Second, there is a need to have good knowledge of the position in question: what tasks need to be done, how they should be done, and what KSAs are needed. Such knowledge is obtained through a work analysis. If we have good information regarding a job, then it is easier to establish criteria for job success.

2-2 PERFORMANCE PLANNING

Armed with knowledge of the organization's strategic goals and information about the position, the supervisor and the employee formally meet to discuss, and agree upon, what needs to be done and how it should be done. This performance planning discussion includes a consideration of both results and behaviors (described in greater detail in Chapter 4), as well as a development plan (described in greater detail in Chapter 8).

2-2-1 Results

Results refer to what needs to be done or the outcomes an employee must produce. A consideration of results needs to include the *key accountabilities*, or broad areas of a job for which the employee is responsible for producing results. This information is typically obtained from the job description. A discussion of results also includes specific *objectives* that the employee will achieve as part of each accountability. Objectives are statements of important and measurable outcomes. Finally, discussing results also means discussing *performance standards*. A performance standard is a yardstick used to evaluate how well employees have achieved each objective. Performance standards provide information about acceptable and unacceptable performance (e.g., quality, quantity, cost, and time).

Consider the job of a university professor. Two key accountabilities are (1) teaching (preparation and delivery of instructional materials to students), and (2) research (creation and dissemination of new knowledge). An objective for teaching could be "to obtain a student evaluation of teaching performance of 3 on a 4-point scale." An objective for research could be "to publish two articles in scholarly refereed journals per year." Performance standards could be "to obtain a student evaluation of teaching performance of at least 2 on a 4-point scale" and "to publish at least one article in scholarly referred journals per year." Thus, the objective is the desired level of performance, whereas the standard is usually a minimum acceptable level of performance.

2-2-2 Behaviors

Although it is important to measure results, an exclusive emphasis on results can give a skewed or incomplete picture of employee performance. For example, for some jobs, it may be difficult to establish precise objectives and standards. For other jobs, employees may have control over how they do their jobs, but not over the results of their behaviors. For example, the sales figures of a salesperson could be affected more by the assigned sales territory than by the salesperson's ability and performance. Behaviors, or how a job is done, thus constitute an important component of the planning phase. This is probably why results from a survey indicated that in addition to sales figures, salespeople would like to be appraised on such behavioral criteria as communications skills and product knowledge.[14]

A consideration of behaviors includes discussing *competencies*, which are measurable clusters of KSAs that are critical in determining how results will be achieved. Examples of competencies are customer service, written or oral communication, creative thinking, and dependability. Returning to the example of the professor, assume that teaching is done online and numerous technology-related problems exist, so that the resulting teaching evaluations are deficient (i.e., lower than the standard of 2). This is an example of a situation in which behaviors should be given more importance than results. In this situation, the evaluation could include competencies such as online communication skills (e.g., in the chat room).

2-2-3 Development Plan

An important step before the review cycle begins is for the supervisor and employee to agree on a development plan. At a minimum, this plan should include identifying areas that need improvement and setting goals to be achieved in each area. Development plans usually include both results and behaviors.

In summary, performance planning includes the consideration of results and behaviors and the development plan. A discussion of results needs to include key accountabilities (i.e., broad areas for which an employee is responsible), specific objectives for each key accountability (i.e., goals to be reached), and performance standards (i.e., what constitutes acceptable and unacceptable levels of performance). A discussion of behaviors needs to include competencies (i.e., clusters of KSAs). Finally, the development plan includes a description of areas that need improving and goals to be achieved in each area. Box 2-1 includes a description of how performance planning is implemented at Discover.

Once the prerequisites are met and the planning phase has been completed, we are ready to begin the actual implementation of the performance management system. This includes performance execution, assessment, and review.

Box 2-1

Company Spotlight: Performance Planning at Discover

The Discover credit card was launched in 1986 and offered an important innovation that no other credit card company was doing at that time: cash back. But today, Discover offers direct bank and electronic payment services. Their direct bank issues the company's flagship credit card business and offers numerous banking products such as private student loans, personal loans, home equity loans, checking and savings accounts, certificates of deposit, and money market accounts. Also, Discover operates PULSE, one of the nation's leading ATM/debit networks; Discover Network, with millions of merchant and cash access locations; and Diners Club International, a global payments network with acceptance in more than 185 countries and territories. Discover is taking several steps to ensure that performance planning and employee development support the organization's business goals. Discover has initiated an approach that addresses the development needs of specific business units by assigning HR professionals to attend business meetings regularly to gain an understanding of what knowledge, skills, and abilities are required. The company asks managers to go through the same curriculum with classroom and online learning opportunities. These managers form discussion groups to talk about what they have learned and how it applies to the challenges of their specific role. In addition, part of the strategy includes meeting with employees to agree upon metrics in the performance planning stage, creating an action plan, and following up with evaluations and ratings to determine to what degree the learning experience was successful. In summary, Discover utilizes the various stages of the performance management process to ensure that employee development is a focus that matches the mission of providing a workplace that supports high performance.[15]

2-3 PERFORMANCE EXECUTION

Once the review cycle begins, the employee strives to produce the results and display the behaviors agreed upon earlier as well as to work on developmental needs. The employee has primary responsibility and ownership of this process. Employee participation does not begin at the performance execution stage, however. As noted earlier, employees need to have active input in the creation of job descriptions, performance standards, and the rating form. In addition, at later stages, employees are active participants in the evaluation process in that they provide a self-assessment, and the performance review interview is a two-way communication process. At the performance execution stage, the following factors must be present[16]:

1. *Commitment to goal achievement.* The employee must be committed to the goals that were set. One way to enhance commitment is to allow the employee to be an active participant in the process of setting the goals.

2. *Check-ins and performance touchpoints.* The employee has performance "touchpoints" with many people inside and outside of the organization on an ongoing basis. So, he should not wait until the review cycle is over to solicit performance feedback in the form of "check-ins." Also, the employee should not wait until a serious problem develops to ask for coaching. The employee needs to take a proactive role in soliciting performance feedback and coaching from her supervisor.[17] Supervisors and others with whom the employee has performance touchpoints (e.g., team members) can provide performance feedback, but are generally busy with multiple obligations. The burden is on the employee to communicate openly and regularly via ongoing check-ins with her performance touchpoints.

3. *Collecting and sharing performance data.* The employee should provide the supervisor with regular updates on progress toward goal achievement, in terms of both behaviors and results.

4. *Preparing for performance reviews.* The employee should not wait until the end of the review cycle approaches to prepare for the review. On the contrary, the employee should engage in an ongoing and realistic self-appraisal, so immediate corrective action can be taken, if necessary. The usefulness of the self-appraisal process can be enhanced by gathering informal performance information from peers and customers (both internal and external).

Although the employee has primary responsibilities for performance execution, the supervisor also needs to do her share of the work. Supervisors have primary responsibility over the following issues[18]:

1. *Observation and documentation.* Supervisors must observe and document performance on a daily basis. It is important to keep track of examples of both good and poor performance.

2. *Updates.* As the organization's goals may change, it is important to update and revise initial objectives, standards, and key accountabilities (in the case of results) and competency areas (in the case of behaviors).

3. *Feedback.* Feedback on progression toward goals and coaching to improve performance should be provided on a regular basis, and certainly before the review cycle is over.

4. *Resources.* Supervisors should provide employees with resources and opportunities to participate in development activities. Thus, they should encourage (and sponsor) participation in training, classes, and special assignments. Overall, supervisors have a responsibility to ensure that the employee has the necessary supplies and funding to perform the job properly.

5. *Reinforcement.* Supervisors must let employees know that their outstanding performance is noticed by reinforcing effective behaviors and progress toward goals. Also, supervisors should provide feedback regarding negative performance and how to remedy the observed problem. Observation and communication are not sufficient. Performance problems must be diagnosed early, and appropriate steps must be taken as soon as the problem is discovered.

The summary list included in Table 2-1 makes it clear that both the employee and the manager are responsible for performance execution. As an example of this shared responsibility, consider the case of International Business Machines (IBM). IBM is one the world's largest multinational technology companies, with more than 400,000 employees in 170 countries. IBM recently transitioned from the previous once-a-year "stack ranking" review that compared employees to a more frequent and personalized review focusing on the employee's own goals. Before deciding on a new performance management system, IBM's HR department asked for employees' input through its internal social media site. Employees reported they wanted more frequent feedback and the ability to change their goals as the year progressed. IBM recognized that the fast-paced business environment meant that new things come along, leading to employees experimenting and iterating. This meant that employees are often not working on what they originally proposed at the beginning of the year. Accordingly, a new system was designed that allows employees to set annual goals and short-term milestones. Based on continuous feedback from managers, employees are able to update their goals and milestones throughout the year. By allowing employees to change and develop their own goals throughout the year, IBM's managers can now avoid irrelevant year-end discussions, and have richer dialogue through frequent check-ins with employees.[19]

Employees	Managers
Commitment to goal achievement	Observation and documentation
Check-ins and performance touchpoints	Updates
Collecting and sharing performance data	Feedback
Preparing for performance reviews	Resources
	Reinforcement

TABLE 2-1
Performance Execution Stage: Areas for Which Employees and Managers Have Primary Responsibility

2-4 PERFORMANCE ASSESSMENT

In the assessment phase, both the employee and the manager are responsible for evaluating the extent to which the desired behaviors have been displayed, and whether the desired results have been achieved. Although many sources can be used to collect performance information (e.g., supervisors, other team members), in most cases, the direct supervisor provides the information. This also includes an evaluation of the extent to which the goals stated in the development plan have been achieved.

It is important that both the employee and the manager take ownership of the assessment process. The employee evaluates his own performance, and so does the manager. The fact that both parties are involved in the assessment provides good information to be used in the review phase. When both the employee and the supervisor are active participants in the evaluation process, there is a greater likelihood that the information will be used productively in the future. Specifically, the inclusion of self-ratings helps emphasize possible discrepancies between self-views and the views that important others (i.e., supervisors, other team members, customers) have of what we are doing, how we are doing it, and what results we are producing. It is the discrepancy between these views that is most likely to trigger development efforts, particularly when feedback from the supervisor and others is more negative than are employee self-evaluations.[20]

The inclusion of self-appraisals is also beneficial regarding important additional factors. Self-appraisals can reduce an employee's defensiveness during an appraisal meeting and increase the employee's satisfaction with the performance management system, as well as enhance perceptions of accuracy and fairness, and therefore, acceptance of the system.[21] Box 2-2 describes how this process is implemented at Google.

In sum, both the employee and the supervisor must evaluate employee performance. As will be described in detail in Chapter 6, employee involvement in the process increases employee ownership and commitment to the system. In addition, it provides important information to be discussed during the performance review, which is discussed next.

Box 2-2

Company Spotlight: Performance Assessment at Google

Google is consistently ranked at the top of Fortune's 100 Best Companies to Work For. Google uses a 360-degree review process, conducted semi-annually. Managers take two things into account when evaluating employees: results (what the employee accomplished), and behaviors (how the employee attained these results). The self-assessment, peer reviews, and manager reviews are based on a five-point scale (1 = needs improvement; 5 = superb) and use the following six criteria (1) "Googleyness"—adherence to Google values, (2) Problem solving—analytical skills applied to work, (3) Execution—delivering great work with great autonomy, (4) Thought leadership—how much an employee is seen as a reference for a specific area of expertise, (5) Leadership—displaying leadership skills such as being proactive and taking the lead on projects, and (6) Presence—the ability to make yourself known in a large organization. To reduce bias, managers meet and review all employee's ratings together. In summary, Google utilizes their performance assessment process to provide a clear link between each individual and team activity and the strategic objectives of the organization.[22]

2-5 PERFORMANCE REVIEW

The performance review stage involves the formal meeting between the employee and the manager to review their assessments. This meeting is usually called the *appraisal meeting* or *discussion*. Although good performance management systems include ongoing check-ins, the formal appraisal meeting is important because it provides a formal setting in which the employee receives feedback on her performance.

In spite of its importance in performance management, the appraisal meeting is often regarded as the "Achilles' heel of the entire process."[23] This is because many managers are uncomfortable providing performance feedback, particularly when performance is deficient.[24] This high level of discomfort, which often translates into anxiety and the avoidance of the appraisal interview, can be mitigated through training those responsible for providing feedback. As will be discussed in detail in Chapters 6 and 9, providing feedback in an effective manner is extremely important because it leads not only to performance improvement, but also to employee satisfaction with the system. For example, a study involving more than 200 teachers in Malaysia, including individuals with distinct Chinese, Malay, and Indian cultural backgrounds, found that when they received effective feedback, they reported greater satisfaction with the system even when they received low performance ratings.[25] At this point, however, let us emphasize that people are apprehensive about both receiving *and* giving performance information, and this apprehension reinforces the importance of a formal performance review as part of any performance management system.[26]

Remember Jack Welch, the famed former chairman and CEO of General Electric (GE)? Although his leadership style was unique, colorful, and often controversial, during his 20-year tenure at GE (1981–2000), the company's value rose about 4,000%. He has addressed the issue of giving honest feedback in many of his public appearances since he retired.[27] At an appearance in front of an audience of about 2,000 managers, he asked them if their organizations had integrity. As was expected, a vast majority of managers, about 95%, raised their hands. Then, he asked the same audience if their organization's leaders provide direct reports with honest and straightforward performance feedback. Only about 5% of the people raised their hands. Avoiding giving negative feedback is very dangerous because it conveys the message that mediocrity is acceptable and damages the morale of the top performers, who can be about four times as productive as the poor performers.[28]

In most cases, the appraisal meeting is regarded as a review of the past, that is, what was done (i.e., results) and how it was done (i.e., behaviors). For example, a survey including more than 150 organizations in Scotland showed that performance management systems in more than 80% of organizations emphasize the past.[29] But the appraisal meeting should also include a discussion of the employee's developmental progress as well as plans for the future. The conversation should include a discussion of goals and development plans that the employee will be expected to achieve over the period before the next formal review session. In addition, a good appraisal meeting includes information on what new compensation and rewards, if any, the employee could receive as a result of her performance. In short, the appraisal discussion focuses on the past (what has been done and how), the present (what compensation is received or denied as a result), and the future (goals to be attained before the upcoming review session).

As noted earlier, the discussion about past performance can be challenging, particularly when performance levels have not reached acceptable levels. Following is a script reflecting what the first few seconds of the appraisal meeting can be like.[30]

Good afternoon, Lucy, please have a seat. As you know, we take performance very seriously and we scheduled our meeting today to talk about the work you have done over the past year. Because we believe in the importance of talking about performance issues, I blocked an hour of my time during which I won't take any phone calls and I also won't be texting or emailing with anyone. I want to be able to focus 100% on our conversation because talking about performance will be helpful to both of us. There should be no surprises, given that we have been communicating about your performance on an ongoing basis. You have also received feedback not only from me, but also from your peers. Let's go through this process step by step. First, I would like you to tell me about your own views about your performance during the past year. Specifically, please share with me what are the things you believe you did particularly well and areas in which you think you may have been able to do better. As a second step, I will tell you about the performance evaluation I prepared. As a third step, we will talk about the issues on which you and I agree. As a fourth step, we can talk about issues for which we may have different perspectives. I will explain the reasoning behind my views and I want to hear the reasoning behind yours. In terms of my evaluation of your work, I want to first make sure we agree on what are the specific goals and objectives of your job. Then, we will talk about the results you achieved this year and the section on the evaluation form about job skills and competencies. After we talk about that, I will tell you what my overall rating is and why I believe this is an appropriate score. Ok, let's go ahead and start. Please tell me about how things went this past year.

We will discuss performance reviews in more detail in Chapter 9. For now, however, consider the following six recommended steps for conducting productive performance reviews[31]:

1. Identify what the employee has done well and poorly by citing specific positive and negative behaviors.
2. Solicit feedback from your employee about these behaviors. Listen for reactions and explanations.
3. Discuss the implications of changing, or not changing, the behaviors. Positive feedback is best, but an employee must be made aware of what will happen if any poor performance continues.
4. Explain to the employee how skills used in past achievements can help him overcome any current performance problems.
5. Agree on an action plan. Encourage the employee to invest in improving his performance by asking questions such as "What ideas do you have for _____ ?" and "What suggestions do you have for _____ ?"
6. Set up a meeting to follow up and agree on the behaviors, actions, and attitudes to be evaluated.

In closing, the performance management process includes a cycle, which starts with prerequisites and ends with the formal performance review. However, the cycle is not over after the formal review. In fact, the process starts all over again: there needs to be a discussion of prerequisites, including the updated organization's mission and strategic goals and the updated job's KSAs. Because markets change, customers' preferences and needs change, and products change, there is a need to continuously monitor the prerequisites so that performance planning, and all the subsequent stages, are consistent with the organization's strategic objectives. Recall that, in the end, one of the main goals of any performance management system is to promote the achievement of organization-wide goals. Obviously, if managers and employees are not aware of what these strategic goals are, it is unlikely that the performance management system will be instrumental in accomplishing the strategic goals.

SUMMARY POINTS

- Performance management is an ongoing and circular process. It never ends. Once established in an organization, it becomes part of an organization's culture. The performance management process includes five closely related components (1) prerequisites, (2) performance planning, (3) performance execution, (4) performance assessment, and (5) performance review.
- Each of the five components of the performance management process plays an important role. If any of these components is implemented poorly, then the entire performance management system suffers. For example, lack of knowledge of the organization's mission and strategic goals and the job in question (i.e., prerequisites) will not allow performance planning (i.e., performance road map) to be aligned with organizational goals, which in turn, will lead to poor performance execution. In short, a performance management system is only as good as its weakest component.
- The links between the various components must be clearly established. For example, performance planning needs to be closely related to performance execution. Performance planning is a futile exercise if execution does not follow from it. The same applies to all the arrows linking the various components, as shown in Figure 2-1.
- The first component of the performance management process involves two prerequisites. First, there is a need to have good knowledge of the organization's mission and strategic goals. This knowledge, combined with knowledge regarding the mission and strategic goals of one's unit, allows employees to make contributions that will have a positive impact on their units and on the organization as a whole. Second, there is a need to have good knowledge of the job in question. A work analysis allows for the determination of the key components of a particular job: what tasks need to be done, how they should be done, and what KSAs are needed. If we have good information regarding a job, then it is easier to establish criteria for job success.
- Work analysis is a technique used to understand employees' tasks and responsibilities and can be implemented using interviews, observation, or off-the-shelf questionnaires. It is important to train individuals to fill out

work analysis instruments so as to minimize biases (i.e., self-serving bias, social projection, false consensus, carelessness responding) in the resulting ratings. Once a list of tasks has been compiled, all incumbents should have an opportunity to review the information and rate each task in terms of its frequency and criticality.

- The second component of the performance management process involves performance planning. Performance planning includes the consideration of results and behaviors, as well as a development plan. A discussion of results needs to include key accountabilities (i.e., broad areas for which an employee is responsible), specific objectives for each key accountability (i.e., goals to be reached), and performance standards (i.e., what are acceptable and unacceptable levels of performance). A discussion of behaviors needs to include competencies (i.e., clusters of KSAs). Finally, the development plan includes a description of areas that need improvement and goals to be achieved in each area.

- The third component involves performance execution. Both the employee and the manager are responsible for performance execution. For example, the employee needs to be committed to goal achievement and should take a proactive role in seeking feedback from his or her supervisor and other performance touchpoints (e.g., other team members, customers). The burden is on the employee to communicate openly and regularly with the supervisor. Also, the employee has a responsibility to be prepared for the performance review by conducting regular and realistic self-appraisals. In addition, the supervisor also has important responsibilities. These include observing and documenting performance, updating the employee of any changes in the goals of the organization, and providing resources and reinforcement so the employee can succeed and continue to be motivated.

- The fourth component involves performance assessment. Both the employee and the supervisor must evaluate employee performance. Involvement of the employee in the process increases his or her ownership and commitment to the system. In addition, it provides important information to be discussed during the performance review. In the absence of self-appraisals, it is often not clear to supervisors if employees have a real understanding of what is expected of them.

- The fifth component involves performance review when the employee and manager meet to discuss employee performance. This formal meeting is usually called the appraisal meeting. This meeting typically emphasizes the past: what the employee has done and how it was done. But a more effective appraisal meeting also focuses on the present and the future. The present involves the changes in compensation that may result from the results obtained. The future involves a discussion of goals and development plans that the employee will be expected to achieve during the period before the next review session.

EXERCISE 2-1   WORK (JOB) ANALYSIS

Conduct a work analysis for the position "wait staff" at a local restaurant. This work analysis may benefit from interviewing incumbents (i.e., wait staff) as well as supervisors (i.e., restaurant's general manager). In addition, of course, you can rely on your own knowledge of this job. By the end of your work analysis, follow the O*NET format and create a summary description for the position as well as a list of tasks, technology skills, abilities, work activities, work context, education, work styles, and work values needed for successful performance. Use Figure 2-3 "Summary Report for Heavy and Tractor-Trailer Truck Drivers (from O*NET)" as a template.

At a minimum, your job description should include four lists—one for tasks, one for knowledge, one for skills, and one for abilities. For each of the four lists, rate the corresponding elements in terms of frequency and criticality. Use the scales provided below to rate each element. Then, multiply the frequency and criticality scores for each of the elements in each list to obtain its overall score. Then, arrange the list of elements in order of importance from high to low.

Frequency and Criticality Scales	
Frequency	**Criticality**
0: not performed	0: not critical
1: every few months to yearly	1: low level of criticality
2: every few weeks to monthly	2: below average level of criticality
3: every few days to weekly	3: average level of criticality
4: every few hours to daily	4: above average level of criticality
5: hourly to many times each hour	5: extremely critical

Have one or more people do the same rating task with the same job description. Then, answer the following questions.

1. Are there any disagreements between or among the resulting orderings? If so, why do you think that is the case?

2. What can be done to mitigate any observed disagreement between or among the resulting orderings? After discussing some possible techniques to reduce disagreement, if there were indeed any disagreements, apply some of those techniques until 100% agreement is reached.

3. Recall that tasks listed in a job description can largely be divided into behaviors (i.e., how to perform) and results (i.e., what outcomes should result from performance). In the job description you created, which of the tasks are behaviors and which tasks are outcomes? Are there more behaviors or more outcomes? Or, is there a strong balance between the two types of tasks? Whether there is such an imbalance or balance, do you think the observed (im)balance is justified? Explain.

EXERCISE 2-2   PERFORMANCE REVIEW MEETING

As part of this exercise, you are asked to conduct a performance review meeting in front of the class. Specifically, you will prepare a performance assessment of student participation in the classroom for a particular student, and then, meet with that student to deliver the performance review face-to-face and real-time in front of the class. You will either play the role of the supervising manager giving the performance review, or the direct report receiving the performance review.

Steps:

1. Conduct a self-appraisal of your own class participation performance
   a. Rate your participation from 0 (lowest level contribution) to 15 (highest possible contribution) on each of the items listed below and note the reasons for the score you assign yourself.
   b. In rating participation, use the following specific eight items:
      i. Being an active participant, but not a dominating participant.
      ii. Being a good listener and demonstrating respect for others' opinions.
      iii. Making thoughtful, insightful comments, and not speaking just to be heard.
      iv. Building on others' comments.
      v. Asking questions, not just giving answers.
      vi. Identifying key assumptions underlying discussion points and arguments.
      vii. Judiciously playing the role of the "devil's advocate".
      viii. Being constructive and positive in one's comments.

2. Choose any five students from the class and prepare an assessment of their participation performance.
   a. Rate their participation from 0 (lowest level contribution) to 15 (highest possible contribution) using the same eight items listed above.

3. Prepare to provide a performance review to each of these five classmates, including ratings and the reasons for the scores you assigned them. (Hint: Consider the steps of the performance management cycle in Figure 2-1 when writing your assessment).
   a. The performance review meeting should not be longer than 10 minutes (Hint: The performance review subsection of the chapter lists the issues typically discussed in a performance review, and provides an example of how to begin a review).
   b. Make sure to include both positive and negative feedback that allows your classmates to improve their performance.

4. The other students in the classroom will then evaluate the performance review meeting and provide feedback on how performance review meetings can be improved in the future.

Disrupted Links in the Performance Management Process at Omega, Inc.[32]

Omega, Inc., is a small manufacturing company whose sales success or failure rests in the hands of sales representatives employed by franchised dealers operating independently. Omega faces a challenging situation because it does not have control over the people working for the independent dealerships. In fact, it is the performance of these individuals that dictates Omega's sales success. To make things even more complicated, until recently, there was no clear understanding of the role of the sales representatives and there were no formal sales processes in place. Sales representatives varied greatly in terms of their level of skill and knowledge; most put in little effort beyond taking orders, and they did not feel motivated to make additional sales. Finally, franchises varied greatly regarding their management strategies and follow-up with Omega.

Recently, understanding the need to improve the performance of sales representatives, Omega agreed to partially fund and support a training program for them. The network of franchise owners, in turn, agreed to work together to implement a performance management system. As a first step in creating the performance management system, the franchise owners conducted a work analysis of the role of the sale representatives, wrote a job description, and distributed it to all sales representatives. The franchise owners also adopted a franchise-wide mission statement based primarily on the need to provide high-quality customer service. This mission statement was posted in all franchise offices, and each franchise owner spoke with his employees about the contribution made by individual sales on achieving their mission. As a second step, the managers set performance goals (i.e., sales quotas) for each employee. Then, all sales representatives attended extensive training sessions. The employees received feedback based on their performance in the training course, and then, were reminded once again of their sales quotas.

Back on the job, managers gave feedback to their employees regarding their standing in relation to their sales quotas. Since the employees had no way of monitoring their own progress toward their quotas, the performance feedback consisted of little more than a reiteration of monthly sales goals. There was no performance appraisal form in place, so discussions were not documented. This lack of feedback continued, and although sales quotas were being met for the first few months, franchise owners received complaints from customers about the low quality of customer service they were receiving. Subsequently, sales began to decline. Furthermore, many orders were often incorrect, forcing customers to return items to Omega.

While the new performance management process was an improvement over no performance management (at least initially), the franchise owners were still far from having a system that included a smooth transition between each of the components of the performance management process. Based on Omega's situation, please answer the following questions.

1. Consider each of the links of the performance management process as shown in Figure 2-1:

    a. prerequisites → performance planning
    b. performance planning → performance execution
    c. performance execution → performance assessment
    d. performance assessment → performance review
    e. performance review → prerequisites

    Discuss whether each of the links is present, and in what form, in the performance management system described.

2. Given your answers to question 1, what can be done to fix each of the disrupted links in the process?

Performance Management at KS Cleaners

KS Cleaners (KSC) is a small company that provides several services to its customers: dry cleaning of clothes, laundry, ironing, and some clothing repair work. KSC specializes in low-cost volume, promising that dry cleaning will be returned to its customers the day after it is turned in. The charge is $2.25 for each item dry-cleaned; there is an extra charge for ironing, although ironing is usually not necessary because the items are placed on clothes hangers immediately after they are removed from the dryers. Laundry is $1.50 per item, with an extra charge for ironing, if desired. Clothing repair, such as hemming, replacement of buttons and zippers, and so on, is charged by the hour.

In addition to Kevin, the owner and manager, there are eight employees: two dry cleaners, a seamstress, and five general duty employees, who rotate where they are needed among front counter customer service and sorting clothes, loading the machines, removing clothes from machines, folding or hanging up the items, and preparing them for pickup. Kevin has found that he can hire teenagers for the general duty positions, because these duties do not require much training. The company needs employees who are focused on customer satisfaction and quick turnaround; when there are slow times, however, these high school students often work on homework, socialize, or spend time on their smart phones, which is acceptable behavior as long as the work gets done and the customers are happy.

Pay ranges from minimum wage for the general duty employees to $20 per hour for the dry cleaners. The seamstress is paid on a negotiated piecework basis, depending on the complexity of the task.

This shop has been doing so well that Kevin is thinking about opening another one. He has done some research and realizes that he will need to formalize procedures that, heretofore, he has run almost by instinct. A new manager will need to operate the new shop in a fashion that is identical to the successful way he has run his current shop. Although he dreads the process, he recognizes that it is time to document procedures and to formalize job descriptions. He has hired you to help him develop a performance management process.

1. In the context of KSC, critically evaluate the availability of any prerequisites to implementing a performance management process.
2. Discuss your plans for developing formal job descriptions for the employees at the second shop.
3. Explain key features of developing performance plans for the employees. Provide examples of factors you would consider in developing such plans for the dry cleaner.
4. In the context of KSC, create two results-oriented performance standards for the general duty employees.
5. The following information was obtained from O*NET.

41-2021.00 - Counter and Rental Clerks

Knowledge: Customer and Personal Service—Knowledge of principles and processes for providing customer and personal services. This includes customer needs assessment, meeting quality standards for services, and evaluation of customer satisfaction.

Technology Skills: Database user interface and query software—Database software.

Abilities: Oral Expression—The ability to communicate information and ideas in speaking so others will understand.

Work Activities—Performing for or Working Directly with the Public—Performing for people or dealing directly with the public. This includes serving customers in restaurants and stores, and receiving clients or guests.

Discuss the factors that should be considered in establishing behavior-oriented performance standards for the general duty employees. Give an example of such a standard.

6. Provide a detailed discussion of both the responsibilities of the manager and the responsibilities of the general duty employees during the performance execution phase.

7. Explain the process that Kevin should use to get information when he is developing the performance assessments for the general duty employees.

ENDNOTES

1. The general framework and labels for these components are based on Grote, D. (1996). *The complete guide to performance appraisal* (Chap. 2). New York: American Management Association.

2. Aguinis, H. (2009). An expanded view of performance management. In J. W. Smither & M. London (Eds.), *Performance management: Putting research into practice* (pp. 1–43). San Francisco, CA: Wiley.

3. Teo, S. (2000). Evidence of strategic HRM linkages in eleven Australian corporatized public sector organizations. *Public Personnel Management, 29*, 557–574.

4. Sanchez, J., & Levine, E. L. (2012). The rise and fall of job analysis and the future of work analysis. *Annual Review of Psychology, 63*, 397–425.

5. Parker, S. K., Morgeson, F. P., & Johns, G. (2017). One hundred years of work design research: Looking back and looking forward. *Journal of Applied Psychology, 102*, 403–420.

6. Van Iddekinge, C. H., Raymark, P. H., & Eidson, J. E. (2011). An examination of the validity and incremental value of needed-at-entry ratings for a customer service job. *Applied Psychology: An International Review, 60*, 24–45.

7. Morgeson, F. P. (2017). Job analysis. In S. G. Rogelberg (Ed.), *The SAGE encyclopedia of industrial/organizational psychology* (2nd ed.,Vol. 2, pp. 765–768). Thousand Oaks, CA: Sage.

8. Rodriguez, D., Patel, R., Bright, A., Gregory, D., & Gowing, M. K. (2002). Developing competency models to promote integrated human-resource practices. *Human Resource Management, 41*, 309–324.

9. DuVernet, A. M., Wilson, M. A., & Dierdorff, E. C. (2015). Exploring factors that influence work analysis data: A meta-analysis of design choices, purposes, and organizational context. *Journal of Applied Psychology, 100*, 1603–1633.

10. Morgeson, F. P., Spitzmuller, M., Garza, A. S., & Campion, M. A. (2016). Pay attention! The liabilities of respondent experience and carelessness when making job analysis judgments. *Journal of Management, 42*, 1904–1933.

11. Aguinis, H., Mazurkiewicz, M. D., & Heggestad, E. D. (2009). Using web-based frame-of-reference training to decrease biases in personality-based job analysis: An experimental field study. *Personnel Psychology, 62*, 405–438.

12. Banner, D. K., & Graber, J. M. (1985). Critical issues in performance appraisal. *Journal of Management Development, 4*, 27–35.

13. Erickson, P. B. (2002, March 24). Performance feedback boosts employee morale, experts in Oklahoma City Say. *The Daily Oklahoman,* OK-Worker-Reviews section.

14. Pettijohn, L. S., Parker, R. S., Pettijohn, C. E., & Kent, J. L. (2001). Performance appraisals: Usage, criteria and observations. *Journal of Management Development, 20*, 754–781.

15. Whitney, K. (2005, August). Discover: It pays to develop leaders. *Chief Learning Officer, 48*.

16. Grote, *The complete guide to performance appraisal*, pp. 22–24.

17. VandeWalle, D., Ganesan, S., Challagalla, G. N., & Brown, S. P. (2000). An integrated model of feedback-seeking behavior: Disposition, context, and cognition. *Journal of Applied Psychology, 85*, 996–1003.

18. Grote, *The complete guide to performance appraisal*, pp. 27–32.

19. Zillman, C. (2016, February 1). IBM is blowing up its annual performance review. *Fortune.* Retrieved January 3, 2018, from http://fortune.com/2016/02/01/ibm-employee-performance-reviews

20. Brown, A., Lin, Y., & Inceoglu, I. (2017). Preventing rater biases in 360-degree feedback by forcing choice. *Organizational Research Methods, 20*, 121–148.

21. Dhiman, A., & Maheshwari, S. K. (2013). Performance appraisal politics from appraisee perspective: A study of antecedents in the Indian context. *International Journal of Human Resource Management, 24*, 1202–1235.

22. Homen de Mello, F. S. (2015). *Google's performance management practices.* Retrieved January 3, 2018, from http://www.qulture.rocks/blog/googles-performance-management-practices-part-1

23. Kikoski, J. F. (1999). Effective communication in the performance appraisal interview: Face-to-face communication for public managers in the culturally diverse workplace. *Public Personnel Management, 28*, 301–322.

24. Cianci, A. M., Klein, H. J., & Seijts, G. H. (2010). The effect of negative feedback on tension and subsequent performance: The main and interactive effects of goal content and conscientiousness. *Journal of Applied Psychology, 95*, 618–630.

25. Rahman, S. A. (2006). Attitudes of Malaysian teachers toward a performance-appraisal system. *Journal of Applied Social Psychology, 36*, 3031–3042.

26. London, M. (2003). *Job feedback: Giving, seeking, and using feedback for performance improvement* (2nd ed.). Mahwah, NJ: Lawrence Erlbaum.

27. Rogers, B. (2006). High performance is more than a dream—It's a culture. *T&D, 60*(1), 12.

28. Aguinis, H., & Bradley, K. J. (2015). The secret sauce for organizational success: Managing and producing star performers. *Organizational Dynamics, 44*, 161–168.

29. Soltani, E. (2003). Towards a TQM-driven HR performance evaluation: An empirical study. *Employee Relations, 25*, 347–370.

30. This material is based on Grote, D. (1998). Painless performance appraisals focus on results, behaviors. *HR Magazine, 43*(11), 52–56.

31. Grossman, J. H., & Parkinson, J. R. (2002). *Becoming a successful manager: How to make a smooth transition from managing yourself to managing others* (pp. 142–145). Chicago, IL: McGraw-Hill Professional.

32. This case study is loosely based on Swinney, J., & Couch, B. (2003). *Sales performance improvement getting results through a franchise sales organization.* International Society for Performance Improvement Case Studies.

3

Performance Management and Strategic Planning

*Strategy is a style of thinking, a conscious and deliberate process,
an intensive implementation system, the science of insuring future success.*

—Pete Johnson

Learning Objectives

By the end of this chapter, you will be able to do the following:

1. Critique the definition and purposes of strategic planning.

2. Create alignment between performance management and an organization's strategic priorities and direction.

3. Assess the critical role of the HR function in the strategic planning process.

4. Devise an environmental (i.e., SWOT) analysis that includes a consideration of both internal (strengths and weaknesses) and external (opportunities and threats) trends.

5. Prepare a gap analysis resulting from a consideration of external and internal trends that identify leverage,

constraints, vulnerabilities, and problems that dictate an organization's mission.

6. Produce state-of-the-science mission and vision statements, objectives, and strategies for the organization and its units.

7. Devise job descriptions that take into account a unit's and the organization's vision, mission, objectives, and strategies.

8. Build up support for the performance management system by using it as a tool to help achieve the organization's strategic priorities.

In Chapters 1 and 2, we discussed the fact that good performance management systems encourage employees to make tangible and important contributions toward the organization's strategic objectives. When these contributions to the top organizational and unit priorities are made clear, performance management systems are likely to receive crucial top management support. Without this support, it is unlikely that a performance management system will even get off the ground. How, then, are these strategic organizational objectives identified? How does an organization know what the "target" should be, what it is trying to accomplish, and how to do it?

The HR function plays a key role as strategic partner in helping to answer these questions. Unfortunately, the HR function is often vilified as being merely operational and not able to think or act strategically. Well, over the past two decades or so, an entire new field of research and practice has emerged, called *strategic human resource management* (SHRM). SHRM is about planning and implementing HR policies and activities with the goal of enabling an organization to achieve its objectives.[1] Performance management is an ideal vehicle to demonstrate the strategic role and contributions of the HR function because it allows for explicit and clear links between what HR is doing and the organization's mission, vision, and objectives. By being involved, and hopefully, leading the rollout of the strategic planning process and linking a firm's objectives with the performance management system, the HR function can serve as an expert internal consultant who has got a "seat at the table" of the top management team. In fact, the few CEOs with a HR background, including Samuel R. Allen at John Deere, James C. Smith at Thomson Reuters, Steven L. Newman at Transocean, and Mary Barra at General Motors, have been able to serve as strategic partners while heading their respective HR units, which is, in large part, what propelled their trajectory into the very top of their organizations. First, let us define strategic planning and describe its purposes.

3-1 DEFINITION AND PURPOSES OF STRATEGIC PLANNING

Strategic planning is a process that involves describing the organization's destination, assessing barriers that stand in the way of that destination, and selecting approaches for moving forward.[2] Among other useful outcomes, strategic planning allows for the allocation of resources in a way that provides organizations with a competitive advantage because they are assigned in a more effective and more targeted manner.[3] Overall, a strategic plan serves as a blueprint that defines how the organization will allocate its resources in pursuit of its most critical and important objectives.

Strategic planning serves the following seven specific purposes. First and foremost, strategic planning allows organizations to define their identity. In other words, it provides organizations with a clearer sense of who they are and what their purpose is. Second, strategic planning helps organizations prepare for the future because it clarifies their desired destination. Knowing where the organization wants to go is a key first step in planning how to get there, and then, doing so. Third, strategic planning allows organizations to analyze their external and internal environment, and doing so enhances their ability to adapt to environmental changes and even anticipate future changes. Although knowledge of the environment does not guarantee that an organization will be more likely to change and adapt, this knowledge is the first and critical step toward possible adaptation. Fourth, strategic planning provides organizations with focus and allows them to allocate resources to what matters most. In turn, the improved allocation of resources is likely to stimulate growth and improve organizational performance and profitability. Fifth, strategic planning helps produce a common perspective and culture of cooperation within the organization, given that a common set of objectives is created. Such a common agenda and culture of cooperation can gain organizations a key competitive advantage. Sixth, strategic planning can be a good corporate eye-opener because it generates new options and opportunities to be considered. For example, new opportunities can include expanding to new markets or offering new products. Finally, strategic planning can be a powerful tool to guide employees' daily activities because it identifies the behaviors and results that are directly linked to the organization's objective and really matter. Thus, a strategic plan provides critical information to be used in the performance management system. To summarize, Table 3-1 lists key purposes of a strategic plan.

TABLE 3-1
Strategic Plan: Purposes

Helps define the organization's identity

Helps organizations prepare for the future

Enhances ability to adapt to environmental changes

Provides focus and allows for better allocation of resources

Produces an organizational culture of cooperation

Allows for the consideration of new options and opportunities

Provides employees with information to direct daily activities

3-2 PROCESS OF LINKING PERFORMANCE MANAGEMENT TO THE STRATEGIC PLAN

The mere presence of a strategic plan does not guarantee that this information will be used effectively as part of the performance management system. In fact, countless organizations spend thousands of hours creating strategic plans that are mostly talk but do not lead to tangible actions. The process then ends up being a huge waste of time and a source of frustration and long-lasting cynicism, particularly in situations when there is frequent leadership turnover and a strategic planning process is put into motion over and over again, leading to nothing more than reports and updated website content. In those situations, it is typical to hear people say: "Oh no, again! Another CEO and another strategic plan!" For example, a worldwide survey of senior executives from 197 companies with combined sales exceeding US$500 million showed that less than 15% spent any time evaluating how the previous year's strategic plan affected current performance. The study also found that corporate strategies routinely only deliver between 50% and 63% of their potential financial performance.[4] Thus, to ensure that strategy cascades down the organization and leads to concrete actions, a conscious effort must be made to link the strategic plan with what everyone does in the organization on a daily basis.

Figure 3-1 provides a useful framework for understanding the relationship between an organization's strategic plan, a unit's strategic plan, and job descriptions (which are the drivers of individual and team tasks and required KSAs—as described in Chapter 2). The organization's strategic plan includes a mission statement and a vision statement, as well as objectives and strategies that will allow for the fulfillment of the mission and vision. The strategies are created with

FIGURE 3-1

Link Among Organization and Unit Strategic Plans, and Job Descriptions

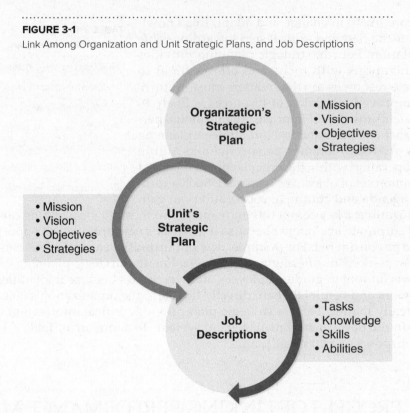

the participation of managers at all levels. The higher the level of involvement, the more likely it is that managers will see the resulting strategies favorably.[5] As soon as the organizational strategies have been defined, senior management proceeds to meet with department or unit managers, who in turn, solicit input from all people within their units to create unit-level mission and vision statements, objectives, and strategies. A critical issue is to ensure that each unit's or department's mission and vision statements, objectives, and strategies are consistent with those at the organizational level. Job descriptions are then revised and updated to make sure they are consistent with unit and organizational priorities. Driven by the job descriptions, results and behaviors as well as development plans are then consistent with the organizational- and department-level priorities.

Does the process of aligning organizational, unit, and individual priorities actually work in practice? Is this doable? The answer to these questions is "yes," and the benefits of doing so are widely documented. Specifically, performance management systems have a critical role in translating strategy into action.[6] In fact, a study including 338 organizations in 42 countries found that performance management is the third most important factor affecting the success of a strategic plan. This is particularly true for organizations that operate in rapidly changing environments, regardless of their size, industry, and age.[7]

One way to formalize the link between strategic planning and performance management is through the implementation of a *Balanced Scorecard*. Although this approach has been revised since it was originally proposed by Kaplan and Norton in 1992,[8] the basic components are largely unchanged. In a nutshell, a balanced scorecard involves creating indicators of individual performance along four separate "perspectives" of an organization's success. For the case of a bank, consider the following: (a) financial (e.g., cost control, sales growth rate, profit growth rate), (b) customer (e.g., service product quality, customer satisfaction, service timing), (c) internal process (e.g., information delivery, interaction between employees and clients, standard operation process), and (d) learning and growth (e.g., corporate image, competitiveness, employee satisfaction).

In addition to including individual performance measures that go beyond pure financial goals, an important feature of balanced scorecards is that each of the indicators should be directly related to a firm's mission and vision. This is usually shown graphically with a *strategy map*, which is a flowchart type diagram with circles and arrows that links objectives developed for each of the four perspectives in a causal chain that eventually leads to a direct impact on the firm's objectives. For example, regarding the illustrative financial indicators mentioned earlier, a strategy map could show the following sequence: employee satisfaction (learning and growth) → interaction between employees and clients (internal processes) → customer satisfaction (customer) → sales growth rate (financial), which leads to achieving the bank's objective of increasing the number of corporate accounts and the total value of commercial loans by the end of the quarter. As a more general example of linking strategy and performance management that does not include the specific balanced scorecard approach, consider the case of KeyBank, a financial services company with assets of US$134.5 billion, which provides investment management, retail and commercial banking, consumer finance, and investment banking products and services. KeyBank has more than 1,200 branches, 1,500 ATMs, and 18,000 employees. In 2015, KeyBank was ranked 540th on the Fortune 500 list. In the state of Utah, KeyBank successfully developed a performance management system that is aligned with the strategic plan of the organization.[9] To do this, the bank first involved managers at all hierarchical levels to develop an organization mission statement. Next, they developed objectives and strategies that would help achieve KeyBank's mission. The mission statement, objectives, and strategies at the organizational level served as the foundation for developing the strategies for individual branches. To develop these, senior managers met with branch managers to discuss the organization's objectives and strategies and to explain the importance of adopting similar ones in each branch. Subsequently, each of the branch managers met with their employees to develop branch mission statements and objectives. One important premise in this exercise was that each branch's mission statement and objectives had to be aligned with the corporate mission statement, objectives, and strategies. After organizational and branch objectives and strategies were aligned, managers and employees reviewed individual job descriptions. That is, each job description was tailored so that individual tasks, duties, and responsibilities were clear and contributed to meeting the department's and the organization's objectives. Involving employees in this process helped them to gain a clear understanding of how their performance affected the branch, and in turn, the organization. A revised version of the process implemented at KeyBank of Utah is shown in Figure 3-2.

Consider KeyBank's overall and branch mission statements in Figure 3-2 and the brief job description for bank teller. Now, re-read the more detailed job description from O*NET for a truck driver in Figure 2-3. What are the critical technology skills and abilities that could be included in the bank teller job description to make it more specific and useful and congruent with organization- and branch-level objectives? What are some key results and behaviors that should be included

FIGURE 3-2

Summary of Alignment of Performance Management and Strategic Plan at KeyBank of Utah

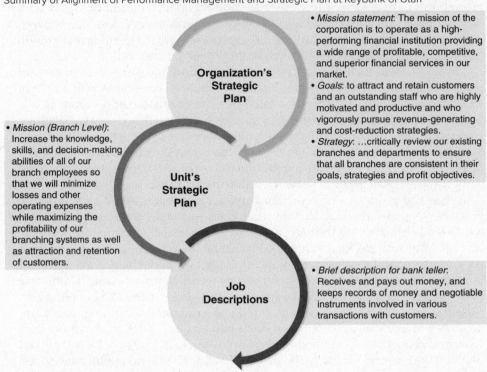

• *Mission statement*: The mission of the corporation is to operate as a high-performing financial institution providing a wide range of profitable, competitive, and superior financial services in our market.
• *Goals*: to attract and retain customers and an outstanding staff who are highly motivated and productive and who vigorously pursue revenue-generating and cost-reduction strategies.
• *Strategy*: …critically review our existing branches and departments to ensure that all branches are consistent in their goals, strategies and profit objectives.

• *Mission (Branch Level)*: Increase the knowledge, skills, and decision-making abilities of all of our branch employees so that we will minimize losses and other operating expenses while maximizing the profitability of our branching systems as well as attraction and retention of customers.

• *Brief description for bank teller*: Receives and pays out money, and keeps records of money and negotiable instruments involved in various transactions with customers.

in the performance management system to make sure there is good alignment between the objectives of the organization and the branch, and individual key accountabilities, performance objectives, and performance standards? (Hint: feel free to look up the job description for bank teller on O*NET.)

What happened after KeyBank of Utah implemented their performance management system? In general terms, KeyBank was able to enjoy several positive consequences of aligning corporate, branch, and individual objectives. After the implementation of its new performance management system, KeyBank found several meaningful benefits, including the following:

• Managers knew that employees were focused on meeting important objectives.
• Employees had more decision-making power.
• Lower-level managers had a better understanding of higher-level managers' decisions.
• Communication increased and improved among managers and between managers and employees.

To sum up, to be most useful and impactful, an organization's performance management system must rely on its strategic plan. The job descriptions, which serve as roadmaps for what individuals are supposed to do, how, and what results will be produced must be aligned with the vision, mission, objectives, and strategies of the organization and unit. Organizations can expect greater returns from implementing a performance management system when such alignment is in place. Also, to the extent that the HR function is involved in the design and implementation of the performance management system, it will gain credibility and will be seen as a strategic and valued contributor to the entire organization.

3-3 STRATEGIC PLANNING PROCESS

Chapter 2 included a brief overview of the strategic planning process. But the development of an organization's strategic plan requires a careful analysis of the organization's competitive situation, the organization's current position and destination, the development of the organization's strategic objectives, the design of a plan of action and implementation, and the allocation of resources (human, organizational, physical) that will increase the likelihood of achieving the stated objectives.[10] And the HR function can, and should, play an important role in this process.

3-3-1 Critical Role of the HR Function

As mentioned in the opening section of this chapter, the HR function can play a critical role in creating and implementing the strategies that will allow the organization to realize its mission and vision. Specifically, the HR function can make the following contributions:

- *Communicate knowledge about the strategic plan.* The HR function can be a good conduit to communicate the various components of the strategic plan (e.g., mission, vision, and objectives) to all the employees.
- *Outline knowledge, skills, and abilities (KSAs) needed for strategy implementation.* The HR function, through work analyses and the resulting job descriptions, serves as a repository of knowledge regarding what KSAs are needed for a successful implementation of the strategic plan. Thus, the HR function is in a unique situation to provide information about whether the current workforce has the KSAs needed to support the strategic plan, and if not, to offer suggestions about what types of employees should be hired and what types of plans (e.g., training and development initiatives) should be put in place to develop the needed KSAs internally.
- *Propose compensation systems.* The HR function can provide useful information on what type of compensation system should be implemented to motivate employees to support the strategic plan.

In addition to serving as a necessary guide for individual and team performance, knowledge of organization- and unit-level mission and vision provides the HR function with information about how to design the performance management system. Specifically, there are many choices in how the system is designed. For example, the system might place more emphasis on behaviors (i.e., processes) than on results (i.e., outcomes), or the system might emphasize more short-term criteria (i.e., quarterly objectives) than long-term criteria (triennial). Some of these choices are presented in Table 3-2.

TABLE 3-2

Some Choices in Performance Management System Design to be Guided by an Organization's Strategic Plan

Criteria: Behavioral criteria vs. results criteria
Participation: Low employee participation vs. high employee participation
Temporal dimension: Short-term criteria vs. long-term criteria
Level of criteria: Individual criteria vs. team/group criteria
System orientation: Developmental orientation vs. administrative orientation
Compensation: Pay for performance (i.e., merit-based) vs. pay for tenure/position

As a result of the strategic planning process, knowledge of the organization and unit vision and mission allows the HR function to serve as an internal consultant and to make informed decisions about performance management design choices. More detailed information on each of the factors guiding each of these design choices is provided in subsequent chapters. For now, as one illustration, assume an organization is producing a mature product in a fairly stable industry. In this situation, an emphasis on behaviors, rather than results, may be preferred because the relationship between processes and outcomes is well known, and the top priority is that employees display reliable and consistent behaviors in making the product. Regardless of the type of criteria used, be it behaviors or results, these must be observable (i.e., the person rating the criteria needs to have the ability to observe what is rated) and verifiable (i.e., there needs to be evidence to confirm the criteria rated).

As a second example, consider the actual case of Dell computers. Dell is one of the top players in the personal computer industry through its mode of online direct selling. Dell's main strategic business strategy is to be a low-cost leader in an industry that deals with a product that has now become a commodity. However, in addition to a low-cost strategy, Dell has a customer relationship business strategy of maintaining customer service at a high level, while reducing costs. Dell's performance management system provides a strong link between individual objectives and organizational performance by including a results component (i.e., cost) and a behavioral component (i.e., customer service).[11] At Dell, both low cost and high levels of customer service (for both internal and external customers) are important dimensions of the performance management system. Also, the system is strongly linked not only to the strategic objectives (i.e., low cost and high levels of customer service), but also to the organization's "winning culture" (i.e., achievement of personal and business objectives through its focus on interaction between managers and team members).

Next, let us discus the several steps involved in the creation of a strategic plan. These include (1) the conduct of an environmental or SWOT analysis (i.e., the identification of the external and internal strengths, weaknesses, opportunities, and threats of the external and internal environment in which the organization operates); (2) the creation of an organizational mission (i.e., statement of what the organization is all about); (3) the creation of an organizational vision (i.e., statement of where the organization intends to be in the long term, say, about 5–10 years); (4) setting objectives (i.e., what the organization intends to do in the short term, say, one to three years); and (5) the creation of strategies that will allow the organization to fulfill its mission and vision and achieve its objectives (i.e., descriptions of game plans or how-to procedures to reach the stated objectives).

Although we will describe these steps sequentially, the strategic planning process is not linear. For example, there may first be a rough draft of the organization's mission and vision, and *then*, the conduct of an environmental or SWOT (strengths, weaknesses, opportunities, and threats) analysis may follow to help define the mission and vision more clearly. In other words, the mission and vision may be drafted first and the environmental analysis may follow second. The important point is that there is a constant back and forth among these issues: the vision and mission affect the type of environmental analysis to be conducted, and the results of an environmental analysis are used to revise the mission and vision. By necessity, we need to discuss them one by one; however, keep in mind that they affect and inform each other on an ongoing basis. Let us begin with a discussion of environmental or SWOT analysis.

3-3-2 External and Internal Environmental (i.e., SWOT) Analysis

In conducting a strategic plan, we need to step back to take in the "big picture." This is accomplished through what is called an environmental or SWOT (i.e., strengths, weaknesses, opportunities, and threats) analysis.[12] An environmental analysis identifies external and internal parameters with the purpose of understanding broad issues related to the context and industry where the organization operates so that decisions can be made against the backdrop of this broader context.[13]

External Environment An examination of the *external environment* includes a consideration of opportunities and threats. Opportunities are characteristics of the environment that can help the organization succeed. Examples of such opportunities might be markets not currently being served, untapped talent pools, and new technological advances. Threats are characteristics of the external environment that can prevent the organization from being successful. Examples of such threats range from economic recession to the launch of innovative products and services on the part of competitors. A common framework for understanding industry-based threats is the now classic work by Michael E. Porter, called "five-force analysis."[14] These include three forces from horizontal competition (i.e., the threat of substitute products or services, the threat of established rivals, and the threat of new entrants), and two forces from vertical competition (i.e., the bargaining power of suppliers and the bargaining power of customers).

For example, consider the case of Frontier airlines, which is an affordable-fare airline headquartered at Denver International Airport, and serving more than 55 cities in the United States, Mexico, the Dominican Republic, and Cuba with approximately 275 daily flights.[15] Frontier commenced operations in July 1994, given two key opportunities in the external environment. First, two major competing airlines (Continental and United, which have actually merged in the year 2012) engaged in a dramatic downsizing of their Denver operations, leading to service gaps in various major markets that Frontier filled. Second, the city of Denver replaced the heavily congested Stapleton Airport with the much larger Denver International Airport. In February 2004, United Airlines, the largest carrier operating out of Denver International Airport, made changes in the environment that resulted in a direct horizontal threat to Frontier: United Airlines launched its own low-fare affiliate. The new affiliate, Ted, was going head-to-head with Frontier. Peter McDonald, then vice president for operations for United Airlines, reported that Ted's cost per available seat mile was in the ballpark of Frontier's 8.3 cents.[16] So, what had been an opportunity for Frontier no longer remained one, given the launching of Ted. To make things even worse for Frontier, Southwest Airlines, another low-cost competitor, also entered the Denver market a few years later—and now, Frontier is only the third largest carrier in Denver after United and Southwest. To complement the more general five-force analysis proposed by Michael Porter, the following is a nonexhaustive list of external factors that should be considered in any environmental analysis:

- *Economic.* For example, is there an economic recession on the horizon? Or, is the current economic recession likely to end in the near future? How would these economic trends affect our business?
- *Political/legal.* For example, how will political changes domestically or in the international markets we are planning on entering affect our entry strategy?

- *Social.* For example, what is the impact of the entry of Millennials in the workforce (and the massive retirement of Baby Boomers)?
- *Technological.* For example, what technological changes are anticipated in our industry and how will these changes affect how we do business?
- *Competitors.* For example, how do the strategies and products of our competitors affect our own strategies and products? Can we anticipate our competitors' next move?
- *Customers.* For example, what do our customers want now, and what will they want in the next five years or so? Can we anticipate such needs?
- *Suppliers.* For example, what is the relationship with our suppliers now and is it likely to change, and in what way, in the near future?

An examination of external trends is critical for businesses of all sizes. But it is particularly challenging for multinational organizations because they are concerned with both domestic and international trends. In fact, monitoring the external environment is so important in the strategic planning of multinational organizations that a survey of U.S. multinational corporations showed that 89% of departments responsible for the assessment of the external environment report directly to a member of the board of directors.[17]

Internal Environment An examination of the *internal environment* includes a consideration of strengths and weaknesses. Strengths are internal characteristics that the organization can use to its advantage. For example, what are the organization's assets and the staff's key skills? At Frontier, several key executives from other airlines were recruited, an important strength that was needed, given the emergence of horizontal threats. These executives created a senior management team with long-term experience in the Denver market.

Weaknesses are internal characteristics that are likely to hinder the success of the organization. These could include an obsolete organizational structure that does not allow for effective organization across units; the misalignment of organizational-, unit-, individual-level objectives; a talent pool with skills that have become obsolete given changes in the industry and in technology.

The following is a nonexhaustive list of internal issues that should be considered in any environmental analysis:

- *Organizational structure.* For example, is the current structure conducive to fast and effective communication?
- *Organizational culture.* Organizational culture includes the unwritten norms and values espoused by the members of the organization. For example, is the current organizational culture likely to encourage or hinder innovation and entrepreneurial behaviors on the part of middle-level managers? Is there a culture in which new ideas and suggestions are quickly suppressed with the argument that "this has never been done before"?
- *Politics.* For example, are the various units competing for resources in such a way that any type of cross-unit collaboration is virtually impossible? Or, are units likely to be open and collaborative in cross-unit projects?
- *Processes.* For example, are the supply chains working properly? Are all touchpoints with customers working properly? Can customers reach

us when they need to and do they receive a satisfying response when they do?

- *Size.* For example, is the organization too small or too large? Are we growing too fast? Will we be able to manage growth (or downsizing) effectively?

Table 3-3 includes a summary list of external and internal trends to be considered in conducting an environmental analysis. Think about your current employer (or last employer). Take a look at Table 3-3. Where does your organization stand in regard to each of these important external and internal issues? Regarding the external issues, what are some of the opportunities and threats? Regarding the internal issues, what are some of the strengths and weaknesses?

TABLE 3-3

Trends to Consider in Conducting an External and Internal Environmental (i.e., SWOT) Analysis

External	Internal
Economic	Organizational structure
Political/legal	Organizational culture
Social	Politics
Technological	Processes
Competitors	Size
Customers	
Suppliers	

Gap Analysis After external and internal issues have been considered, information is collected regarding opportunities, threats, strengths, and weaknesses. This information is used to conduct a *gap analysis*, which analyzes the external environment in relation to the internal environment. The pairing of external opportunities and threats with internal strengths and weaknesses leads to the following situations (ranked from most to least competitive):

1. *Opportunity + Strength = Leverage.* The best combination of external and internal factors occurs when there is an opportunity in the environment and a matching strength within the organization to take advantage of that opportunity. These are obvious directions that the organization should pursue. Consider the case of IBM, the world's largest information technology company, as well as the world's largest business and technology services provider with a revenue from continuing operations of US$21.8 billion. IBM has concluded that the personal computer-driven model no longer applies and that network-based computing is taking over. As noted by IBM's CEO Virginia (Ginni) Rometty, "Digital is the wires, but digital intelligence, or artificial intelligence as some people call it, is about much more than that. This next decade is about how you combine those and become a cognitive business. It's the dawn of a new era." This realization shifted the focus to servers, databases, and software for transaction and data management. Furthermore, IBM recognized the upsurge of network-connected devices, including smartphones and tablets. To take advantage of this external opportunity, IBM now focuses its resources on supporting network systems, developing software for the network-connected devices, and manufacturing specialized components. Consider the categories of products that IBM offers today (a) Cloud, (b) Cognitive, (c) Data and Analytics, (d) Internet of Things, (e) IT Infrastructure, (f) Mobile, and (g) Security.[18] This is a long way from IBM's first products involving clocks and cash registers! IBM built up its software capabilities through internal development and outside acquisitions. In short, IBM developed a leverage factor by identifying internal strengths that matched external opportunities, which in turn, leads to a successful business model.

2. *Opportunity + Weakness = Constraint.* In a constraint situation, the external opportunity is present; however, the internal situation is not conducive to taking advantage of the external opportunity. At IBM, this situation could have taken place if IBM did not have the internal capabilities to develop software and other products for the network-connected devices and specialized components. The external opportunity would still be there, but, absent the internal capabilities, it would not turn into an advantageous business scenario.

3. *Threat + Strength = Vulnerability.* In this situation, there is an external threat, but this threat can be contained because of the presence of internal strengths. If this had been the case at IBM, the company would not have been able to take advantage of a new situation; nevertheless, existing strengths would have allowed IBM to continue to operate in other areas.

4. *Threat + Weakness = Problem.* In the worst scenario, there is an external threat and an accompanying internal weakness. For example, in the 1980s, IBM refused to adapt to the demands of the emerging microcomputer market (i.e., today's personal systems including desktops, laptops, and notebooks). IBM did not have the internal capability to address customers' needs for personal systems, and instead, continued to focus on its internal strength: the mainframe computer. IBM's poor performance in the early 1990s was a direct consequence of this problem situation: the external threat (increasing demand for personal systems and dwindling demand for mainframe computers) was met with an internal weakness (lack of ability to shift internal focus from the mainframe to the personal systems and devices).

Consider the organization you are currently working for, or the organization for which you have worked most recently. Try to identify one leverage and one problem, based on an analysis of opportunities, threats, strengths, and weaknesses. What was the situation like? What were the outcomes?

In sum, the process of creating a strategic plan begins with an environmental analysis, also called SWOT analysis, which considers internal as well as external trends. Internal trends can be classified as either strengths or weaknesses, and external trends can be classified as either opportunities or threats. A gap analysis consists of pairing strengths and weaknesses with opportunities and threats, and determining whether the situation is advantageous (i.e., leverage), disadvantageous (i.e., problem), or somewhere in between (i.e., constraint and vulnerability). A SWOT analysis offers critical information for all organizations—as illustrated with the case of Airbnb in Box 3-1.

3-3-3 Mission

After the environmental analysis has been completed and the gap analysis reveals an organization's leverage, constraints, vulnerabilities, and problems, the members of the organization must determine who they are and what they do. This information will then be incorporated into the organization's mission statement. The mission statement summarizes the organization's most important reason for its existence. Mission statements provide information on the purpose

Box 3-1

Company Spotlight: SWOT and Gap Analysis at Airbnb[a]

Airbnb is an online hospitality service broker that allows customers to rent short-term lodging from local residents. Launched in 2008, it has more than 3 million listings in 65,000 cities and 191 countries, 150 million users, and was recently valued at over US$30 billion.[b]

Strengths	Weaknesses
• First to market • Host incentive (hosts can make money) • Ease of use (search by price, location, dates) • Website design • Profiles (browse hosts and review them) • No daily updates required for listings	• Lack of brand awareness in new markets • Company quality dependent on hosts and customers • Ease of competitor entry • Legal costs to deal with zoning laws (e.g., prohibiting people from running a business) • Insurance costs to protect hosts and customers

Opportunities	Threats
• Lower prices than hotels • More connected to city and its culture • Easy to become a host and connect with local residents • Large market for temporary housing • Growing use of online booking	• Established lodging providers (e.g., hotels) • Online rooms (e.g., Craigslist, couchsurfing.com) • Competitors copying business model • Bad press surrounding poor room, poor customers, or poor hosts

Gap Analysis (Leverage):

• **Provide alternative to hotels by providing temporary housing that allows hosts to make money and users to save money and experience local culture.**

• **Provide easy-to-use web platform that allow hosts to easily list temporary housing by posting their listing once, and users to easily search and filter.**

[a] This analysis is based loosely on the pitch deck of Airbnb: Dishman, L. (2015, September). *Lessons from the early pitch decks of Airbnb, Buzzfeed, and Youtube.* Retrieved from https://www.fastcompany.com/3050985/lessons-from-the-early-pitch-decks-of-airbnb-buzzfeed-and-youtubeo
[b] Fast Company. (2017). *Most innovative companies: Airbnb.* Available online at: https://www.fastcompany.com/company/airbnb

of the organization and its scope. State-of-the-science mission statements provide answers to the following questions:

• Why does the organization exist?
• What is the scope of the organization's activities?
• Who are the customers served?
• What are the products or services offered?

As an example, consider the mission statement for the Coca-Cola Company:

• To refresh the world mind, body, and spirit.
• To inspire moments of optimism and happiness through our brands and actions.
• To create value and make a difference.[19]

Presumably, this mission statement was preceded by an environmental analysis examining external and internal trends. We do not have information on this. But what we do know is that this mission statement provides some information regarding the four questions noted earlier. Based on this mission statement, we have information about why the company exists (i.e., "to refresh the world") and the scope of the organization's activities (i.e., "to inspire moments of optimism and happiness, create value, and make a difference"). The mission statement does not, however, include information about who are the customers served. Also, there is no information about specific products (e.g., Fanta, Sprite, Minute Maid, Powerade, Dasani, Fresca).

More specific and detailed information would be needed if Coca-Cola's mission statement is to be used by its various units to create their own mission statements. More detailed information is also needed if both the organization and unit mission statements are to be used as input for individual job descriptions, which will, in turn, be used for managing individual and team performance. State-of-the-science mission statements include the following components:

- Basic product or service to be offered (does what?)
- Primary markets or customer groups to be served (to whom?)
- Unique benefits and advantages of products or services (with what benefits?)
- Technology to be used in production or delivery
- Fundamental concern for survival through growth and profitability

Mission statements can also include information about the organization's values and beliefs, but these are sometimes listed separately, including the following:

- Managerial philosophy of the organization
- Public image sought by the organization
- Self-concept of business adopted by employees, shareholders, and other stakeholders

In short, a mission statement defines why the organization exists, the scope of its activities, the customers served, and the products and services offered. Mission statements also include specific information, such as the technology used in production or delivery, and the unique benefits or advantages of the organization's products and services. Finally, a mission statement can include a statement of values and beliefs, such as the organization's managerial philosophy, or these can be presented separately. Table 3-4 lists the characteristics of good mission statements.

TABLE 3-4
Characteristics of Good Mission Statements

Characteristics
Basic product/service to be offered (does what)
Primary markets or customer groups to be served (to whom)
Unique benefits, features, and advantages of products/services (with what benefits)
Technology to be used in production or delivery
Fundamental concern for survival through growth and profitability
Managerial philosophy of the organization
Public image sought by organization
Self-concept of business adopted by employees, shareholders, and other stakeholders

3-3-4 Vision

An organization's vision is a statement of future aspirations. In other words, the vision statement includes a description of what the organization would like to become in the future—about 5–10 years out. Vision statements are typically written after the mission statement is completed because the organization needs to know who they are and what their purpose is before they can figure out who they want to be in the future. Note, however, that mission and vision statements are often combined, and therefore, in many cases, it is difficult to differentiate one from the other. In such cases, the vision statement usually includes two components: a *core ideology*, which is referred to as the mission, and an *envisioned future*, which is what is referred to as the vision per se. The core ideology contains the core purpose and core values of an organization, and the envisioned future specifies long-term objectives and a picture of what the organization aspires to in the long term.

Spectrum Brands provides an example of combining mission and vision into one statement. Spectrum Brands is a global consumer products company and a leading supplier of batteries, kitchen appliances, shaving and grooming products, personal care products, pet supplies, and home and garden products. Originally founded in 1906 as the French Battery Company in Madison, Wisconsin, and renamed Rayovac Company during the 1930s, the company changed its name to Spectrum Brands to reflect its diverse portfolio and position as a publicly held company. Some of its more recognizable brands include Rayovac, VARTA, Remington, George Foreman, Black+Decker, Nature's Miracle, Littermaid, and Liquid Fence. Based in Middleton, Wisconsin, Spectrum Brands' products are sold by the world's top 25 retailers and are available in more than one million stores in approximately 160 countries. Spectrum Brands' combined mission and vision statement is the following:

> Spectrum Brands is a rapidly growing, global, diversified, market-driven consumer products company.
>
> We will continue to grow our company through a combination of strategic acquisitions and organic growth.
>
> We will strengthen our brands and generate growth through emphasis on brand strategy/marketing and innovative product technology, design and packaging.
>
> We will leverage IT infrastructure, distribution channels, purchasing power and operational structure globally to continue to drive efficiencies and reduce costs.
>
> We will profitably expand distribution in all served markets.[20]

This statement includes components of a mission statement (i.e., "a rapidly growing, global, diversified, market-driven consumer products company") as well as components of a vision statement (e.g., "will strengthen our brands and generate growth through emphasis on brand strategy/marketing and innovative product technology, design and packaging"). Thus, this statement combines the present (i.e., who the company is, what it does) with the future (i.e., aspirations).

Other organizations make a more explicit differentiation between the mission and vision statements. Consider the vision statement for Greif, a global company headquartered in Delaware, Ohio, with approximately 13,000 employees and more than 200 operating locations in more than 50 countries. Greif offers rigid industrial packaging and services (e.g., steel, rigid intermediate bulk containers; blending, filling and other packaging services), flexible products and services (e.g., flexible intermediate bulk containers, shipping sacks; reconditioning flexible intermediate bulk containers), paper packaging (e.g., containerboard, corrugated sheets and other corrugated products; packaging services), and land management (e.g., timber, timberland and special use properties). Greif's vision statement is the following[21]:

Vision

In industrial packaging, be the best performing customer service company in the world.

Our Core Values. Our people are our past, present and future. We will honor The Greif Way, building upon our rich history as a special place to work. We will operate within a culture of integrity, character and respect. We will maintain a safe working environment. We will attract and cultivate a responsible, competent, efficient and empowered workforce. We will provide opportunities to excel. We will communicate. We will listen.

Our customers are our reason for being. We will keep our promises to our customers. We will be synonymous with quality and service. We will solve their packaging challenges. We will prove the value of our relationship by being the best at what we do.

Our products are our livelihood. We will be a low-cost manufacturer and the high-value supplier in our business segments. We will innovate, using our ingenuity and creativity to provide better solutions. We will maintain our focus on where we can be the best and apply our expertise to do it better.

Our shareholders are our support. We will conduct our business ethically and with transparency. We will establish rigorous financial goals that will drive our business decisions and measure our progress. We will strive to attain a superior rate of return and maintain trust with our investors.

Our stage is the world. Our communities and the environment are our backdrop. We will be a conscientious global citizen, a responsive community neighbor and a responsible steward of the earth's natural resources.

Greif's vision statement is clearly future-oriented. It provides direction and focus. In addition, it includes several features that are required of useful vision statements. First, it focuses attention on what is most important, and thus, eliminates unproductive activities. Second, it provides a context from which to evaluate new external opportunities and threats. For example, the vision statement indicates that new opportunities for profitable growth in the industrial packaging and services business should be pursued. In addition, state-of-the-science vision statements have the following characteristics, not all of which are present in Greif's vision statement:

- *Brief.* A vision statement should be brief so that employees can remember it.
- *Verifiable.* A good vision statement should be able to stand the reality test. For example, how can we verify if Greif indeed becomes "one of the most desirable companies to work for in our industries, focusing on establishing a work atmosphere in which our employees can excel"?

- *Bound by a timeline.* A good vision statement specifies a timeline for the fulfillment of various aspirations.
- *Current.* Outdated vision statements are not useful. Vision statements should be updated on an ongoing basis, ideally as soon as the old vision is fulfilled.
- *Focused.* A good vision statement is not a laundry list of aspirations, but rather, focuses on just a few (perhaps not more than three or four) aspects of an organization's performance that are important to future success.
- *Understandable.* Vision statements need to be written in a clear and straightforward manner so that they are understood by all employees.
- *Inspiring.* Good vision statements make employees feel good about their organization's direction and motivate them to help achieve the vision.
- *A stretch.* Consider Microsoft's vision statement in the 1980s of "putting a computer on every desk and in every home," which was the vision when CEO Bill Gates started the MS-DOS operating system. This vision statement was such a stretch that it was considered ludicrous at a time when the mainframe computer still reigned supreme and the first personal computers were being made and sold. But that vision became a reality. Two decades later, Microsoft revised their vision as follows: "putting a computer in every car and every pocket." Once again, this vision has now become a reality—in the form of car dashboards and smartphones.

TABLE 3-5
Characteristics of Good Vision Statements
Brief
Verifiable
Bound by a timeline
Current
Focused
Understandable
Inspiring
A stretch

In sum, a vision statement includes a description of future aspirations. Whereas the mission statement emphasizes the present, the vision statement emphasizes the future. Table 3-5 includes a summary list of the features that should be present in a good vision statement. Think about your current or last employer. Take a look at Table 3-5. How many of these features are reflected in your organization's vision statement? What should be added to the vision statements to make it more congruent with an ideal one?

3-3-5 Objectives

After an organization has analyzed its external opportunities and threats as well as internal strengths and weaknesses and has defined its mission and vision, it can realistically establish objectives that will further its mission. The purpose of setting such objectives is to formalize statements about what the organization hopes to achieve in the medium- to long-range period (i.e., within the next three to five years). Objectives provide more specific information regarding how the mission will be implemented. Objectives also provide a good basis for making decisions by keeping the desired outcomes in mind. Objectives provide the basis for performance measurement because they allow for a comparison of what needs to be achieved versus what each unit, group, and individual is achieving. Moreover, objectives can also be a source of motivation and provide employees with a more tangible target for which to strive.

Consider the case of Harley-Davidson, Inc., the motorcycle manufacturer. Matthew S. Levatich, president and CEO since May 2015, said that a major objective is to

> . . . deliver those customer-growth objectives, not chassis-growth objectives. It sounds kind of trite: We're not really in the business of manufacturing motorcycles. We're in the business of building customers. When I joined

[in 1994], we had made 86,000 motorcycles the prior year. Compare that to the peak in 2006 at about 350,000. It's less today, but we're working hard to get that volume back up. But the emphasis has shifted from making motorcycles to what I would say is identifying and finding customers—with product, with distribution, with everything we do at the company.[22]

Operationally speaking, this means that Harley Davidson is trying to achieve the following[23]:

- Lead in every market: Harley-Davidson plans to achieve the leadership position in the 601cc motorcycle segment. As the company's CEO Matt Levatich put it, "This is not just about competing, but winning."
- Grow sales at a faster rate: Harley-Davidson plans to grow its retail sales in the United States as well as internationally at a faster pace. In the next five years, the company plans to add 150–200 dealers globally to achieve this objective.
- Grow earnings faster than revenues: Harley-Davidson has stated an objective of growing its revenues over the next five years. It is also aiming at growing its earnings faster than its revenues through 2020.

These objectives provide a clear direction for Harley-Davidson. In fact, they provide useful information to guide unit-level objectives as well as individual and team performance. The entire organization has a clear sense of focus because all members know that there are clear objectives in terms of market presence, growth, sales, earnings, and financial performance.

3-3-6 Strategies

At this point, we know what the organization is all about (mission), what it wants to be in the future (vision), and what it needs to do to get there (objectives). What remains is a discussion of *how* to fulfill the mission and vision and *how* to achieve the stated objectives. This is done by creating strategies, which are descriptions of game plans or how-to procedures to reach the stated objectives. The strategies could address issues of growth, survival, turnaround, stability, innovation, talent acquisition, and leadership, among others.

There is an entire field of study called "strategic management studies" devoted to the development and implementation of strategies. In fact, Deloitte, Boston Consulting Group, Bain & Company, KPMG, and Accenture offer consulting services in the domain of business strategy. Also, there are hundreds of books written on this topic. To give you a brief overview of some possibilities, consider the following strategies, out of many, that could be implemented[24]:

- *Operations*: Addressing issues about the global economic environment in terms of market, capital, interest rates, labor costs, taxes, regulations, and available infrastructure.
- *Competitiveness*: Operating at optimum levels of productivity and efficiency: Continuous benchmarking, use of statistical tools for process optimization, total quality model, gathering data on customer expectations and experiences.
- *Optimal use of resources*: Optimization of global collaboration with suppliers, parts standardization and reduction, and flexible manufacturing and services.

- *Global corporate culture*: Respecting cultural values of different regions, constant training at all levels, policies of respect and recognition to individuals, and selecting highly qualified employees.
- *Research and development*: Ongoing initiatives aimed at innovation and creativity.

3-3-7 Developing Strategic Plans at the Unit Level

As shown in Figure 3-1, the organization's strategic plan has a direct impact on the units' strategic plans. The case of KeyBank of Utah described earlier illustrates how the branches had a mission statement that was aligned with the overall organizational mission statement. Similarly, the vision statement, objectives, and strategies of the various units need to be congruent with the overall organizational vision, objectives, and strategies. Consider the case of Microsoft Corporation's mission statement[25]:

Our Mission: Our mission is to empower every person and every organization on the planet to achieve more.

What We Value
- *Innovation*: Learn about innovations from our computer science research organization. With more than 1,000 researchers in our labs, it's one of the largest in the world.
- *Diversity and Inclusion*: Explore how we maximize every person's contribution—from our employees to our customers—so that the way we innovate naturally includes diverse thought.
- *Corporate Social Responsibility*: See how we work to be a responsible partner to those who place their trust in us, conducting business in a way that is inclusive, transparent, and respectful of human rights.
- *Philanthropies*: Find out how we empower people by investing technology, money, employee talent, and the company's voice in programs that promote digital inclusion.
- *Environment*: Discover how we lead the way in sustainability and use our technologies to minimize the impact of our operations and products.
- *Trustworthy Computing*: Check out how we deliver secure, private, and reliable computing experiences based on sound business practices.

Now, consider the mission statement of one of Microsoft's units, Training and Education:

With the charter to enable Microsoft engineering workgroups to realize their full potential for innovation and performance through world-class learning strategies, Microsoft Training and Education (MSTE) provides performance support strategies to support the overall corporation's software engineering efforts. Our efforts include the design, development, and delivery of learning programs, on-line information, and resources for Microsoft employees. MSTE's integrated suite of technical offerings supports our objective of having a significant impact on Microsoft's business. We promote best practices, cross-group communication, Microsoft expertise and Industry expertise.

As you can see, the mission of the training and education unit regarding the realization of people's full potential for innovation and performance is consistent with the overall mission to empower every person, which plays a central role. Of course, MSTE's mission is more focused on issues specifically relevant to the training and education function. Nevertheless, the link between the two mission statements is clearly apparent.

The congruence between the mission of the organization and its various units is important, regardless of the type of industry and the size of the organization. High-performing organizations have a clear alignment in the mission and vision of the overall and unit-level mission and vision statements. Consider the case of Norfolk State University (NSU), located in Norfolk, Virginia. NSU, the seventh largest historically African American university in the United States, serves many students who are the first in their families to attend college. It offers about 50 academic programs, including 16 Master's and 2 Doctoral degree programs. NSU has seven main schools offering courses to their approximately 6,200 and 800 undergraduate and graduate students, respectively: School of Business, School of Education, School of Liberal Arts, College of Engineering, Science & Technology, School of Social Work, and School of Extended Learning. The university's mission statement is the following:

> Through exemplary teaching, scholarship, and outreach, Norfolk State University transforms lives and communities by empowering individuals to maximize their potential, creating life-long learners equipped to be engaged leaders and productive global citizens.[26]

The mission statement of the School of Business indicates that its objective is to:

> . . . be your path to an amazing future. At Norfolk State's School of Business, high character combines with high expectations, excellence in instruction and a global perspective to prepare students to succeed personally and professionally. Our graduates will be known for mastery of their academic specialties and the ability to apply their knowledge in the workplace and in service to others. It is precisely this type of preparation that has allowed our graduates to assume leadership roles in great organizations worldwide.[27]

Note that both mission statements are aligned and refer to similar issues. Specifically, they include the (1) delivery of a high-quality education and academic achievement, and (2) educating productive citizens who will contribute to a (3) global society.

In sum, the organization's strategic plan, including the mission, vision, objectives, and strategies, cascades down to all organizational levels. Thus, each division, branch, department, or unit also creates its own strategic plan, which should be consistent with the organization's overall plan.

3-3-8 Job Descriptions

Continuing with the sequence of components shown in Figure 3-1, job descriptions also need to be congruent with the organization and unit mission, vision, objectives, and strategies. We discussed the work analysis process leading to the creation of job descriptions in Chapter 2. Recall that job descriptions are important because they serve as a roadmap for what individuals are supposed to do, how, and what results will be produced. Moreover, job descriptions are

Operates gasoline- or diesel-powered truck or truck tractor equipped with two or more driving wheels and with four or more forward speed transmissions, which may include two or more gear ranges. These vehicles are coupled to a trailer or semi-trailer by use of a turntable (fifth wheel) or pintle (pivot) hook. Drives over public roads to transport materials, merchandise, or equipment. Performs difficult driving tasks such as backing truck to loading platform, turning narrow corners, negotiating narrow passageways, and keeping truck and trailer under control, particularly on wet or icy highways. May assist in loading and unloading truck. May also handle manifest, bills of lading, expense accounts, and other papers pertinent to the shipment.

FIGURE 3-3
Job Description for Trailer Truck Driver: Civilian Personnel Management Service, U.S. Department of Defense

important for new employees because they set clear expectations from day one. So, if job descriptions are consistent with the organization and unit mission, vision, objectives, and strategies, it is more likely that results produced by individuals and teams will contribute to the success of their units and organization as a whole. Chapter 4 will address how to define behaviors and results and Chapters 5 and 6 will address how to measure them in great detail. For now, let us continue to address the links between strategic business priorities and job descriptions.

After the strategic plan is completed, some rewriting of the existing job descriptions may be in order. Recall the job description for trailer truck driver as used by the Civilian Personnel Management Service (U.S. Department of Defense) (see Figure 3-3).

This description provides information about the various tasks performed, together with a description of some of the KSAs required for the position. But what is the link with the organization and unit strategic plans? How do the specific tasks make a contribution to the strategic priorities of the transportation division and the organization as a whole? This description includes only cursory and indirect information regarding these issues. For example, one can assume that the proficient handling of bills of lading, expense accounts, and other papers pertinent to the shipment contributes toward a smooth shipping operation, and therefore, makes a contribution to the transportation division. However, this link is not sufficiently clear.

However, consider a job announcement describing the position of Performance Solutions Group Manager in Microsoft's training and education unit (see Figure 3-4). This job description makes the link between the individual position and MSTE quite clear. First, the description includes MSTE's mission statement so that individuals become aware of how their specific role fits within the overall mission of the department. Second, the job description includes language to the effect that the work must lead to an "industry leading" product, which is consistent not only with MSTE's mission, but also with Microsoft's overall mission. Third, in the needed qualifications section, there is a clear overlap between those needed for this specific position and those mentioned in MSTE's as well as in Microsoft's overall mission. In short, the person working as performance solutions group manager has a clear sense not only of her position, but also of how behaviors and expected results are consistent with expectations about MSTE and Microsoft in general.

In sum, the tasks and KSAs included in individual job descriptions must be congruent with the organization's and unit's strategic plans. In other words, job descriptions should include activities that, if executed well, will help execute the

As the Performance Solutions Group Manager, you will be accountable for developing and delivering on a portal strategy that touches over 20,000 employees worldwide and involves a complex data delivery system. Additionally, the person is responsible for defining the cutting-edge tool suite used by the team to develop and maintain the portal, the content housed by the group, and all e-learning solutions. Key initiatives include redesigning the Engineering Excellence Guide within the next 6 months and evolving it over the next 18 months to 3 years to become the industry-leading performance support site. Key challenges include maintaining and managing the cutting-edge tool suite used by the team and driving a clear vision for an industry-leading portal and content delivery plan.

Qualifications for this position are a minimum of five years of senior management experience, preferably in knowledge management, e-learning, or Web-based product development roles; ability to think strategically and exercise sound business judgment on behalf of Microsoft; excellent leadership, communication, interpersonal, and organizational skills; firsthand experience delivering/shipping Web-based learning and content management solutions; proven record of successful team management; and ability to work well independently and under pressure, while being flexible and adaptable to rapid change. Knowledge of performance support and training procedures, standards, and processes is preferred.

With the charter to enable Microsoft engineering workgroups to realize their full potential for innovation and performance through world-class learning strategies, Microsoft Training and Education (MSTE) provides performance support strategies to support the overall corporation's software engineering efforts. Our efforts include the design, development, and delivery of learning programs, online information, and resources for Microsoft employees. MSTE's integrated suite of technical offerings supports our objective of having a significant impact on Microsoft's business. We promote best practices, cross-group communication, Microsoft expertise and Industry expertise.

mission and vision. Job descriptions that are detached from strategic priorities will lead to performance evaluations focused on behaviors and results that are not central to an organization's success, and the performance management system will be seen as irrelevant and a big waste of time by managers and employee alike.

3-4 BUILDING SUPPORT AND ANSWERING THE "WHAT'S IN IT FOR ME" QUESTION

Given the many competing projects and the usual scarcity of slack resources, some organizations may be reluctant to implement a performance management system. Primarily, the reasons include a lack of any perceived value added, an initiative that requires many resources (particularly, time from supervisors), and something that, simply put, is perceived to produce little tangible payoffs and even causes more harm than good. The need to align organization and unit priorities with the performance management system is one of the key factors contributing to obtaining the much-needed top management support for the system.

A good question that top management is likely to, and frankly, should ask is: "Why is performance management important and even necessary?" One answer to this question is that performance management is the primary tool that will allow top management to carry out their vision. The performance management system, when aligned with organization and unit priorities, is a critical tool to (1) allow all employees to understand where the organization stands and where it wants to go, and (2) provide tools to employees (e.g., motivation, developmental resources) so that their behaviors and results will help the organization achieve its targets. Fundamentally, the implementation of any performance management system requires that the "What's in it for me?" question be answered convincingly. In the case of top management, the answer to the "What's in it for me?" question is that performance management can serve as a primary tool to realize their vision and achieve strategic objectives.

Building support for the system does not stop with top management, however. All participants in the system need to understand the role they play and also receive a clear answer to the "What's in it for me?" question. Accordingly, communication about the system is key. This includes a clear description of the system's mechanics (e.g., when the performance planning meetings will take place, how to handle disagreements between supervisor and employees) and the system's consequences (e.g., relationship between performance evaluation and compensation). As discussed in Chapter 1, not involving people in the process of system design and implementation can create resistance, and the performance management system may result in more harm than good.

Consider the role that good communication played in the launching of a revamped performance management system at Bankers Life and Casualty, an insurance company specializing in insurance for seniors and headquartered in Chicago. When Edward M. Berube was appointed as its president and CEO, he understood that Bankers Life and Casualty was facing important challenges, including new customer demands, the impact of the Internet, outsourcing, and increased competition. So, Bankers Life and Casualty engaged in a very aggressive marketing campaign, which included retaining actor Dick Van Dyke as its company spokesperson. In spite of these efforts, however, internal focus groups revealed that while employees understood the organization's strategic plan, they did not understand what role each person was supposed to play in helping the organization execute its strategy. In other words, employees did not have a clear understanding of how each person could help achieve the organization's strategic objectives, including focusing on the following three key areas (1) distribution scope, scale, and productivity; (2) home office productivity and unit costs; and (3) product revenue and profitability.

Bankers Life and Casualty realized that a better link between strategy and job descriptions could be established by improving its performance management process. The HR function, therefore, proceeded to overhaul the performance management system so that the three areas of strategic importance just outlined would be part of everyone's job descriptions. The design and implementation of the new system was a *joint venture* between the HR and the communications departments. First, the HR and communications teams spoke candidly with the CEO about his expectations. The CEO responded with overwhelming support, stating that the performance management system would be implemented for every employee on pre-established dates, and that he would hold his team accountable for making this happen. Then, to implement the performance management system, each unit met with its VP. During these meetings, each VP discussed how his or her unit's objectives were linked to the corporate objectives. Next, HR and communications led discussions surrounding objective setting, giving feedback, and writing development plans. Managers were then given the opportunity to share any feedback, concerns, or questions that they had about the program. During this forum, managers exchanged success stories and offered advice to one another. These success stories were then shared with the CEO. The CEO then shared these stories with those who reported directly to him to strengthen the visibility of his support for the program.

In short, the performance management system at Bankers Life and Casualty helped all employees understand their contributions to the organization's strategic plan. This was a key issue that motivated the CEO to lend unqualified support to the system. This support gave a clear message to the rest of the organization that the performance management system was an important initiative that added value to the entire organization. The support of the CEO and other top executives, combined with a high degree of participation from all employees and their ability to voice concerns and provide feedback regarding the system, was a critical factor in the success of the performance management system at Bankers Life and Casualty.

SUMMARY POINTS

- Strategic planning involves defining the organization's present and future identity. Overall, the strategic plan serves as a blueprint that allows organizations to allocate resources in a way that provides the organization with a competitive advantage.
- The HR function can play a critical role as a strategic partner and expert internal consultant in creating the strategic plan. Also, performance management is an ideal vehicle to demonstrate the strategic role of the HR function because it allows for explicit and clear links with the organization's mission, vision, and objectives. By helping implement the strategic planning process and linking a firm's objectives with the performance management system, the HR function can get a "seat at the table" of the top management team.
- Strategic planning serves several specific purposes, including defining an organization's identity, preparing for the future, analyzing the environment, providing focus, creating a culture of cooperation, generating new options, and serving as a guide for the daily activities of all organizational members.
- Performance management systems must rely on the strategic plan to add value and be useful. The job descriptions of all employees must be aligned with the vision, mission, objectives, and strategies of the organization and unit. It is critical to align organizational, unit, and individual priorities, and one formal approach to do this is the balanced scorecard approach.
- The process of creating a strategic plan begins with an environmental (SWOT) analysis, which considers internal (e.g., organizational structure, processes) as well as external (e.g., economic, technological) trends. Internal trends can be classified as either strengths or weaknesses, and external trends can be classified as either opportunities or threats. A gap analysis consists of pairing strengths and weaknesses with opportunities and threats and determining whether the situation is advantageous (i.e.,

leverage), disadvantageous (i.e., problem), or somewhere in-between (i.e., constraint and vulnerability).

- The second component in creating a strategic plan is to write a mission statement based on the results of the gap analysis. A state-of-the-science mission statement defines why the organization exists, the scope of its activities, the customers served, and the products and services offered. Mission statements also include information about what technology is used in production or delivery, and the unique benefits or advantages of the organization's products and services. Finally, a mission statement can include a statement of values and beliefs, such as the organization's managerial philosophy, although some organizations choose to create separate value statements.

- The third component of a strategic plan is the vision statement, which includes a description of future aspirations. Whereas the mission statement emphasizes the present, the vision statement emphasizes the future. In many cases, however, the mission and vision statements are combined into one statement. State-of-the-science vision statements are brief, verifiable, bound by a timeline, current, focused, understandable, inspiring, and a stretch.

- After the mission and vision statements are created, the fourth step in the strategic planning process is to generate objectives that will help fulfill the mission and vision. Objectives provide more specific information regarding how the mission and vision will be implemented. Typically, objectives span a three- to five-year period.

- The fifth and final step in the strategic planning process is to identify strategies that will help achieve the stated objectives. These strategies are game plans and usually address issues surrounding growth, survival, turnaround, stability, innovation, and leadership.

- The organization's strategic plan, including the mission, vision, objectives, and strategies, cascades down to all organizational levels. Thus, each division, department, or unit also creates its own strategic plan, which should be consistent with the organization's overall plan. The most effective sequence for doing so is for the units to first agree on common strategies, and then, specify unit-level objectives.

- The tasks and KSAs included in individual job descriptions must be congruent with the organization's and unit's strategic plans. In other words, job descriptions should include activities that, if executed well, will help realize the mission and vision. Job descriptions that are detached from strategic priorities will lead to performance evaluations focused on behaviors and results that are not central to an organization's success.

- To build support for the performance management system, top management must be aware that it is a primary tool and ideal conduit to execute an organization's strategic plan. This awareness will lead to top management's support for the system. In addition, all organizational members need to be able to answer the "What's in it for me?" question regarding the system. Implementing the performance management system will require considerable effort on the part of all those involved. Those doing the evaluation and those being evaluated should know how the system will benefit them directly.

EXERCISE 3-1 LINKING INDIVIDUAL WITH UNIT AND ORGANIZATIONAL PRIORITIES

Obtain a copy of the job description for your current or most recent job. If this is not feasible, obtain a copy of a job description of someone you know. Then, obtain a copy of the mission statements for the organization and unit in question.

Revise the job description so that it is aligned with the unit and organizational strategic priorities. Revisions may include adding tasks and KSAs important in the mission statement that are not already included in the job description.

EXERCISE 3-2 BUILDING SUPPORT FOR A PERFORMANCE MANAGEMENT SYSTEM AT THE GAP, INC.

You have just been appointed the Chief Human Resource Office (CHRO) for The Gap, Inc., a large retail clothing company with more than US$1 billion in sales, 3,000 retail stores in the United States, and over 130,000 employees. The mission of the company is "to create emotional connections with customers through our brands, unique designs, and enjoyable store experiences."

The current performance management system is not delivering results in terms of business performance, with the company posting a 10% decline in sales during the previous month, the 12th monthly decrease in a row. The Chief Executive Officer (CEO) believes that this is because of a lack of strategic alignment between the company's overall mission and its retail stores.

Imagine the class instructor is the CEO of the company, and the other students are members of the top management team. Your task is to devise a new strategic plan that achieves the CEO's goal of greater alignment between organizational- and store-level strategies. Based on the mission statement of the company and other information provided:

1. Develop a mission and vision statement that translates the organization's mission statement for the retail stores using the guidelines below. (Hint: Sections 3-3-3 "Mission" and 3-3-4 "Vision" provide detailed guidance and examples of mission and vision statements.)
   - Mission statements should include: The product offered (clothing); the target customer group (young adults and casual wear for professionals); benefits of the product (cost, quality, style); technology used (if applicable); and a focus on sales growth and profitability (increasing revenue).
   - Vision statements should be: brief, verifiable, bound by a timeline, current, focused, understandable, inspiring, and a stretch.
2. Develop 2–3 retail store objectives and the strategies to achieve those objectives. These should be closely linked to the new mission and vision statement. (Hint: Sections 3-3-5 "Objectives," 3-3-6 "Strategies," and 3-3-7

"Developing Strategic Plans at the Unit Level" provide detailed guidance and examples of setting objectives and strategies.)

- Objectives should address the next three to five years, and provide a clear performance target to aim for. They might address issues such as sales revenue, payroll, or advertising.
- Strategies should address *how* the objectives will be achieved. They might address issues such as operations, customer surveys and benchmarking, or inventory management.

3. Prepare a brief (5–10 minute) presentation that:
   - Presents the new strategic plan (mission, vision, objectives, and strategies) to the CEO and the top management team.
   - Convinces the CEO and the top management team to support the new plan
     - Your presentation should clearly answer the question *"What's in it for me?"* for both the CEO and the rest of the top management team.
     - Articulate how the new plan aligns with the organization's overall mission and how it will lead to greater sales.
     - Consider how you can make the CEO and the rest of the top management team feel a sense of involvement and ownership (e.g., allow top management team members to provide suggestions about the verbiage of the mission or vision; allow them to take responsibility for some part of the process).

* This exercise is loosely based on *Gap Inc. encouraging employees to grow, perform and succeed—Without ratings*. Retrieved January 3, 2018, from https://www.e-reward.co.uk/uploads/editor/files/GapInc_Case_Study.pdf

Evaluating Vision and Mission Statements at PepsiCo

Consider the mission and vision statements for PepsiCo, and then, answer the questions included below:

PepsiCo's Mission Statement[a]

As one of the largest food and beverage companies in the world, our mission is to provide consumers around the world with delicious, affordable, convenient and complementary foods and beverages from wholesome breakfasts to healthy and fun daytime snacks and beverages to evening treats. We are committed to investing in our people, our company, and the communities where we operate to help position the company for long-term, sustainable growth.

PepsiCo's Vision Statement

At PepsiCo, we aim to deliver top-tier financial performance over the long term by integrating sustainability into our business strategy, leaving a positive imprint on society and the environment. We call this Performance with Purpose. It starts with what we make—a wide range of foods and beverages from the indulgent to the more nutritious; extends to how we make our products—conserving precious natural resources and fostering environmental responsibility in and beyond our operations; and considers those who make them—striving to support communities where we work and the careers of generations of talented PepsiCo employees.

	Characteristics	Y/N
	Basic product/service to be offered (does what)	
	Primary markets or customer groups to be served (to whom)	
	Unique benefits, features, and advantages of products/services (with what benefits)	
	Technology to be used in production or delivery	
Mission Statement—who we are and what we do	Fundamental concern for survival through growth and profitability	
	Managerial philosophy of the organization	
	Public image sought by organization	
	Self-concept of business adopted by employees, shareholders, and other stakeholders	
	Brief—so that employees can remember it	
	Verifiable—able to stand the reality test	
	Bound by a timeline—specifies a timeline for fulfillment of the various aspirations	
	Current—updated on an ongoing basis	
Vision Statement—future aspirations	Focused—lists a few (3–4) aspects of organization's performance that are important for future success	
	Understandable—written in a clear and straightforward manner so that they are understood by all employees	
	Inspiring—makes employees feel good about their organization's direction and motivates them to help achieve the vision	
	Stretch—objective not easily attained	

[a] PepsiCo. (2017). *What we believe*. Retrieved January 3, 2018, from http://www.pepsico.com/purpose. Used with permission from PepsiCo, Inc.

1. The table below summarizes the key characteristics of ideal mission and vision statements as discussed in Chapter 3. Use the Y/N columns in the table to indicate whether each of the features is present or not in the mission and vision statements of PepsiCo.

2. How do the mission and vision statements relate to the eight characteristics of an ideal mission statement and the eight characteristics of an ideal vision statement? What are the gaps?

3. How useful are the mission and vision statements of PepsiCo in terms of linking organizational priorities with individual and team performance? In creating such a link, which ideal mission/vision statement characteristics (shown in the table earlier) seem to be more important than others? What other places might the HR department at PepsiCo look for information regarding how to more effectively cascade firm-level strategy to each individual's objectives?

CASE STUDY 3-2

Linking Performance Management to Strategy at Procter & Gamble

Consider the following description of a firm-wide strategy pursued by Procter & Gamble[a]:

Procter & Gamble (P&G), the world's largest consumer products company, follows a fairly unique strategy: P&G appeals to the heart and cares about human needs. In other words, P&G attempts to touch and improve the lives of its consumers all over the world. As an example, take the razor-and-blade innovation pioneered by Gillette's Himalaya team, which focuses on India but is a global group based partly in Boston, USA. The team received information about how men in India shave: about half of them use barbershops and barbers usually break double-sided blades in two and used them repeatedly, which crates unsanitary conditions. With the strategic objective of improving the lives of its customers, the team created a razor-and-blade innovation that simplified the essential features of the shaving done in barbershops. The products were a success in terms of improving both the human condition and profitability. As a second example, consider a situation in P&G Brazil, where P&G feared a shutdown due to decreased business volume. Low-income consumers were the fastest growing segment of the population, but P&G's global premium products were too expensive for this market segment. Local P&G teams decided to live with families, scrutinized every P&G process in an attempt to reduce costs, and ended up creating an innovative product line they dubbed "basico" (for "essential" in Portuguese). The team members felt that they were doing good for the world, not just making money for the corporation. Demand immediately outpaced supply when the first "basico" products were launched, which included women's hygiene, diapers, and greener laundry detergent. The company quickly captured market share through small neighborhood shops and premium products were no longer offered. The business in Brazil became a profitable global growth model, and not just for emerging countries. As a consequence, "Tide Basic" was recently introduced in the United States.

In sum, P&G's strategy inspires employees to add their hearts to their heads and aims at finding creative solutions when purpose-inspired opportunities and commercial considerations seem to collide.

Imagine you are an HR executive at P&G. Given the company's strategic orientation toward purpose and values, what would you do to help align a new performance management system with the strategic plan? How would you explain this relationship? What would you say and do to garner company-wide support for your performance management system?

[a] The description is adapted from the following source: Kanter, R. M. (2009, September 14). Inside Procter & Gamble's new values-based strategy. *Harvard Business Review*. Retrieved January 3, 2018, from https://hbr.org/2009/09/fall-like-a-lehman-rise-like-a.html

ENDNOTES

1. Wright, P. M., & Ulrich, M. D. (2017). A road well traveled: The past, present, and future journey of strategic human resource management. *Annual Review of Organizational Behavior and Organizational Psychology, 4*, 45–65.

2. Wolf, C., & Floyd, S. W. (2017). Strategic planning research: Toward a theory-driven agenda. *Journal of Management, 43*, 1754–1788.

3. Mankins, M., & Steele, R. (2005). Turning great strategy into great performance. *Harvard Business Review*. Retrieved January 2, 2018, from https://hbr.org/2005/07/turning-great-strategy-into-great-performance

4. Rao, A. S. (2007). Effectiveness of performance management systems: An empirical study in Indian companies. *International Journal of Human Resource Management, 18*, 1812–1840.

5. McCauley, M. A. (2017). How to weave strategic planning into your day-to-day work. *Communication World*, 1–4.

6. Nistor, C. S., Stefanescu, C. A., & Sintejudeanu, M. A. (2017). Performance management and balanced scorecard—A link for public sector. *Journal of Accounting and Management, 6*(3), 5–25.

7. Pierce, J. R., & Aguinis, H. (2013). The too-much-of-a-good-thing effect in management. *Journal of Management, 39*, 313–338.

8. Kaplan, R. S., & Norton, P. (1992). The balanced scorecard: Measures that drive performance. *Harvard Business Review, 70*(1), 71–79.

9. This example is loosely adapted from Addams, H. L., & Embley, K. (1988). Performance management systems: From strategic planning to employee productivity. *Personnel, 65*, 55–60.

10. Adapted from Fisher, C. D., Schoenfeldt, L. F., & Shaw, J. B. (2003). *Human resource management* (5th ed.). Boston, MA: Houghton Mifflin.

11. *Performance management at Dell*. Retrieved January 2, 2018, from https://prezi.com/d3d_hvlvs8te/performance-management-at-dell/

12. Kolbina, O. (2015). SWOT analysis as a strategic planning tool for companies in the food industry. *Problems of Economic Transition, 57*, 74–83.

13. The discussion regarding environmental analysis is adapted from Drohan, W. (1997). Principles of strategic planning. *Association Management, 49*, 85–87.

14. Porter, M. E. (1979). How competitive forces shape strategy. *Harvard Business Review, 57*(2), 137–156.

15. About us: Low fares done right. Retrieved January 2, 2018, from https://www.flyfrontier.com/about-us

16. Low-cost Ted may help United fly out of bankruptcy. (2004, February 13). *USA Today*. Retrieved January 2, 2018, from http://www.usatoday.com/travel/news/2004-02-13-ted-wrap_x.htm

17. Prudential: Planning strategic direction for global operations. (2016). *Profiles in Diversity Journal, 153*.

18. IBM Products. Retrieved January 2, 2018, from https://www.ibm.com/products

19. About us: Mission, vision and values. Retrieved January 2, 2018, from http://www.coca-cola.co.uk/about-us/mission-vision-and-values

20. Our mission. Retrieved January 2, 2018, from http://www.spectrumbrands.com/AboutUs/Mission.aspx

21. About Greif. Retrieved January 2, 2018, from http://www.greif.com/company

22. Cycle World Interview: Matt Levatich, Harley-Davidson President & CEO. Retrieved January 2, 2018, from http://www.cycleworld.com/2015/04/30/cycle-world-interview-matt-levatich-harley-davidson-president-and-ceo

23. *An Investor's Guide to Harley-Davidson's 3Q15 Earnings*. Retrieved January 2, 2018, from http://marketrealist.com/2015/10/harley-davidsons-5-objectives-investor-takeaways/

24. Vargas-Hernández, J. G. (2017). Strategies for organizational intervention to develop a world-class company. *Scholedge International Journal of Business Policy & Governance, 4*(1), 1–6.

25. About Microsoft. Retrieved January 2, 2018, from https://www.microsoft.com/en-us/about/default.aspx

26. Mission statement of NSU. Retrieved January 2, 2018, from https://www.nsu.edu/president/mission-statement

27. The School of Business mission statement. Retrieved January 2, 2018, from https://www.nsu.edu/business/about-us

part two

System Implementation

4

Defining Performance and Choosing a Measurement Approach

You have to measure to understand

—*Ginni Rometty*

Learning Objectives

By the end of this chapter, you will be able to do the following:

1. Argue that performance involves both behaviors and results and that performance is evaluative and multidimensional in nature.

2. Prepare a list of the factors that determine performance, including abilities and other traits, knowledge and skills (including declarative knowledge and procedural knowledge), and context.

3. Propose a list of contextual factors (e.g., HR policies, organizational and national culture) that have a direct impact on performance.

4. Plan interventions involving deliberate practice and extreme ownership with the goal of improving performance.

5. Propose how to address and anticipate performance problems.

6. Create a performance management system that includes key performance indicators (KPIs) of each of the four types or dimensions of performance: (a) task, (b) contextual, (c) counterproductive, and (d) adaptive.

7. Set up a behavior approach to measuring performance (e.g., competency modeling), which basically focuses on how the job is done, as opposed to the results produced.

8. Set up a results approach to measuring performance, which basically focuses on the outcomes of work, as opposed to the manner in which the work is done.

This chapter marks the beginning of Part II of this text, which describes how to implement a performance management system. Whereas Part I addressed strategic and organizational and other macro-level issues, Part II addresses operational concerns. In this chapter, we begin with an issue that, at first glance, may seem simple, but it is not: What exactly is performance and how can we measure it? Answering this question is absolutely key if we want to implement a successful performance management system, because if we do not have a good answer, we will not be able to craft actual measures—a topic that will be addressed in Chapter 5. Let us begin by defining performance.

4-1 DEFINING PERFORMANCE: BEHAVIORS AND RESULTS

As shown in Figure 4-1, performance includes (a) behaviors and actions (what an employee does) and (b) results and products (the outcomes of an employee's behavior).[1] Both of these components are important and they influence each other. For example, if a student allocates a sufficient amount of efficient time to preparing for an exam (behavior), it is likely that he will receive a good grade (result). In turn, receiving a good grade (result) will serve as a motivating factor for continuing to allocate sufficient time to studying in the future (behavior). So behaviors and results create a virtuous and self-reinforcing cycle that together constitute performance.

There are two characteristics of the behaviors and results we label "performance."[2] First, they are *evaluative*. This means that they can be judged as negative, neutral, or positive for individual and organizational effectiveness. In other words, the value of these behaviors and results can vary depending on the extent to which they make a contribution toward the accomplishment of individual, unit, and organizational goals. Second, performance is *multidimensional*.[3] This means that there are many different types of behaviors and results that have the capacity to advance (or hinder) organizational goals.

As an example, consider a set of behaviors that can be grouped under the general label "contribution to effectiveness of others in the work unit." This set of behaviors can be defined as follows:

Works with others within and outside the unit in a manner that improves their effectiveness; shares information and resources; develops effective working relationships; builds consensus; constructively manages conflict.

Contribution to the effectiveness of others in the work unit could be assessed by using a scale that includes anchors demonstrating various levels of competence. For example, anchors could be words and phrases such as "outstanding," "significantly exceeds standards," "fully meets standards," "does not fully meet standards," and "unacceptable." This illustrates the evaluative nature of performance because this set of behaviors is judged as positive, neutral, or negative. In addition, this example illustrates the multidimensional nature of performance because there are several behaviors that, combined, affect the overall perceived contribution that an employee makes to the effectiveness of others in the work unit. In other words, we would be missing important information if we only considered, for example, "shares information and resources" and did not consider the additional behaviors listed earlier.

FIGURE 4-1

Performance: Combination of Behaviors and Actions, and Results and Products

Performance management systems also include measures of results or products that we infer are the direct result of employees' behaviors. Take the case of a salesperson whose job consists of visiting clients to offer them new products or services. The salesperson's supervisor is back in the home office and does not have an opportunity to observe the salesperson's behaviors firsthand. In this case, sales volume may be used as a performance measure. In other words, the supervisor makes the assumption that if the salesperson is able to produce high sales figures, then she is probably engaging in the right behaviors.

4-2 DETERMINANTS OF PERFORMANCE: ABILITIES AND OTHER TRAITS, KNOWLEDGE AND SKILLS, AND CONTEXT

Why do certain individuals perform better than others? What factors cause an employee to perform at a certain level? A combination of three factors allows some people to perform at higher levels than others: (1) *abilities and other traits*, (2) *knowledge and skills*, and (3) *context*.[4]

Abilities and other traits include such things as cognitive abilities (i.e., intelligence), personality, stable motivational dispositions, and physical characteristics and abilities. Also, knowledge and skills include job-related knowledge and skills, attitudes, and malleable motivational states. Knowledge and skills can be divided into *declarative knowledge*, which is information about facts and things, including information regarding a given task's requirements, labels, principles, and goals; and *procedural knowledge*, which is a combination of knowing what to do and how to do it and includes cognitive, physical, perceptual, motor, and interpersonal skills. Finally, contextual issues include HR policies and procedures (e.g., compensation system), managerial and peer leadership, organizational and national culture, issues about time and timing of performance, and resources and opportunities given to employees to perform.

As shown in Figure 4-2, performance results from a combination of all three factors. Also, the three factors have an additive relationship. This means that two employees can achieve the same level of performance by having different combinations of factors. For example, one employee can be more motivated and spend more hours at work, whereas another can work fewer hours, but have higher levels of skill.[5]

In addition, however, if any of the determinants has a value of 0, then overall performance is unlikely to be satisfactory. For example, consider the case of Jane, a sales associate who works in a national clothing retail chain. Jane has excellent declarative knowledge regarding the merchandise. In particular, she knows the names of all of the brands; the prices for all products; sizing charts for clothes for women, men, and children; and sales promotions. So her declarative knowledge is very high. Jane is also intelligent and physically able to conduct all of the necessary tasks—both considered important traits for the job. However, her interactions with customers are not so good (i.e., procedural knowledge regarding interpersonal skills). She does not pay much attention to them because she is busy restocking clothes on shelves and hangers. She does not greet customers and is also not good at providing answers to their questions. Her overall performance, therefore, is likely to be poor because although she has the declarative knowledge necessary to do the job, as well as cognitive and physical traits, she lacks procedural knowledge. In short, it is necessary to have at least some level of each of the determinants of performance.

FIGURE 4-2

Determinants of Performance: Abilities and Other Traits, Knowledge and Skills, and Context

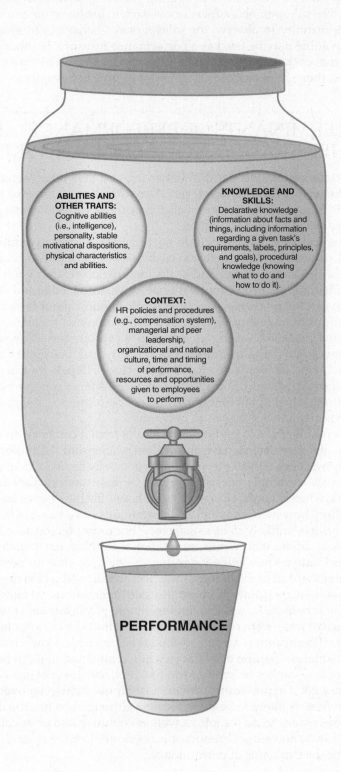

4-2-1 Abilities and Other Traits, and Knowledge and Skills

An important difference between abilities and other traits and knowledge and skills is that knowledge and skills are more malleable—meaning that they are easier to change. For example, cognitive abilities and personality traits are fairly stable.[6] For example, the following personality traits are called the "Big Five"[7]:

1. *Extroversion*: being sociable, gregarious, assertive, talkative, and active (the opposite end of extroversion is labeled *introversion*)

2. *Neuroticism*: being anxious, depressed, angry, embarrassed, emotional, worried, and insecure (the opposite pole of neuroticism is labeled *emotional stability*)

3. *Agreeableness*: being curious, flexible, trusting, good-natured, cooperative, forgiving, and tolerant

4. *Conscientiousness*: being dependable (i.e., being careful, thorough, responsible, and organized), as well as hardworking, achievement-oriented, and persevering

5. *Openness to experience*: being imaginative, cultured, curious, original, broad-minded, intelligent, and artistically sensitive

In general, individual differences that are less malleable are called "traits." Those that are easier to change, for example, through a training program or other organizational interventions, are called "states." For example, consider the fact that employees vary in terms of their motivation: how much energy and effort they allocate. Specifically, consider the following three choices:

1. Choice to expend effort (e.g., "I will go to work today")

2. Choice of level of effort (e.g., "I will put in my best effort at work" versus "I will not try very hard")

3. Choice to persist in the expenditure of that level of effort (e.g., "I will give up after a little while" versus "I will persist no matter what")

The first two are more malleable and therefore considered state motivation. For example, we could influence an employee's choice regarding whether she shows up at work—and on time—using HR policies regarding absenteeism and tardiness. We could influence the second choice by setting clear goals. But the third is less malleable and more likely to be a stable individual trait (rather than a state). This type of trait motivation is considered a fairly stable personality trait, called "achievement motivation," and is a facet of conscientiousness.

What can we do to improve our own knowledge and skills and therefore improve our performance? Let us think about those individuals who have achieved the top level of performance in their fields. Think about Leo Messi and Cristiano Ronaldo as soccer ("football" outside of North America) players, Beyoncé as a singer and songwriter, Bill Gates as Microsoft's founder, Magnus Carlsen as a chess player, Thomas Edison as an inventor, Marie Curie as a physicist and chemist, and Socrates as a philosopher. How did they achieve such excellence? What made these individuals' performance so extraordinary? How were they able to improve their performance constantly even when others would believe they had reached a plateau and could not possibly improve their performance? What these individuals have in common is that they devoted a large number of hours to *deliberate practice*.[8] Deliberate practice is different from regular practice and from simply working many hours a week. Professor K. Anders Ericsson of Florida State University gives the following example: "Simply hitting a bucket of balls is not deliberate practice, which is why most golfers don't get better. Hitting an eight-iron 300 times with a goal of leaving the ball within 20 feet of the pin 80% of the time, continually observing results and making appropriate adjustments, and doing that for hours every day—that's deliberate practice." Top performers in all fields engage in deliberate practice consistently, daily, including weekends. The famous pianist Vladimir Horowitz was quoted as saying: "If I don't practice for a day, I know it; if I don't practice for two days, my wife knows it; if I don't practice for three days, the world knows it." Deliberate practice involves the following five steps:

1. Approach performance with the goal of getting better and better.
2. As you are performing, focus on what is happening and why you are doing things the way you do.
3. Once your task is finished, seek performance feedback from expert sources, and the more sources, the better.
4. Build mental models of your job, your situation, and your organization.
5. Repeat steps 1–4 continually and on an ongoing basis.

Think about a particular task at which you would like to do better. This could be job-related, school-related, or a hobby (e.g., music, sports, cooking, playing poker). Now, create a deliberate practice program for yourself. Who are the experts from whom you could solicit feedback? How often would you practice? For how long? What would be some of your specific goals you would like to achieve, and by when?

4-2-2 Context

The third determinant of performance is context because performance is also determined by what is happening around the employee. For example, HR policies and practices can have an important impact on employee performance. Take the case of IBM. In December 2016, Ginni Rometty, IBM's CEO, said that over the next four years, the company will invest US$1 billion in training and develop-ment in the United States.[9] In contrast to IBM, working for a company with an HR function that does not offer much in terms of training means that, sooner or later, performance will suffer as skills become obsolete.

As a second example, an organizational culture that does not promote excellence will also have negative consequences on performance. Take the case of a compensation system that includes paying everyone the same, regardless of employee performance—this is unlikely to motivate employees to do better.

As a third example, time and the timing of performance is another contextual factor that also plays a role. Specifically, *typical performance* refers to the average level of an employee's performance, whereas *maximum performance* refers to the peak level of performance an employee can achieve. Employees are more likely to perform at maximum levels when they understand they are being evaluated, when they accept instructions to maximize performance on the task, and when the task is of short duration.[10] A key issue is that the relationship between typical (i.e., what employees will do) and maximum (i.e., what employees could do) performance is very weak. What this means is that measuring performance during short time intervals may be assessing maximum, and not typical, performance. Most organizations are more interested in what employees will do on a regular basis, rather than what they could do during the short period of time when they are observed and evaluated. In short, the time and timing of performance observation and measurement also affect the observed levels of performance.

Fourth, resources and opportunities to perform are important contextual issues as well. There is a harsh reality in organizations that involves some employees receiving less resources and opportunities than others.[11] For example, within the same firm, some consultants may have more opportunities to work with important clients than others. This issue is quite obvious in sports: there is a limited amount of playing time during each game. So some athletes have more playing time than others. In both of these cases, although employees may have the same levels of abilities and other traits as well as knowledge and skills, differential levels of opportunities will have a direct impact on their performance.

Finally, consider the issues of organizational and national culture. Take the case of WorldCom, a company that was the second largest long-distance phone company in the United States before it collapsed in 2002. One of the reasons for its collapse was its "cult-like corporate culture" around a charismatic leader, former basketball coach Bernie Ebbers.[12] Ebbers exercised unquestioned authority and demanded unquestioned loyalty from employees. Within this context, it was difficult, if not impossible, for employees to do anything different from what they were told—even if this meant doing things that were clearly unethical. This was an important contextual factor that affected the performance of all employees at WorldCom, regardless of their levels of abilities and traits as well as knowledge and skills. National culture can also affect performance in meaningful ways. For example, cultures that are more hierarchical and power centered are less likely to lead to outstanding performance regarding such issues as creativity and innovation. On the other hand, these types of cultures can result in outstanding performance regarding standardization, speed, and efficiency.[13]

4-2-3 Implications for Addressing and Anticipating Performance Problems

The fact that performance is affected by the combined effect of three different factors has implications for addressing as well as anticipating performance problems. To do so properly, managers must find information that will allow them to understand whether the source of the problem is abilities and other traits; knowledge and skills; contextual issues; or some combination of these three factors. If an employee lacks procedural knowledge but the manager believes the source of the problem is declarative knowledge, the manager may give the employee a manual with facts and figures about products so he can acquire the knowledge that is presumably lacking. In the example of Jane discussed earlier, this would obviously be a waste of time and resources for the individual, manager, and organization because it is lack of procedural knowledge, and not lack of declarative knowledge, that is causing her poor performance. This is why performance management systems should not only measure performance, but also be a tool to understand the source of any performance deficiencies.

Another issue regarding the identification of performance problems relates to what is called ownership, or what Jocko Willink, retired United States Navy SEAL and former commander in the Battle of Ramadi in Iraq, calls *extreme ownership*.[14] Willink served in SEAL Task Unit Bruiser, the most highly decorated Special Operations unit from the war in Iraq. They faced tremendous difficulties along the way, including being involved in a "blue-on-blue": friendly fire—the worst thing that could happen. One of the American soldiers was wounded, an Iraqi soldier was dead, and others were seriously wounded. This incident led to asking very difficult questions, and the most critical one was: "Who was responsible for this debacle?" Willink notes that the very first step is to take ownership of poor performance, no matter how painful this process may be. What he learned in war can be extrapolated to other contexts: Acknowledging that we have performed under par is never easy. It hurts our egos. It hurts our self-esteem. But these are short-term effects only. Unless we engage in this process, it will be very difficult to address any type of performance problem. Willink said that he "had to take complete ownership of what went wrong. That is what a leader does—even if it means getting fired." We will continue to address this important issue of extreme ownership in other chapters, including the discussion of coaching in Chapter 9.

In short, when addressing and anticipating performance problems, managers first need to identify whether abilities and other traits, knowledge and skills (i.e., declarative and procedural knowledge), or context are hampering performance, and then, help the employee improve his performance. Think about the last time when you or a coworker showed a level of performance that was not considered adequate. What were the causes of this substandard level of performance—Lack of abilities and traits, knowledge and skills, or contextual issues? Which were the two most important factors?

4-3 PERFORMANCE DIMENSIONS

As noted earlier, performance is multidimensional, meaning that we need to consider many different types of behaviors and results to understand performance. We can classify performance into four types or dimensions (a) task performance, (b) contextual performance (also called prosocial or organizational citizenship performance), (c) counterproductive performance, and (d) adaptive performance. A good performance management system should include Key Performance Indicators (KPIs), or observable measures, for each of these types.

4-3-1 Task and Contextual Performance

Contextual and task performance must be considered separately because they do not necessarily occur in tandem. An employee can be highly proficient at her task, but be an underperformer regarding contextual performance.[15] Task performance is defined as:

- Activities that transform raw materials into the goods and services that are produced by the organization
- Activities that help with the transformation process by replenishing the supply of raw materials; distributing its finished products; or providing important planning, coordination, supervising, or staff functions that enable the organization to function effectively and efficiently.

Contextual performance is defined as those behaviors that contribute to the organization's effectiveness by providing a good environment in which task performance can occur. Contextual performance includes behaviors such as the following:

- Persisting with enthusiasm and exerting extra effort as necessary to complete one's own task activities successfully (e.g., being punctual and rarely absent, expending extra effort on the job)

- Volunteering to carry out task activities that are not formally part of the job (e.g., suggesting organizational improvements, making constructive suggestions)
- Helping and cooperating with others (e.g., assisting and helping coworkers and customers)
- Following organizational rules and procedures (e.g., following orders and regulations, showing respect for authority, complying with organizational values and policies)
- Endorsing, supporting, and defending organizational objectives (e.g., organizational loyalty, representing the organization favorably to outsiders).

Both task and contextual performance are important dimensions to take into account in performance management systems. Imagine what would happen to an organization in which all employees are outstanding regarding task performance, but do not perform well regarding contextual performance. What if a colleague whose cubicle is next to yours needs to take a restroom break and asks you to answer the phone if it rings, because an important client will call at any moment? What if we said, "That is not MY job?" See Box 4-1, which describes a system including both task and contextual performance at Sprint.

Many organizations now realize that there is a need to focus on both task and contextual performance because organizations cannot function properly without a minimum dose of positive contextual behaviors on the part of all employees. Consider the case of ZF TRW Automotive Holdings Corp., which designs, manufactures, and sells automotive systems, modules, and components to automotive

Box 4-1

Company Spotlight: Task and Contextual Performance at Sprint

Sprint is a communications services company serving 59.7 million connections. Sprint is widely recognized for developing, engineering, and deploying innovative technologies, including the first wireless 4G service from a national carrier in the United States, leading no-contract brands, including Virgin Mobile USA, Boost Mobile, and Assurance Wireless, instant national and international push-to-talk capabilities, and a global Tier 1 Internet backbone. The company is headquartered in Reston, Virginia. At Sprint, all employees are evaluated and development plans are created through the use of five core dimensions: acting with integrity, focusing on the customer, delivering results, building relationships, and demonstrating leadership. The dimensions are used not only for business strategy and objectives, but also as a template for what successful performance looks like at the company. These dimensions include the consideration of both task and contextual performance, and employees in the evaluation and development process are asked to write behavioral examples of how they have performed on each dimension. For example, the delivering results dimension clearly links to performing specific tasks of one's job. Each employee has certain tasks to complete on a regular basis to keep the business moving. On the other hand, the company is concerned about how the work gets done and contributing to a good work environment that allows for greater effectiveness. This is apparent through the dimensions that look at how employees develop relationships with others and act with integrity in their day-to-day functioning. In summary, Sprint has recognized the importance of considering both task and contextual components of a job in its performance management system. Employees are evaluated not only on results, but also on how they are achieved through working with others.[16]

original equipment manufacturers. The company was founded in 1904, is based in Livonia, Michigan, and has approximately 67,000 employees. With increasing market pressures and sluggish growth, the company wanted to become more performance driven, experiment in new markets, and offer greater value to its shareholders. To do so, the senior management team developed what they labeled the "key behaviors." These behaviors are communicated throughout the company and have a prominent role in the performance management process. The majority of these key behaviors actually focus on *contextual performance*. Specifically, the ZF TRW behaviors emphasize many of the elements of contextual performance, including teamwork and trust.

Table 4-1 summarizes the main differences between task and contextual performance. First, task performance varies across jobs. For example, the tasks performed by an HR manager are different from those performed by a line manager. The tasks performed by a senior HR manager are more strategic in nature compared to those performed by an entry-level HR analyst, which are more operational in nature. On the other hand, contextual performance is fairly similar across functional and hierarchical levels. All employees, regardless of job title, function, and responsibilities, are equally responsible for, for example, volunteering to carry out task activities that are not formally part of the job. Second, task performance is likely to be role prescribed, meaning that task performance is usually included in one's job description. In contrast, contextual performance behaviors are usually not role prescribed, but are typically expected without making them explicit. Finally, task performance is influenced mainly by abilities and skills (e.g., cognitive, physical), whereas contextual performance is influenced mainly by personality (e.g., conscientiousness, agreeableness).[17]

There are numerous pressing reasons why both task and contextual performance dimensions should be included in a performance management system. First, global competition is raising the levels of effort required of employees. Thus, whereas it may have sufficed in the past to have a workforce that was competent in task performance, today's globalized world and accompanying competitive forces make it imperative that the workforce also engage in positive contextual performance. It is difficult to compete if an organization employs a workforce that does not engage in contextual behaviors. Second, related to the issue of global competition is the need to offer outstanding customer service. Contextual performance behaviors can make a profound impact on customer satisfaction. Imagine what a big difference it makes, from a customer perspective, when an employee puts in extra effort to satisfy a customer's needs. Third, many organizations are forming employees into teams. Although some teams may not be permanent because they are created to complete specific short-term tasks, the reality of today's world of work is that teams are here to stay. Interpersonal cooperation is a key determinant of team effectiveness. Thus, contextual

TABLE 4-1
Main Differences Between Task and Contextual Performance

Task Performance	Contextual Performance (also called Prosocial or Organizational Citizenship Performance)
Varies across jobs	Fairly similar across jobs
Likely to be role prescribed	Not likely to be role prescribed
Antecedents: abilities and skills	Antecedent: personality

performance becomes particularly relevant for teamwork. Fourth, including both task and contextual performance in the performance management system provides an additional benefit: Employees being rated are more satisfied with the system and also believe the system is more fair if contextual performance is measured in addition to task performance.[18] It seems that employees are aware that contextual performance is important in affecting organizational effectiveness, and therefore, believe that these types of behaviors should be included in a performance management system in addition to the more traditional task performance. Finally, when supervisors evaluate performance, it is difficult for them to ignore the contextual performance dimension, even though the evaluation form they are using may not include any specific questions about contextual performance.[19] Consequently, because contextual performance has an impact on ratings of overall performance even when only task performance is measured, it makes sense to include contextual performance more explicitly.

Finally, there is an additional type of behavior that is another facet of contextual performance but is different from traditional ways of thinking about it: *voice behavior*.[20] Voice behavior is a type of behavior that emphasizes expression of constructive challenge with the goal to improve, rather than merely criticize; it challenges the status quo in a positive way and is about making innovative suggestions for change and recommending modifications to standard procedures even when others, including an employee's supervisor, disagree.

Consider an employee who has just been hired into your organization. This new colleague was recruited from a competitor, which is known to implement top-notch performance management practices. This employee, having the benefit of an outsider perspective, can point to processes that could be improved. For example, the new colleague may suggest that more feedback be given to the members of the team regarding their performance. This employee may even send an e-mail message to all members of her team and to her supervisor, including suggestions for improvement based on proven practices directly observed elsewhere. Some of these suggestions may not be applicable in the new organizational environment owing to different equipment, processes, products, and clients. However, others, if implemented, may produce immediate and highly beneficial results. Although such type of behavior can be included as part of the broader category of contextual behavior, it is different in that it is not conformist in nature. In fact, voice behavior can be seen as a threat by the new employee's supervisor, who is used to "doing things the same way we've done them before." Such supervisors may perceive the suggestions for changes and improvements as a threat to the status quo. Moreover, more senior organizational members may also feel personally threatened by the knowledge, energy, and innovative ideas of the new employee. These reactions to voice behavior can be a sign that the wrong people are occupying leadership positions in the organization, and also, a sign of imminent organizational decline.[21] In contrast, healthier organizational environments that are more adaptive and promote innovation and improvements are more receptive to voice behavior and even reward it.[22]

4-3-2 Counterproductive Performance

The third type or dimension of performance is labeled counterproductive performance.[23] Counterproductive performance is behaviors and results that are voluntary and that violate organizational norms, and consequently, threaten the well-being of the organization, its members, or both. It may seem that counterproductive performance is simply the opposite of contextual performance, but it is not. Specifically, the same employee can engage in both contextual and counterproductive performance. Some KPIs of counterproductive performance include the following[24]:

- Exaggerating hours worked
- Falsifying a receipt to get reimbursed for more money than was spent on business expenses
- Starting negative rumors about the company
- Gossiping about coworkers and one's supervisor
- Covering up one's mistakes
- Competing with coworkers in an unproductive way
- Staying out of sight to avoid work
- Blaming one's coworkers for one's mistakes
- Intentionally working slowly or carelessly
- Being intoxicated during working hours
- Seeking revenge on coworkers
- Cyberloafing
- Presenting colleagues' ideas as if they were one's own

Consider the corporate scandal of Enron, which led to the bankruptcy of the Enron Corporation. This was a large American energy company based in Houston, Texas, and the "Enron scandal" was the largest bankruptcy reorganization in American history, as well as the biggest audit failure. A book by McLean and Elkind, based on hundreds of interviews and details from personal calendars, performance reviews, e-mails, and other documents, showed that one of the primary reasons for the company's collapse was widespread counterproductive performance.[25] In fact, Enron executives were described as "supersmart." For example, its former CEO, Jeffrey Keith "Jeff" Skilling, and many other top executives, had earned their MBAs from top-ranked business schools such as Harvard Business School and The University of Texas. A performance management system that included not only task performance but also counterproductive performance could have detected unethical behaviors and accounting practices before they became widespread and led to the collapse of the entire company—including a loss of 99.5 percent of its market value in a year. Not surprisingly, when he became dean of the Harvard Business School a few years after Enron's collapse, Professor Nitin Nohria posed the core question for the school: "Are we educating people who have the competence and character to exercise leadership in business?"[26]

4-3-3 Adaptive Performance

Adaptive performance is the fourth type and is related to an individual's adaptability to changes—be it in the organization and its goals, in the requirements of the job, or the overall work context.[27] Given the rapid pace of technology and other factors that are constantly changing the nature of work and organizations, adaptive performance is becoming an increasingly important performance dimension. For example, an organization may change its strategic priorities, merge or be acquired, and have more or less resources. The way employees react to and anticipate these changes is, therefore, an important performance component.

There are several KPIs of adaptive performance. Consider the following eight[28]:

1. *Handling emergencies or crisis situations.* To what extent can employees react with appropriate and proper urgency in dangerous or emergency situations; quickly analyze options for dealing with danger or crises; maintain emotional control and objectivity while staying focused on the situation at hand; and step up to take action and handle danger or emergencies?

2. *Handling work stress.* To what extent can employees remain composed and cool when faced with difficult circumstances or a highly demanding workload or schedule; not overreact to unexpected news or situations; and manage frustration well by directing effort to constructive solutions rather than blaming others?

3. *Solving problems creatively.* To what extent can employees use unique types of analyses to generate new, innovative ideas in complex areas; turn problems upside down and inside out to find fresh, new approaches; integrate seemingly unrelated information to develop creative solutions; and entertain wide-ranging possibilities others may miss?

4. *Dealing with uncertain and unpredictable work situations.* To what extent can employees take effective action without knowing all the facts at hand; change gears in response to unpredictable or unexpected events; adjust plans, goals, actions, or priorities to deal with changing situations; not need things to be black and white; and refuse to be paralyzed by uncertainty or ambiguity?

5. *Learning work tasks, technologies, and procedures.* To what extent can employees demonstrate enthusiasm for learning new approaches and technologies; do what is necessary to keep knowledge and skills current; learn new methods; adjust to new work processes and procedures, and anticipate changes in the work demands; and search for and participate in assignments or training that will prepare them for these changes?

6. *Demonstrating interpersonal adaptability.* To what extent can employees be flexible and open-minded when dealing with others; listen to and consider others' viewpoints and opinions and alter their own opinion when it is appropriate to do so; be open and accepting of negative or developmental feedback regarding work; and work well and develop effective relationships with people with diverse personalities?

7. *Demonstrating cultural adaptability.* To what extent can employees take action to learn about and understand the climate, orientation, needs, and values of other groups, organizations, or cultures; integrate well into and be comfortable with different values, customs, and cultures; and understand the implications of one's actions and adjust their approach to maintain positive relationships with other groups, organizations, and cultures?

8. *Demonstrating physically oriented adaptability.* To what extent can employees adjust to challenging environmental states such as extreme heat, humidity, cold, or dirt; accommodate frequent physical pressure to complete strenuous or demanding tasks and adjust weight and muscular strength; and become proficient in performing physical tasks as necessary for the job?

In summary, performance includes four types or dimensions: task, contextual, counterproductive, and adaptive. All four should be considered because they have separate and important effects on organizational success. In the case of all dimensions, each behavior and result should be defined clearly so that employees understand what is expected of them. Organizations that include all four dimensions are likely to be more successful, as in the case of Three Ireland, Ireland's second largest mobile phone operator. Headquartered in Dublin, it operates 67 retail stores and currently has over 1,400 employees throughout Ireland. A few years ago, Three Ireland implemented a performance management system in its 320 seat customer care center in Limerick. Three Ireland's performance management system includes several performance dimensions—for example, task-related facets centered in hard metrics regarding productivity. Also, contextual-related facets include involvement in staff socialization and contribution to team development. The targets set for each employee are also aligned with company objectives. Three Ireland believes that this focus on both task and contextual performance has led to higher levels of customer service and employee satisfaction.

4-4 APPROACHES TO MEASURING PERFORMANCE

We must once again remember that performance involves both results and behaviors (see Figure 4-1). So good systems include measures of both behaviors and actions as well as results and products, as described next.

4-4-1 Behavior Approach

The behavior approach emphasizes what employees do on the job and does not consider the outcomes or products resulting from their behaviors. This is basically a process-oriented approach that emphasizes *how* an employee does the job, and not what is produced.

The behavior approach is most appropriate under the following circumstances:

- *The link between behaviors and results is not obvious.* Sometimes, the relation between behaviors and the desired outcomes is not clear. In some cases, the desired result may not be achieved in spite of the fact that the right behaviors are in place. For example, a salesperson may not be able to close a deal because of a downturn in the economy. In other cases, results may be achieved in spite of the absence of the correct behaviors. For example, a pilot may not check all the items in the preflight checklist, but the flight may nevertheless be successful (i.e., take off and land safely and on time). When the link between behaviors and results is not always obvious, it is beneficial to focus on behaviors, as opposed to outcomes.

- *Outcomes occur in the distant future.* When the desired results will not be seen for months, or even years, the measurement of behaviors is beneficial. Take the case of NASA's Mars Exploration Rover Mission program. NASA launched the exploration rover Spirit on June 10, 2003, which landed on Mars on January 3, 2004, after traveling 487 million kilometers (302.6 million miles). Its twin, the exploration rover, Opportunity, was launched on July 7, 2003, and landed on the opposite side of Mars on January 24, 2004. From launch to landing, this mission took about six months to complete. In this circumstance, it is certainly appropriate to assess the performance of the engineers involved in the mission by measuring their behaviors in short intervals during this six-month period, rather than waiting until the final result (i.e., successful or unsuccessful landing) is observed. Now, NASA has the goal of sending humans to the

Red Planet in the 2030s. That journey is already well under way. But we will have to wait more than 10 years until we are able to evaluate performance based on results. So a behavior approach is appropriate in this case.

- *Poor results are due to causes beyond the performer's control.* When the results of an employee's performance are beyond the employee's control, it makes sense to emphasize the measurement of behaviors. For example, consider a situation involving two assembly line workers, one of them working the day shift, and the other, the night shift. When the assembly line gets stuck because of technical problems, the employee working during the day receives immediate technical assistance, so the assembly line is back in motion in less than five minutes. By contrast, the employee working the night shift has very little technical support, and, therefore, when the assembly line breaks down, it takes about 45 minutes for it to be up and running again. If we measured results, we would conclude that the performance of the day-shift employee is far superior to that of the night-shift employee, but this would be an incorrect conclusion. Both employees may be equally competent and do the job equally well. The results produced by these employees are uneven because they depend on the amount and quality of technical assistance they receive when the assembly line is stuck.

A popular type of behavior approach used mostly for managerial positions is called *competency modeling*.[29] In a nutshell, competencies are clusters of knowledge, skills, abilities, and other characteristics (KSAOs) that, together, determine how results are achieved. As such, competencies are not directly observable, but we can measure them by assessing behavioral indicators. For example, to measure the competency "leadership," we can measure the behaviors that a manager uses in mentoring and developing her direct reports. For an example of competency modeling at Dollar General, see Box 4-2. We discuss the specific steps involved in developing measures of behaviors, including competencies, in Chapter 5. Next, let us discuss the results approach to measuring performance.

4-4-2 Results Approach

The results approach emphasizes the outcomes produced by the employees. It does not consider how employees do the job. This is basically a bottom-line approach that is not concerned about employee behaviors and processes but instead focuses on what is produced (e.g., sales, number of accounts acquired, time spent with clients on the telephone, number of errors). Defining and measuring results usually takes less time than defining and measuring behaviors needed to achieve these results. In fact, given the ongoing collection of employee data in the form of employee monitoring (what we described in Chapter 1 as "Big Data"), the results approach is usually seen as more cost-effective because results can be less expensive to track than behaviors. Overall, data resulting from a results approach seem to be objective and are intuitively very appealing.

The results approach is most appropriate under the following circumstances:

- *Workers are skilled in the needed behaviors.* An emphasis on results is appropriate when workers have the necessary abilities, knowledge, and skills to do the work. In such situations, workers know what specific behaviors are needed to achieve the desired results, and they are also sufficiently skilled to know what to do to correct any process-related problems when the desired results are not obtained. Consider the example

Box 4-2

Company Spotlight: Competency-Based Behavior Approach at Dollar General

Dollar General uses a behavior approach to measure performance. Tennessee-based Dollar General operates about 13,000 stores in 43 states in the United States. The company sells consumable basics, such as paper products, cleaning supplies, health and beauty products, foods and snacks, housewares, toys, and basic apparel. As part of the performance management system, Dollar General has identified behaviors that serve as indicators of underlying competencies. These behaviors are reviewed and utilized to encourage certain outcomes and provide feedback and rewards to staff members. For example, the company management sought to improve attendance among employees. In order to encourage employees to arrive at work on time, a system was developed to group employees into teams who earn points. A wall chart was created displaying a racetrack, and each team was given a car that would be moved forward by the number of points earned each day. After a certain number of laps around the track, employees on the teams with the most points would be given a choice about how to celebrate. The program was successful within the first two weeks and increased attendance significantly. In summary, Dollar General's performance management system includes the use of a behavior approach to measuring performance.[30]

of a professional basketball player. A free throw is an unhindered shot made from the foul line and is given to one team to penalize the other team for committing a foul. Free throw shooting can make the difference between winning and losing in a close basketball game. Professional players know that there is really no secret to becoming a great free throw shooter: just hours and hours of dedicated practice besides actual basketball play, per our earlier discussion about deliberate practice. In assessing the performance of professional basketball players, the free throw shooting percentage is a key results-oriented performance indicator because most players have the skills to do it. It is just a matter of assessing whether they do it well or not.

- *Behaviors and results are obviously related.* In some situations, certain results can be obtained only if a worker engages in certain specific behaviors. This is the case of jobs involving repetitive tasks such as assembly line work or newspaper delivery. Take the case of a person delivering newspapers. Performance can be measured adopting a results approach: whether the newspaper is delivered to every customer within a particular time frame. For the employee to obtain this result, she needs to pick up the papers at a specific time and use the most effective delivery route. If these behaviors are not present, the paper will not be delivered on time.
- *Results show consistent improvement over time.* When results improve consistently over time, it is an indication that workers are aware of the behaviors needed to complete the job successfully. In these situations, it is appropriate to adopt a results approach to assessing performance.
- *There are many ways to do the job right.* When there are different ways in which one can do the tasks required for a job, a results approach is appropriate. An emphasis on results can be beneficial because it could encourage employees to achieve the desired outcomes in creative and innovative ways.

Table 4-2 summarizes the conditions under which a behavior or a results wapproach may be best suited for assessing performance. Let us emphasize again that these approaches are not mutually exclusive. Measuring *both* behavior and results is the approach adopted by many organizations. Consider the case of L Brands Inc., a retailer that owns the brands Victoria's Secret, Bath & Body Works, PINK, La Senza, and Henri Bendel. L Brands operates more than 3,000 company-owned specialty stores in the United States, Canada, the United Kingdom, and Greater China; its brands are sold in more than 700 franchised locations worldwide; and it employs more than 88,000 associates, who produced combined sales of US$12.6 billion. L Brands aims to foster an entrepreneurial culture for its managers; therefore, managers who thrive in the company have a history of delivering impressive business results. They decided to design a new performance management system that is now used uniformly by all L Brands companies. With the involvement of outside consultants and employees, L Brands developed a performance management system wherein managers are measured on business results, including total sales, market share, and expense/sale growth ratio, as well as leadership competencies that are tailored to L Brands. A few of these competencies include developing a fashion sense, financial acumen, and entrepreneurial drive. Overall, L Brands has been pleased with the new system because it helps align individual goals with business strategy and results. Raters like the new system because behavioral anchors help define the competencies, which make ratings more straightforward. Finally, employees comment that they appreciate the new focus on *how* results are achieved as opposed to the earlier focus on only *what* is achieved (i.e., sales).

The results approach is used not only in large companies but, in fact, in many small as well as start-up organizations as well, where results are key. For example, Box 4-3 includes an illustration of the use of a results approach in a very different type of organization: Basecamp.

TABLE 4-2

Behavior Approach Versus Results Approach to Measuring Performance

Adopting a behavior approach to measuring performance is most appropriate when
• The link between behaviors and results is not obvious
• Outcomes occur in the distant future
• Poor results are due to causes beyond the performer's control

Adopting a results approach to measuring performance is most appropriate when
• Workers are skilled in the needed behaviors
• Behaviors and results are obviously related
• Results show consistent improvement over time
• There are many ways to do the job right

Box 4-3

Company Spotlight: Results Approach to Measuring Performance at Basecamp

Basecamp, a web and mobile project management company, generates more than US$25 million in revenue with only 52 employees. It was recognized in Forbes' 2017 Small Giant List as being among the top 25 small businesses in the United States. Since it was founded in 1999, they have lost only four employees. The company divides its work into six-week work cycles containing one or two "big batch projects," and four to eight "small batch projects" that take anywhere from a day to two weeks to complete. As founder and CEO Jason Fried explains: "We don't measure efficiency, compare actuals vs. estimates. We have six weeks to get something done. However, a team decides to get it done during that time is up to them." In summary, Basecamp utilizes a performance management system focusing on outcomes or results in order to motivate employees and bring about business results. The company looks at what is produced in the work, rather than at behaviors or how the job gets done.[31]

SUMMARY POINTS

- Performance is about behavior or what employees do and what employees produce or the outcomes of their work. Thus, performance management systems typically include the measurement of both behaviors (how the work is done) and the results (the outcomes of one's work). Performance is evaluative (i.e., we judge it on the basis of whether it advances or hinders organizational goals) and multidimensional (i.e., there are different types or dimensions of performance).

- Performance is determined by a combination of (1) abilities and other traits (i.e., fairly stable individual differences), (2) knowledge and skills (i.e., more malleable information and know-how), and (3) context (i.e., situational factors). Lack of ideal values for any of these factors can be compensated by higher levels of the other factors. However, if any of the three determinants of performance has a very small value (e.g., very little knowledge of how to treat customers right), then overall performance will also be at a low level. All three determinants of performance must be present for performance to reach satisfactory (and better) levels.

- The role of context is particularly noteworthy because it includes organizational and national culture, HR policies, time and the timing of performance (i.e., maximum versus typical performance), resources and opportunities to perform, and other situational factors that are often outside of the employee's control. Thus, it is important to be able to know whether a performance problem is due to lack of abilities and traits, knowledge and skills, or contextual issues.

- Two ways to improve our own performance is to engage in deliberate practice and assume extreme ownership. Deliberate practice involves approaching performance with the goal of getting better and better; focusing on what is happening and why you are doing things the way you do; seeking performance feedback from expert sources; and building mental models of your job, your situation, and your organization. Extreme ownership involves taking responsibility for poor performance, no matter how painful this process may be. Acknowledging that we have performed under par is never easy; it hurts our egos and our self-esteem. But these are short-term effects only. Unless we engage in this process, it will be very difficult to address any type of performance problem.

- There are four important facets of performance: task, contextual, counterproductive, and adaptive. Unless we understand the reasons for poor performance, we will not be able to address or anticipate performance problems. All four types or dimensions of performance have an important impact on organizational success and should be included in a performance management system:

  - Task performance refers to the specific activities required by one's job. It varies across jobs, is likely to be role prescribed, and its main antecedents are abilities, knowledge, and skills.
  - Contextual performance refers to the activities required to be a good "organizational citizen," and examples are helping coworkers, supporting company initiatives, and expressing voice behavior (i.e.,

issuing constructive challenge with the goal to improve, rather than merely criticize even when others, including an employee's supervisor, disagree).

- Counterproductive performance is behaviors and results that are voluntary and violate organizational norms, and consequently, threaten the well-being of the organization, its members, or both. Examples include starting negative rumors about the company, gossiping about coworkers, cyberloafing, covering up one's mistakes, and intentionally working slowly or carelessly.
- Adaptive performance is related to an individual's adaptability to changes—be it in the organization and its goals, in the requirements of the job, and in the overall work context. Examples include handling emergencies or crisis situations, handling work stress, solving problems creatively, and dealing with uncertain and unpredictable work situations.

- An emphasis on behaviors leads to a behavior-based approach to assessing performance (including competency modeling). An emphasis on results leads to a results-based approach to assessing performance.

- A behavior approach emphasizes what employees do (i.e., how work is done). This approach is most appropriate when (1) the link between behaviors and results is not obvious, (2) outcomes occur in the distant future, and (3) poor results are due to causes beyond the employee's control. A behavior approach may not be the best choice if most of these conditions are not present. In most situations, however, the inclusion of at least some behavior-based measures is beneficial. A common behavior approach is called competency modeling, which involves creating bundles of knowledge, skills, and abilities, and then measuring them by creating observable behavioral indicators.

- A results approach emphasizes the outcomes and results produced by employees. This is a bottom-line approach that is not concerned with how the work is done as long as certain specific results are obtained. This approach is most appropriate when (1) workers are skilled in the needed behaviors, (2) behaviors and results are obviously related, (3) results show consistent improvement over time, and (4) there are many ways to do the job right. An emphasis on results can be beneficial because it could encourage employees to achieve the desired outcomes in creative and innovative ways. However, measuring only results is typically not welcomed by employees even in types of jobs for which the expected result is very clear (e.g., sales jobs).

EXERCISE 4-1   DO YOU HAVE WHAT IT TAKES? ASSESSING YOUR OWN EXTREME OWNERSHIP

Watch the 13-minute Ted Talk on Extreme Ownership by Jocko Willink delivered at the University of Nevada. It is available on YouTube at https://www.youtube.com/watch?v=ljqra3BcqWM. Then, think about a recent situation in which your own performance was not satisfactory. This could involve a situation involving task, contextual, counterproductive, or adaptive performance. Also, it may involve performance defined as behaviors, results, or both.

Applying the concept of extreme ownership, what went wrong? What was your own responsibility in this situation? What did you do or not do that should be improved in the future? What will you do in the future to try to avoid making these same mistakes?

EXERCISE 4-2 ROLE PLAY: DIAGNOSING CAUSES OF POOR PERFORMANCE

Heather works in the training department of a large information technology organization. She is in charge of designing and delivering interpersonal skills training, including communication skills, networking, and new manager training classes. Heather has excellent knowledge of how to design a training class. She incorporates deliberate practice into all of her classes. She has also conducted research on what good communication consists of, how to network, and what new managers need to know to be successful. However, individuals who attend Heather's training classes often give her low ratings, stating that she has a hard time answering specific questions in classes and that she does not seem approachable after the classes when individuals want to ask questions.

You are Heather's manager. You are meeting with Heather to discuss her poor performance and will try to determine what is going on.

1. In your opinion, what is causing Heather's poor performance? Is it due to a deficiency in abilities and traits, knowledge, and skills (declarative and procedural), or contextual issues?

2. What can be done to remedy the performance problem?

Differentiating Task from Contextual Performance at Pharma Co. Company

Consider the following adaptation of a job description for the position of a district business manager for a sales organization in a pharmaceutical company (Pharma Co.). Pharma Co. produces pharmaceuticals, infant formulas and nutritional products, ostomy and advanced wound care products, cardiovascular imaging supplies, and over-the-counter products. Their stated mission is to "extend and enhance human life by providing the highest-quality pharmaceutical and related health care products." In addition, all employees live by the Pharma Co. pledge: "We pledge—to our patients and customers, to our employees and partners, to our shareholders and neighbors, and to the world we serve—to act on our belief that the priceless ingredient of every product is the honor and integrity of its maker."

Job Responsibilities of the District Business Manager

The following are the core performance objectives for the district business manager (DBM) position: Create the environment to build an innovative culture, create and articulate a vision, drive innovation by embracing diversity and change, set the example, and thereby shape the culture. Develop and communicate the business plan, understand and explain Pharma Co. strategies, translate national plan to business plans for districts and territories, set goals and expectations of performance, set priorities, and allocate resources. Execute and implement the business plan, maximize rank order lists of medical education professional relationships, achieve optimum coverage frequency of highest potential physicians, take accountability, and achieve results. Build relationships focused on customer retention, develop relationships (i.e., networks), influence others (i.e., internal and external), and develop self and others. Strong skills are acquired in the following areas: written and oral communication, negotiation, strategic analysis, leadership, team building, and coaching. (*Source*: Pharma Co.)

1. Based on the DBM job description, extract a list of KPIs in each of the following four dimensions (a) task, (b) contextual, (c) counterproductive, and (d) adaptive.

Choosing a Performance Measurement Approach at Show Me the Money

The following job description is for an account executive at Show Me the Money, a payroll and HR solution providers similar to ADP, AmCheck, BenefitMall, Big Fish Payroll Services, Fuse Workforce Management, GetPayroll, Gusto, and others. Show Me the Money offers payroll, human resources, and benefits outsourcing solutions for small- to medium-sized businesses. Because account executives often make sales calls individually, their managers do not always directly observe their behavior. Furthermore, managers are also responsible for sales in their markets and for staying up-to-date on payroll laws. However, account executives are responsible for training new account executives and networking in the industries in which they sell products. For example, if an account manager is responsible for retail companies, then that account executive is expected to attend retail trade shows and professional meetings to identify potential clients and to stay current with the issues facing the retail industry.

Account Executive Job Responsibilities

- Performing client needs analysis to ensure that the major market services product can meet a client's requirements and expectations
- Establishing clients on the host processing system
- Acting as primary contact for the client during the conversion process
- Supporting clients during the first few payrolls
- Completing the required documentation to turn the client over to customer service for ongoing support
- Scheduling and making client calls, and when necessary, supporting sales representatives in presales efforts
- Keeping abreast of the major market services system and software changes, major changes and trends in the PC industry, and changes in wage and tax law.
  1. Based on the above description, assess whether Show Me the Money should use a behavior approach, a results approach, or a combination of both to measure performance.
  2. Using the accompanying tables as a guide, place check marks next to the descriptions that apply to the job of account executive. Explain why you chose the approach you did.

Behavior approach to measuring performance is most appropriate when
the link between behaviors and results is not obvious
outcomes occur in the distant future
poor results are due to causes beyond the performer's control

Results approach to measuring performance is most appropriate when
workers are skilled in the necessary behaviors
behaviors and results are obviously related
results show consistent improvement over time
there are many ways to do the job right

ENDNOTES

1. Cascio, W. F., & Aguinis, H. (2019). *Applied psychology in talent management* (8th ed.). Thousands Oaks, CA: SAGE Publications.

2. Motowidlo, S. J., Borman, W. C., & Schmit, M. J. (1997). A theory of individual differences in task and contextual performance. *Human Performance, 10*, 71–83.

3. Borman, W. C., Brantley, L. B., & Hanson, M. A. (2014). Progress toward understanding the structure and determinants of job performance: A focus on task and citizenship performance. *International Journal of Selection & Assessment, 22*, 422–431.

4. Campbell, J. P., & Wiernik, B. M. (2015). The modeling and assessment of work performance. *Annual Review of Organizational Psychology and Organizational Behavior, 2*, 47–74.

5. Van Iddekinge, C. H., Aguinis, H., Mackey, J. D., & DeOrtentiis, P. S. (2017). A meta-analysis of the interactive, additive, and relative effects of cognitive ability and motivation on performance. *Journal of Management, 44*(1), 249–279. doi:10.1177/0149206317702220

6. Borghuis, J., Denissen, J. A., Oberski, D., Sijtsma, K., Meeus, W. J., Branje, S., & . . . Bleidorn, W. (2017). Big five personality stability, change, and codevelopment across adolescence and early adulthood. *Journal of Personality and Social Psychology, 113*, 641–657.

7. Woods, S. A., & Anderson, N. R. (2016). Toward a periodic table of personality: Mapping personality scales between the five-factor model and the circumplex model. *Journal of Applied Psychology, 101*, 582–604.

8. Eskreis-Winkler, L., Shulman, E. P., Young, V., Tsukayama, E., Brunwasser, S. M., & Duckworth, A. L. (2016). Using wise interventions to motivate deliberate practice. *Journal of Personality and Social Psychology, 111*, 728–744.

9. *IBM's $1 Billion Training Investment.* Retrieved January 2, 2018, from https://www .trainingindustry.com/workforce-development/articles/ibms-1-billion-training-investment.aspx

10. Beus, J. M., & Whitman, D. S. (2012). The relationship between typical and maximum performance: A meta-analytic examination. *Human Performance, 25*, 355–376.

11. Huselid, M. A., & Becker, B. E. (2011). Bridging micro and macro domains: Workforce differentiation and strategic human resource management. *Journal of Management, 37*, 421–428.

12. Rosenbush, S. (2005). *Five lessons of the WorldCom debacle*. Retrieved January 2, 2018, from https://www.bloomberg.com/news/articles/2005-03-15/ five-lessons-of-the-worldcom-debacle

13. Eisend, M., Evanschitzky, H., & Gilliland, D. I. (2016). The influence of organizational and national culture on new product performance. *Journal of Product Innovation Management, 33*, 260–276.

14. Willink, J., & Babin, L. (2015). *Extreme ownership: How Navy SEALS lead and win*. New York, NY: St. Martin's Press.

15. Kmicinska, M., Zaniboni, S., Truxillo, D. M., Fraccaroli, F., & Wang, M. (2016). Effects of rater conscientiousness on evaluations of task and contextual performance of older and younger co-workers. *European Journal of Work & Organizational Psychology, 25*, 707–721.

16. Ellis, K. (2004). Individual development plans: The building blocks of development. *Training, 41*(12), 20–25.

17. Schmitt. N. (2014). Personality and cognitive ability as predictors of effective performance at work. *Annual Review of Organizational Psychology and Organizational Behavior, 1*, 45–65.

18. Ahmed, I., Mohammad, S. K., & Islam, T. (2013). The relationship between perceived fairness in performance appraisal and organizational citizenship behavior in the banking sector of Pakistan: The mediating role of organizational commitment. *International Journal of Management and Innovation, 5*, 75–88.

19. DeNisi, A. S., & Murphy, K. R. (2017). Performance appraisal and performance management: 100 years of progress? *Journal of Applied Psychology, 102*, 421–433.

20. Liang, S. (2017). Linking leader authentic personality to employee voice behaviour: A multilevel mediation model of authentic leadership development. *European Journal of Work & Organizational Psychology, 26*, 434–443.

21. Bedeian, A. G., & Armenakis, A. A. (1998). The cesspool syndrome: How dreck floats to the top of declining organizations. *Academy of Management Executive, 12*, 58–63.

22. Aguinis, H., Davis, G. F., Detert, J. R., Glynn, M. A., Jackson, S. E., Kochan, T., . . . Sutcliffe, K. M. (2016). Using organizational science research to address U.S. Federal Agencies' management and labor needs. *Behavioral Science & Policy, 2*, 67–76.

23. Marcus, B., Taylor, O. A., Hastings, S. E., Sturm, A., & Weigelt, O. (2016). The structure of counterproductive work behavior. *Journal of Management, 42*, 203–233.

24. Stewart, S. M., Bing, M. N., Davison, H. K., Woehr, D. J., & McIntyre, M. D. (2009). In the eyes of the beholder: A non-self-report measure of workplace deviance. *Journal of Applied Psychology, 94*, 207–215.

25. McLean, B., & Elkind, P. (2004). *The smartest guys in the room: The amazing rise and scandalous fall of Enron*. New York, NY: Penguin.

26. Olster, S. (2011). From Harvard success story to accused insider trader. *Poets and Quants*. Retrieved January 2, 2018, from http://fortune.com/2011/02/09/from-harvard-success-story-to-accused-insider-trader/

27. Jundt, D. K., Shoss, M. K., & Huang, J. L. (2015). Individual adaptive performance in organizations: A review. *Journal of Organizational Behavior, 36*, S53–S71.

28. Pulakos, E. D., Arad, S., Donovan, M. A., & Plamondon, K. E. (2000). Adaptability in the workplace: Development of a taxonomy of adaptive performance. *Journal of Applied Psychology, 85*, 612–624.

29. Stone, T. H., Webster, B. D., & Schoonover, S. (2013). What do we know about competency modeling? *International Journal of Selection and Assessment, 21*, 334–338.

30. Daniels, A. (2005, October). Daniels' scientific method. *Workforce Management, 84*, 44–45.

31. Signal v. Noise. (2017). *How we structure our work and teams at Basecamp*. Available from https://m.signalvnoise.com/how-we-set-up-our-work-cbce3d3d9cae; Forbes. (2017). *Forbes small giants 2017: America's best small companies*. Available from https://www.forbes.com/sites/boburlingham/2017/05/09/forbes-small-giants-2017-americas-best-small-companies/#564b1bd44c32

5

Measuring Results and Behaviors

The reason most people never reach their goals is that they don't define them, or ever seriously consider them as believable or achievable. Winners can tell you where they are going, what they plan to do along the way, and who will be sharing the adventure with them.

—Denis Waitley

Learning Objectives

By the end of this chapter, you will be able to do the following:

1. Devise a results approach to measuring performance, including the development of key accountabilities, objectives, and standards.

2. Formulate key accountabilities and their relative importance.

3. Produce performance objectives that are specific and clear, challenging, agreed upon, significant, prioritized, bound by time, achievable, fully communicated, flexible, and limited in number.

4. Develop performance standards that are related to the position, concrete, specific, measurable, practical to measure, meaningful, realistic and achievable, and reviewed regularly.

5. Devise a behavior approach to measuring performance, including the identification and assessment of competencies.

6. Create competencies that are defined clearly, propose specific behavioral indicators that can be observed when someone demonstrates a competency effectively,

propose specific behaviors that are likely to occur when someone doesn't demonstrate a competency effectively (what a competency is not), and include suggestions for developing them further.

7. Design comparative performance measurement systems such as simple rank order, alternation rank order, paired comparisons, relative percentile, and forced distribution being aware of the relative advantages and disadvantages of each and critique the assumption that performance is normally distributed and recommend how to produce star performers. Design absolute performance measurement systems such as essays, behavior checklists, critical incidents, and graphic rating scales being aware of the relative advantages and disadvantages of each.

8. Appraise how choices in performance measurement approaches are affected by an organization's culture, industry, and strategic direction established by its leadership.

Chapter 4 provided a definition of performance and described the results and behavior approaches to measuring performance. In this chapter, we provide a more detailed description of how to measure performance, adopting the results and behavior approaches. Recall that most systems include a combination of both results and behaviors. Also, regardless of whether performance is assessed using results or behaviors, all systems rely on observable measures, which are usually referred to as key performance indicators (KPIs).

5-1 MEASURING RESULTS

Chapter 2 included a brief preview of how to assess performance when using a results approach. Specifically, we need to answer the following key questions:

- What are the different areas in which this individual is expected to focus efforts (*key accountabilities*)?
- Within each area, what are the expected *performance objectives*?
- How do we know how well the results have been achieved (*performance standards*)?[1]

As a reminder, key accountabilities are broad areas of a job for which the employee is responsible for producing results. A discussion of results also includes specific objectives that the employee will achieve as part of each accountability. Objectives are statements of important and measurable outcomes. Finally, discussing results also means discussing performance standards. A performance standard is a yardstick used to evaluate how well employees have achieved each objective. Performance standards provide information on acceptable and unacceptable performance—for example, regarding quality, quantity, cost, and time.

Organizations that implement a management by objectives (MBO) philosophy are likely to implement results-based performance management systems that include objectives and standards. For example, as part of Kraft Heinz's MBO system, employees' personal goals are publically displayed on their desks, while top executives' goals (including those of the CEO) are posted on the wall. The goals are data-driven, measurable, and linked to other employees' goals, to encourage teamwork as well as the company's values of ownership and transparency.[2] Several other companies have also made MBOs an integral part of their performance management systems. For example, Bill Packard, one of the founders of the computer company Hewlett-Packard (HP), has said that no operating policy contributed more to HP's success than MBOs.[3] Google uses MBOs to set "stretch" goals, and asks that employees achieve 65% of these seemingly unachievable goals. Business networking site LinkedIn uses MBOs to set 3–5 objectives for the quarter that are difficult to achieve, and then, uses weekly meetings to monitor progress made toward achieving the objectives. Zynga, maker of the popular computer game FarmVille, uses MBOs to encourage focus and urgency by asking employees to set three objectives each week and attempt to achieve at least two out of the three, and then, track how they performed.[4] Overall, an emphasis on objectives and standards is likely to allow employees to translate organizational goals into individual goals, which is a key purpose of MBO philosophies.[5]

5-1-1 Determining Accountabilities

The first step in determining accountabilities is to collect information about the job. The primary source is, of course, the job description that has resulted from the work analysis and a consideration of unit- and organization-level strategic priorities. The job description provides information on the tasks performed. Tasks included in the job description can be grouped into clusters, based on their degree of relatedness. Each of these task clusters or accountabilities is a broad area of the job for which the employee is responsible for producing results.

After the accountabilities have been identified, we need to determine their relative degree of importance. To understand this issue, we need to answer the following key questions:

- What percentage of the employee's time is spent performing each accountability?
- If the accountability were performed inadequately, would there be a significant impact on the work unit's mission?
- Is there a significant consequence of error? For example, could inadequate performance of the accountability contribute to the injury or death of the employee or others, serious property damage, or loss of time and money?

Although determining accountabilities may, at first, seem like a daunting task, it is not that difficult. Let us discuss an example based on a real job in a real organization to illustrate how it is done. Consider the position of Training Specialist/ Consultant—Leadership & Team Development for Target Corporation. Target focuses exclusively on general merchandise retailing and is the second largest discount store retailer in the United States, behind Walmart. Target employs a workforce of 341,000 employees in its more than 1,800 stores and generates US$69.495 billion in revenue. A brief summary of the job description is provided below:

> Identifies the training and development needs of Target Corporation's work force (in collaboration with partners), with primary emphasis on exempt team members. Designs and delivers training and development workshops and programs and maintains an ongoing evaluation of the effectiveness of those programs. Assumes leadership and strategic responsibility for assigned processes. May supervise the non-exempt staff.

Based on the job description, and additional information found on Target's web page regarding the company's strategic priorities, a list of the accountabilities, consequences of performing them inadequately, consequences of making errors, and percentage of time spent in each follows:

- *Process leadership.* Leads the strategy and direction of assigned processes. Coordinates related projects and directs or manages resources. This is extremely important to the functioning of Target leadership and the ability of executives to meet strategic business goals. If this position is managed improperly, then it will lead to a loss of time and money in training costs and leadership ineffectiveness. (40% of time)
- *Supervision of nonexempt staff.* Supervises nonexempt staff working in the unit. This is relatively important to the functioning of the work unit. If nonexempt staff members are supervised improperly, then the development of the employees and the ability to meet business targets will be compromised. (10% of time)

- *Coaching.* Conducts one-on-one executive coaching with managers and executives. This is extremely important to the development of internal leaders. If managers and executives are not coached to improve their performance, there is a loss of time and money associated with their poor performance as well as the cost of replacing them, if necessary. (20% of time)
- *Team-building consultation.* Assists company leaders in designing and delivering their own team-building sessions and other interventions. This is relatively important to the success of teams at Target. Mismanagement of this function will result in teams not meeting their full potential and wasting time and resources on conducting team sessions. (10% of time)
- *Assessment instrument feedback.* Delivers feedback based on scores obtained on assessment instruments of skills, ability, personality, and other individual characteristics. This is relatively important to the development of leaders. If assessment is incorrect, it could derail leader development. (10% of time)
- *Product improvement.* Continuously seeks and implements opportunities to use technology to increase the effectiveness of leadership and team development programs. This is important to the effectiveness of training delivery and could result in significant gains in efficiencies of the systems if carried out effectively. (10% of time)

5-1-2 Determining Objectives

After the accountabilities have been identified, the next step is to determine specific objectives. Objectives are statements of an important and measurable outcome that, when accomplished, will help ensure success for the accountability. The purpose of establishing objectives is to identify a limited number of highly important results that, when achieved, will have a dramatic impact on the overall success of the organization. After objectives are set, employees should receive feedback on their progress toward attaining the objective. Also, rewards should be allocated to those employees who have reached their objectives.

Objectives are clearly important because they help employees guide their efforts toward a specific target. To serve a useful function, objectives must have the following characteristics[6]:

1. *Specific and clear.* Objectives must be easy to understand. In addition, they must be verifiable and measurable—for example: "Cut travel cost by 20%."
2. *Challenging.* Objectives need to be challenging but not impossible to achieve. They must be a stretch, but employees should feel that the objective is reachable.
3. *Agreed upon.* To be most effective, objectives need to result from an agreement between the manager and the employee. Employees need an opportunity to participate in setting objectives. Participation in the process increases objective aspirations and acceptance, and decreases objective resistance.
4. *Significant.* Objectives must be important to the organization. Employees must believe that if the objective is achieved, it will have a critical impact on the overall success of the organization. In addition, achieving the objective should give the employee a feeling of congruence between the employee's performance and the goals of the organization. This, in turn, is likely to enhance feelings of value to the organization.
5. *Prioritized.* Not all objectives are created equal; therefore, objectives should be prioritized and tackled one by one.

6. *Bound by time.* Good objectives have deadlines and mileposts. Objectives lacking a time dimension are likely to be neglected.

7. *Achievable.* Good objectives are doable; that is, employees should have sufficient skills and training to achieve them. If they do not, then the organization should make resources available so that the necessary skills are learned and technology is made available to achieve the goals.

8. *Fully communicated.* In addition to the manager and employee in question, the other organizational members who may be affected by the objectives need to be aware of them.

9. *Flexible.* Good objectives are not immutable. They can, and likely will, change based on changes in the work or business environments.

10. *Limited in number.* Too many objectives may become impossible to achieve, but too few may not make a sufficient contribution to the organization. Objectives must be limited in number. Between 5 and 10 objectives per review period is a manageable number, but this can change, based on the position and organization in question.

Several organizations set goals following these guidelines. For example, Microsoft Corporation has a long history of using individual goals in its performance management system. The goals at Microsoft are described by the acronym SMART: specific, measurable, achievable, results-based, and time-specific. Research based on more than 1,000 empirical studies has demonstrated that setting goals that are specific and challenging leads to higher performance than setting an easy or vague goal, such as "I will do my best."[7]

Why does setting goals work? There are four main reasons why goal setting leads to better performance. First, setting a goal establishes a clear priority and clear *focus* over other less important tasks. Second, a specific and difficult goal increases *effort* over and above an easy, vague, or nonexistent goal. Third, setting goals improves *persistence* because there is a clear target in sight. Finally, and perhaps the most critical reason, a specific and difficult goal forces people to create and implement specific *strategies*, such as how to allocate time and resources, to reach the goal.

Table 5-1 summarizes the characteristics of good objectives. Using this list as our guide, let us return to the position Training Specialist/Consultant— Leadership & Team Development at Target Corporation.

Examples of objectives (one or two per accountability) are the following:

- *Process leadership.* Establish leadership development processes and training programs within budget and time commitments. Meet budget targets and improve executive leaders' "leadership readiness" scores across organization by 20% in the coming fiscal year.
- *Supervision of nonexempt staff.* Receive acceptable managerial effectiveness rating scores from your nonexempt staff in the coming fiscal year.
- *Coaching.* Improve the managerial effectiveness scores of executive coaching clients in the coming fiscal year.
- *Team-building consultation.* Deliver necessary team-training sessions throughout the year within budget and with an acceptable satisfaction rating (as measured by the follow-up survey that is sent to every team) for team-training sessions in the coming fiscal year.
- *Assessment instrument feedback.* Deliver assessment feedback with an acceptable approval rating from your coaching clients in the coming fiscal year.

TABLE 5-1
Characteristics of Good Objectives

Specific and clear
Challenging
Agreed upon
Significant
Prioritized
Bound by time
Achievable
Fully communicated
Flexible
Limited in number

- *Product improvement.* Improve satisfaction with training delivery in the coming fiscal year by receiving acceptable scores while staying on budget.

Now, compare the objectives listed above with the criteria listed in Table 5-1. Do these objectives comply with each of the 10 characteristics of good objectives? Which objectives could be improved? How, specifically?

5-1-3 Determining Performance Standards

After accountabilities and objectives have been determined, the next step is to define performance standards. These are yardsticks designed to help people understand to what extent the objective has been achieved. The standards provide raters with information about what to look for to determine the level of performance that has been achieved. Standards can refer to various aspects of a specific objective, including quality, quantity, and time. Each of these aspects can be considered a criterion to be used in judging the extent to which an objective has been achieved.

- *Quality*: how well the objective has been achieved. This can include usefulness, responsiveness, effect obtained (e.g., problem resolution), acceptance rate, error rate, and feedback from users or customers (e.g., ≈customer complaints, returns), and cost of spoiled or rejected work.
- *Quantity*: how much has been produced, how many units, how often, and at what cost. For example, commission earnings, dollar volume of sales, and number of new patents or creative/innovative inventions and projects.
- *Time*: due dates, adherence to schedule, cycle times, and deadlines (how quickly) (e.g., timetables, progress reports).

Standards must include an action, the desired result, a due date, and some type of quality or quantity indicator. For example, a standard might be the following: "Reduce overtime from 150 hours/month to 50 hours/month, 6 months from now at a cost not to exceed US$16,000." The action is *reduce*, the due date is 6 months from now and the indicators are the *reduction in hours from 150 to 50* and *at a cost not to exceed US$16,000*.

Standards usually describe fully satisfactory performance. As soon as a standard has been created, one can create standards that describe *minimum performance* and *outstanding performance*. For example, the minimum standard could be the following: "Reduce overtime from 150 hours/month to 75 hours/month by 6 months from now at a cost not to exceed US$16,000." The standard suggesting outstanding performance could be the following: *Reduce overtime from 150 hours/ month to 40 hours/month by 4 months from now at a cost not to exceed US$16,000.*

In writing standards, consider the following characteristics that often determine their usefulness:

1. *Related to the position.* Good standards are based on the job's key elements and tasks, not on individual traits or person-to-person comparisons.
2. *Concrete, specific, and measurable.* Good standards are observable and verifiable. They allow us to distinguish between different performance levels. A good standard allows raters to measure the employee's actual performance to determine if it is below expectations, fully satisfactory, or above expectations. Standards are specific and concrete so that there should be no dispute over whether and how well they were met.
3. *Practical to measure.* Good standards provide necessary information about performance in the most efficient way possible. Good standards are created

by taking into account the cost, accuracy, and availability of the needed data.

4. *Meaningful.* Good standards are about what is important and relevant to the purpose of the job, to the achievement of the organization's mission and objectives, and to the user or recipient of the product or service.

5. *Realistic and achievable.* Standards are possible to accomplish, but they require a stretch. There should be no apparent barriers to achieving the standard. Employees should be able to reach the standards within the specified time frame.

6. *Reviewed regularly.* Information should be available on a regular basis to determine whether the employee has reached the standard, and if not, remedial action should be taken.[8]

TABLE 5-2
Characteristics of Good Performance Standards
Related to the position
Concrete, specific, and measurable
Practical to measure
Meaningful
Realistic and achievable
Reviewed regularly

Table 5-2 lists the aforementioned characteristics that are typical of good standards. Using this list as a guide, let us once again return to the position of Training Specialist/Consultant—Leadership & Team Development at Target Corporation. Examples of standards (one per objective for each accountability) are the following:

- *Process leadership.* Increase the executive leaders' "leadership readiness" scores across the organization by 20% by 5 months from now at a cost not to exceed US$70,000.
- *Supervision of nonexempt staff.* Receive managerial effectiveness rating scores of 80% approval from the nonexempt staff 5 months from now.
- *Coaching.* Improve the managerial effectiveness scores of executive coaching clients by 5%, 5 months from now.
- *Team-building consultation.* Design and deliver 95% of scheduled team-building sessions with a cost not to exceed US$30,000 for an 85% satisfaction rating with team-training sessions by 5 months from now.
- *Assessment instrument feedback.* Deliver assessment feedback with an 85% approval rating from the coaching clients by 5 months from now.
- *Product improvement.* Improve satisfaction scores with training delivery by 5% by 5 months from now at a cost not to exceed US$30,000.

Now, compare the standards listed above with the characteristics of good performance standards in Table 5-2. Do they meet each of the six characteristics of good standards? Which of the six standards could be improved? How, specifically?

5-2 MEASURING BEHAVIORS

Chapter 2 provided a brief introduction to the topic of measuring behaviors. Also, as mentioned in Chapter 4, a behavior approach to measuring performance usually includes the assessment of competencies. Competencies are measurable clusters of knowledge, skills, and abilities (KSAs) that are critical in determining how results will be achieved.[9] Examples of competencies are customer service, written or oral communication, creative thinking, and dependability.

We can consider two types of competencies. First, *differentiating competencies* are those that allow us to distinguish between average and superior performers.

Second, *threshold competencies* are those that everyone needs to display to do the job to a minimally adequate standard. For example, for the position Information Technology (IT) Project Manager, a differentiating competency is process management. Process management is defined as "managing project activities." For the same position, a threshold competency is change management.[10] The change management competency includes knowledge of behavioral science, operational and relational skills, and sensitivity to motivators. Therefore, for an IT project manager to be truly effective, she has to possess process management and change management competencies.

As noted earlier, competencies should be defined in behavioral terms. Take the case of a professor teaching an online course. An important competency is "communication." This competency is defined as the set of behaviors that enables a professor to convey information so that students are able to receive it and understand it. For example, one such behavior might be whether the professor is conveying information during preassigned times and dates. That is, if the professor is not present at the chat room at the prespecified dates and times, no communication is possible. Box 5-1 includes an example of how the assessment of competencies is a critical component in the leadership development program at XCS.

To understand the extent to which an employee possesses a competency, we measure indicators. Each indicator is an observable behavior that gives us information regarding the competency in question. In other words, we do not measure the competency directly, but we measure indicators that tell us whether the competency is present or not.

Figure 5-1 shows the relationship between a competency and its indicators. A competency can have several indicators. Figure 5-1 shows a competency with five indicators. An indicator is a behavior that, if displayed, suggests that the competency is present. In the example of the competency communication for a professor teaching an online course, one indicator is whether the professor shows up at the chat room at the preestablished dates and times. Another behavioral indicator of the competency communication could be whether the responses provided by the professor address the questions asked by the students or whether the answers are only tangential to the questions asked.

BOX 5-1

Company Spotlight: Leadership Competencies at Xerox Capital Services

At Xerox Capital Services (XCS), identifying leadership competencies was the first step in a successful leadership development program. XCS is jointly owned by the Xerox Corporation and General Electric. The company offers financing, risk analysis, credit approval, order processing, billing, and collection services. It employs 1,800 people in the United States and generates an estimated US$146.5 million in annual revenue. A leadership development program at XCS was focused on high-potential future leaders that were currently in pre-management roles. An important step in developing training sessions was to identify the key competencies of leaders in the organization. This process involved senior managers giving their opinions about what was most critical for leadership success in the company. After a clearly defined list of 12 competencies was identified, a curriculum was developed that included readings and a specific course each week on each topic. In summary, XCS provides an example of the importance of identifying competencies and how the competencies can be used within the context of a performance management system.[11]

FIGURE 5-1

Competency and Behavioral Indicators

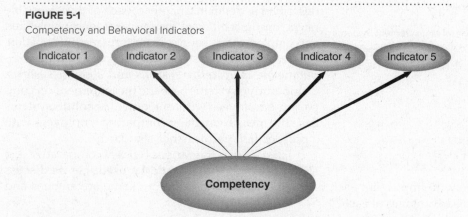

As another example, consider the two competencies that define good leadership: consideration and initiation structure.[12] Consideration is the degree to which the leader looks after the well-being of his followers. Initiating structure is the degree to which the leader lays out task responsibilities. Five indicators whose presence would indicate the existence of the consideration competency are the following:

- Supports direct reports' projects
- Asks about the well-being of employees' lives outside of work
- Encourages direct reports to reach their established goals
- Gets to know employees personally
- Shows respect for employees' work and personal lives

In describing a competency, the following components must be present:

1. Definition of competency
2. Description of specific behavioral indicators that can be observed when someone demonstrates a competency effectively
3. Description of specific behaviors that are likely to occur when someone does not demonstrate a competency effectively (what a competency is not)
4. List of suggestions for developing the competency in question[13]

Using "consideration," let us discuss the four essential elements in describing a competency. We defined consideration: it is the degree to which a leader shows concern and respect for followers, looks out for their welfare, and expresses appreciation and support. Next, we listed five indicators or behaviors that can be observed when a leader is exhibiting consideration leadership. Leaders who do not show consideration may speak with direct reports only regarding task assignments, repeatedly keep employees late with no consideration of social lives, take no interest in an employee's career goals, and assign tasks based only on current expertise. Finally, how do leaders develop the consideration competency? One suggestion would be to ask employees, on a regular basis, how their lives outside of work are going. This may lead to knowledge about an employee's family and interests outside of work.

In contrast to the measurement of results, the measurement of competencies is intrinsically judgmental. In other words, competencies are measured using data provided by individuals who make a judgment regarding the extent to which the competency is present. That is, the behaviors displayed by the employees are observed and judged by raters such as the direct supervisor, peers, customers, the employee himself, and direct reports (for the case of managers). As will be

TABLE 5-3

Comparative and Absolute Behavioral Measurement Systems

Comparative	Absolute
Simple rank order	Essays
Alternation rank order	Behavior checklists
Paired comparisons	Critical incidents
Relative percentile	Graphic rating scales
Forced distribution	

described in detail in Chapter 6, each of these possible raters constitute different "performance touchpoints" and are complementary sources of performance information.

Two types of systems are used to evaluate competencies: *comparative systems* and *absolute systems*. Comparative systems base the measurement on comparing employees with one other. Absolute systems base the measurement on comparing employees with a prespecified performance standard.

Table 5-3 lists the various types of comparative and absolute systems that could be used. Let us discuss how to implement each of these systems and point out some advantages and disadvantages of each.[14]

5-2-1 Comparative Systems

Comparative systems of measuring behaviors imply that employees are evaluated relative to one other. If a *simple rank order* system is used, employees are simply ranked from best performer to worst performer. Alternatively, in an *alternation rank order* procedure, the result is a list of all employees. Then, raters selects the best performer (#1), then the worst performer (#n), the second best (#2), the second worst (#n−1), and so forth, alternating from the top to the bottom of the list until all employees have been ranked.

Paired comparisons is another comparative system. In contrast to the simple and alternation rank order procedures, explicit comparisons are made between all pairs of employees to be evaluated.[15] In other words, raters systematically compare the performance of each employee against the performance of all other employees. The number of pairs of employees to be compared is computed by the following equation: where n is the number of employees to be evaluated. If a rater needs to evaluate the performance of 8 employees, she would have to make $[8(8−1)]/2 = 28$ comparisons. The rater's job is to choose the better of each pair, and each individual's rank is determined by counting the number of times he was rated as better.

Another type of comparison method is the *relative percentile method*.[16] This type of measurement system asks raters to consider all employees at the same time and to estimate the relative performance of each by using a 100-point scale. The 50-point mark on this scale (i.e., 50th percentile) suggests the location of an

$$\frac{n(n-1)}{2}$$

average employee—about 50% of employees are better performers and about 50% of employees are worse performers than this individual. Relative percentile methods may include one scale for each competency and also include one scale on which raters evaluate the overall performance of all employees. Figure 5-2 includes an example of a relative percentile method scale to measure the competency "communication."

FIGURE 5-2

Example of Relative Percentile Method Scale

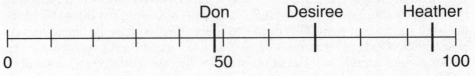

In this illustration, the rater has placed Heather at roughly the 95th percentile, meaning that Heather's performance regarding communication is higher than 95% of other employees. On the other hand, Don has been placed around the 48th percentile, meaning that about 52% of employees are performing better than him.

A fifth comparison method is called *forced distribution*. In this type of system, employees are apportioned according to an approximately normal distribution—a curve that looks like a bell and has approximately the same number of performers to the right and the left of the mean score (i.e., the center of the distribution). For example, 20% of employees must be classified as exceeding expectations, 70% must be classified as meeting expectations, and 10% must be classified as not meeting expectations.

General Electric (GE) is one organization that adopted a forced distribution system under the leadership of former CEO Jack Welch. This forced distribution system was called the "vitality curve." In Welch's view, forced ranking enables managers to "take care of your very best, make sure the valued middle is cared for, and weed out the weakest." GE's success in implementing a forced ranking system is cited as the model by many of the 20% of U.S. companies that have adopted it in the past three decades. At GE, each year 10% of managers were assigned the "C" grade, and if they did not improve, they were asked to leave the company.[17] Box 5-2 describes the evolution of this type of forced distribution system at GE and Box 5-3 describes Deloitte's journey.

BOX 5-2

Company Spotlight: The Evolution of the Forced Distribution System at General Electric (GE)

General Electric (GE) is one of the most frequently cited companies to have utilized a comparative rating system with a forced distribution. GE, based in Fairfield, Connecticut, provides a wide array of products and services globally to customers in the areas of financial services, media entertainment, health care, and energy technologies, and products such as appliances and plastics. In recent years, the rigid system of requiring managers to place employees into three groups (top 20%, middle 70%, and bottom 10%) has been revised to allow managers more flexibility. While the normal distribution curve is still referenced as a guideline, the reference to the 20/70/10 split has been removed, and work groups are now able to have more "A players" or "no bottom 10's." The company did not view the forced distribution system of the past as a match for fostering a more innovative culture in which taking risks and failure are part of the business climate. As a result, the company has begun evaluating employees relative to certain traits, including one's ability to act in an innovative manner or have an external business focus. In summary, GE's performance management system and revisions to the system provide an example of how decisions about how to measure performance need to consider the ramifications and resulting behaviors that are encouraged or discouraged. The consideration of culture and overall business strategy is also crucial in determining how to measure performance.[18] More recently, GE has revised its measurement system again. Specifically, GE has moved from a formal "once-a-year" performance review to an app-based system. Using this system allows managers to provide feedback and coaching on a more frequent basis to their employees. Performance management tasks such as recognizing employee contributions, identifying areas of concern, and offering developmental opportunities can now be offered in near real-time, rather than waiting until the annual performance appraisal.[19] In addition, performance appraisal meetings are themselves more productive as there are few surprises. Rather than an exclusive backward-looking system, the new system is forward-looking and emphasizes development by focusing on guiding, coaching, and providing feedback to employees that helps them on their path to achieving their goals.[20] These changes at GE reflect a shift from a performance appraisal system focused on ratings to a performance management system involving a constant and ongoing evaluation and improvement of performance.

BOX 5-3

Company Spotlight: The Evolution of the Forced Distribution System at Deloitte

Deloitte Touche Tohmatsu Limited (Deloitte), headquartered in New York City, is one of the world's largest professional services firms, providing a host of services in areas such as audit, tax, financial advisory, consulting, and enterprise risk management. It employs over 200,000 professionals and has consistently been ranked as one of the best companies to work for by Fortune magazine. Previously, the performance management system at Deloitte had utilized a forced distribution system for assessing and reviewing employee performance. In this system, all departments were required to compare employees to one another using a "forced curve" methodology and classify them as "underperformers," "average performers," and "high performers," based on a predetermined percentage that must fall in each category, with the goal being to "weed" out the bottom performers.[21] In 2015, however, Deloitte announced a new performance management system with only four metrics for managers to fill out at the end of every project or on a quarterly basis. The three objectives of this new system are to (1) "Recognize" performance through variable compensation,

(2) "See" performance by reshaping the manner in which supervisors evaluate performance, and (3) "Fuel" performance by improving the ongoing performance management conversation between supervisor and employee. Leaders now provide feedback on measures such as "I would always want him or her on my team" and "I would award this person the highest possible compensation increase and money" at the end of each project or quarter, which helps them "see" performance in terms of their future interactions with the employee. To "fuel" performance, managers are expected to check in with each team member at least once a week, and to document their conversation. Data on these ratings and check-ins is provided back to the leaders at the end of the year, enabling them to give deliver better performance reviews.[22] In summary, although Deloitte has moved away from forced distribution, it does not mean that performance evaluation has been eliminated. Instead, the company has moved to a more robust performance management system that includes ongoing evaluation and feedback with the goal of improving employee performance.

You will see that these companies, and many others, are going through a similar process of transitioning from a performance appraisal (i.e., dreaded once-a-year evaluation and review) to a performance management system (i.e., ongoing evaluation and feedback). Also, you may have noticed quite a bit of popular business press hype about the "demise of performance evaluation and measurement." However, contrary to the way this trend is usually described with such headlines as "Performance Evaluation is Dead" and "The End of Performance Reviews," the evaluation of performance is not going away. In fact, it is becoming a normal, routine, built-in, and ever-present aspect of work in twenty-first-century organizations. Clearly, as described in Chapter 1, performance management systems play a critical role and serve important purposes. So, to paraphrase Mark Twain, the death of performance management has been vastly exaggerated.

What are some of the advantages of using comparative measurement methods? First, these types of measurement procedures are usually easy to explain. Second, decisions resulting from these types of systems are fairly straightforward: it is easy to see which employees are where in the distributions. Third, they tend to control several biases and errors made by those rating performance better than do those in absolute systems. Such errors include leniency (i.e., giving high scores to most employees), severity (i.e., giving low scores to most employees), and central tendency (i.e., not giving any above-expectations or below-expectations ratings). Fourth, they are particularly beneficial for jobs that are very autonomous (i.e., employees perform their duties without much interdependence).[23] Finally, a recent study found that individuals high in cognitive abilities are more attracted to organizations that have forced distribution systems.[24] Clearly, those individuals are attracted to it because they expect to perform well and benefit directly from this type of system. Also, to them, it is an important signal that the organization values high achievement.

On the other hand, there are also disadvantages associated with the use of comparative systems, which may explain why only about 17% of HR executives (e.g., vice presidents of HR, vice presidents for global talent development, HR directors, and HR managers) report that their companies use these types of systems (but 32% use a combination of comparative and absolute systems, as described in Section 5-2-2 Absolute Systems).[25] First, employees usually are compared only in terms of a single overall category. Employees are not compared based on individual behaviors, or even individual competencies, but instead, are compared based on an overall assessment of performance. As a consequence, the resulting rankings are not sufficiently specific so that employees can receive useful feedback, and also, these rankings may be subject to legal challenge. Second, because the resulting data are based on rankings and not on actual scores, there is no information about the relative distance between employees. All we know is that employee A received a higher score than employee B, but we do not know if this difference is, for example, similar to the difference between employee B and employee C.

Some of these disadvantages were experienced by Microsoft and were noticed by Lisa E. Brummel, former vice president for HR.[26] She noted that by using a forced distribution system, "people were beginning to feel like their placement in one of the buckets was a larger part of the evaluation than the work the person actually did." Similarly, a posting on an anonymous Microsoft employee's blog called MiniMicrosoft read as follows: "I LOVE this company, but I hate the Curve."

If these criticisms of forced distribution systems ring a bell, they should. The reason is that they should remind you of our discussion of performance ratings serving the role of "canary in the coal mine" in Chapter 1. Many of the criticisms against forced distribution systems, and comparative systems in general, are similar to those raised against the use of performance ratings. After all, ratings are often the building blocks for making employee comparisons. And although many of the criticisms may seem directed at comparative rating systems, they are actually about how the system is designed and used. For example, much like our discussion regarding performance ratings in Chapter 1, criticisms involve saying that forced distributions are biased, unjustified, inaccurate, and may even lead to litigation. But much like performance ratings, the problem is often not the forced distribution per se, but what is measured, how, the extent to which employees participate in the process, and consequences associated with the resulting ratings. Forced distribution systems that are perceived as being unfair and even cruel are indicators (i.e., the canary in the coal mine) that the performance management system is broken. For example, it is likely that there is no clear explanation of how ratings were produced. Also, it is likely that employees not rated at the top of the distribution feel that their contributions are not valued by their organizations.

Many organizations that initially ditched forced distributions and even ratings altogether are using them again—although they use different labels and terms to refer to them.[27] For example, Cargill introduced its "Everyday Performance Management" system, designed to incorporate daily encouragement and feedback into on-the-job conversations. Managers offer performance evaluations and feedback on an ongoing basis. As another example, consider Adobe, which is probably one of the most frequently discussed cases regarding their performance management system because it is argued that they were able to reduce voluntary employee turnover by about 30% after introducing a frequent "check-in program." Again, performance is evaluated on an ongoing basis. As noted by Adobe's Senior Vice President for People and Places, Donna Morris, the new system "requires executives and managers to have regular tough discussions with employees who are struggling with performance issues—rather than putting them off until the next performance review cycle comes around." And consider the case of Google, where employee set goals called OKRs: objectives and key results. So, as mentioned earlier, contrary to what one may conclude based on reading the popular business press, it is *not* the case that companies are abandoning distributions and ratings.[28] They are actually implementing performance systems more clearly aligned with best practices, as described in this text, that involve a *constant and ongoing evaluation of performance*! These and many other companies may have eliminated the label "performance evaluation," "performance review," and even "performance management." Instead, they use labels such as "performance achievement," "check-ins," and "employee development." But at the end of the day, they are implementing performance management using new labels.

5-2-1-1 The Nature of the Performance Distribution

The use of a forced distribution system implies that performance scores are forced to fit under a particular distribution shape. As mentioned earlier, companies such as GE, Yahoo, and many others have used the normal distribution for decades. And today, it is used in many colleges and universities as part of the student grading system.

Let us think about the following: If the distribution of performance is truly bell-shaped, this means that the majority of employees are grouped toward the center (i.e., are average), and there is a very small minority of individuals who are very poor and very good performers, as shown in Figure 5-3. Also, if we use a normal curve to assign ratings, we ration the number of top performers. For example, if we use a five-point scale, many companies would tell managers that "no more than 10% of the direct reports gets the highest rating of 5." But what if this is an outstanding unit that had an excellent applicant pool, recruited the best among the best, and then, offered training and development opportunities resulting in even better performance? Why should we limit the highest ratings to just the top 10% if we have, say, 40% of star performers?

Research conducted over the past few years has challenged the common practice of using the normal curve. In fact, several studies based on more than 600,000 workers, including the number of publications authored by more than 25,000 researchers across more than 50 scientific fields, as well as productivity metrics collected from movie directors, writers, musicians, athletes, bank tellers, call center employees, grocery checkers, electrical fixture assemblers, and wirers have revealed that performance is distributed following a heavy-tail.[29]

Figure 5-3 shows a critical difference between these two types of distributions. Specifically, under a heavy-tailed distribution, we expect to see many "star performers" (i.e., those very far to the right of the mean). However, under a normal distribution, the presence of such extreme scores is considered an anomaly. Also, Figure 5-3 shows that performance (i.e., area under the curves) is such that under a heavy-tailed distribution, differences between the top and average performers are much greater under a heavy-tailed compared to normal distribution.

The existence of normal performance distributions is expected in certain situations, however. For example, workers in a manufacturing plant cannot work faster than the speed of the assembly line. So, this type of situational constraint will impede the emergence of star performers, and the performance distribution is likely to be normal or close to it. But in the twenty-first-century economy dominated by the services industry, ceilings on performance are the exception, rather than the rule.[30] Constraints such as geographic distances, lack of good communications, inability to access information and knowledge, and slow technological dispersion are now disappearing, given the pervasiveness of the Internet and the virtually unimpeded flow of information. Consequently, normal distributions are the exception, rather than the rule.

FIGURE 5-3

Normal versus Heavy-tailed Performance Distribution

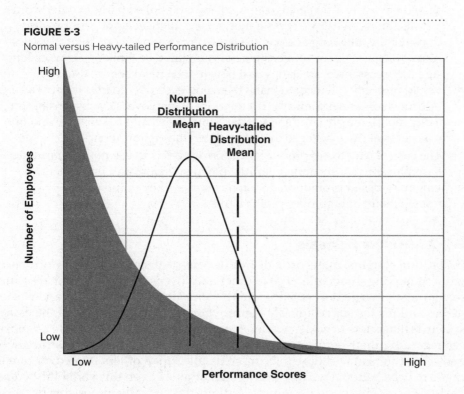

An important consequence of "debunking the myth of the normal curve" is that we are now more aware of the existence of star performers—those individuals whose contributions are much larger than the rest.[31] Star performers not only do well in terms of their individual performance, but more importantly, they have a large positive influence on numerous key outcomes, such as firm survival, retention of clients, new product development, and many other indicators of organizational performance.[32] How can an organization produce more star performers? Consider the following recommendations[33]:

- Identify, and if possible, eliminate situational constraints (i.e., ceiling constraints) faced by workers to allow for the emergence of star performers. For example, what are the resources needed to facilitate the emergence of stars?
- Allow star performers to rotate across teams because this widens their network and takes full advantage of knowledge transfer to rising stars.
- Make sure sufficient resources are invested in star performers who are making clear contributions to an organization's core strategic objectives.
- Take care of star retention by paying attention to their developmental network (e.g., employment opportunities for significant others and long-term contracting with a star's direct reports).
- In times of financial challenges and budget cuts, pay special attention to star performers because once they leave, an organization's recovery will be very difficult. In fact, star departure can create a downward spiral of performance when average and even mediocre performers deliberately replace stars with inferior workers.
- Star performers should be given preferential treatment, but these perks should be clearly articulated to all workers and applied fairly. In other words, anyone can receive those perks if they achieve high levels of performance. Consider the following analogy. If a large proportion of your company sales come from just 30% of your customers, you would be thinking about making sure these customers are happy and how to treat them better. Also, you would probably call them to thank them and even offer to treat them to a very nice lunch or dinner. Similarly, if a minority of employees are responsible for a disproportionately large amount of results, we should talk to them and find ways to treat them better so they stay within the organization.[34]
- The easiest way to *not* produce star performers is to use non-performance-based incentives, encourage limited pay dispersion, and implement longevity-based promotion decisions because they emphasize homogeneity of employee performance.

5-2-2 Absolute Systems

In absolute systems, raters provide evaluations of an employee's performance without making direct reference to other employees. In the simplest absolute system, a rater writes an *essay* describing each employee's strengths and weaknesses and makes suggestions for improvement. One advantage of the essay system is that raters have the potential to provide detailed feedback to employees regarding their performance. But, essays are almost totally unstructured and some raters may choose to be more detailed than others. Moreover, some raters may be better at writing essays than others. Given this variability, comparisons across individuals, groups, or units are virtually impossible because essays written by different raters, and even by the same rater regarding different employees, may address different aspects of an employee's performance. Finally, essays do not provide any quantitative information, making it difficult to use them in some personnel decisions (e.g., allocation of rewards).

A second type of absolute system involves a *behavior checklist*, which consists of a form listing behavioral statements that are indicators of the various competencies to be measured. The rater's task is to indicate ("check") statements that describe the employee being rated. When this type of measurement system is in place, raters are not so much evaluators as they are "reporters" of employee behavior. Because it is likely that all behaviors rated are present to some extent, behavior checklists usually include a description of the behavior in question (e.g., "the employee arrives at work on time"), followed by several response categories, such as "always," "very often," "fairly often," "occasionally," and "never." The rater simply checks the response category she feels best describes the employee. Each response category is weighted—for example, from 1 ("never") to 5 ("always") if the statement describes desirable behavior such as arriving at work on time. Then, an overall score for each employee is computed by adding the weights of the responses that were checked for each item. Figure 5-4 includes an example of an item from a form using a behavior checklist measurement approach.

How do we select response categories for behavior checklist scales? Often, this decision is fairly arbitrary and equal intervals between scale points are simply assumed. For example, in Figure 5-4, we would assume that the distance between "never" and "sometimes" is the same as the distance between "fairly often" and "always" (i.e., 1 point in each case). However, great care must be taken in how the anchors are selected. Table 5-4 includes anchors that can be used for scales involving frequency and amount.[35]

FIGURE 5-4

Example of Behavior Checklist Item.

1	2	3	4	5
Never	Sometimes	Often	Fairly often	Always

TABLE 5-4

Anchors for Checklists of Frequency and Amount

Anchors for Checklists of Frequency		Anchors for Checklists of Amount	
Seven-point scale	**Five-point scale**	**Seven-point scale**	**Five-point scale**
Always	Always	All	All
Constantly	Very often	An extraordinary amount of	An extreme amount of
Often	Fairly often	A great amount of	Quite a bit of
Fairly often	Occasionally	Quite a bit of	Some
Sometimes	Never	A moderate amount of	None
Once in a while		Somewhat	
Never		None	

TABLE 5-5

Anchors for Checklists of Evaluation and Agreement

Anchors for Checklists of Evaluation		Anchors for Checklists of Agreement	
Anchor	Rating	Anchor	Rating
Terrible	1.6	Slightly	2.5
Bad	3.3	A little	2.7
Inferior	3.6	Mildly	4.1
Poor	3.8	Somewhat	4.4
Unsatisfactory	3.9	In part	4.7
Mediocre	5.3	Halfway	4.8
Passable	5.5	Tend to	5.3
Decent	6.0	Inclined to	5.4
Fair	6.1	Moderately	5.4
Average	6.4	Generally	6.8
Satisfactory	6.9	Pretty much	7.0
Good	7.5	On the whole	7.4
Excellent	9.6	Very much	9.1

Table 5-4 includes anchors to be used in both seven-point and five-point scales. For most systems, a five-point scale should be sufficient to capture an employee's performance on the behavior being rated. One advantage of using five-point scales is that they are less complex than seven-point scales. Also, five-point scales are superior to three-point scales because they are more likely to motivate performance improvement because employees believe it is more doable to move up one level on a five-point scale than it is on a three-point scale.[36]

Table 5-5 includes anchors that can be used in scales involving agreement and evaluation.[37] This table includes 13 anchors that can be chosen if one uses a scale of evaluation and 13 anchors that can be used if a scale of agreement is used.

Table 5-5 also includes ratings that can be used to choose anchors for a scale of evaluation or agreement. In creating scales, we must choose anchors that are approximately equally spaced based on the ratings included in Table 5-5. So, if we were to create a five-point scale of evaluation using the information provided in this table, one possible set of anchors might be the following:

1. Terrible
2. Unsatisfactory
3. Decent
4. Good
5. Excellent

In this set of anchors, the distance between all pairs of adjacent anchors ranges from 1.5 to 2.3 points. Note, however, that the use of the anchor "terrible" has a very negative connotation, so we may want to use a less negative anchor, such as "bad" or "inferior." In this case, we would be choosing an anchor that is closer to the next one ("unsatisfactory") than we may wish, but using the new anchor may lead to less defensive and overall negative reactions on the part of employees who receive this rating.

In summary, behavior checklists are easy to use and to understand. But, detailed and useful feedback is difficult to extract from the numerical rating provided. Overall, however, the practical advantages of checklists probably account for their current use.

Every job includes some critical behaviors that make a crucial difference between doing a job effectively and doing it ineffectively. The *critical incidents* measurement approach involves gathering reports of situations in which employees exhibited behaviors that were especially effective or ineffective in accomplishing their jobs.[38] The recorded critical incidents provide a starting point for assessing performance. For example, consider the following incident as recorded by a high school principal regarding the performance of Tom Jones, the head of the disability services office:

> A sophomore with learning disabilities was experiencing difficulty in writing. Her parents wanted an iPad for her. Tom Jones ordered an iPad and it was delivered to the student's teacher. No training was provided to the child, her teacher, or her parents. The iPad was never used.

This recorded incident is actually the synthesis of a series of incidents:

1. A problem was detected (a student with a special need was identified).
2. Corrective action was taken (the iPad was ordered).
3. Corrective action was initially positive (the iPad was delivered).
4. Corrective action was subsequently deficient (the iPad was not used because of the lack of training).

When critical incidents are collected, this measurement method allows raters to focus on actual job behavior, rather than on vaguely defined traits. But, collecting critical incidents is very time-consuming. Also, as is the case with essays, it is difficult to attach a score quantifying the impact of the incident (either positive or negative). So, a revised version of the critical incidents technique involves summarizing critical incidents and giving them to raters in the form of scales (e.g., behavior checklist). One example following up on the critical incident involving Tom Jones might be the following:

Addresses learning needs of special-needs students efficiently				
Strongly Agree	Agree	Undecided	Disagree	Strongly Disagree

A second variation of the critical incidents technique is the approach adopted in the performance management system implemented by the city of Irving, Texas.[39] First, the city identified core competencies and classified them as core values, skill group competencies, or performance essentials. Then, the team in charge of implementing the system wrote dozens of examples of different levels of performance on each competency—from ineffective to highly effective. In other words, this team was in charge of compiling critical incidents illustrating various performance levels for each competency. Then, managers used this list by simply circling the behavior that best described each of the employees in the work unit.

As an example, consider the competency Adaptability/Flexibility. For this competency, critical incidents were used to illustrate various performance levels:

Completely Ineffective	Somewhat Ineffective	Effective	Highly Effective	Exceptional
Able to focus on only one task at a time	Easily distracted from work assignments/ activities	Handles a variety of work assignments/ activities with few difficulties	Handles a variety of work assignments/ activities concurrently	Easily juggles a large number of assignments and activities
Avoids or attempts to undermine changes	Complains about necessary changes	Accepts reasons for change	Understands and responds to reasons for change	Encourages and instructs others about the benefits of change
Refuses to adopt changed policies	Makes only those changes with which they agree	Adapts to changing circumstances and attitudes of others	Adapts to changes and develops job aids to assist others	Welcomes change and looks for new opportunities it provides
Considers only own opinion when seeking solution	Occasionally listens to others but supports own solutions	Listens to others and seeks solutions acceptable to all	Ensures that everyone's thoughts and opinions are considered in reaching a solution	Actively seeks input in addition to recognized sources and facilitates implementation of solution

A third variation of the critical incidents technique is the use of behaviorally anchored rating scales (BARS), which are described next, as one of several types of graphic rating scales.

The *graphic rating scale* is a popular tool used to measure performance. The aim of graphic rating scales is to ensure that the response categories (ratings of behavior) are clearly defined, that interpretation of the rating by an outside party is clear, and that the rater and the employee understand the rating. An example of a graphic rating scale used to rate the performance of a project manager is the following:

Project management awareness is the knowledge of project management planning, updating status, working within budget, and delivering project on time and within budget. Rate _____'s project management awareness using the following scale:

1	2	3	4	5
Unaware or not interested	Needs additional training	Aware of responsibilities	Excellent knowledge and performance of skills	Superior performance of skill; ability to train others

BARS use graphic rating scales that use critical incidents as anchors.[40] BARS improve on the graphic rating scales by first having a group of employees identify all of the important dimensions of a job. Then, another group of employees generates critical incidents illustrating low, average, and high skills of performance for each dimension. A third group of employees and supervisors takes each dimension and the accompanying definitions and a randomized list of critical incidents. They must match the critical incidents with the correct dimensions. Finally, a group of judges assigns a scale value to each incident. Consider the following BARS for measuring job knowledge:

Job Knowledge: The amount of job-related knowledge and skills that an employee possesses.

Consider the following BARS which assess one of 10 performance dimensions identified as important for auditors[41]:

5	Exceptional: Employee consistently displays high level of job knowledge in all areas of his or her job. Other employees go to this person for training.
4	Advanced: Shows high levels of job knowledge in most areas of his or her job. Consistently completes all normal tasks. Employee continues searching for more job knowledge, and may seek guidance in some areas.
3	Competent: Employee shows an average level of job knowledge in all areas of the job. May need assistance completing difficult tasks.
2	Improvement Needed: Does not consistently meet deadlines or complete tasks required for this job. Does not attempt to acquire new skills or knowledge to improve performance.
1	Major Improvement Needed: Typically performs tasks incorrectly or not at all. Employee has no appreciation for improving his or her performance.

Knowledge of Accounting and Auditing Standards/Theory: Technical foundation, application of knowledge on the job, ability to identify problem areas and weigh theory vs. practice.

3	High-Point Performance: Displays very strong technical foundation, able to proficiently apply knowledge on the job, willingly researches areas, able to identify problems, can weigh theory vs. practice considerations.
2	Mid-Point Performance: Can resolve normal accounting issues, has adequate technical foundation and skills, application requires some refinement, has some problems in weighing theory vs. practice, can identify major problem areas.
1	Low-Point Performance: Displays weak accounting knowledge and/or technical ability to apply knowledge to situations/issues on an engagement, has difficulty in identifying problems and/or weighing factors of theory vs. practice.

For graphic rating scales to be most useful and accurate, they must include the following features:

- The meaning of each response category is clear.
- The individual who is interpreting the ratings (e.g., a human resources manager) can tell clearly what response was intended.
- The performance dimension being rated is defined clearly for the rater.

Compare the two examples of BARS shown earlier. Which is better regarding each of these three features? How can these BARS be revised and improved?

In summary, several types of methods are available for assessing performance. These methods differ in terms of practicality (i.e., some take more time and effort to be developed than others), usefulness for administrative purposes (i.e., some are less useful than others because they do not provide a clear quantification of performance), and usefulness for users (i.e., some are less useful than others in terms of the feedback they produce that allows employees to improve performance in the future). Practicality and usefulness are key considerations in choosing one type of measurement procedure over another. But there are additional, contextual, issues that also determine choices regarding the performance measurement approach. We describe these next.

5-3 THE ROLE OF CONTEXT

Chapter 4 described how context plays an important role in determining performance. Similarly, context plays an important role in determining how performance is measured—including the relative emphasis on results and behaviors, the use of comparative or absolute systems, and the many other choices and options that we discussed in this chapter, such as types and the nature of accountabilities, objectives, and standards.

For example, consider the role of organizational culture. In some organizations, the culture is highly competitive and there is a win-lose mentality such that employees know that to succeed and receive the rewards they want, they need to be concerned about themselves first and others last. In those organizations, it is unlikely that the performance management system will include measures of contextual performance such as competencies regarding cooperation and working with others.

As a second example, the culture in some firms is such that employees know, although this will not be found in the "employee manual," that they are not rewarded for establishing long-term relationships with customers. Rather, the name of the game is to "squeeze as much out the customer as possible—here and now." In fact, many financial advisors working for investment banks are fully aware that pushing the products of their own banks (e.g., mutual funds) to clients is seen favorably because this helps their organization's bottom line. So, a performance management system in an organization such as this one is likely to include measures of results in the form of sales volume. Because of this, many of the largest brokerage firms in the United States are now trying to shrug off "their lingering boiler room images and sales-driven cultures, which have contributed to their loss of market share to independent peers the past several years."[42] For example, in the recent Wells Fargo scandal, employees created as many as 2.1 million phony deposit and credit cards accounts, and branch managers were told that they "would end up working for McDonald's" if they missed sales quotas.[43]

Another contextual factor that affects choices in terms of performance measurement is the issue of industry trends. To continue with the financial brokerage industry, an important change is that consumers are starting to recognize that investment "advisers" actually have a conflict of interest when they recommend their bank's own products. Accordingly, many firms are changing their performance management systems, and specifically, the way in which they measure performance. For example, early in 2017, Merril Lynch, which has US$2 trillion in client assets, abandoned the traditional model in which employees' performance is measured based on the amount of charges to customers on each transaction in a retirement account. Performance is no longer measured based on revenue generated from the number of transactions and, instead, customers are charged a flat fee based on a percentage of a portfolio's asset. This change in how performance is now measured was a direct result of changes in the industry.

Leadership also plays an important role in how performance is measured. To continue with the Merril Lynch example, Andy Sieg, Head of Merrill Lynch Wealth Management, sees this change in the way performance is measured as a critical strategic move. In fact, he hopes that this change in how the performance of financial advisers is measured "will help raise the level of trust in our industry because clients are going to be assured that when it comes to their retirement savings, there's no one's interest that is being put in front of the interest of a client."

In closing, we earlier discussed reasons for measuring performance as results or behaviors and these focused on the nature of the job and the nature of work. However, there are also contextual factors that play an important role in how performance is measured and these are related to the culture of the organization, characteristics of the industry, and the strategic direction chosen by the organization's leadership. Next, in Chapter 6, we will consider the important topic of performance analytics—the process of collecting and compiling performance data.

SUMMARY POINTS

- A results approach to measuring performance involves an assessment of what employees produce and not how they do so. The first step in measuring performance by adopting a results approach is to identify key accountabilities. Accountabilities are broad areas of a job for which the employee is responsible for producing results.

- After all key accountabilities have been identified, the second step in the results approach is to set objectives for each. Objectives should be (1) specific and clear, (2) challenging, (3) agreed upon, (4) significant, (5) prioritized, (6) bound by time, (7) achievable, (8) fully communicated, (9) flexible, and (10) limited in number. Goal-setting leads to superior performance compared to vague or "do your best" goals because it helps establish a clear priority and focus, increases effort over and above an easy and vague goal, improves persistence because there is a clear target in sight, and forces people to create and implement specific strategies, such as how to allocate time and resources to reach the goal.

- The third and final step in the results approach involves determining performance standards. These yardsticks are designed to help people understand to what extent the objective has been achieved. In creating standards, we must consider the dimensions of quality, quantity, and time. Good standards are (1) related to the position; (2) concrete, specific, and measurable; (3) practical to measure; (4) meaningful; (5) realistic and achievable; and (6) reviewed regularly.

- A behavior approach to measuring performance involves assessing how the employee does the job and not the outcomes produced. Adopting a behavior approach involves identifying competencies. Competencies are measurable clusters of KSAs that are critical in determining how results will be achieved. Examples of competencies are customer service, written or oral communication, creative thinking, and dependability.

- The second step in the behavior approach involves identifying observable indicators that will allow us to understand the extent to which each individual possesses the competency in question. These indicators are behavioral manifestations of the underlying (unobservable) competency.

- In describing a competency, one must first clearly define it, then describe behavioral indicators showing the presence of the competency, describe behavioral indicators showing the absence of the competency, and list suggestions for developing the competency.

- After the behavioral indicators have been identified, the third and final step in the behavior approach includes choosing an appropriate measurement system, either comparative or absolute.

- Comparative systems base the measurement on comparing employees relative to one another and include simple rank order, alternation rank order, paired comparisons, relative percentile, and forced distribution. Comparative systems are easy to explain and the resulting data are easy to interpret, which facilitates administrative decisions. Also, employees are usually compared to one another in terms of one overall single category, instead of in terms of specific behaviors or competencies. This reduces the usefulness of the feedback for employees in their future improvement.

- The performance distribution is usually not normal (i.e., bell-shaped). This means that there is a minority of employees who perform at substantially higher levels than others. These star performers are critical for an organization's success. To produce more star performers, it is useful to identify and eliminate situational constraints, allow star performers to rotate across teams, make sure sufficient resources are invested in star performers who are making clear contributions to an organization's core strategic objectives, take care of star retention by paying attention to their developmental network, pay special attention to star performers because an organization's recovery will be difficult if they leave, and use performance-based incentives.

- Absolute systems include evaluations of employees' performance without making direct reference to other employees. Such systems include essays, behavior checklists, critical incidents, and graphic rating scales. Essays are difficult to quantify, but produce useful and often detailed feedback. Behavior checklists are easy to use and understand, but the scale points used are often arbitrary and we cannot assume that a one-point difference has the same meaning along the entire scale (i.e., the difference between an employee who scores 5 and an employee who scores 4 may not have the same meaning as the difference between an employee who scores 3 and one who scores 2). Critical incidents allow raters to focus on actual job behavior rather than on vaguely defined traits, but gathering critical incident data may be quite time-consuming. Graphic rating scales are arguably the measurement method most frequently used to assess performance. For this type of measurement to be most useful, the meaning of each response category should be clear, the individual interpreting the ratings (e.g., the human resources manager) should be able to tell clearly what response was intended, and the performance dimension being rated should be defined clearly for the rater.

- Much like performance is affected by context, choices in terms of how to measure performance are also affected by such factors as an organization's culture, industry, and leadership. To understand why an organization makes certain choices in terms of how to measure performance, we must understand not just the job in question, the nature of work, and the relation between results and behaviors, but also the context within which individuals and organizations are situated.

EXERCISE 5-1 MEASURING COMPETENCIES AT MIDWESTERN UNITED STATES DEPARTMENT OF TRANSPORTATION

The Department of Transportation (DOT) of a large Midwestern state uses core competencies to measure performance in its organization. Two of its core competencies on which all employees are measured are "organizational knowledge" and "learning and strategic systems thinking." Organizational knowledge is defined as follows: (1) "Understands the DOT's culture. (2) Accurately explains the DOT's organizational structure, major products/services, and how various parts of the organization contribute to one other. (3) Gets work done through formal channels and informal networks. (4) Understands and can explain the origin and reasoning behind key policies, practices, and procedures. (5) Understands, accepts, and communicates political realities and implications."

Learning and strategic systems thinking is defined as follows: (1) "Accepts responsibility for continued improvement/learning. (2) Appreciates and can explain the mission of each individual work unit and the importance of the tie between them to make the entire operation whole. (3) Acquires new skills and competencies and can explain how they benefit the DOT. (4) Regularly takes all transportation forms (e.g., bicycle, light rail, highway) into account in planning and problem solving. (5) Seeks information and ideas from multiple sources. (6) Freely and intentionally shares ideas with others."

Using the accompanying table as a guide, evaluate each of these two competencies and place a check mark next to each of the components of a good competency description if the component is present.

Next, using the organizational knowledge and learning and strategic systems thinking competencies, create a five-point graphic rating scale for each indicator using anchors of frequency, amount, agreement, or evaluation.

In describing a competency, the following components must be present:
Definition
Description of specific behavioral indicators that can be observed when someone demonstrates a competency effectively
Description of specific behaviors that are likely to occur when someone does not demonstrate a competency effectively (what a competency is not)
List of suggestions for developing the competency in question

Source: Adapted from D. Grote, "Public Sector Organizations: Today's Innovative Leaders in Performance Management," *Public Personnel Management* 29 (Spring 2000): 1–20.

EXERCISE 5-2   CREATING BEHAVIORALLY ANCHORED RATING SCALES (BARS) FOR EVALUATING BUSINESS STUDENT PERFORMANCE IN TEAM PROJECTS

In many universities, students are required to conduct team projects. A description of these "job" duties is the following:

Work with team members to deliver project outcomes on time and according to specifications. Complete all individual assignments to the highest quality, completing necessary background research, making any mathematical analysis, and preparing final documents. Foster a good working environment.

Please do the following:

1. Generate a list of competencies for the position described.
2. Identify a list of critical behavioral indicators for each competency.
3. Generate critical incidents (high, average, and poor performance) for each behavioral indicator.
4. Create graphic rating scales using BARS to measure each competency.

Accountabilities, Objectives, and Standards at Disney

Below is an actual job description for a purchasing and procurement internship position that was available at Disney Consumer Products/Studios. Based on the information in the job description, create accountabilities, objectives, and standards for this position.

Title

Graduate Associate, Purchasing & Procurement (Disney Consumer Products/Studios)

The Position

- Provide analytical support for projects impacting business units, specifically targeting Disney Consumer Products & Studios.
- Survey current pricing models and develop new approaches to pricing/buying various products and services that yield creative and business advantage.
- Support the continuing efforts to increase the percentage of spend influenced, specifically as it relates to business units where we have had only a minor impact.
- Assist in the development of key stakeholder lists and savings opportunities regarding existing contracts.
- Assist in developing overall Purchasing & Procurement strategy for partnering with business units, specifically targeting Disney Consumer Products & Studios.

The Company

The Walt Disney Company is a diversified, international family entertainment and media company with 2016 annual revenues of US$55.63 billion. Its operations include theme parks and resorts, filmed entertainment, including motion pictures and television shows, home video and DVD products, records, broadcast and cable networks, Internet and direct marketing, consumer products, radio and television stations, theatrical productions, publishing activities, and professional sports enterprises.

The Ideal Candidate

- Ability to conceptualize issues and problems and develop hypotheses around appropriate responses.
- Intellectual curiosity and professional commitment to excellence.
- Superior analytical skills defined by an ability to identify and rearticulate critical aspects of a business situation from a large data pool (both qualitative and quantitative).
- Superior Microsoft Excel modeling skills.
- Strong written and verbal communication skills with the ability to build relationships.
- Ability to work independently.
- Demonstrated ability to manage multiple tasks, meanwhile retaining focus on project deliverables and strategic priorities.

The Opportunity

This will be an opportunity for an MBA intern to utilize project management skills he or she has learned in the classroom. The intern will be faced with difficult and/or skeptical clients and will learn how to work with them. This will also be an opportunity for those individuals who have not experienced working in Corporate America, and for those that have had some experience, to further their learnings. The intern will gain experience from working in the Media and Entertainment industry. Through these various experiences, we hope the intern will find value in the internship we are offering.

Evaluating Objectives and Standards at Disney

Using the results from Case Study 5-1, use the accompanying checklist to evaluate each objective and standard you produced. For each objective and standard, use the first column in the checklist and place a check mark next to each of the ideal characteristics if the characteristic is present. Then, use the Comments column to provide a description of why or why not each objective and standard meets the ideal. Finally, review your tables and provide an overall assessment of the quality of the objectives and standards you created.

Objectives must have the following characteristics:	Comments
Specific and clear	
Challenging	
Agreed upon	
Significant	
Prioritized	
Bound by time	
Achievable	
Fully communicated	
Flexible	
Limited in number	
Performance standards must have the following characteristics:	Comments
Related to the position	
Concrete, specific, and measurable	
Practical to measure	
Meaningful	
Realistic and achievable	
Reviewed regularly	

ENDNOTES

1. The following discussion of accountabilities, objectives, and standards is based on Grote, D. (1996). *The complete guide to performance appraisal* (Chap. 4). New York, NY: AMACOM.

2. Trotter, G. & Elejalde-Ruiz, A. (2017). Working at Kraft Heinz means competition, cost-cutting, and, for some, Reward. LaCrosse Tribune. Retrieved from http://lacrossetribune.com/working-at-kraft-heinz-means-competition-cost-cutting-and-for/article_55601020-092e-597c-aff6-0a8af735dd81.html

3. Hindle, T. (2009). Management by objectives. *The Economist*. Retrieved from http://www.economist.com/node/14299761

4. Bryant, A. (2010). Are you a C.E.O. of something? *New York Times*. Retrieved from http://www.nytimes.com/2010/01/31/business/31corner.html?pagewanted=2&_r=4&, and McCloskey, H. (2015). How organizations like Google, LinkedIn and Zynga do OKRs. UserVoice. Retrieved from https://community.uservoice.com/blog/google-okrs/

5. Stanley, T. L. (2017). The best management ideas are timeless. *Supervision, 78*(2), 15–17.

6. Adapted from Grote, D. (1996). *The complete guide to performance appraisal* (pp. 91–94). New York, NY: AMACOM.

7. Latham, G., Seijts, G., & Slocum, J. (2016). The goal setting and goal orientation labyrinth: Effective ways for increasing employee performance. *Organizational Dynamics, 45*, 271–277.

8. Adapted from Kirkpatrick, D. L. (1982). *How to improve performance through appraisal and coaching* (pp. 35–36). New York, NY: AMACOM.

9. Stone, T. H., Webster, B. D., & Schoonover, S. (2013). What do we know about competency modeling? *International Journal of Selection and Assessment, 21*, 334–338.

10. Kendra, K. A., & Taplin, L. J. (2004). Change agent competencies for information technology project managers. *Consulting Psychology Journal: Practice & Research, 56*, 20–34.

11. Chughtai, J. (2006). Identifying future leaders at Xerox Capital Services. *Strategic HR Review*. Retrieved January 2, 2018, from www.allbusiness.com/periodicals/article/892962-1.html

12. Gottfredson, R. K. & Aguinis, H. (2017). Leadership behaviors and follower performance: Deductive and inductive examination of theoretical rationales and underlying mechanisms. *Journal of Organizational Behavior, 38*, 558–591.

13. Grote, D. (1996). *The complete guide to performance appraisal* (p. 118). New York, NY: AMACOM.

14. The material that follows on comparative and absolute systems is based primarily on Cascio, W. F., and Aguinis, H. (2019). *Applied psychology in talent management* (8th ed.). Thousand Oaks, CA: Sage Publication.

15. Marin-Garcia, J. A., Ramirez Bayarri, L., & Atares Huertas, L. (2015). Comparing advantages and disadvantages of rating scales, behavior observation scales and paired comparison scales for behavior assessment of competencies in workers: A systematic literature review. *Working Papers on Operations Management, 6*(2), 49–63.

16. Goffin, R. D., Jelley, R. B., Powell, D. M., & Johnston, N. G. (2009). Taking advantage of social comparisons in performance appraisal: The relative percentile method. *Human Resource Management, 48*, 251–268.

17. Davis, P., & Rogers, B. (2003). Managing the "C" performer: An alternative to forced ranking of appraisals. Retrieved January 2, 2018, from http://www.workinfo.org/index.php/articles/item/674-managing-the-c-performer-an-alternative-to-forced-ranking-of-appraisals

18. McGregor, J. (2006, January). The struggle to measure performance. *Business Week*. Retrieved January 2, 2018, from http://www.businessweek.com/magazine/content/06_02/b3966060.htm

19. Baldassarre, L. & Finken, B. (2015). GE's real-time performance development. *Harvard Business Review*. Retrieved from https://hbr.org/2015/08/ges-real-time-performance-development

20. Duggan, K. (2015). Six Companies that are Redefining Performance Management. *FastCompany*. Retrieved from https://www.fastcompany.com/3054547/six-companies-that-are-redefining-performance-management

21. Wall Street Journal. (2014). It's official: Forced ranking is dead. Retrieved from http://deloitte.wsj.com/cio/2014/06/10/its-official-forced-ranking-is-dead/

22. Buckingham, M., & Goodall, A. (2015). Reinventing performance management. *Harvard Business Review, 93*(4), 40–50.

23. Moon, S. H., Scullen, S. E., & Latham, G. P. (2016). Precarious curve ahead: The effects of forced distribution rating systems on job performance. *Human Resource Management Review, 26,* 166–179.

24. Blume, B. D., Rubin, R. S., & Baldwin, T. T. (2013). Who is attracted to an organization using a forced distribution performance management system? *Human Resource Management Journal, 23,* 360–378.

25. Gorman, C. A., Meriac, J. P., Roch, S. G., Ray, J. L., & Gamble, J. S. (2017). An exploratory study of current performance management practices: Human resource executives' perspectives. *International Journal of Selection and Assessment, 25,* 193–202.

26. Holland, K. (2006, September 10). Performance reviews: Many need improvement. *The New York Times, Section 3-Money and Business/Financial Desk,* 3.

27. Duggan, K. (2015). Six companies that are redefining performance management. *Fast Company.* Retrieved January 2, 2018, from https://www.fastcompany.com/3054547/six-companies-that-are-redefining-performance-management

28. Hunt, S. (2016). Rating performance may be difficult, but it is also necessary. *Industrial and Organizational Psychology, 9,* 296–304.

29. Aguinis, H., O'Boyle, E., Gonzalez-Mulé, E., & Joo, H. (2016). Cumulative advantage: Conductors and insulators of heavy-tailed productivity distributions and productivity stars. *Personnel Psychology, 69,* 3–66.

30. Aguinis, H., & O'Boyle, E. (2014). Star performers in twenty-first-century organizations. *Personnel Psychology, 67,* 313–350.

31. Bersin. J. (2014). The myth of the bell curve: Look for the hyper-performers. *Forbes.* Retrieved January 2, 2018, from https://www.forbes.com/sites/joshbersin/2014/02/19/the-myth-of-the-bell-curve-look-for-the-hyper-performers/#2b92e62c6bca

32. Kehoe, R. R., & Tzabbar, D. (2015). Lighting the way or stealing the shine? An examination of the duality in star scientists' effects on firm innovative performance. *Strategic Management Journal, 36,* 709–727.

33. Aguinis, H., & Bradley, K. J. (2015). The secret sauce for organizational success: Managing and producing star performers. *Organizational Dynamics, 44,* 161–168.

34. Finnegan, R. P. (2012). *The Power of Stay Interviews.* Alexandria, VA: Society for Human Resource Management.

35. This table is based on Bass, B. M., Cascio, W. F., & O'Connor, E. J. (1974). Magnitude estimations of expressions of frequency and amount. *Journal of Applied Psychology, 59,* 313–320.

36. Bartol, K. M., Durham, C. C., & Poon, J. M. L. (2001). Influence of performance evaluation rating segmentation on motivation and fairness perceptions. *Journal of Applied Psychology, 86,* 1106–1119.

37. This table is based on Spector, P. (1976). Choosing response categories for summated rating scales. *Journal of Applied Psychology, 61,* 374–375.

38. Ruiz, C. E., Hamlin, R. G., & Carioni, A. (2016). Behavioural determinants of perceived managerial and leadership effectiveness in Argentina. *Human Resource Development International, 19,* 267–288.

39. Grote, D. (2000, Spring). Public sector organizations: Today's innovative leaders in performance management. *Public Personnel Management, 29,* 1–20.

40. Hauenstein, N., Brown, R., & Sinclair, A. (2010). BARS and those mysterious, missing middle anchors. *Journal of Business and Psychology, 25,* 663–672.

41. Harrell, A., & Wright, A. (1990). Empirical evidence on the validity and reliability of Behaviorally Anchored Rating Scales for auditors. *Auditing, 9,* 134–149.

42. Wursthorn, M. (2017, January 7). Brokerages tack to the adviser model. *The Wall Street Journal,* B7.

43. Colvin, G. (2017). Can Wells Fargo get well? *Fortune, 175*(8), 138–146.Addresses learning needs of special-needs students efficiently

6

Performance Analytics

The goal is to turn data into information,
and information into insight

—*Carly Fiorina*

Learning Objectives

By the end of this chapter, you will be able to do the following:

1. Argue about the ubiquity and inescapability of judgments about performance in organizations even if they are not made explicit or called "performance ratings."

2. Design appraisal forms that include all major features to make them a useful component of the performance management system (e.g., accountabilities, objectives, and standards; competencies and behavioral indicators; developmental needs, plans, and goals; multiple performance touchpoints, employee comments).

3. Design appraisal forms that are simple, relevant, descriptive, adaptable, comprehensive, include clear definitions, are communicated well, and have a clear time orientation.

4. Use different methods to combine performance data to arrive at an overall score for each person being rated.

5. Choose an appropriate appraisal period and an appropriate number of formal performance meetings.

6. Collect performance information involving all of the relevant performance touchpoints, such as supervisors, peers, direct reports, self, and customers, as well as employee performance monitoring systems that are involved in collecting Big Data.

7. Appraise the reasons for disagreements in the data collected from different performance touchpoints.

8. Propose ways to motivate raters to provide performance information that minimizes intentional distortion of ratings.

As discussed in Chapter 2, the performance management process includes several stages: prerequisites, performance planning, performance execution, performance assessment, and performance review. An important component of the performance assessment stage is *performance analytics*. This involves the systematic collection and compilation of performance data, usually in the form of performance ratings, which are collected from all the relevant performance touchpoints, such as supervisors, peers, direct reports, self, and customers, as well as employee performance monitoring systems that are involved in collecting Big Data.

Chapters 4 and 5 provided a description of the various approaches and techniques that can be used to define and measure performance and this chapter addresses performance analytics, including the use of specific tools (i.e., appraisal forms, employee performance monitoring) to gather data. For example, this chapter describes how to choose the performance touchpoint from which to collect data (i.e., supervisors, self, direct reports, peers, or customers), and the use of electronic performance monitoring. The chapter concludes with a discussion of reasons why those who provide performance data may intentionally distort information and what can be done to improve the accuracy of performance data.

Before we begin, let us address once again the hotly debated issue of performance ratings. Although many companies such as Adobe, Microsoft, Eli Lilly, and The Gap have announced that they are abandoning performance ratings, let us clarify that *they actually engage in various forms of performance analytics and continue to collect and compile performance data*. But instead of using the term "performance ratings," they use terms such as "judgments," "achievement metrics," and "expectations." In other words, managers and employees continue to gather and compile data about performance, and those data are used to make administrative decisions about employees and evaluations of employees' on-the-job behaviors and results.

For example, consider the frequently talked about case of Juniper as an example of a company that has supposedly "abandoned" performance ratings. Juniper is based in California and develops and markets networking products such as routers, switches, and network security software. Juniper uses the label "J Players" to refer to the performance of employees who meet expectations against four performance elements. Also, the performance of employees is calibrated based on relative contribution.[1] Similarly, other companies use different labels in their performance analytics efforts, such as "don't have it," "have it," or "knock it out of the park." Moreover, companies continue to ask managers about their recommendations regarding who should receive a pay increase or bonus, and of what size, based on employee performance—regardless of whether they call this a "rating" or not. For an additional example that has received quite a bit of popular business press and media coverage, see Box 6-1 describing the performance management system at The Gap.

The inescapable reality in organizations is that evaluations about performance are made all the time—explicitly or implicitly—because, simply put, an organization cannot be successful in accomplishing its goals if the performance of its employees is not measured in some way. Performance analytics is also critical for managing individual and team performance. Absent performance analytics, how can an organization understand if its employees are making progress? How can an organization make decisions about promotions and compensation? How can an organization that wants to create a "personal growth and development culture" offer meaningful development and coaching opportunities absent knowledge about who is doing what—and how?[2] And, even if they do not say it openly, managers and peers form impressions and evaluate the performance of

Box 6-1

Company Spotlight: Performance Management "Without Ratings" at the Gap? Not Really . . .

The Gap, Inc., is one of the companies frequently talked about as being the leader in implementing a performance management system "without ratings."[3] Gap, Inc. is an American clothing store that includes renowned brands such as Gap, Banana Republic, Old Navy, Athleta, Intermix, and Weddington Way. In 2014, the company decided to revamp their performance management system by "eliminating performance ratings." Their new system is called GPS, which stands for grow, perform, and succeed (not co-incidentally Gap's New York Stock Exchange stock symbol is also GPS). GPS includes many of the features of best-in-kind performance management systems described throughout this text. For example, performance management does not take place once a year, and instead, is a year-long process that involves monthly "touch base" sessions between supervisors and direct reports. Also, each employee has a limited, yet meaningful, number of goals and this includes not only what has been achieved, but also how—which involves behaviors and competencies. Also, employee goals are updated throughout the year and are closely linked to company goals. For example, the touch base sessions involve answering the question of whether an employee's performance is "demonstrating the values of the company." How about performance ratings? Rob Ollander-Krane, Senior Director, Organization Performance Effectiveness, said that "With the removal of ratings, employees are no longer awarded a grade at the end of the year." So, how do managers make decisions about compensation and development needs? Can these decisions be made fairly and accurately without performance ratings? Is it really true that the system is "ratingless"? Well, not really. As noted by Ollander-Krane, managers "are not giving an A, B, or C, but *they still need to rank their employees* [emphasis added] . . . They still need to say here's my number one employee, here's my number two, here's my number three—and to allocate their merit and bonus pot accordingly." How about documentation? Ollander-Krane said that "We've had a new CEO and CHRO since we introduced GPS, and they have questioned whether we need to have a bit more of a written record of employee performance." The lesson? It is simply not possible to implement a performance management system that does not include measures of performance—regardless of whether those measures are called ratings, rankings, grades, scores, achievement metrics, or anything else. As the saying goes, if it looks like a duck, swims like a duck, and quacks like a duck, then it probably is a duck. This applies quite well to metrics used by many companies that have seemingly abandoned "performance ratings." Ratings are still very much part of their process, in one way or another.

people around them on a daily basis—even if these evaluations are not written down or said out loud. So, the fact is that judgments and evaluations of performance are part of organizational life. This chapter is about adopting a systematic, transparent, and effective approach to performance analytics.

6-1 USEFUL COMPONENTS OF APPRAISAL FORMS

Information on performance is collected formally by using forms, which are most often administered online. The availability of apps, and off-the-shelf software to collect performance data has produced a veritable revolution. Specifically, performance data are collected in real-time using Web and mobile apps, and the information can easily be shared, also in real-time. In this way, other team members, supervisors, direct reports, and also, the HR function have access to the same data.

The availability of performance data gathered electronically also facilitates subsequent analyses. For example, this makes comparisons of the relative average performance levels of various units within the organization more straightforward. Finally, using online forms is also beneficial because as changes take place in the organization (e.g., a new strategic direction) or job in question (e.g., new tasks), forms need to be revised and updated, and this can be done fast and efficiently.

Good appraisal forms usually include a combination of the following components[4]:

- *Basic employee information.* This section of the form includes basic employee information such as job title, division, department and other work group information, employee ID number, and pay grade or salary classification. In addition, forms usually include the dates of the evaluation period, the number of months and years the rater has supervised or worked with the employee, an employee's starting date with the company and starting date in the current job, the reason for appraisal, current salary and position in range, and the date of the next scheduled formal evaluation.

- *Accountabilities, objectives, and standards.* If the organization adopts a results approach, this section of the form would include the name and description of each accountability, objectives agreed upon by manager and employee, and the extent to which the objectives have been achieved. In many instances, the objectives are weighted in terms of importance, which facilitates the calculation of an overall performance score. Finally, this section can also include a subsection describing conditions under which performance was achieved, which may help explain why the employee achieved a particular level (high or low) of performance. For example, a supervisor may have the opportunity to describe specific circumstances surrounding performance during the review period, including a tough economy, the introduction of a new line of products, and so forth.

- *Competencies and behavioral indicators.* If the organization adopts a behavior approach, this section of the form includes a definition of the various competencies to be assessed, together with their behavioral indicators.

- *Major achievements and contributions.* Some forms include a section in which a rater is asked to list the two or three major accomplishments of the individual being rated during the review period. These could refer to results, behaviors, or both.

- *Developmental achievements.* This section of the form includes information about the extent to which the developmental goals set for the review period have been achieved. For example, this can include a summary of activities, such as workshops attended and online courses taken, as well as results, such as a description of new skills learned. Evidence of having learned new skills can be documented, for example, by obtaining a professional certification or designations (e.g., human resource management certifications, information systems certifications). Although some organizations include developmental achievements in the appraisal form, others choose to include them in a separate form. Sun Microsystems is an example of an organization that separates these forms. Some organizations do not include development content as part of the appraisal form because it is often difficult for employees to focus constructively on development if they have received a less-than-ideal performance review.

- *Developmental needs, plans, and goals.* This section of the form is future-oriented and includes information about specific goals and timetables in terms of employee development. As noted earlier, some organizations choose to create a separate development form and do not include this information as part of the performance appraisal form.

- *Multiple performance touchpoints.* Some forms include sections to be completed by different raters involved in different types of performance touchpoints, such as customers with whom the employee interacts. Those involved in performance touchpoints are people who have *firsthand knowledge of and are affected by the employee's performance*. In most cases, input is collected by using forms separate from the main appraisal because not all sources of performance information are in the position to rate the same performance dimensions. For example, an employee may be rated on the competency "teamwork" by peers and on the competency "reliability" by customers. A more detailed discussion of the use of information derived from different performance touchpoints is offered later in this chapter.
- *Employee comments.* This section includes reactions and comments provided by the employee being rated. In addition to allowing formal employee input, which improves the perceived fairness of the system, the inclusion of this section helps with legal issues because it documents that the employee has had an opportunity to participate in the evaluation process.
- *Signatures.* The final section of most forms includes a section in which the employee being rated, the rater, and the rater's supervisor provide their signatures to show they have seen and discussed the content of the form. The HR function may also provide approval of the content of the form.

Table 6-1 summarizes the major components of appraisal forms. Let us consider some examples to see which of these components is present in each. The goal of including these illustrations is that you examine them critically. So, these forms purposely do not include all of the major components. Let us discuss them in detail to understand the extent to which they deviate from including all necessary components.

First, consider the form included in Figure 6-1. This is a fairly generic form that can be used for almost any position in a company. Let us evaluate this form in relation to the components listed in Table 6-1. First, the form asks for the employee's basic information. Second, while the form asks the manager to list the expected versus the actual accountabilities, it does not include objectives or standards. Third, the form includes five competencies including teamwork and leadership, but it does not include a definition of those competencies nor does it

Basic employee information
Accountabilities, objectives, and standards
Competencies and behavioral indicators
Major achievements and contributions
Developmental achievements (could be included in a separate form)
Developmental needs, plans, and goals (could be included in a separate form)
Performance touchpoints
Employee comments
Signatures

TABLE 6-1
Major Components of Comprehensive Appraisal Forms

FIGURE 6-1
Basic Performance Review Form

PERFORMANCE REVIEW FORM

Employee Name:

Title:

Manager:

Date of Appraisal Meeting:

Employee Performance Reviews improve employee performance and development by encouraging communication, establishing performance expectations, identifying developmental needs, and setting goals to improve performance. Performance reviews also provide an ongoing record of employee performance, which is helpful for both the supervisor and employee.

Use the form below to list examples of outstanding performance or achievements as well as areas of performance that need improvement. Please provide open comments on your employee's performance. Complete each section and list examples of performance where applicable.

❐ Job description/key responsibilities/required tasks:

❐ Note expected accomplishments vs. actual accomplishments:

❐ List the areas where the employee developed in ways enabling him or her to take on additional responsibilities or be eligible for high-profile assignments:

FIGURE 6-1 (*Continued*)

☐ Areas of development for upcoming quarter (i.e., communication skills, teamwork, project management skills, budgeting experience, etc.):

☐ Goals for upcoming quarter (Please list S.M.A.R.T. goals):

Please circle the number below that best describes the employee's performance in the following areas:

Areas of concentration	Did not meet expectations	Achieved most expectations	Achieved expectations	Achieved expectations and exceeded on a few	Significantly exceeded expectations
Teamwork	1	2	3	4	5
Leadership	1	2	3	4	5
Business acumen	1	2	3	4	5
Customer service	1	2	3	4	5
Project management	1	2	3	4	5

Average Performance Score	

Employee Use Only:

Please provide comments and examples of behaviors to describe your performance in the past quarter.

Manager Signature: _____   Date : ☐ / ☐ / ☐

Employee Signature: _____   Date: ☐ / ☐ / ☐

list the indicators to look for to determine whether the employee has mastered the relevant competencies. The form does include space to list major developmental achievements, developmental needs, and employee comments. The form does not include information regarding different performance touchpoints and it seems that the supervisor is the only source of performance data. The following table summarizes which of the components are present:

Major Components of Appraisal Forms: Critical Evaluation of Basic Performance Review Form in Figure 6-1	
X	Basic employee information
	Accountabilities, objectives, and standards
	Competencies and indicators
X	Major achievements and contributions
X	Developmental achievements
X	Developmental needs, plans, and goals
	Multiple performance touchpoints
X	Employee comments
X	Signatures

As a second example, consider the form included in Figure 6-2, which is used to evaluate the performance of managers at a university hospital. This form has a section for basic employee information. Also, there is a section on objectives (i.e., "goals"), but no specific section for accountabilities and standards—although these could be included in the text boxes. The form includes several behavioral indicators for each competency, but there is no section for developmental achievements. Also, the form includes open-ended sections for developmental needs, plans, and goals. Similar to Figure 6-1, it seems that the form is directed at supervisors only, rather than multiple performance touchpoints. Finally, the form includes a box for the ratee to discuss thoughts on the evaluation. In short, the following components are present:

Major Components of Appraisal Forms: Critical Evaluation of Manager/Supervisor Appraisal Form in Figure 6-2	
X	Basic employee information
	Accountabilities, objectives, and standards
X	Competencies and indicators
	Major achievements and contributions
	Developmental achievements
X	Developmental needs, plans, and goals
	Multiple performance touchpoints
X	Employee comments
X	Signatures

FIGURE 6-2
Performance Appraisal form used for Managers and Supervisors (Lacking Some Components of an Ideal Form)

MANAGER/SUPERVISOR PERFORMANCE APPRAISAL FORM

Employee Name: _____   Hospital ID: _____

Position Title: _____

Department: _____

Appraisal Type: Probationary ☐ Annual ☐ Reappraisal ☐   Evaluation Period: From ____ To ____
Month/Year   Month/Year

INSTRUCTIONS:

1. At the beginning of each annual evaluation period list the performance goals for the coming year on page three. Also place a check mark to the left of any competency statement on page two requiring particular attention by the Manager/Supervisor. Give a copy to the Manager/Supervisor.

2. At the end of the evaluation period, make a determination of the extent to which the Manager/Supervisor met the Competency standards for each category. Enter a numeric score for each category, using the Ratings Guidelines below.

3. For each standard indicate in the right margin, a plus (+) where performance deserves recognition, or a minus (-) where performance needs attention.

4. Complete the Performance Goals section by following the instructions on page 3.

5. Review the entire evaluation. Using the Rating Guidelines, place the corresponding number that best describes your assessment of overall performance in the Overall Rating section on page 4.

6. Identify any increase in salary on page 4. Give the Manager/Supervisor the opportunity to record his/her comments.

RATING GUIDELINES:

(5) This staff member has made significant contributions to advance the position of the department and/or Hospital toward excellence and prominence. Only a small percentage of staff members who exhibit uniform excellence and initiative will receive this rating.

(4) This staff member has been instrumental to the department's success and has performed in an exemplary manner.

(3) This staff member is proficient. Performance is what is expected of a fully qualified and experienced person.

(2) This staff member occasionally fails to exhibit proficiency in the job. Improvement is necessary to meet the expectations for acceptable performance.

(1) This staff member has serious deficiencies in key areas. Performance fails to meet expectations and is not acceptable.

(Continued)

FIGURE 6-2 (*Continued*)

MANAGER/SUPERVISOR COMPETENCIES

ADMINISTRATIVE COMPETENCIES   RATING   **+   -**

☐ Creates effective work plans; identifies the appropriate resources and processes; sets priorities; delegates authority and meets deadlines.   ☐ ☐

☐ Incorporates control systems that monitor workflow and ensure task completion.   ☐ ☐

☐ Ensures department compliance with regulatory standards such as Joint Commission, OSHA, DOH, EEOC, etc., so that no serious citations exist.   ☐ ☐

☐ Understands and adheres to University Hospital's compliance standards as they appear in University Hospital's Corporate Compliance Policy, Code of Conduct, and Conflict of Interest Policy; sponsors and implements initiatives to achieve the Hospital's compliance goals.   ☐ ☐

☐ Enforces for all subordinates and personally complies with all Hospital disease prevention and control, including tuberculosis and hepatitis B.   ☐ ☐

☐ Ensures that budget dollars are used responsibly; introduces innovative ways to reduce costs.   ☐ ☐

☐ Identifies customer needs and takes action to meet those needs; continually searches for ways to increase customer satisfaction.   ☐ ☐

☐ Emphasizes the need to deliver quality services; defines standards for quality and evaluates processes against those standards in an effort to improve departmental performance.   ☐ ☐

CATEGORY SCORE: ☐

LEADERSHIP/STAFF MANAGEMENT: RATING   **+   -**

☐ Demonstrates knowledge of the Hospital's mission and values and their relationship to the department's work.   ☐ ☐

☐ Demonstrates the ability to take charge; gains support and commitment; initiates actions and makes logical decisions.   ☐ ☐

☐ Fosters team spirit through cooperation and trust; leads by example   ☐ ☐

☐ Initiates new and unique ideas; assumes risk and accepts responsibility for results.   ☐ ☐

☐ Acts professionally and responsibly within and outside of the Hospital; contributes to a positive image.   ☐ ☐

☐ Hires competent staff; creates and develops work teams through coaching, training, and education.   ☐ ☐

☐ Provides staff with continual feedback; conducts all performance appraisals on time; recognizes and celebrates exceptional performance and takes corrective action to improve poor performance.   ☐ ☐

☐ Recognizes the existence of, and the need for, diversity in the workplace; supports the employment, education, and development of minorities and protected classes; ensures that decisions are based on the principles of equal employment opportunity.   ☐ ☐

CATEGORY SCORE: ☐

WORK METHODS AND QUALITIES: RATING   **+   -**

☐ Expresses self well in verbal and written communication; keeps all appropriate individuals informed regarding progress or problems.   ☐ ☐

☐ Accepts the perspectives of others and maintains a positive attitude.   ☐ ☐

☐ Analyzes own departmental needs and improves capabilities to meet the changing requirements of the job; ensures or enhances professional position.   ☐ ☐

☐ Demonstrates flexibility; adjusts to shifting priorities; stays focused during stressful or difficult situations.   ☐ ☐

☐ Works effectively as a member of a team; contributes to the achievement of joint objectives.   ☐ ☐

CATEGORY SCORE: ☐

EVALUATOR'S COMMENTS:

FIGURE 6-2 (*Continued*)

PERFORMANCE GOALS

INSTRUCTIONS:

· List goals by order of importance.

· Review goals periodically and make changes to this section if goals or priorities change during the year.

· At the end of the evaluation period, rate each goal individually using the Rating Guidelines listed on page one of the form.

· Consider your individual rating for each goal relative to its priority. Assign a numeric category score for overall goal achievement.

PRIORITY RATING	GOAL DESCRIPTION	RESULTS and COMMENTS	RATING
1			
2			
3			
4			
5			
6			

CATEGORY SCORE FOR PERFORMANCE GOALS: [ ]

(Continued)

FIGURE 6-2 (*Continued*)

EVALUATOR: Discuss your assessment of the Manager's/Supervisor's developmental needs, suggest ways the Manager/Supervisor can meet those needs, and how you plan to help.

MANAGER/SUPERVISOR: Discuss your thoughts on this evaluation and identify the specific ways the Hospital can help you optimize your performance.

OVERALL RATING:

I have reviewed my job description as of this date and it is consistent with my present position responsibilities.

Staff Member's Signature: _____ Date: [ ] / [ ] / [ ]
                                                                      mm   dd   yy

Note: Staff member's signature indicates review and discussion.

Evaluator's Name: _____ Signature: _____ Date: [ ] / [ ] / [ ]
                                                                      mm   dd   yy

Next Level Manager's Name: _____ Signature: _____ Date: [ ] / [ ] / [ ]
                                                                                  mm   dd   yy

Source: http://www.uhnj.org/hrweb/forms/managersupervisorform.pdf

This analysis shows that although the forms included in Figures 6-1 and 6-2 seem, at first glance, to be quite complete and thorough, they are not. Thus, before implementing appraisal forms, make sure that all their necessary components are present. From your own perspective, do you agree with these conclusions about which of the major components is present in each of these forms? What is missing and should be added? What would the revised and improved versions of these forms look like?

6-2 DESIRABLE FEATURES OF APPRAISAL FORMS

We should be aware that there is no such thing as a universally correct appraisal form that can be used for all purposes and in all situations. In some cases, a form may emphasize competencies, rather than results. This would be the case if the system adopted a behavior approach as opposed to a results approach to measure performance. In others, the form may emphasize developmental issues and minimize, or even completely ignore, both behaviors and results. In such cases, the form would be used for developmental purposes only and not for administrative purposes.[5] In yet other cases, there may be a very short form used for weekly check-ins and a separate and more comprehensive form used for a quarterly, semi-annual, or even annual review. One size does not fit all, and different components are appropriate, based on the purposes of the appraisal.

In spite of the large variability in terms of format, components, and length, there are certain desirable features that make appraisal forms particularly effective for all types of jobs and hierarchical positions in the organization:

- *Simplicity.* Forms must be easy to understand, easy to administer, quick to complete, clear, and concise. If forms are too long, convoluted, and complicated, it is likely that the performance assessment process will not be effective or may not even happen at all.
- *Relevancy.* Good forms include information related directly to the tasks and responsibilities of the job; otherwise, they will be regarded as an administrative burden and not as a tool for performance improvement. This information is derived directly from the work analysis described in Chapter 2.
- *Descriptiveness.* Good forms require that the raters provide evidence of performance regardless of the performance level. The form should be sufficiently descriptive that an outside party (e.g., supervisor's supervisor or HR department) has a clear understanding of the performance information conveyed.
- *Adaptability.* Good forms allow managers in different functions and departments to adapt them to their particular needs and situations. Also, this feature allows for changes over time to reflect changes in the nature of work and an organization's strategic direction. This feature encourages widespread use of the form.

....

TABLE 6-2
Desirable Features of All Appraisal Forms

Simplicity
Relevancy
Descriptiveness
Adaptability
Comprehensiveness
Definitional clarity
Communication
Time orientation

- *Comprehensiveness.* Good forms include all the major areas of performance for a particular position for the entire review period.
- *Definitional clarity.* Desirable competencies (and behavioral indicators) and results are clearly defined for all raters so that everyone evaluates the same attributes. This feature enhances the consistency of ratings across raters and levels of the organization.
- *Communication.* The meaning of each of the components of the form must be clearly and successfully communicated to all people participating in the evaluation process. This enhances acceptance of the system and motivation to participate in it, both as rater and ratee.
- *Time orientation.* Good forms help clarify expectations about performance. They address not only the past, but also the future.[6]

Table 6-2 includes a summary of the features that are desirable in all forms, regardless of specific content and format. Let us consider the two illustrative forms discussed earlier to see how they fare in relation to these desirable features.

First, consider the form shown in Figure 6-1. It is simple because it is easy to understand and clear. The fact that it includes an essay format implies that it would take a little more time to complete, but the number of essays is kept to a minimum. The form is also relevant, but only if the supervisor enters the correct job description and actual accountabilities. This form can be extremely descriptive owing to its narrative nature. The form encourages the manager to give examples of relevant behavior. Next, the first portion of the form is also adaptable, perhaps too adaptable; it would be hard to compare performance across employees because the manager can adapt and change the content of the form to each employee. This form is comprehensive, but again only if the manager lists all of the expected accountabilities. This form does not have definitional clarity. Because the competencies listed are not clearly defined, ratings are likely to be inconsistent across raters. Next, this form can be communicated across the organization. Manager acceptance may be hard to gain, however, because of the amount of detail required by the essay answers. Finally, the form is time-oriented. It asks for past and future performance expectations and goals. In short, the following table summarizes which of the desirable features are present in this form:

	Desirable Features of Appraisal Forms: Critical Evaluation of Basic Performance Review Form in Figure 6-1
X	Simplicity
X	Relevancy
X	Descriptiveness
X	Adaptability
X	Comprehensiveness
	Definitional clarity
X	Communication
X	Time orientation

Next, let us evaluate the form shown in Figure 6-2 in relation to the desirable features listed in Table 6-2. First, it is not that simple in that it includes many different types of behavioral indicators. Yet, it seems quite relevant and descriptive. It is particularly relevant for the job of manager/supervisor, specifically regarding behavioral indicators for each competency. This form is easier to administer than the form shown in Figure 6-1 because it does not include an essay format. Although there is a comprehensive list of competencies and behavioral indicators, the actual expectations of the individual employees are not clear, and there is a lack of definitional clarity regarding goals. The form seems adaptable. For example, it would be quite easy to add or delete behavioral indicators and it would also be easy to change the set of indicators across units and departments. Next, the form could be communicated throughout the organization. Finally, the form mentions time in the section on developmental goals and needs. The table below summarizes this analysis:

	Desirable Features of Appraisal Forms: Evaluation of Manager/Supervisor Performance Appraisal Form in Figure 6-2
	Simplicity
X	Relevancy
X	Descriptiveness
X	Adaptability
X	Comprehensiveness
	Definitional clarity
	Communication
X	Time orientation

From your own perspective, do you agree with the above conclusions about which desirable features are present in each of these forms? What is missing and should be added? What would the revised and improved versions of these forms look like?

Many organizations use forms very similar to those presented in Figures 6-1 and 6-2. A careful analysis of these forms against the desired features indicates that the forms could be improved. An important point to consider regarding these and other forms is that an exclusive emphasis on the appraisal form should be avoided; it is just one component of the performance management system.

6-3 DETERMINING OVERALL RATING

After performance data have been gathered for each employee, there is usually a need to compute an overall performance score. This is particularly necessary for making administrative decisions such as the allocation of rewards. Computing overall performance scores is also useful in determining whether employees, and groups of employees, are improving their performance over time. This is a critical aspect and advantage of approaching performance management with a *performance analytics mindset*: We use performance data collected on an ongoing basis to create useful and meaningful insights that help individuals grow and develop, and data serve the purpose of improving individual and team performance in terms of both behaviors and results.

Two main strategies are used to obtain an overall performance score for each employee: judgmental and mechanical. The judgmental procedure consists of considering every aspect of performance, and then, arriving at a defensible summary. This holistic procedure relies on the ability of the rater to arrive at a fair and accurate overall score. The mechanical procedure consists of first considering the scores assigned to each section of the appraisal form, and then, combining them up to obtain an overall score. When adding scores from each section, weights are typically used based on the relative importance of each performance dimension measured.

Consider the performance evaluation form shown in Figure 6-3, which is used to evaluate the performance of sales associates at a supermarket chain.[7] This form includes the hypothetical ratings obtained by a sales associate on just two competencies and just two key results (the complete form probably includes more than four performance dimensions). You can see that in the Competencies section, each competency is weighted according to its value to the organization. Specifically, Follow-Through/Dependability is given a weight of 0.7 whereas Decision Making/Creative Problem-Solving is given a weight of 0.3. For the competency Follow-Through/Dependability, Patricia Carmello obtained a score of 4 for the first half of the review period and a score of 3 for the second half of the review period; consequently, the scores for this competency are $4 \times 0.7 = 2.8$ for the first half and $3 \times 0.7 = 2.1$ for the second half of the review period. Adding up the scores obtained for the first and second halves in each competency leads to a total of 3.7 points for the first half and 2.7 for the second half of the review period.

The form also indicates that the key results have different weights. Specifically, KR #1 has a weight of 0.6 whereas KR #2 has a weight of 0.4. Consider KR #1. The objective for the first half was to achieve a sales figure of US$78,000. The actual sales figure achieved by Patricia was US$77,000, representing a 98.71% achievement, which is a score of 2. Multiplying this score times the weight of 0.6 yields 1.2 points for the first half of the review period. Similarly, for the second

FIGURE 6-3

Performance Appraisal Form Used by Grocery Retailer

PERFORMANCE EVALUATION FORM

For use by Store Director; Co-Director; Meat, Seafood, Produce, Deli/Bakery, Floral and Grocery Managers

Name	Patricia Carmello	Review Period	2018
Position	Sales Associate	Store	#25
Evaluator	ames Garcia	Date	12/15/18

Competencies: Please rate the Associate on the following competencies. Determine the point total and multiply by the weight factor to achieve the point total for the competencies.

				1st	2nd	Wgt	Pts	Pts
Follow-Through/Dependability		Points:		4	3	0.7	2.8	2.1

4	3	2	1
Work is completed correctly and on time without supervision. Anticipates needs Extremely organized.	Work is usually completed correctly and on a timely basis with some supervision. Very organized.	Work is completed as assigned and results can usually be relied upon with normal supervision. Organized.	Work can seldom be relied upon. Often fails to complete tasks correctly. Unorganized.

Comments:

				1st	2nd	Wgt	Pts	Pts
Decision Making/Creative Problem Solving		Points:		3	2	0.3	0.9	0.6

4	3	2	1
Anticipates, recognizes, and confronts problems with extraordinary skill. Perseveres until solution is reached. Extremely innovative and takes risks.	Defines and addresses problems well. Typically reaches useful solutions and decisions are sound. Innovative, with above-average risk taking.	Acknowledges and attempts to solve most problems when presented. Usually comes to conclusions on solving basic issues. Little innovation and sometimes takes risks.	Has difficulty recognizing problems and making decisions. Always needs guidance. No innovation and never takes risks.

Comments:

Total Score for Competencies Section	3.7	2.7

(Continued)

FIGURE 6-3 (*Continued*)

Key Results: Rate each area to the performance demonstrated in the achievement of budgeted numbers.

KR #1: Achieved Budgeted Sales (U.S. dollars)

	Budgeted	Actual	% of achievement (1, 2, 3, 4)		Wgt 0.6
1st half objective	$78,000	$77,000	2		
2nd half objective	$80,000	$83,000	3		Pts
	4 = 108%+ 3 = 107–103%		2 = 102–98%	1 = Below 97%	1.2 | 1.8

Comments:

KR #2: Margin Balance (gain/loss in U.S. dollars)

	Budgeted	Actual	% of achievement (1, 2, 3, 4)		Wgt 0.4
1st half objective	$30,000	$29,000	1		
2nd half objective	$31,000	$34,000	4		Pts
	4 = 108%+ 3 = 107–103%		2 = 102–98%	1 = Below 97%	0.4 | 1.6

Comments:

TOTAL SCORE FOR KEY RESULTS:						1.6	3.4
	Comp. Score 1st half	Comp. Score 2nd half	KR Score 1st half	KR Score 2nd half		Subtotal	
Circle Rating:	3.7	2.7	1.6	3.4		11.4/4 = 2.85	
Excellent	**Above Average**	Average	Unsatisfactory				
3.6–4.0	**2.6–3.5**	1.6 – 2.5	1 – 1.5				

Associate _____   Date _____

Store Director _____   Date _____

half, the goal was US$80,000 and Patricia surpassed it by achieving a figure of US$83,000, which represents a score of 3 (i.e., 103.75% achievement); therefore, the score for the second half is $3 \times 0.6 = 1.8$. Finally, the form shows that the total score for the first half for all key results combined is 1.6, whereas the score for the second half is 3.4. These scores were computed by simply adding the scores obtained in each half.

In the end, the form shows the scores obtained for the competencies and the key results in each of the two halves of the review period. To obtain the overall performance score, we simply take an average of these four numbers: $(3.7 + 2.7 + 1.6 + 3.4)/4 = 2.85$. This puts Patricia in the 2.6–3.5 range, which represents a qualification of "above average."

Now, suppose that we do not follow a mechanical procedure to compute the overall performance score, and instead, we use a judgmental method. That is, suppose raters have no information on weights. How would James Garcia, Patricia's supervisor, compute the overall performance score? One possibility is that he might give equal weights to all competencies and would therefore consider that Follow-Through/Dependability is as important as Decision Making/Creative Problem-Solving. This would lead to different scores compared to using weights of 0.7 and 0.3. Or, as an alternative, the supervisor may have his own ideas about what performance dimensions should be given more weight and decide to ignore how the work is done (i.e., behaviors), and instead, assign an overall score based primarily on the key results (i.e., sales and margin balance).

The use of weights allows the supervisor to come to an objective and clear overall performance score for each employee. As this example illustrates, the use of clearly specified weights allows the supervisor to obtain a verifiable score for each employee. Thus, the supervisor and the employees can be sure that the overall performance rating is reflective of the employee's performance in each category.

Which strategy is best, judgmental or mechanical? In most cases, the mechanical method is superior to the judgmental method.[8] A supervisor is more likely to introduce her own biases in computing the overall perform-ance score when no clear rules exist regarding the relative importance of the various performance dimensions and there is no direction on how to combine the various performance dimensions in calculating the overall score.[9] As far as the computation of overall scores goes, the mechanical method is superior to the judgmental method.

Finally, you will notice that the form included in Figure 6-3 has sections labeled comments. These open-ended sections are common in most appraisal forms. However, this information is typically not used effectively.[10] Likely, there are two chief reasons why this is the case. First, it is not easy to systematically categorize and analyze such comments. Second, the quality, length, and content of these comments may be more a function of the culture of the organization and the writing skills of the person filling out the form than actual KSAs of the employee being rated. Regarding the first challenge, a recent analytics innovation is the increasing sophistication of computer-aided text analysis (CATA) software that allows for an analysis of text (as opposed to numbers) and more and better use of such information. For example, the software package DICTION 5.0 allows for the analysis of text by first creating categories of terms or phrases, and then, counting the relative frequency of each.[11] So, an organization may wish to classify the comments in terms of, for example, task and contextual performance. Then, a "dictionary" of terms and phrases related to each of these performance dimensions is created and the software automatically counts the number of times that such types of behaviors are mentioned in the comments. The second challenge is more difficult to overcome because if raters are not given any training or general instructions on what to write, comments may range from none at all to very detailed descriptions of what employees have done (i.e., past orientation) and very detailed descriptions of what employees should do (i.e., future orientation). Thus, to overcome this second challenge, it is important to first establish the goals of the information that raters are asked to include in these open-ended sections, and then offer raters training on how to do that in a systematic and standardized fashion across ratees. If these two challenges are overcome, then the information included in the open-ended sections can be used to supplement the quantitative information offered on the forms.

6-4 APPRAISAL PERIOD AND NUMBER OF FORMAL MEETINGS

Let us be clear that this section addresses the issues of the appraisal period and *formal* sit-down reviews. If we want to create a culture of performance and encourage everyone to improve performance on an ongoing basis, conversations about performance should be part of everyone's routine. This is why so many companies currently implement check-in systems in which employees can talk about what they are doing and how and the results they are generating with several performance touchpoints such as peers and supervisors. Again, Web-based and mobile apps now make this easier. In fact, there are dozens of vendors that offer these products. All you need to do is Google "performance appraisal apps" and you will find them right away.

Regarding the evaluation period, the first question we should answer is: How long should the appraisal period be? In other words, what period of time should be included in the appraisal form? Most organizations typically conduct a formal annual review. However, others choose to conduct semiannual or even quarterly formal reviews. Conducting only an annual review is usually not sufficient for most employees to discuss performance issues in a formal setting. In particular, Millennials value more frequent feedback about how they are doing.[12]

The recommendation then is to conduct formal sit-down reviews semiannually or quarterly. For example, Colorado-based Hamilton Standard Commercial Aircraft uses a semiannual review system.[13] Twice a year, the company performs a modified 360-degree appraisal, meaning that performance information is collected from performance touchpoints from all around (hence, the "360-degree" label). This type of system allows individuals to receive feedback and adjust goals or objectives, if necessary, in preparation for the more in-depth annual review. An example of a company implementing formal quarterly reviews is Synygy, Inc., a Philadelphia-based compensation software and services company.[14] Each quarter, employees receive a summary of comments and specific examples from coworkers about how they are performing. Synygy states that the goal of the system is to encourage open communication. Employees are trained to write effective comments to their coworkers that will facilitate growth by pointing out positive and negative areas of performance. In areas that need improvement, coworkers are encouraged to suggest ways that employees could improve their performance.

When is the best time to complete formal sit-down reviews? Most organizations adopt one of two possibilities. First, the appraisal form could be completed on or around the annual anniversary date. In the case of semiannual reviews, the first review would be six months before the annual anniversary date and the second review would be on or around the annual anniversary date. The biggest advantage of this choice is that the supervisor does not have to fill out everyone's forms at the same time. The disadvantage of this choice is that because results are not tied to a common cycle for all employees, resulting rewards cannot be tied to the fiscal year.

The second choice is to complete the appraisal forms toward the end of the fiscal year. In the case of a system including semiannual reviews, one review would be completed halfway through the fiscal year and the other one toward the end of the fiscal year. Adopting this approach leads to the completion of the appraisal form for all employees at about the same time, which facilitates cross-employee comparisons as well as the distribution of rewards. An additional advantage of following the fiscal year cycle is that individual goal setting can be more easily tied to corporate goal setting because most companies align their goal cycle with their fiscal year. This helps employees synchronize their work and objectives with those of their unit and organization. But what about the additional work imposed on the supervisors who need to evaluate all employees at once during a short period of time? This can be a major problem if the performance management system is not implemented using the best practices described in this book, and instead, performance appraisal is a once-a-year event. If there is ongoing communication between the supervisor and the employee about performance issues throughout the year, completing appraisal forms should not uncover any major surprises and filling out the appraisal form should not create a major time burden for the supervisors.

Performance management systems can include six formal meetings between the direct reports and the supervisor[15]:

- System inauguration
- Self-appraisal
- Classical performance review
- Merit/salary review
- Development plan
- Objective setting

Recall that informal performance discussions take place throughout the year and involve ongoing check-ins. In addition, however, there should be regularly scheduled formal meetings for the specific purpose of discussing the various aspects of performance and the performance management system. The fact that the supervisor allocates time to this activity sends a message that performance management is important.

The first meeting, system inauguration, includes a discussion of how the system works and the identification of the requirements and responsibilities resting primarily on the employee and on the supervisor. This discussion includes the role of self-appraisal and the dates when the employee and supervisor will meet formally to discuss performance issues. This meeting is particularly important for new employees, who should be introduced to the performance management system as soon as they become members of the organization.

The second meeting, the self-appraisal, involves the employee's assessment of herself. This meeting is informational in nature, and at this point, the supervisor does not pass judgment on how the employee regards her own performance. This meeting provides an opportunity for the employee to describe how she sees her own performance during the review period. It is helpful if the employee is given the same form to be filled out later by the supervisor so that she can provide self-ratings using the same dimensions that will be used by the supervisor.

The third meeting, the classical performance review meeting, during which employee performance is discussed, includes both the perspective of the supervisor and the employee. Most performance management systems include this type of meeting only. No other formal meetings to discuss performance are usually scheduled. This meeting is mainly past-oriented and typically does not focus on what performance should look like in the future.

The fourth meeting, the merit/salary review, discusses what, if any, compensation changes will result as a consequence of the period's performance. It is useful to separate the discussion of rewards from the discussion of performance so that the employee can focus on performance first, and then on rewards. If these meetings are not separated, employees may not be very attentive during the discussion of performance and are likely to feel it is merely the price they must pay to move on to the part of the meeting that really matters: the discussion about rewards. Although these meetings are separate, supervisors should explain clearly the link between the employee's performance, discussed in detail in a previous meeting, and the rewards given. Rewards are not likely to carry their true weight if they are not linked directly to performance.

The fifth meeting, the development plan, discusses the employee's developmental needs and what steps will be taken so that performance will be improved during the following period. This meeting also includes information about what types of resources will be provided to the employee to facilitate the development of any required new skills.

The sixth and final meeting, objective setting, includes setting goals, both behavioral and results-oriented, regarding the following review period. At this point, the employee has received very clear feedback about her performance during the past review period, knows what rewards will be allocated (if any), understands developmental needs and goals, and knows about resources available to help in the process of acquiring any required skills.

Although these six meetings are possible, not all six take place separately. For example, the self-appraisal, classical performance review, merit/salary review, development plan, and objective setting meetings may all take place during one umbrella meeting. Nonetheless, it is best to separate the various types of information discussed so that the employee and the supervisor will focus on each of the components separately.

Take the case of Johnsonville Foods, one of the largest sausage-making producers in the Unites States, making such products as brats, Italian sausage, breakfast sausage in fully cooked and fresh varieties, chicken sausage, meatballs, and summer sausage. Johnsonville Foods has a performance management system that includes the following meetings: self-appraisal, classical performance review, merit/salary review, development plan, and objective setting.[16] Team members (i.e., employees) and coaches (i.e., supervisors) write six-month contracts stating their goals for the following six months and how they plan to meet those goals (objective setting). This contract also asks the employee to state developmental goals for the upcoming six months (development plan). These goals may include reading a book on leadership or learning a new computer software program. In addition, each month, the employee writes up a contract with his goals for the month. That contract is posted on the company electronic bulletin board and sent to three internal customers, who evaluate that employee's performance over the

Box 6-2

Company Spotlight: Performance Review Meetings at McCoy Federal Credit Union

McCoy Federal is a nonprofit organization that provides financial services to those who join on a membership basis. It is the result of a merger with Central Florida Healthcare Federal Credit Union and one of the largest credit unions in Central Florida, with over 63,000 members, assets over US$565 million, and 14 locations. The credit union utilizes a Web-based system that allows tailoring each position's performance evaluation to specific duties performed. The performance management system also involves quarterly meetings and goal setting, which allow both supervisor and employee to track progress. The frequent performance reviews, including self-appraisals, were instituted in order to ensure that all employees receive regular performance feedback from supervisors, who might otherwise spend more time focusing on those whose performance is considered substandard. This allows employees and supervisors to focus regularly on progress toward goals. The information systems facilitate the process by allowing both supervisor and employee to keep track of progress in almost real-time. In summary, McCoy Federal utilizes a performance management system that includes frequent performance review meetings, combined with an emphasis on setting goals and tracking progress to ensure all employees and supervisors are focused on performance management.[17]

month. The next month, employees and their coaches discuss how the goals were met (classical performance review) and how much bonus the employee should receive (merit/salary review), and they set new goals for the upcoming month (objective setting). If the employee does not expect to meet his goals, a meeting is scheduled halfway through the month to discuss options.

In short, Johnsonville Foods includes all the formal meetings that can take place in a performance management system; however, it does not involve six separate meetings. Instead, the company holds only two formally scheduled meetings, but the system allows for the addition of more meetings if the need arises. Box 6-2 includes an example of how performance reviews are implemented in an organization in the nonprofit sector: McCoy Federal Credit Union.

6-5 PERFORMANCE TOUCHPOINTS: SOURCES OF PERFORMANCE DATA

So far, we referred to the supervisor as a primary source of performance information. This is the case in many organizations because the supervisor usually observes employees directly and has good knowledge about performance standards. However, there are multiple performance touchpoints, which are all the relevant sources that have firsthand knowledge of the employee's performance. Let us consider the use of the direct supervisor as a source of performance information, followed by the use of other sources, including peers, direct reports, self, and customers.[18] Then, we will discuss the issue of electronic performance monitoring, which is used by many organizations to collect Big Data about their employees.

6-5-1 Supervisors

An advantage of using supervisors as a source of performance information is that they are usually in the best position to evaluate performance in relation to strategic organizational goals. Also, supervisors are often those making decisions about rewards associated with performance evaluation. Moreover, in some cultural contexts, supervisors are seen as the exclusive source due to the pervasiveness of hierarchical organizational structures. For example, a survey of 74 HR directors in Jordan revealed that in every one of these organizations, the supervisor had almost exclusive input in terms of providing performance information; 95% of respondents reported that peers had no input; 82% reported that employees had no input; and 90% reported that customers had no input either.[19] Accordingly, supervisors are often the most important source of performance information because they are knowledgeable about strategic issues, understand performance, and are usually in charge of managing employee performance.

Although supervisors are usually the most important—and sometimes, only—source of performance information, other sources should be considered as well. For example, we have already seen that self-appraisals are an important component in the performance review process. In addition to self-appraisals and supervisor appraisals, performance information can be collected from peers, customers, and direct reports (assuming there are any). Alternative sources are usually considered because for some jobs, such as teaching, law enforcement, or sales, supervisors may not be performance touchpoints because they do not observe direct reports' performance on a regular basis. Also, performance evaluations given by the supervisor may be biased because the supervisor may evaluate performance based on whether the ratee is contributing to goals valued by the supervisor as opposed to goals valued by the organization as a whole. For example, a supervisor may provide high performance ratings to employees who help the supervisor advance his career aspirations within the company, as opposed to those who engage in behaviors conducive to helping achieve organizational strategic goals.

6-5-2 Peers

Many organizations use performance evaluations provided by peers. Take, for example, the system implemented at a large international financial services bank.[20] Through acquisitions, the bank has been growing rapidly and has as its strategic goal the consolidation of its offices. Change management is extremely important to the successful implementation of this consolidation. The company is therefore revising how it assesses the competency "teamwork" at the senior and middle management levels, with the belief that successful teamwork is crucial to change management initiatives. Specifically, one-third of the score for this competency is determined by ratings provided by peers. As an additional example, the Australian National University Medical School recently introduced a system in which students rate their peers in terms of personal and professional performance. Students begin to provide anonymous ratings online at the end of their first year in medical school. The system allows students to share their assessment of their peers and provides faculty with early-warning signs to assist students who may not be performing up to personal or professional standards.[21]

Although the use of peers as a source of performance data is often described as a "breakthrough" or "new" feature in many performance management systems, they have been around for quite some time. For example, in the 1940s and 1950s, they were called "buddy ratings" and were used to select military leaders.[22]

Peer evaluations suffer from three problems, however. First, such evaluations may not be readily accepted when employees believe there is *friendship bias* at work.[23] In other words, if an employee believes that ratings provided by his peers will be lower than those provided for another employee because the other employee has more friends than he does, then performance evaluations will not be taken seriously. In this situation, it is not likely that the employee will use the feedback received to improve his performance. A second problem with peer evaluations is that peers are less discriminating among performance dimensions compared to supervisors. In other words, if one is rated high on one dimension, one is also likely to be rated high on all the other dimensions, even though the performance dimensions rated may not be related to one another and may require very different knowledge, skills, and abilities. This is what is called the *halo effect*. Finally, peer evaluations are likely to be affected by what is called *context effects*.[24] For example, consider the situation in which peers evaluate communication behaviors. The salience of such behaviors will be affected by context: these behaviors are much more salient when there is a conflict as compared to routine daily work. The resulting peer evaluations can thus be quite different, based on whether the peer providing the rating is thinking about one specific situation versus another one, or communication behaviors across situations in general. This issue should remind you of the description of maximum versus typical performance described in Chapter 4.

Given these weaknesses of peer evaluations, it would not be wise to use them as the sole source of performance information. Peer evaluations can be part of the system, but information should also be obtained from additional sources involved in performance touchpoints.

6-5-3 Direct Reports

Direct reports are a good source of information regarding the performance of their managers. For example, direct reports are in a good position to evaluate leadership competencies, including delegation, organization, and communication. In addition, direct reports may be asked to rate their manager's ability to (1) remove barriers that employees face, (2) shield employees from politics, and (3) raise employees' competence. Be aware that direct reports may hesitate to provide upward feedback if put on the spot; however, if managers take the time to involve employees in the process by soliciting their input, employees are more likely to give honest feedback.[25]

Many organizations take upward feedback very seriously because it provides tangible benefits—especially long-term benefits—as demonstrated by results of a study in a Korean public institution with about 2,500 employees that performs research, development, tests and evaluation.[26] Managers received upward feedback once a year during a period of seven years. Then, the data were analyzed, based on whether managers were classified as low, medium, or high-performers. Results showed that those in the low-performing group benefited the most.

For an example of a company that you may know well because of the pervasiveness of its products, take the case of computer giant Dell. Dell employs over 100,000 individuals worldwide. More than 30 years ago, Michael Dell founded Dell, based on the simple concept of selling computer systems directly to customers. At Dell, all employees rate their supervisors, including Michael Dell himself, who is currently chairman and CEO, every six months, using "Tell Dell" surveys. Michael Dell said, "If you are a manager and you're not addressing [employee] issues, you're not going to get compensation. And if you consistently score in the bottom rungs of the surveys, we're going to look at you and say 'Maybe this isn't the right job for you.'"[27]

The intended purpose of the evaluation provided by direct reports has an impact on the accuracy of the information provided. Overall, performance information provided by direct reports is more accurate when the resulting ratings are to be used for developmental purposes, rather than administrative purposes. When evaluation data are intended for administrative purposes (i.e., whether the manager should be promoted), direct reports are likely to inflate their ratings.[28] Most likely, this is because direct reports may fear retaliation if they provide low performance scores. Confidentiality is key if direct reports are to be used as a useful and valid source of performance information.

6-5-4 Self

As discussed earlier, self-appraisals are an important component of any performance management system. They have become particularly prominent, given the increasingly popular view regarding the need to shift from performance appraisal to performance management. If the only focus is appraisal, collecting data from supervisors may suffice. However, if we want to implement a state-of-the-science performance management system that serves as a tool for continuously identifying, measuring, and developing the performance of individuals and teams, it is crucial to include self-evaluations as well.

When employees are given the opportunity to participate in the performance management process, their acceptance of the resulting decision is likely to increase and their defensiveness during the appraisal interview is likely to decrease. An additional advantage associated with self-appraisals is that the employee is in a good position to keep track of activities during the review period, whereas a supervisor may have to keep track of the performance of several employees. On the contrary, self-appraisals should not be used as the sole source of information in making administrative decisions because they are more lenient and biased than ratings provided by other sources, such as a direct supervisor.[29] This may explain why only 16% of HR managers report that their organizations include self-appraisals as part of their performance management systems.[30] Fortunately, self-ratings tend to be less lenient when they are used for developmental as opposed to administrative purposes. In addition, the following suggestions are likely to improve the quality of self-appraisals:

- *Use comparative as opposed to absolute measurement systems.* For example, instead of asking individuals to rate themselves using a scale ranging from "poor" to "excellent," provide a relative scale that allows them to compare their performance with that of others (e.g., "below average," "average," "above average"). Other options in terms of comparative systems were discussed in Chapter 5.

- *Allow employees to practice their self-rating skills.* Provide multiple opportunities for self-appraisal because the skill of self-evaluation may well be one that improves with practice.
- *Assure confidentiality.* Provide reassurance that performance information collected from oneself will not be disseminated and shared with anyone other than the direct supervisor and other relevant parties (e.g., members of the same work group).
- *Emphasize the future.* The development plan section of the form should receive substantial attention. The employee should indicate his plans for future development and accomplishments.

6-5-5 Customers

Customers provide yet another source of performance information because they participate in performance touchpoints in many types of industries, occupations, and jobs.[31] Although collecting information from customers can be a costly and time-consuming process, performance information provided by customers is particularly useful for jobs that require a high degree of interaction with the public. Moreover, performance information can also be collected from *internal* customers. For example, line managers may provide performance data regarding their HR representative.

Although the clients served may not have full knowledge of the organization's strategic direction, they can nevertheless provide useful performance data. For example, consider how this is done at Federal Express (FedEx), which has revised its performance management system to include measures of customer service.[32] FedEx employees 400,000 employees; has a total income of US$1.82 billion; and on average, it ships more than 13 million packages every business day. In 2017, it was ranked as one of Fortune's "100 Best Places to Work For." The company uses a six-item customer-satisfaction survey which is evaluated by a representative sample of the employee's customers at the end of the year. As a result of adding customer input and customer-developed goals to the performance review process, employees are more focused on meeting customer expectations.

FedEx already uses external customer input in evaluating performance, but organizations in other industries have some catching up to do. For example, a study examining appraisal forms used to evaluate the performance of account executives in the largest advertising agencies in the United States found that much more emphasis is placed on internal than on external customers.[33] Specifically, external client feedback was measured in only 12% of the agencies studied. About 27% of agencies do not evaluate the contributions that account executives make to client relationships and to growing the client's business. In a yet more recent study involving individuals in charge of the HR function, only 8% reported that clients and customers provide performance evaluations of employees.[34] In short, many companies might benefit from assessing the performance of employees—including managers—from the perspective not only of internal, but also external customers.

6-5-6 Employee Performance Monitoring and Big Data

In Chapter 1, we discussed the concept of electronic performance monitoring (EPM) briefly. In the past, EPM included surveillance camera systems and computer and phone monitoring systems. At present, EPM includes wearable technologies and smartphones, including Fitbits and mobile GPS tracking applications. Indeed, in the contemporary workplace, every email, instant message, phone call, and mouse click leaves a digital footprint, all of which can be used as data to be included in the performance management system.

EPM sparked a lot of enthusiasm about the availability of Big Data, a generic label used to describe large datasets. Essentially, Big Data is a fancy label for "a lot of data." The availability of Big Data related to the behavior of people in organizations has led to the emergence of "people analytics," "HR analytics," "talent analytics," and "workforce analytics."[35] Essentially, these are different labels used to describe how to collect and analyze Big Data.

But the key issue in terms of collecting, compiling, and analyzing performance data is not Big Data, but *Smart Data*. An analytics mindset means that we collect, compile, and analyze data with the goal of gaining insights that can be used to enhance individual, team, and organizational performance, as well as individual well-being. Having a lot of data does not mean we have good data. We should not be enamored by the presence of Big Data, and instead, should think about the criteria that make data useful and accurate. For example, is the information related to the position in question; are the issues measured specific, concrete, meaningful, and under the control of the employee? From the perspective of employees, is EPM considered useful, or a nuisance and an invasion of privacy? The motto "garbage in–garbage out" is particularly relevant in the domain of Big Data and performance analytics.[36]

When implemented well, EPM can lead to very useful data. For example, it can used to collect information on the various dimensions of performance we discussed in previous chapters, including task performance (e.g., productivity) and counterproductive performance such as cyberloafing (i.e., spending time on the Internet engaging in non-work behaviors such as online shopping or gaming). As an illustration, consider tracking software such as WorkIQ and Desk Time, which allows companies to condense real-time employee behavior data into weekly or quarterly reports that are emailed directly to the employee, outlining how she used her computer time throughout the week. Also, mobile tracking systems can yield useful time-oriented data to help employees engage in safer behaviors. This is precisely what semi-truck company Ryder implemented recently: A driver-facing camera and a satellite-based monitoring system to record both positive and negative personal driver behaviors, such as speeding, safe turning, abrupt braking, and authorized and unauthorized stops.[37]

But EPM certainly has challenges, as was learned the hard way by Intermex, a money transfer company based in the United States. For example, EPM can result in feelings of invasion of privacy, perceptions of unfairness, decreased job satisfaction and organizational commitment, and even increased counterproductive performance—just the opposite of what EPM is trying to achieve.[38] You can learn more about some unintended consequences of EPM by reading Box 6-3.

Clearly, EPM and Big Data are becoming more and more prominent in organizational life as we continue to see technological advancements. So, given that EPM is likely to be part of most firms, consider the following four evidence-based suggestions to improve the chances that EPM will lead to positive results[39]:

Box 6-3

Company Spotlight: Employee Performance Monitoring at Intermex

Intermex is licensed in 49 states in the United States to send money to 17 countries in Latin America. Intermex offers customers the ability to send money online or in any of over 4,400 locations. The company's management required employees to download a mobile resource management application called Xora that provided useful on-the-go web services for employees that often engage in client-related communication and travel. The goal was for the app to gather useful information about employee whereabouts and transportation metrics during work hours. But Xora also collected location information via GPS 24 hours a day, 7 days a week in order to function efficiently. Myrna Arias, an Intermex employee, objected to the constant surveillance and requested that the application only be activated during work hours. Her manager insisted that Xora be active at all times for client call purposes, but also bragged to Arias about the exceptional accuracy of the application, claiming that he could see how fast she was driving at any given time, including outside of working hours. Perturbed by the manager's indiscreet use of the application and her now perceived loss of privacy, she decided to deactivate the application for her own privacy concerns. Despite being an excellent employee, Arias was scolded for her actions and was soon fired for noncompliance, leading to a lengthy lawsuit with damages of more than US$500,000 for lost wages. The lesson? It is critical to consider employee reactions before implementing employee performance monitoring systems.[40]

1. *Be transparent.* Employees need to know that they are being monitored. In fact, employee reactions will be affected by their perceptions of justice and the most negative reactions to EPM come from employees who do not know whether they are being monitored, why they are being monitored, or how they are being monitored.

2. *Be aware of all potential employee reactions.* Even when perceived as fair, EPM is nevertheless likely to be perceived as invasive. Also, employees respond differently to two types of EPM because they target different aspects of the employee. First, *passive monitoring* typically concerns artifacts of employee behavior, such as emails and number of phone calls. Second, *active monitoring* involves evaluating real-time location (i.e., GPS, surveillance cameras), computer (i.e., time spent on computer), or Internet use (i.e., website tracking). Consider making sure you do the following to minimize negative reactions: (1) if there is a choice, use the least invasive technique possible, (2) make sure employees understand the reasoning behind the decision and have an opportunity to voice their opinions and concerns, and (3) make sure employees understand the details of the monitoring system (e.g., what information is collected and stored and how is it used).

3. *Use EPM for learning and development.* Employees are more likely to accept EPM when it is used for learning and development purposes. For example, in the case of Ryder, it would be important to use the resulting data in subsequent training programs teaching drivers how to improve their safe-turning skills.

4. *Restrict EPM to job-related behaviors and behaviors.* As in the case described in Box 6-3, EPM can blur the boundaries between work and personal life. Make sure that data collected are job-related.

6-5-7 Disagreement Across Sources of Performance Data: Is This Really a Problem?

If performance information is collected from more than one source, it is likely that there will be some overlap in the dimensions measured.[41] For example, a manager's peers and direct supervisor may rate him on the same competency "communication." In addition to the overlapping dimensions across sources, each source is likely to evaluate performance dimensions that are unique to each source. For example, direct reports may evaluate "delegation," but this competency may not be included on the form used by the direct supervisor. Once the competencies and results that need to be measured are identified for a particular position, a decision needs to be made regarding which source of information will be used to assess each dimension. Regardless of the final decision, it is important that employees take an active role in deciding which sources will rate which dimensions. Active participation in the process is likely to enhance acceptance of results and perceptions that the system is fair.

When the same dimension is evaluated across sources, we should not necessarily expect ratings to be similar.[42] Different sources disagreeing about an employee's performance is not necessarily a problem. For example, self-ratings of salespeople do not necessarily agree with the ratings given by their direct supervisor, which may indicate misunderstandings regarding the nature of performance.[43] Also, those rating the same employee may be drawn from different organizational levels, and they probably observe different facets of the employee's performance, even if they are evaluating the same general competency (e.g., "communication" or "sales behavior"). In fact, the behavioral indicators for the same competency may vary across sources. For example, an employee may be able to communicate very well with his superior, but not very well with his direct reports. The important issue to take into account is that for each source, the behaviors and results to be rated must be defined clearly so that biases are minimized. In terms of feedback, however, there is no need to come up with one overall conclusion regarding the employee's performance. On the contrary, it is important that the employee receive information on how her performance was rated by each of the sources used. This is the crux of what are called 360-degree feedback systems, which are discussed in more detail in Chapter 8. When feedback is broken down by source, the employee can place particular attention and effort on the different performance touchpoints.

If disagreements are found, a decision must be made regarding the relative importance of the rating provided by each source. For example, is it equally important to please external and internal customers? Is communication an equally important competency regarding direct reports and peers? Answering these questions can lead to assigning differential weights to the scores provided by the different sources in computing the overall performance score used for administrative purposes.

6-6 UNDERSTANDING INTENTIONAL RATING DISTORTION: A MODEL OF RATER MOTIVATION

Regardless of who rates performance, performance ratings may be intentionally distorted or inaccurate. When this happens, incorrect decisions may be made; employees are likely to feel they are treated unfairly; and the organization is more prone to litigation. In other words, when performance ratings are distorted, the performance management system not only fails to result in desired outcomes, but also, may lead to very negative consequences for employees and the organization. To prevent these negative outcomes, we need to understand why raters are likely to provide distorted ratings. We address intentional distortion here and unintentional distortion in Chapter 7.

Intentional rating behaviors are influenced by (1) the motivation to provide accurate ratings and (2) the motivation to distort ratings.[44] The motivation to provide accurate ratings is determined by whether the rater expects positive and negative consequences of accurate ratings and by whether the probability of receiving these rewards and punishments will be high if accurate ratings are provided. Similarly, the motivation to distort ratings is determined by whether the rater expects any positive and negative consequences of rating distortion and by the probability of experiencing such consequences if ratings are indeed distorted. Consider a supervisor and his motivation to provide accurate ratings. What will the supervisor gain if ratings are accurate? What will he lose? Will his own performance be rated higher and will he receive any rewards if this happens? Or will the relationship with her direct reports suffer? The answers to these questions provide information about whether this supervisor is likely to be motivated to provide accurate ratings. Similarly, are there any positive and negative consequences associated with rating distortion? What is the probability that this will indeed happen? The answers to these questions will determine the supervisor's motivation to distort ratings.

There are motivational barriers that prevent raters from providing accurate performance information. Raters may be motivated to distort performance information and provide inflated or deflated ratings.[45] Rating inflation is usually called *leniency error* (i.e., when raters assign high lenient ratings to most or all employees) and deflation is usually called *severity error* (i.e., raters assign low ratings to most or all employees).[46] In fact, supervisors may not even be trying to measure performance accurately, and instead, may attempt to use performance ratings for other goals that are unrelated, and often run completely counter, to what a good performance management system is trying to accomplish.[47] For example, a supervisor may be motivated to provide inflated ratings to:

- *Maximize the merit raise and rewards.* A supervisor may want to produce the highest possible reward for her employees and she knows this will happen if she provides the highest possible performance ratings.
- *Encourage employees.* A supervisor may believe that employees' motivation will be increased if they receive high performance ratings.
- *Avoid creating a written record.* A supervisor may not want to leave a "paper trail" regarding an employee's poor performance because such documentation may eventually lead to negative consequences for the employee in question. This situation is possible if the supervisor and employee have developed a friendship.
- *Avoid confrontation with employees.* A supervisor may feel uncomfortable providing negative feedback, and to avoid a possible confrontation with the employee, he may decide to take what may seem like a less painful path and give inflated performance ratings.
- *Promote undesired employees out of unit.* A supervisor may believe that if an employee receives very high ratings, he may be promoted out of the

unit. The supervisor may regard this as an effective way to get rid of undesirable or disliked employees.

- *Make the manager look good to his own supervisor.* A supervisor may believe that if everyone receives very high performance ratings, she will be considered an effective unit leader. Moreover, when the performance ratings for the manager himself depend on the performance of her direct reports, managers are likely to inflate their direct reports' ratings.[48]

We can understand each of the reasons for a supervisor's choosing to inflate ratings using a *model of rater motivation*. For example, looking good in the eyes of one's own supervisor can be regarded as a positive consequence of providing inflated ratings. Avoiding a possible confrontation with an employee can also be regarded as a positive consequence of providing inflated ratings. Thus, given these anticipated positive consequences of rating inflation, the supervisor may choose to provide distorted ratings.

Supervisors may also be motivated to provide ratings that are artificially deflated. Some reasons for this are to:

- *Shock an employee.* A supervisor may believe that giving an employee a "shock treatment" and providing deflated performance ratings will jolt the employee, demonstrating that there is a problem.
- *Teach a rebellious employee a lesson.* A supervisor may wish to punish an employee or force an employee to cooperate with the supervisor and believes that the best way to do this is to give deflated performance ratings.
- *Send a message to the employee that he should consider leaving.* A supervisor lacking communication skills may wish to convey the idea that an employee should leave the unit or organization. Providing deflated performance ratings may be seen as a way to communicate this message.
- *Build a strongly documented, written record of poor performance.* A supervisor may wish to get rid of a particular employee and decides that the best way to do this is to create a paper trail of substandard performance.

We can also understand the psychological mechanisms underlying the decision to provide deflated ratings. For example, if shocking employees and building strongly documented records about employees are considered to be positive consequences of rating deflation, it is likely that the supervisor will choose to provide distorted ratings.

Fundamentally, this discussion should allow us to see that the process of evaluating performance can be filled with emotional overtones and hidden political and personal agendas that are driven by the goals and motivation of the person providing the rating.[49] If raters are not motivated to provide accurate ratings, they are likely to use the performance management system to achieve political and other goals, such as rewarding allies and punishing enemies or competitors, instead of using it as a tool to improve employee, and ultimately, organizational performance.[50] Thus, it is important to understand the influence of context on the accuracy of performance ratings and also be aware that performance measurement does not take place in a vacuum, but as mentioned throughout this text, in an organizational context with written and unwritten norms.[51]

Rating Inflation	Rating Deflation
Maximize the merit raise and rewards	Shock employees
Encourage employees	Teach a rebellious employee a lesson
Avoid creating a written record	Send a message that employee should
Avoid a confrontation with employees	consider leaving
Promote undesired employees out of unit	Build a record of poor performance
Make manager look good to his or her supervisor	

TABLE 6-3
Reasons for Rating Distortion

Table 6-3 summarizes the reasons discussed earlier for why raters are likely to inflate or deflate ratings. What can be done to prevent conscious distortion of ratings? Considering a model of rater motivation, we need to provide *incentives* so that raters will be convinced that they have more to gain by providing accurate ratings than they do by providing inaccurate ratings.[52] For example, if a supervisor is able to see the advantages of a well-implemented performance management system, as opposed to one dominated by office politics, she will be motivated to help the system succeed. Also, if a supervisor believes there is accountability in the system, and ratings that are overly lenient are likely to be easily discovered, resulting in an embarrassing situation for the supervisor, leniency is also likely to be minimized. Lenient ratings may be minimized when supervisors understand they will have to justify their ratings to their own supervisors.[53] In terms of increasing accountability, specific recommendations include the following[54]:

1. *Have raters justify their ratings.* Ratings are more accurate when raters are told they will have to justify their ratings to someone with authority, such as their own supervisors. However, rating accuracy does not necessarily improve if raters need to justify their ratings to others with less authority, such as their own direct report.

2. *Have the raters justify their ratings in a face-to-face meeting.* Ratings are also more accurate when the rating justifications are offered in a face-to-face meeting, compared to justifications offered in writing only.

In a nutshell, a supervisor asks herself, "What's in it for me if I provide accurate ratings versus inflated or deflated ratings?" The performance management system needs to be designed in such a way that the benefits of providing accurate ratings outweigh the benefits of providing inaccurate ratings. This may include assessing the performance of the supervisor in how she is implementing performance management within her unit, and communicating that performance management is a key part of a supervisor's job. Also, supervisors need to have tools available to make their job of providing accurate ratings and feedback easier. This includes training on, for example, how to conduct the appraisal interview so that supervisors are able to provide both positive and negative feedback and are skilled at conveying both positive, and especially, negative news regarding performance.

In sum, raters are likely to make intentional errors in rating performance. To understand intentional distortion of ratings, it is critical to consider the motivation of raters and to provide a clear answer to the "What's in it for me?" question. In other words, raters need to be able to see the benefit of providing accurate ratings compared to providing inaccurate ones.

In addition to conscious and intentional errors in the rating process described in this chapter, raters are likely to make unintended errors. Observing information about performance, storing this information in memory, and then recalling it when it is time to fill out the appraisal form is a complex task. This task becomes more difficult with more complex jobs that include several unrelated performance dimensions. Because of the cognitive complexity of the performance evaluation process, raters are likely to make not only intentional, but also unintentional errors in evaluating performance.[55] These errors, and training programs aimed at minimizing these unintentional errors, are discussed in detail in Chapter 7.

SUMMARY POINTS

- Judgments and evaluations of performance are ubiquitous and inescapable in organizations, even if they are not made explicit or called "performance ratings," and instead, labeled "judgments," "achievement metrics," or "expectations." Even if they do not say it openly, supervisors and peers form impressions and evaluate the performance of people around them on a daily basis—although these evaluations are not written down or said out loud. Performance analytics involves the systematic use of techniques for collecting and compiling performance data. Performance analytics is critical to be able to manage individual and team performance. Absent performance analytics, it is difficult to understand whether employees are making progress, to make decisions about promotions and compensation, and to create a "personal growth and development culture" that offers meaningful development and coaching opportunities.
- Appraisal forms are the key data collection tools used to measure performance. Care and attention are required to ensure that the forms include all the necessary components. The most useful forms include the following components (1) basic employee information; (2) accountabilities, objectives, and standards; (3) competencies and behavioral indicators; (4) major achievements and contributions; (5) developmental achievements; (6) developmental needs, plans, and goals; (7) performance touchpoints; (8) employee comments; and (9) signatures. Note, however, that one size does not fit all, and different components are appropriate, based on the purposes of the appraisal.
- Regardless of the specific components included in the appraisal form, there are several features that make appraisal forms particularly effective. These are (1) simplicity, (2) relevancy, (3) descriptiveness, (4) adaptability, (5) comprehensiveness, (6) definitional clarity, (7) communication, and

(8) time orientation. Before it is used, each form needs to be evaluated, based on the extent to which it complies with each of these characteristics.

- For administrative purposes, it is usually desirable to compute an employee's overall performance score. Two approaches are available: judgmental and mechanical. The judgmental procedure considers every aspect of performance, and then, arrives at a fair and defensible summary. The mechanical procedure consists of combining the scores assigned to each performance dimension, usually taking into account the relative weight given to each dimension. The mechanical procedure is recommended over the judgmental procedure, which is more prone to biases. Rounding of overall scores can be implemented (upward or downward), based on the information included in the "Comments" section of the appraisal forms. However, for this to happen, there must be a systematic analysis of this text-based information and raters must be provided clear guidelines regarding what to include in these "Comments" sections.

- It is recommended that the period for the formal review be six months (i.e., semiannual) or three months (i.e., quarterly). This provides fairly frequent opportunities for a formal discussion about performance issues. It is more convenient if the completion of the appraisal form coincides with the fiscal year so that rewards can be allocated shortly after the employee has received her performance review.

- Performance management systems can include up to six separate formal meetings between the supervisor and the direct report (1) system inauguration, (2) self-appraisal, (3) classical performance review, (4) merit/salary review, (5) development plan, and (6) objective setting. In practice, these meetings are usually condensed into two or so meetings during each review cycle. One point that should be emphasized is that these are *formal* meetings. Informal "check-in" meetings involving a discussion of performance issues should take place on an ongoing basis. To create a culture of performance improvement, conversations about performance should be routine and part of everyone's job.

- Several sources can be used to obtain performance information and these include all of the relevant performance touchpoints: supervisors, peers, direct reports, self, and customers, as well as performance monitoring systems that produce Big Data. Before selecting a source, one needs to be sure that it has firsthand knowledge of the employee's performance (i.e., that it is indeed a performance touchpoint). Using each of these sources has advantages and disadvantages, none of which is foolproof, and not all may be available in all situations. However, it is important that employees take part in the process of selecting which sources will evaluate which performance dimensions. Active employee participation in the process is likely to enhance acceptance of results and perceptions that the system is fair.

- Employee performance monitoring (EPM) is now pervasive, given technological advancements. However, to make sure that the resulting Big Data are "Smart Data" (i.e., useful, accurate, and fair), it is important to be transparent (i.e., employees need to know that they are being monitored), to be aware of all potential employee reactions (i.e., even when perceived as fair, EPM is nevertheless likely to be perceived as invasive so it is important to explain how data are collected and how they will be used), use EPM for learning and development purposes, and restrict EPM to job-related behaviors and behaviors.

- When multiple performance touchpoints are used to collect performance data, there may be disagreements in the resulting ratings, even if these multiple sources are rating the same performance dimension. The people rating the same employee may be drawn from different organizational levels, and they may observe different facets of the employee's performance, even if they are evaluating the same general competency (e.g., "communication"). If an overall score is needed that considers all sources, then a weighting mechanism is needed. For example, a decision needs to be made regarding whether performance information provided by the supervisor has more or less relative importance than that provided by customers. There is no need to summarize the information across the sources for feedback purposes; in fact, it is beneficial for the employee to receive feedback broken down by source so the employee can place particular attention and effort on the interactions involving any source that has detected performance deficiencies.

- In providing performance information, raters may make intentional errors. These errors may involve inflating or deflating performance scores. For example, a supervisor may want to avoid a confrontation with his employees, and so, inflate ratings. A peer may believe that providing accurate ratings may jeopardize the relationship with a colleague, and may, consequently, provide inflated ratings.

- When raters provide performance ratings, they are faced with providing either accurate or inaccurate ratings. They weigh the costs and benefits of choosing one or the other path. If the cost/benefit equation does not favor providing accurate ratings, it is likely that ratings will be distorted. When this happens, incorrect decisions may be made, employees are likely to feel they have been treated unfairly, and the organization is more prone to litigation. In other words, when performance ratings are distorted because raters are not motivated to provide accurate scores, the performance management system not only will fail to achieve desired outcomes, but also may lead to very negative consequences for employees and the organization.

- Intentional distortion in ratings can be minimized by providing raters with information about how rating employees accurately will provide them with direct and tangible benefits. No performance management system is foolproof, and performance ratings are inherently subjective; however, implementing interventions that enhance accountability such as having to justify ratings to superiors in a face-to-face meeting and incentives associated with accurate ratings provides raters with the needed motivation to minimize intentional distortion.

EXERCISE 6-1 CHOOSING A PERFORMANCE APPRAISAL FORM VENDOR

The goal of this exercise is to critically review the performance appraisal forms offered by various vendors. At the end of your exercise, you will present your findings to the rest of the class.

Steps:

1. Conduct a Google search for performance appraisal vendors and identify five that you will use for this exercise.

   a. Useful websites include, for example, those maintained by the Society for Human Resource Management (SHRM),[a] HR-Guide,[b] and Capterra[c]

2. Evaluate the performance appraisal forms that the vendors provide.

   a. As a first step, examine if the forms contain the following components: (Hint: Section 6-1 Useful Components of Appraisal Forms provides greater detail about each of these components.)
      * Basic employee information
      * Accountabilities, objectives, and standards
      * Competencies and behavioral indicators
      * Major achievements and contributions
      * Developmental achievements
      * Developmental needs, plans, and goals
      * Performance touchpoints
      * Employee comments
      * Signatures

   b. Second, assign a score from 0 (lowest) to 10 (highest) to each form on each of the features listed below, and note the reasons for the score you assign. Total the score for each form. (Hint: Section 6-2 Desirable Features of Appraisal Forms provides greater detail about each of these features.)
      * Simplicity
      * Relevancy
      * Descriptiveness
      * Adaptability
      * Comprehensiveness
      * Definitional clarity
      * Communication
      * Time orientation

[a] Society for Human Resource Management. (2017). *Performance management*. Available at: http://vendor-directory.shrm.org/category/talent-management/performance-management
[b] HR-Guide.com. (2017). Performance appraisal systems/vendors. Available at: http://www.hr-guide.com/Performance/Appraisal_Systems_Vendors.htm
[c] Capterra. (2017). Top performance appraisal software products. Available at: http://www.capterra.com/performance-appraisal-software/

    c. Next, review how the form computes the overall performance score. (Hint: Section 6-3 Determining Overall Rating clarifies and provides examples of these strategies.)

- ◆ Does it use a judgmental or mechanical strategy?
- ◆ Does it include space for "Comments" or "Feedback?"

3. Examine the vendor's website to determine what other performance management software/applications/solutions they offer. These may include, for example:

    a. Skills-matrices and competency worksheets

    b. App-based software that allows for real-time performance measurement entry

    c. Observation checklists

    d. Employee evaluation dashboards

    e. Rater training programs

4. Based on your critical assessment, identify the top two appraisal forms and the top two performance appraisal vendors (Note: The top two forms may or may not come from the top two vendors).

    a. For the forms, remember to take into account all three aspects listed in Step 2 (i.e., components, total score for features, and overall score computing method)

    b. For the vendors, consider issues such as customizability, ease-of-use and implementation, and cost.

5. Prepare a brief report, including a 10-minute presentation describing the best vendors and forms you found.

    a. Make sure to highlight why you chose the particular forms/vendors.

    b. Note at least two improvements that could be made to each of the top-two forms.

EXERCISE 6-2 EMPLOYEE PERFORMANCE MONITORING AT TUMGO: GOOD OR BAD IDEA?

Tumgo, a leading energy drink maker, was facing a challenge in managing its sales force and distributing its drinks to customers and retailers spread throughout the nation. As the company's sales force continued to grow, it needed a better way to manage its distribution network and the growing number of remote employees. Faced with this challenge, Tumgo's Vice President of Sales decided to implement TumStreetsmart (Tum), an employee performance monitoring system (EPM) that uses mobile phones' GPS to track employees' locations.

Tum allows dispatchers to see the exact location of remote employees on a map, and uses mobile forms to gather data from the field, such as how fast employees are driving at any given point of time to assist and automate dispatch decisions.[a,b] By doing so, Tum enables companies to improve dispatch decisions, reduce fuel consumption and overtime, and increase the productivity and efficiency of the fleet. The system also allows the employer to know exactly when employees sign in using mobile apps, rather than paper time sheets, and their location (e.g., whether someone signs in from home).[c] Finally, information from the system is integrated with payroll software, simplifying the payment process and saving administrative time, thus allowing for more accurate billing. Overall, the system increases efficiency by saving time, saving fuel, providing faster customer service. In order to function as efficiently as possible, Tum needs to collect information via its GPS technology 24 hours a day, 7 days a week.

By implementing Tum, Tumgo will be able to track how many miles per hour are covered by its sales force, how many stops they made each day, and how long they spent at each stop. This will also enable the company to improve customer service by making sure every store is visited regularly. To implement Tum, Tumgo required all employees to download the application onto their mobile devices, and to ensure the efficiency of the software, keep the application activated 24 hours a day.

Steps:
One group of students will argue in favor of the employee performance management system (Tum), while the other group will argue against the system. As you develop arguments against or for Tum, consider the following issues:

- Usefulness in achieving the company's goals (Is the data being collected useful and accurate? Is the information being collected related to the position in question?)
- Effectiveness in delivering goals (Will the EPM provide data on issues that are specific, meaningful, and under the control of the employees?)
- Employee reactions to the system (e.g., perceptions of fairness, job satisfaction/morale, commitment, stress and employee well-being)
- Effect of system on employee performance (effects on counterproductive workplace behaviors, such as absenteeism or tardiness, productivity changes)
- Acceptability of the system
- Legal and ethical issues
- Privacy concerns
- Implementation of the system

[a] This case is based loosely on Rockstar Energy: Xora. (n.d.). Retrieved January 3, 2018, from http://wwwstg .xora.com/blog/success-stories/rockstar-energy/
[b] Tomczak, D. L., Lanzo, L. A., & Aguinis, H. (2018). Evidence-based recommendations for employee performance monitoring. *Business Horizons, 61*, 251–259.
[c] Zetlin, M. (2009, May). Keeping tabs on mobile workers. *Inc.* Retrieved January 3, 2018, from https:// www.inc.com/telecom/articles/200905/tracking.html

Judgmental and Mechanical Methods of Assigning Overall Performance Score at *The Daily Planet*

The form here shows performance ratings obtained by David Kuhn, a hypothetical reporter at a major newspaper in the United States. First, use the judgmental method to come up with his overall performance score. What is Kuhn's overall[a] performance score?

Second, the form below actually omitted weight information for the various competencies. The weights are the following:

Now, compute Kuhn's overall performance score using the weights in the table. Is there a difference between the score computed using a subjective, rather than the mechanical method? If yes, what are the implications of these differences for the employee being rated, for the supervisor, and for the organization?

Competency	Weight
Producvtivity	.15
Quality of work	.50
Dependability and adherence to company values and policies	.25
Contribution to effectiveness of others/unit	.10

Name: David Kuhn	Job Title: Reporter			
Dept.: International	Supervisor: John DuBoss			
Performance Period:	from Jan 19	to Dec 19		
Job Description: Researches and writes news, features, analyses, human interest stories. Develops and cultivates news sources and contacts. Completes assignments by deadlines, ensuring accuracy by verifying sources. Attends newsworthy events and interviews key sources. Respects confidentiality as appropriate.				
	Unacceptable	Does not fully meet standards	Fully meets standards	Significantly exceeds standards	Outstanding
Productivity—Production is high relative to time and resources consumed; develops expected number of stories and covers beat adequately to ensure stories are detected as they break; stories are developed within time frame that enables deadlines to be met; and appropriate reviews are performed as they are refined.	1	②	3	4	5

[a]Adapted from R. J. Greene, 2003, "Contributing to Organizational Success Through Effective Performance Appraisal," Alexandria, VA, Society for Human Resource Management.

Quality of work—Work meets quality standards and established editorial standards; stories are written in clear and appropriate manner, are consistent with editorial policy, and are fair and balanced; research is thorough and encompasses all relevant sources, which are verified to ensure accuracy; works with editors to revise and improve content; develops and maintains network of contacts who can provide early notification of breaking stories.	1	2	3	④	5
Dependability and adherence to company values and policies—Consistently meets deadlines; conforms to attendance policies; adapts to work demands; conforms to established values and policies; adheres to ethical standards of the paper and the profession; respects confidentiality as appropriate; behaves in manner that enhances the image of the paper.	1	2	3	4	⑤
Contribution to effectiveness of others/unit—Works with others within and outside the unit in a manner that improves their effectiveness; shares information and resources; develops effective working relationships; builds consensus; constructively manages conflict; contributes to the effectiveness of own unit/group and the paper.	1	②	3	4	5

CASE STUDY 6-2

Minimizing Distortions in Performance Data at Expert Engineering, Inc.

Under various engineer titles, veteran engineer Demetri worked for Expert Engineering, Inc. for almost 15 years. He has recently been promoted to the position of Principal at the engineering firm. The firm's performance evaluation history is both unique and long. All principals are involved in evaluating engineers because the founders of the firm believed in multiple source evaluation and feedback to prevent favoritism and promote a merit-based culture. At the same time, the firm has a long history of using quality performance appraisal forms and review meetings to better ensure accurate performance evaluations. Several months ago, however, the firm initiated a big hiring initiative of a dozen new engineers, nine of whom turn out to be graduates from Purdue University, which is the same university from which Demetri graduated. Indeed, Demetri was active in moving forward the hiring initiative. There is tension and discontent among the other principals, who fear that a time of unchecked favoritism, biased performance ratings, and unfair promotion decisions is on the rise.

1. Provide a detailed discussion of the intentional rating distortion factors that may come into play in this situation.
2. Evaluate the kinds of interventions you could implement to minimize intentional rating distortion, and its reasons, that you have described. What do you recommend and why?

ENDNOTES

1. Kadakia, C. (2016). *Eliminating performance reviews: Those who do it well vs. those who don't.* Retrieved January 2, 2018, from http://www.huffingtonpost.com/crystal-kadakia/eliminating-performance-r_b_8595610.html

2. *Gap Inc. encourages employees to grow, performance and succeed without ratings.* Retrieved January 2, 2018, from https://www.e-reward.co.uk/uploads/editor/files/GapInc_Case_Study.pdf

3. Adler, S., Campion, M., Colquitt, A., Grubb, A., Murphy, K., Ollander-Krane, R., & Pulakos, E. (2016). Getting rid of performance ratings: Genius or folly? A debate. *Industrial and Organizational Psychology, 9,* 219–252.

4. Adapted from Grote, D. (1996). *The complete guide to performance appraisal* (Chap. 10). New York, NY: AMACOM.

5. Cambon, L., & Steiner, D. (2015). When rating format induces different rating processes: The effects of descriptive and evaluative rating modes on discriminability and accuracy. *Journal of Business and Psychology, 30,* 795–812.

6. Grote, D. (1996). *The complete guide to performance appraisal.* New York, NY: AMACOM.

7. Adapted from Workforce Research Center. (2003, April). Busch performance evaluations. *Workforce Online.* Retrieved January 2, 2018, from http://www.workforce.com/2003/03/27/buschs-performance-evaluations

8. Kuncel, N. R., Connelly, B. S., Klieger, D. M., & Ones, D. S. (2013). Mechanical versus clinical data combination in selection and admissions decisions: A meta-analysis. *Journal of Applied Psychology, 98,* 1060–1072.

9. Kraiger, K., & Aguinis, H. (2001). Training effectiveness: Assessing training needs, motivation, and accomplishments. In M. London (Ed.), *How people evaluate others in organizations* (pp. 203–220). Mahwah, NJ: Lawrence Erlbaum.

10. Brutus, S. (2010). Words versus numbers: A theoretical exploration of giving and receiving narrative comments in performance appraisal. *Human Resource Management Review, 20,* 144–157.

11. McKenny, A. F., Aguinis, H., Short, J. C., & Anglin, A. H. (2016). What doesn't get measured does exist: Improving the accuracy of computer-aided text analysis. *Journal of Management.* doi:10.1177/0149206316657594

12. Moriarty-Siler, E. (2017). 10 Tips for next generation benefits. *Benefitspro, 4.*

13. Milliman, J. F., Zawacki, R. A., Schulz, B., Wiggins, S., & Norman, C. A. (1995). Customer service drives 360-degree goal setting. *Personnel Journal, 74,* 136–142.

14. Workforce Research Center. Writing effective co-worker comments. *Workforce Online.* Retrieved January 2, 2018, from http://www.workforce.com/archive/feature/22/28/68/223579.php

15. Adapted from from Grote, D. (1996). *The complete guide to performance appraisal* (Chap. 10). New York, NY: AMACOM.

16. Talbott, S. P. (1994). Peer review drives compensation at Johnsonville. *Personnel Journal, 73,* 126–132.

17. Courter, E. (2006). Measuring up. *Credit Union Management, 29*(6), 30–33.

18. The discussion of the various sources of performance information is based in part on Cascio, W. F., & Aguinis, H. (2019). *Applied psychology in talent management* (8th ed.). Thousand Oaks, CA: Sage Publication.

19. Abu-Doleh, J., & Weir, D. (2007). Dimensions of performance appraisal systems in Jordanian private and public organizations. *International Journal of Human Resource Management, 18,* 75–84.

20. Workforce Research Center. Dear workforce: How are peer reviews used for compensation? *Workforce Online.* Retrieved January 2, 2018, from http://www.workforce.com/archive/article/22/13/94.php

21. Ramsey, W., & Owen, C. (2006). Is there a role for peer review in performance appraisal of medical students? *Medical Education, 40*(2), 95–96.

22. Hollander, E. P. (1954). Buddy ratings: Military research and industrial implications. *Personnel Psychology, 7,* 385–393.

23. Sol, J. (2016). Peer evaluation: Incentives and coworker relations. *Journal of Economics and Management Strategy, 25,* 56–76.

24. Dierdoff, E. C., & Surface, E. A. (2007). Placing peer ratings in context: Systematic influences beyond rate performance. *Personnel Psychology, 60*, 93–126.

25. Jelley, R. B., & Goffin, R. D. (2001). Can performance-feedback accuracy be improved? Effects of rater priming and rating-scale format on rating accuracy. *Journal of Applied Psychology, 86*, 134–145.

26. Jhun, S., Bae, Z., & Rhee, S. (2012). Performance change of managers in two different uses of upward feedback: A longitudinal study in Korea. *International Journal of Human Resource Management, 23*, 4246–4264.

27. Serwer, A. (2005). The education of Michael Dell. *Fortune, 151*(5), 76.

28. Greguras, G. J., Robie, C., Schleicher, D. J., & Goff, M. (2003). A field study of the effects of rating purpose on the quality of multisource ratings. *Personnel Psychology, 56*, 1–21.

29. Hoffman, B., Lance, C. E., Bynum, B., & Gentry, W. A. (2010). Rater source effects are alive and well after all. *Personnel Psychology, 63*, 119–151.

30. Gorman, C. A., Meriac, J. P., Roch, S. G., Ray, J. L., & Gamble, J. S. (2017). An exploratory study of current performance management practices: Human resource executives' perspectives. *International Journal of Selection and Assessment, 25*, 193–202.

31. Simmons, J., & Lovegrove, I. (2005). Bridging the conceptual divide: Lessons from stakeholder analysis. *Journal of Organizational Change Management, 18*, 495–513.

32. Milliman, J. F., Zawacki, R. A., Schulz, B., Wiggins, S., & Norman, C. A. (1995). Customer service drives 360-degree goal setting. *Personnel Journal, 74*, 136–142.

33. Franke, G. R., Murphy, J. H., & Nadler, S. S. (2003). Appraising account executive performance appraisals: Current practices and managerial implications. *Journal of Current Issues & Research in Advertising, 25*, 1–11.

34. Gorman, C. A., Meriac, J. P., Roch, S. G., Ray, J. L., & Gamble, J. S. (2017). An exploratory study of current performance management practices: Human resource executives' perspectives. *International Journal of Selection and Assessment, 25*, 193–202.

35. Handa, D., & Garima. (2014). Human Resource (HR) analytics: Emerging trend in HRM. *International Journal of Research in Commerce & Management, 5*(6), 59–62.

36. Feinzig, S. (2015). Workforce analytics: Practical guidance for initiating a successful journey. *Workforce Solutions Review, 6*(6), 14–17.

37. Bowman, R. (2014, February 11). Is new truck-monitoring technology for safety—Or spying on drivers? *Forbes*. Retrieved January 2, 2018, from http://www.forbes.com/sites/robertbowman/2014/02/11/is-new-truck-monitoring-technology-for-safety-or-spying-on-drivers

38. McNall, L. A., & Stanton, J. M. (2011). Private eyes are watching you: Reactions to location sensing technologies. *Journal of Business and Psychology, 26*, 299–309.

39. Tomczak, D. L., Lanzo, L. A., & Aguinis, H. (2018). Evidence-based recommendations for employee performance monitoring. *Business Horizons, 61*, 251–259.

40. Newman, L. H. (2015). Sales exec says she was fired for uninstalling GPS app that tracked her constantly. *Slate*. Retrieved January 2, 2018, from http://www.slate.com/blogs/future_tense/2015/05/11/intermex_employee_says_she_was_fired_for_deleting_xora_gps_apps.html

41. Bynum, B., Hoffman, B., Meade, A., & Gentry, W. (2013). Reconsidering the equivalence of multisource performance ratings: Evidence for the importance and meaning of rater factors. *Journal of Business and Psychology, 28*, 203–219.

42. Semeijn, J. H., Van Der Heijden, B. M., & Van Der Lee, A. (2014). Multisource ratings of managerial competencies and their predictive value for managerial and organizational effectiveness. *Human Resource Management, 53*, 773–794.

43. Jaramillo, F., Carrillat, F. A., & Locander, W. B. (2005). A meta-analytic comparison of managerial ratings and self-evaluations. *Journal of Personal Selling & Sales Management, 25*, 315–328.

44. Murphy, K. R., & Cleveland, J. N. (2005). *Understanding performance appraisal: Social, organizational, and goal-based perspectives*. Thousand Oaks, CA: Sage Publications.

45. Longenecker, C. O., Sims, H. P., & Gioia, D. A. (1987). Behind the mask: The politics of employee appraisal. *Academy of Management Executive, 1*, 183–193.

46. Dewberry, C., Davies-Muir, A., & Newell, S. (2013). Impact and causes of rater severity/leniency in appraisals without postevaluation communication between raters and rates. *International Journal of Selection and Assessment, 21*, 286–293.

47. Murphy, K. R. (2008). Perspectives on the relationship between job performance and ratings of job performance. *Industrial and Organizational Psychology, 1*, 197–205.

48. Spence, J. R., & Keeping, L. M. (2010). The impact of non-performance information on ratings of job performance: A policy-capturing approach. *Journal of Organizational Behavior, 31*, 587–608.

49. Rosen, C. C., Kacmar, K. M., Harris, K. J., Gavin, M. B., & Hochwarter, W. A. (2017). Workplace politics and performance appraisal: A two-study, multilevel field investigation. *Journal of Leadership and Organizational Studies, 24*, 20–38.

50. Xiaoye May, W., Kin Fai Ellick, W., & Kwong, J. Y. (2010). The roles of rater goals and ratee performance levels in the distortion of performance ratings. *Journal of Applied Psychology, 95*, 546–561.

51. Murphy, K. R. (2008). Explaining the weak relationship between job performance and ratings of job performance. *Industrial and Organizational Psychology, 1*, 148–160.

52. Harari, M. B., & Rudolph, C. W. (2017). The effect of rater accountability on performance ratings: A meta-analytic review. *Human Resource Management Review, 27*, 121–133.

53. Curtis, A. B., Harvey, R. D., & Ravden, D. (2005). Sources of political distortions in performance appraisals: Appraisal purpose and rater accountability. *Group & Organization Management, 30*, 42–60.

54. Mero, N. P., Guidice, R. M., & Brownlee, A. L. (2007). Accountability in a performance appraisal context: The effect of audience and form of accounting on rater response and behavior. *Journal of Management, 33*, 223–252.

55. Ohme, M., & Zacher, H. (2015). Job performance ratings: The relative importance of mental ability, conscientiousness, and career adaptability. *Journal of Vocational Behavior, 87*, 161–170.

7

Rolling Out the Performance Management System

*Good governance with good intentions is the hallmark of our government.
Implementation with integrity is our core passion.*

—*Narendra Modi*

Learning Objectives

By the end of this chapter, you will be able to do the following:

1. Prepare the rollout and implementation of a new or up-dated and revised performance management system by setting up a communication plan, appeals process, rater training program, and pilot test.

2. Create a communication plan that answers the following key questions: What is performance management? How does performance management fit in the organization's strategy? How does everyone benefit from the system? How does the performance management system work? What are everyone's responsibilities? How is performance management related to other key organizational initiatives?

3. Prepare interventions aimed at dealing with cognitive biases (i.e., selective exposure, selective perception, selective retention) and resistance to change, involve all employees and understand their needs, provide facts and consequences of the system, and use multiple channels of communication and credible communicators.

4. Devise an appeals process to enhance the integrity of the performance management system that involves the human resources (HR) department, a panel of managers and peers,

and possibly, a senior-level manager in the role of arbitrator and final decision maker.

5. Anticipate unintentional rating errors such as similar to me, contrast, halo, primacy, recency, negativity, first impression, stereotype, and attribution.

6. Design and implement rater errors, frame of reference, and behavioral observation training programs to minimize the impact of unintentional rating errors.

7. Devise a pilot test of the performance management system using a selected group of employees and managers from the organization.

8. As soon as the performance management system is in place, collect various measurements, such as number of individuals evaluated, quality of performance information gathered, quality of performance discussion meetings, user satisfaction with the system, overall cost/benefit ratio, and unit- and organization-level performance indicators—all of these will provide information regarding the system's effectiveness and the extent to which it is working the way it should and whether it is producing the expected results.

Chapters 4 and 5 described operational details about how to define and measure performance. Chapter 6 described operational details about performance analytics—the process of collecting and compiling performance data. This chapter, the last one in Part II, continues to address operational issues in implementing a performance management system. Specifically, it addresses the steps needed to roll out the system, such as setting up good communication and appeals procedures that will gain system acceptance, implement training programs to minimize unintentional rating errors, and pilot test the system. Finally, the chapter describes how to monitor the system as soon as it is in place to make sure it is working properly. Taken together, these steps are necessary to make sure that performance management is implemented with integrity.

Before we begin, here is an important clarification: The term "implementation" of the performance management system does not refer only to launching an entirely new system. In most cases, an organization will already have some type of performance management system, although it may be closer to a once-a-year performance appraisal system and not very effective. So, by using the term "implementation" we are referring not only to launching a new system from scratch, but also to revising and improving an existing one. For example, it may be the case that the organization is under new leadership, and this new leadership wants to implement a better system.

7-1 COMMUNICATION PLAN

In general, having more and better knowledge of the performance management system leads to greater employee acceptance and satisfaction.[1] Organizations often design a communication plan to ensure that information regarding the performance management system is disseminated widely in the organization. A good communication plan answers the following questions[2]:

- *What is performance management?* Answering this question involves providing general information about performance management, how performance management systems are implemented in other organizations, and the general goals of performance management systems.
- *How does performance management fit into our strategy?* To answer this question, we should provide information on the relation between performance management and strategic planning. Specifically, information is provided on how the performance management system will help accomplish strategic goals. Recall that Chapter 3 addressed this issue in detail.
- *What is in it for me?* A good communication plan describes the benefits of implementing performance management for all those involved.
- *How does it work?* Answering this question entails giving a detailed description of the performance management process and time line: for example, when meetings will take place, what the purposes of each meeting are, and when decisions about rewards will be made.
- *What are my responsibilities?* The communication plan should include information on the role and responsibilities of each person involved at

each stage of the process. For example, it includes a description of the employees' and supervisors' main responsibilities in the performance management process.

- *How is performance management related to other initiatives?* The communication plan should include information on the relationship between performance management and other initiatives and systems, such as training, promotion, and succession planning.

Figure 7-1 summarizes the questions that should be answered in a state-of-the science performance management communication plan. As an example, consider the performance management system for the position of Senior Executive Service (SES), which is a position in U.S. federal agencies such as the Department of Justice, Department of Interior, Department of Energy, and Department of Commerce.[3] SES members serve in key leadership positions directly below the top presidential

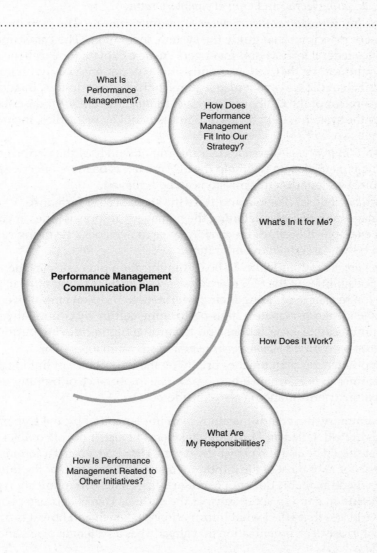

FIGURE 7-1
Performance Management
Communication Plan: Basic
Components

appointees. SES members link the appointees to the rest of the federal government, and they are charged with overseeing various governmental functions in U.S. federal agencies.

The communication plan that the Department of Justice implemented for this performance management system answers each of the questions described earlier and included in Figure 7-1:

- *What is performance management?* The plan states the reasons for the department's implementing a performance management system and discusses what it is expected to accomplish. For example, it explains that performance management aims at promoting efficient and effective attainment of the department's mission, program objectives, and strategic planning initiatives, and it also aims at motivating high levels of achievement and accountability. It also includes definitions of several key terms, including *performance management system*, *performance*, *progress review*, *rating levels*, and *annual summary rating*.

- *How does performance management fit into our strategy?* The plan includes a list of principles that guide the system, including, "The Department of Justice federal leaders and managers create a climate for excellence by communicating their vision, values and expectations clearly." It goes on to detail all of the ways in which leaders in the agency do this. In addition, the director of the Office of Personnel Management (OPM) describes how the system would be used to implement key principles, including excellence.

- *What is in it for me?* There is clear information on how the performance management system will help the SES members be more effective leaders so that the department's mission can be achieved.

- *How does it work?* The plan outlines the steps in a performance management process, detailing the managers' responsibilities at each step. For example, it outlines the performance dimensions, the rating categories, and how to assign an overall rating.

- *What are my responsibilities?* The communication plan outlines the responsibilities of the SES members as well as their rating official, the person in charge of rating their performance. The plan emphasizes that leaders must create a high-performing culture by continually communicating expectations and rewarding high-achieving performers.

- *How is performance management related to other initiatives?* The communication plan touches briefly on the importance of linking system outcomes to performance-based pay. The importance of training to maximize performance is also considered.

In summary, the communication plan implemented by the Department of Justice is quite detailed and provides answers to most, if not all, of the key questions that should be addressed by a good plan. However, even if a communication plan answers all or most of the important questions, the fact that the information has been made available does not necessarily mean the communication plan will be successful in gaining acceptance of the system. This is because people have cognitive biases that affect what information is taken in and how it is processed. Also, in the case of an organization that already has a system in place, and a better one is being rolled out, it is likely that many people will not be comfortable with the change, and might engage in what is called *resistance to change*.[4] We discuss these issues next.

7-1-1 Dealing with Cognitive Biases and Resistance to Change

There are three types of biases that affect the effectiveness of a communication plan, regardless of whether it includes the six components shown in Figure 7-1. Also, these biases are accentuated when people are not willing or interested in change. The biases are *selective exposure*, *selective perception*, and *selective retention*.[5] First, selective exposure is a tendency to expose our minds only to ideas with which we already agree. Those employees who already agree that performance management is a good idea may become involved in the communication plan activities, including reading about the system and attending meetings describing how the system works. On the contrary, those who do not see much value in a performance management system may choose not to read information about it and to not attend meetings about it. Second, selective perception is a tendency to perceive a piece of information as meaning what we would like it to mean even though the information, as intended by the communicator, may mean the exact opposite. Someone who believes performance management is about only rewards and punishments may incorrectly interpret that receiving formal performance feedback at the end of each quarter translates exclusively into receiving a pay increase or a bonus. Third, selective retention is a tendency to remember only those pieces of information with which we already agree. If an employee perceives his employer as vindictive, that employee is not likely to remember information about how the appeals process works or about other fair and equitable aspects of the system.

Selective exposure, selective perception, and selective retention biases are pervasive and could easily render the communication plan ineffective. Fortunately, there are several ways to minimize the negative impact of these biases, and therefore, help gain support for the system. Consider the following[6]:

- *Involve employees.* Involve employees in the design of the system. People support what they help create. The higher the level of participation is in designing the system, the greater the support for the system will be.
- *Understand employee needs.* Understand the needs of the employees and identify ways in which these needs can be met through performance management. For example, do they want more feedback? Are they interested in development activities that would eventually lead to a promotion or a different job within the organization?
- *Strike first.* Create a positive attitude toward the performance system before any negative attitudes and rumors are created. Make communications realistic and do not set up expectations you cannot deliver. Discuss some of the arguments that might be used against the system and provide evidence to counter them.
- *Provide facts and consequences.* Because of the presence of cognitive biases, facts do not necessarily speak for themselves. Clearly explain facts about the system and also explain what they mean or what the consequences are. Do not let employees draw their own conclusions because they may differ from yours.

- *Put it in writing.* In Western cultures, written communications are usually more powerful and credible than spoken communications because they can be carefully examined and challenged for accuracy. Create documentation, which is often posted online for everyone to download, describing the system.
- *Use multiple channels of communication.* Use multiple methods of communication, including face-to-face (especially in the case of small and medium-size organizations) and virtual meetings, email, TED talks, and short video clips. In other words, allow employees to be exposed repeatedly to the same message delivered using different communication channels. Of course, make sure that all channels convey consistent information.
- *Use credible communicators.* Use credible sources to communicate the performance management system. In companies where HR department members are perceived as "HR cops" because they continually emphasize what cannot be done as opposed to how one's job can be done better, it may be better to use a different department or group. In such situations, communication should be delivered by people who are trusted and admired within the organization. It also helps if those delivering the communication and endorsing the system are regarded as key and powerful organizational players.
- *Say it, and then, say it again.* Repeat the information frequently. Because people can absorb only a small amount of information at a time, and may be resistant to change, the information must be repeated frequently.

Table 7-1 summarizes what can be done to minimize cognitive biases, including selective exposure, selective perception, and selective retention. Consider the Department of Justice communication process, described earlier in this chapter. That plan attempts to minimize negative biases and gain support for the performance management system. For example, although it is a government agency and the performance management system is a federal mandate, the Office of Personnel Management (OPM) offered to help managers tailor the systems to their specific agencies. This is likely to help employees become more involved and is also helpful in addressing the specific needs of the employees in the various agencies.

The director of the OPM, who is a credible source of information on the performance management system, set a positive tone and even appealed to employees' patriotism by including a message from the United States President, reminding them of the importance of serving the "American people." The communication plan also provides facts and conclusions about the system. For example, it explains the reasoning for realigning the performance management system with the fiscal year, how to carry out this time line, and the importance of

TABLE 7-1

Interventions to Minimize the Effects of Cognitive Biases and Resistance to Change

Involve employees
Understand employee needs
Strike first
Provide facts and consequences
Put it in writing
Use multiple channels of communication
Use credible communicators
Say it, and then, say it again

doing so. The communication plan is also posted on the department's website. There are also links to other websites with information about performance management. It is not clear whether the Department of Justice disseminated the information using other media, such as short video clips. But all in all, the plan implemented by the Department of Justice is a good example of a communication plan that attempts to minimize the detrimental impact of cognitive biases and resistance to change.

In addition to implementing a communication plan, support for the performance management system can be gained by implementing an appeals process. This topic is discussed next.

7-2 APPEALS PROCESS

The inclusion of an appeals process is important in gaining employee acceptance for the performance management system. The reason is that it allows employees to understand that if there is a disagreement regarding performance ratings or any resulting decisions, then such disagreements can be resolved in an amicable and nonretaliatory way. In addition, the inclusion of an appeals process increases the system's fairness.[7]

When an appeals process is in place, employees have the ability to question two types of issues: judgmental and administrative.[8] Judgmental issues center on the validity of the performance evaluation. For example, an employee may believe that a manager's performance ratings for that employee do not reflect his actual performance. Administrative issues involve whether the policies and procedures were followed. For example, an employee may argue that her supervisor did not meet with her as frequently as he had with her coworkers and that the feedback she is receiving about her performance is not as thorough as that received by her coworkers. Figure 7-2 includes a summary of the three main levels involved in an appeals process.

Typically, when an appeal is first filed, the HR department serves as a mediator between the employee and the supervisor. An appeal sent to the HR department is usually called a Level 1 appeal. The HR department is in a good position to judge whether policies and procedures have been implemented correctly, and also, has good information about the various jobs, levels of performance expected, and levels of performance of other employees within the unit and organization. The HR department gathers the necessary facts and brings them to the attention of either the rater to encourage reconsideration of the decision that caused the appeal or to the complainant to explain why there have been no biases or violations. In other words, the HR department either suggests corrective action to the supervisor or informs the employee that the decision or procedures were correct.

If the rater does not believe corrective action should be taken or if the employee does not accept the HR decision, and the appeal continues, then the process moves to Level 2. In Level 2, there is an outside arbitrator that usually consists of a panel of peers and managers. The panel reviews the case, asks questions, interviews witnesses, researches precedents, and reviews policy. Then, they simply take a vote to make the decision. In some cases, the vote represents

FIGURE 7-2

Steps in Appeals Process

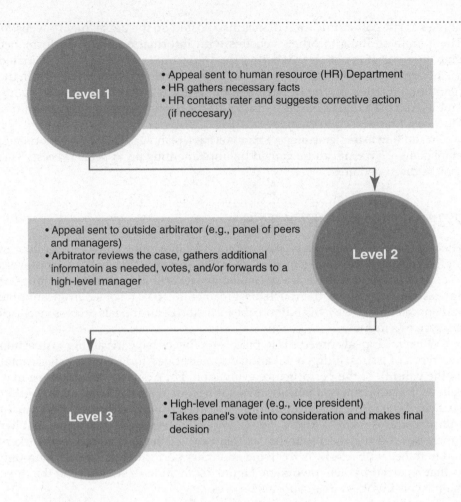

Level 1
- Appeal sent to human resource (HR) Department
- HR gathers necessary facts
- HR contacts rater and suggests corrective action (if neccesary)

- Appeal sent to outside arbitrator (e.g., panel of peers and managers)
- Arbitrator reviews the case, gathers additional informatoin as needed, votes, and/or forwards to a high-level manager

Level 2

Level 3
- High-level manager (e.g., vice president)
- Takes panel's vote into consideration and makes final decision

the final decision. In other cases, the vote is forwarded to a high-level manager (vice president or higher level), who takes the panel's vote into consideration in making the final decision.

Box 7-1 shows some of the key sections of the performance management appeals process for employees at the University of Lethbridge in Canada. The appeals process is intended to air concerns and to resolve disagreements. The purpose of this specific policy is to provide employees and management with a means for resolving disagreements involving performance evaluations.

The information shown in the box describing the appeals process at the University of Lethbridge spells out the steps involved, the time line that should be followed, and the various outcomes that could be expected. Given that such a policy is in place, employees are given assurances that if there is an appeal, the case will be treated fairly and as objectively as possible. Once again, this should help gain support for the performance management system. From your perspective, how does this process compare to the one summarized in Figure 7-2? Is there anything missing that the University of Lethbridge should consider adding?

Box 7-1

Company Spotlight: University of Lethbridge Performance Management Appeals Process

Purpose

The Appeal Process is a means for Employees and Supervisors to resolve disagreements involving the Performance Evaluation process. This Appeal Process does not in any way circumvent or prohibit an employee from the invocation of Article 12; Grievance Procedure.

Principles

All appeals:

1. Are to be conducted with diplomacy and impartiality.
2. Aspire to construct and provide the best possible information.
3. Maintain confidentiality and respect for the individual.

Process

If an Employee disagrees with the result of their Performance Evaluation, as conducted by their Supervisor, the Employee may appeal in writing to the Office of Human Resources. A request for appeal must be received within ten (10) Work Days of the date of the Employee's signature on the Performance Evaluation. The deadline for all written appeals is the last work day in June. Late applications shall not be subject to appeal except under extraordinary circumstances as determined by the Associate VP HR and Admin. Submission of an appeal must be with the use of the Performance Evaluation Appeal Form.

Level 1

Following the receipt of an appeal, a member of the Human Resources Department will conduct a confidential investigation, gathering information in discussion with the Employee, the Supervisor, and where necessary other informed parties. A recommendation for resolution will be put forward by HR to the Supervisor and Employee. If an agreement cannot be reached at Level 1 then the appeal will move to Level 2 of the Appeals Process.

Level 2

The appeal will be brought before a Performance Evaluation Committee whose membership shall consist of three (3) AUPE (Alberta Union of Provincial Employees) Representatives, three (3) Representatives of the Board and a Facilitator from Human Resources. The committee members will remain consistent for all appeals relating to the evaluation period except in circumstances where members with a substantial personal or professional relationship with the employee under appeal shall not participate in the review.

The committee will consider the information collected by Human Resources in Level 1, as well as any relevant evidence that may be offered by the Employee and the Supervisor, and may seek out other sources that the committee deems to be of relevance to the appeal. The committee will have five (5) Work Days from the date the committee was convened to review the evidence and then formally issue a ruling.

Level 3

In the event that an agreement is not achieved in Level 2 the matter will continue as a grievance commencing at Step 2 of Article 12: Grievance Procedure.

Once a consensus has been reached and signed by all parties involved, at any point in the appeal process, the revised Performance Evaluation will be final and not subject to further appeal. All documentation will be forwarded to the Human Resources department and will remain confidential. The employee may at anytime withdraw the appeal request by writing to the Associate VP HR and Admin who will inform the members of the committee.

Source: Performance Management—Appeals Process & Appeals Form. Available online at https://www.uleth.ca/hr/performance-management-appeals-process-appeals-form. Retrieved on January 2, 2018.

7-3 TRAINING PROGRAMS FOR MINIMIZING UNINTENTIONAL RATING ERRORS

Training the raters is another necessary step to prepare for the rollout of the performance management system. Training not only provides participants in the performance management system with needed skills and tools to do a good job implementing it, but also helps increase satisfaction with the system.[9]

In Chapter 6, we discussed what to do to minimize intentional rating distortion. But *unintentional errors* also affect the accuracy of ratings. Specifically, before rolling out the performance management system, we should consider implementing rater training programs that address how to identify and rank job activities and how to observe, record, and measure performance.

7-3-1 Rater Error Training

Many performance management systems can be plagued with rating errors. In fact, rating errors are usually the reason why so many performance management systems are usually criticized.[10] Accordingly, the goal of rater error training (RET) is to make raters aware of what rating errors they are likely to make and to help them develop strategies to minimize those errors. In other words, the goal of RET is to increase rating accuracy by making raters aware of the unintentional errors they are likely to make.

RET programs generally include definitions of the most typical errors and a description of possible causes for those errors. Such programs also allow trainees to view examples of common errors and to review suggestions on how to avoid making errors. This can be done by showing video vignettes designed to elicit rating errors and asking trainees to fill out appraisal forms regarding the situations they observed on the video clips. Finally, a comparison is made between the ratings provided by the trainees and the correct ratings. The trainer then explains why the errors took place, which specific errors were made, and ways to overcome the errors in future.

RET does not guarantee increased accuracy. Raters do become aware of the possible errors they can make, but precisely because many of the errors are unintentional, simple awareness of the errors does not mean that errors will not be made. Nevertheless, it may be useful to expose raters to the range of possible errors. These errors include the following:

- *Similar to me error.* Similarity leads to attraction, so we tend to favor those who are similar to us. Consequently, in some cases, raters are more likely to give higher performance ratings to those employees who are perceived to be more similar to them in terms of attitudes, preferences, personality, and demographic variables, including race and gender.
- *Contrast error.* Contrast error occurs when, even if an absolute measurement system is in place, raters compare individuals with one another, instead of against predetermined standards. For example, when a rater rates an individual of only average performance, the rating may actually be higher than deserved if the other individuals rated by the same rater display substandard performance levels: the average performer may seem to be much better in comparison to the others. This error is most likely to occur

when raters complete multiple appraisal forms at the same time because, in such situations, it is difficult to ignore the ratings given to other employees.

- *Halo error.* Halo error occurs when raters fail to distinguish between the different aspects of performance being rated. Recall, we described this error in Chapter 6 in the context of peer evaluations. If an employee receives a high score on one dimension, she also receives a high score on all other dimensions, even though performance may not be even across all dimensions. For example, if an employee has a perfect attendance record, then the rater may give her a high mark on dedication and productivity. The perfect attendance record, however, may be caused by the fact that the employee has large loan payments to make and cannot afford to miss work, not because the employee is actually an excellent overall performer. In other words, being present at work is not the same as being a productive employee. This error is typically caused by the rater's assigning performance ratings based on an overall impression about the employee instead of evaluating each performance dimension independently.

- *Primacy error.* Primacy error occurs when performance evaluation is influenced mainly by information collected during the initial phases of the review period. For example, in rating communication skills, the rater gives more weight to incidents involving communication that took place toward the beginning of the review period, as opposed to incidents taking place at all other times.

- *Recency error.* Recency error occurs when performance evaluation is influenced mainly by information gathered during the last portion of the review period. This is the opposite of the primacy error: raters are more heavily influenced by behaviors taking place toward the end of the review period, instead of giving equal importance and paying attention to incidents occurring throughout the entire review period.

- *Negativity error.* Negativity error occurs when raters place more weight on negative information than on positive or neutral information. For example, a rater may have observed one negative interaction between the employee and a customer and several positive interactions in which customers' expectations were surpassed. The rater may focus on the one negative incident in rating the "customer service" dimension. The negativity error explains why most people have a tendency to remember negative rather than positive news that they read online or watch on television.

- *First impression error.* First impression error occurs when raters make an initial favorable or unfavorable judgment about an employee, and then, ignore subsequent information that does not support the initial impression. This type of error can be confounded with the "similar to me error" because first impressions are likely to be based on the degree of similarity: the more similar the person is to the rater, the more positive the first impression will be.

- *Spillover error.* Spillover error occurs when scores from previous review periods unjustly influence current ratings. For example, a rater makes the assumption that an employee who was an excellent performer in the previous period ought to be an excellent performer during the current period also, and provides performance ratings consistent with this belief.

- *Stereotype error.* Stereotype error occurs when a rater has an oversimplified view of individuals, based on group membership. That is, a rater may have a belief that certain groups of employees (e.g., women) are unassertive in their communication style. In rating women, therefore, he may automatically describe communication as being "unassertive" without actually having any behavioral evidence to support the rating.[11] This type of error can also lead to biased evaluations of performance when an individual (e.g., woman) violates stereotypical norms by working in an occupation that does not fit the stereotype (e.g., assembly of airplane parts).[12] This type of error can also result in consistently lower performance ratings for members of certain groups. For example, a study including an identical sample of black and white workers found that white raters gave higher ratings to white workers relative to black workers than did black raters. In other words, if a white worker is rated, then it does not really matter whether the rater is black or white; however, if a black worker is rated, the rater's ethnicity matters because this worker is likely to receive a higher rating from a black rater than from a white rater.[13]

- *Attribution error.* The attribution error takes place when a rater attributes poor performance to an employee's dispositional tendencies (e.g., personality, abilities) instead of features of the situation (e.g., malfunctioning equipment). In other words, different raters may place different relative importance on the environment in which the employee works in making performance evaluations. If raters make incorrect inferences about the employees' dispositions and ignore situational characteristics, actions taken to improve performance may fail because the same situational constraints may still be present (e.g., obsolete equipment).[14]

As a recap, Table 7-2 includes a summary list of unintentional errors that raters may make in assigning performance ratings. RET exposes raters to the different errors and their causes; however, being aware of unintentional errors does not mean that raters will no longer make these errors.[15] Awareness is certainly a good first step, but we need to go further if we want to minimize unintentional errors. One fruitful possibility is the implementation of a frame of reference training.

7-3-2 Frame of Reference Training

Frame of reference (FOR) training helps improve rater accuracy by thoroughly familiarizing raters with the various performance dimensions to be assessed.[16] The

TABLE 7-2

Unintentional Errors Likely to Be Made in Providing Performance Ratings

Similar to me
Contrast
Halo
Primacy
Recency
Negativity
First impression
Spillover
Stereotype
Attribution

overall goal is to give raters skills so that they can minimize unintentional errors and provide accurate ratings on each performance dimension by developing a common FOR.

A typical FOR training program includes a discussion of the job description for the individuals being rated and the duties involved. Raters are then familiarized with the performance dimensions to be rated by reviewing the definitions for each dimension and discussing examples of good, average, and poor performance. Raters are then asked to use the appraisal forms to be used in the actual performance management system to rate fictitious employees usually shown in video practice vignettes. The trainees are also asked to write a justification for the ratings. Finally, the trainer informs trainees of the correct ratings for each dimension and the reasons for such ratings and discusses differences between the correct ratings and those provided by the trainees. Typically, FOR training programs include the following formal steps[17]:

1. Raters are told that they will evaluate the performance of three employees on three separate performance dimensions.

2. Raters are given an appraisal form and instructed to read it as the trainer reads aloud the definition for each of the dimensions and the scale anchors.

3. The trainer discusses various employee behaviors that illustrate various performance levels for each rating scale included in the form. The goal is to create a common "performance theory" (frame of reference) among raters so that they will agree on the appropriate performance dimension and effectiveness level for different behaviors.

4. Participants are shown a video clip of a practice vignette, including behaviors related to the performance dimensions being rated, and are asked to evaluate the employee's performance using the scales provided.

5. Ratings provided by each participant are shared with the rest of the group and discussed. The trainer seeks to identify which behaviors participants used to decide on their assigned ratings and to clarify any discrepancies among the ratings.

6. The trainer provides feedback to participants, explaining why the employee should receive a certain rating (target score) on each dimension, and shows discrepancies between the target score and the score given by each trainee.

Consider how the Canadian military uses FOR training.[18] First, the training program includes a session regarding the importance of performance management systems in the military. In the next session, raters are told that they will be evaluating the performance of four direct reports. They are given the appraisal form to be used and information on each of the scales included in the form. As the trainer reads through each of the scales, participants are encouraged to ask questions. At the same time, the trainer gives examples of behaviors associated with each level of performance. The trainer thus makes sure that the trainees come to a common FOR concerning what behaviors constitute the different levels of performance. Participants are shown a video clip of a soldier and are asked to evaluate the performance using the appraisal form explained earlier. Next, the ratings are discussed as a group, focusing on the behaviors exhibited in the video clip and the ratings that would be most appropriate in each case. This process is repeated several times. Finally, the participants are given three more samples of behavior to rate, as displayed by three hypothetical soldiers, and they receive feedback on how well they evaluated each soldier.

It should be evident by now that FOR training can take quite a bit of time and effort to develop and administer, but it is well worth it. Specifically, as a consequence of implementing this type of training, raters not only are more likely to provide consistent and more accurate ratings, but they are also more likely to help employees design effective development plans. This is because sharing a common view of what constitutes good performance allows supervisors to provide employees with better guidelines to employ to reach such performance levels.[19]

7-3-3 Behavioral Observation Training

Behavioral observation (BO) training is another type of program implemented to minimize unintentional rating errors. BO training focuses on how raters observe, store, recall, and use information about performance. Fundamentally, this type of training improves raters' skills at observing performance.

For example, one type of BO training involves showing raters how to use observational aids such as notes or diaries. These observational aids help raters record a preestablished number of behaviors on each performance dimension. Using these aids helps raters increase the sample of incidents observed and recorded during a specific time period. In addition, an aid such as a diary is an effective way to standardize the observation of behavior and record of critical incidents throughout the review period. In addition, it serves as a memory aid when filling out evaluation forms. Memory aids are beneficial because ratings based on memory alone, without notes or diaries, are likely to be distorted due to factors of social context (e.g., friendship bias) and time (i.e., duration of supervisor–direct report relationship).[20]

Consider how BO training is also implemented by the Canadian military. The Canadian military has found that a combination of FOR and BO training works best. Earlier, we described how the Canadian military uses FOR training. BO training is added to the FOR training program. In addition to FOR training, there are sessions on the importance of BO and common BO errors, including first impression, stereotypes, and halo effects. Finally, the participants are trained in the importance of keeping diaries and taking notes on their direct reports throughout the year. Furthermore, the trainer explains the criteria for each performance dimension and provides written descriptions of the different levels of performance. The participants are given a chance to practice keeping a diary while watching the video clips used in the FOR training section of the training program. After watching each video clip, participants are given tips on note-taking and recording behaviors as well as the resulting outcomes.

In summary, raters are likely to make several types of unintentional errors when providing performance information. Unintentional errors are the product of the complex tasks of observing, encoding, storing, and retrieving performance information—and resistance to change exacerbates these errors. Through the implementation of three different types of training programs, these errors can be substantially minimized. Training programs focus on describing the errors that raters usually make (i.e., RET programs). In addition, they should allow raters to generate a common FOR to be used in evaluating performance as well as offer raters tools to improve observation and memory skills and help mitigate the discomfort generated by the interpersonal demands of the performance management process. FOR training is particularly beneficial when performance measurement emphasizes behaviors. On the contrary, BO training is particularly beneficial when performance measurement emphasizes results because raters learn not only how to observe behaviors, but also how these behaviors are linked to results.

Thus far, this chapter has described how to prepare for the launching of a performance management system by designing a communication plan and an appeals process and by delivering training programs that will minimize unintentional rating distortions. Next, we turn to the final set of activities required before the performance management system is put into practice: pilot testing.

7-4 PILOT TESTING

Before the performance management system is fully rolled out, it is a good idea to test a version of the entire system so that adjustments and revisions can be made as needed.[21] In the pilot test of the system, evaluations are not recorded in employee files; however, the system is implemented in its entirety from beginning to end, including all the steps that would be included if the system had actually been implemented. In other words, meetings take place between supervisor and employee, performance data are gathered, developmental plans are designed, and feedback is provided. The most important aspect of the pilot test is that all participants maintain records, noting any difficulties they encountered, ranging from problems with the appraisal form and how performance is measured to the feedback received. The pilot test allows for the identification and early correction of any flaws before the system is implemented throughout the organization.

We should not assume that the performance management system will necessarily be executed or that it will produce the anticipated results. The pilot test allows us to gain information from the perspective of users on how well the system works, to learn about any difficulties and unforeseen obstacles, to collect recommendations on how to improve all aspects of the system, and to understand personal reactions to it. In addition, conducting a pilot test is yet another way to achieve early acceptance from a small group who can then act as champions for the performance management system, rather than putting the burden on the HR department to sell the idea. A final reason for conducting a pilot test is that users are likely to have a higher system acceptance rate, knowing that stakeholders in the company had a say in its design, rather than feeling that the system was created by the HR department alone.

In larger organizations, an important decision to be made is the selection of the group of employees with whom the system will be tested. In choosing this group, we need to understand that the managers who will be participating should be willing to invest the resources required to do the pilot test. In addition, this group should be made up of managers who are flexible and willing to try new things. Thus, managers should know what the system will look like and receive a realistic preview before they decide to participate in the pilot test.

In selecting the group, we must also consider that it should be sufficiently large and representative of the entire organization so that reactions will be generalizable to the rest of the organization. Thus, in selecting the group, we should select jobs that are similar to those throughout the company, and the group selected should not be an exception in either a positive or a negative way. Specifically, the group should not be regarded as particularly productive, hardworking, lazy, and so forth. For example, at The Gap, Inc., the pilot testing of their revamped performance management system was conducted in one store, given that it is a self-contained business unit.[22]

Pilot tests provide crucial information to be used in improving the system before it is actually put in place. Pilot testing the system can provide huge savings and identify potential problems before they become irreversible and the credibility of the system is ruined permanently. For example, consider the case of the Washington State Patrol.[23] This organization realized that several changes were occurring, just like similar changes were occurring in patrol departments in other states, which prompted the revision of its performance management system. It established a committee to develop the new appraisals. Before implementing the system, the state patrol pilot tested it in two districts. First, the committee prepared a training chapter that included a pre-appraisal work group meeting. In this meeting, employees discussed their roles and expectations surrounding the performance management system and applied those discussions to a common goal. The training also focused on how new developments in the patrol led to new elements in the performance management system. During the training, the trainers encouraged the participants to ask questions regarding the shift to the new approach. The trainers then used the feedback received in these sessions to fix specific operational issues before introducing the training to the entire agency. After the appraisal process was fine-tuned, it was submitted for the approval of the troopers' and sergeants' associations. A select number of individuals across the districts received "train the trainer" training. Finally, the system was instituted agency-wide. Each of these steps allowed for the identification of potential barriers that could have prevented the system from being successful.

7-5 ONGOING MONITORING AND EVALUATION

When the testing period is over and the performance management system has been implemented organization-wide, it is important to use clear measurements to monitor and evaluate the system.[24] This also involves understanding the extent to which the training programs are achieving the objective of minimizing rating errors. In a nutshell, a decision needs to be made about how to evaluate the system's effectiveness, how to evaluate the extent to which the system is being implemented as planned, and how to evaluate the extent to which it is producing the intended results. As an illustration, the U.S. federal government takes the evaluation of performance management systems very seriously. Specifically, several laws have been passed and bills are being prepared that mandate federal agencies to develop a strategic plan, a performance plan, and a performance report.[25] Although these initiatives concern agencies and not individuals, ultimately, the performance of any agency depends on the performance of the individuals working in that agency.[26] The net result of such laws as the Government Performance and Results Act is an increase in accountability and funding allocation based on performance. Thus, federal agencies are required to evaluate the relative efficiency of their various management practices and initiatives including performance management systems.

Evaluation data should include reactions to the system and assessments of the system's operational and technical requirements. For example, a confidential survey could be administered to all employees, asking about perceptions and attitudes regarding the system. This survey can be administered during the initial stages of implementation, and then, at the end of the first review cycle to find out if there have been any changes. In addition, regarding the system's results, one can assess performance ratings over time to see what positive effects the implementation of the system is having. Finally, interviews can be conducted with key stakeholders, including managers and employees who have been involved in developing and implementing the performance management system.[27]

Several additional measures can be used on a regular basis to monitor and evaluate the system:

- *Number of individuals evaluated.* One of the most basic measures is to assess the number of employees who are actually participating in the system. If performance evaluations have not been completed for some employees, we need to find out who they are and why a performance review has not been completed.

- *Quality of non-quantitative performance data.* An indicator of quality of the performance data refers to the information provided in the open-ended sections of the appraisal forms. For example, how much did the rater write? What is the relevance of the examples provided?

- *Quality of follow-up actions.* A good indicator of the quality of the system is whether it leads to important follow-up actions in terms of development activities or improved processes. For example, to what extent do follow-up actions involve exclusively the supervisor as opposed to the employee? If this is the case, then the system may not be working as intended because it may be an indicator that employees are not sufficiently involved.[28] Also, to what extent have employees learned from their successes and failures and applying those lessons to the future?

- *Quality of performance discussion meeting.* A confidential survey can be distributed to all employees on a regular basis to gather information about how the supervisor is managing the performance discussion meetings. For example, is the feedback useful? Has the supervisor made resources available so the employee can accomplish the developmental plan objectives? How relevant was the performance review discussion to one's job? To what degree have developmental objectives and plans been discussed? To what extent does the supervisor's way of providing feedback encourage direct reports to receive more feedback in the future?[29]

- *System satisfaction.* A confidential survey could also be distributed to assess the perceptions of the system's users, both raters and ratees. This survey can include questions about satisfaction with equity, usefulness, and accuracy.

- *Overall cost/benefit ratio or return on investment (ROI).* A fairly simple way to address the overall impact of the system is to ask participants to rate the overall cost/benefit ratio for the performance management system. This is a type of bottom-line question that can provide convincing evidence for the overall worth of the system. The cost/benefit ratio question can be asked in reference to an individual (employee or manager), her job, and her organizational unit.

- *Unit-level and organization-level performance.* Another indicator that the system is working well is provided by the measurement of unit- and organization-level performance. Such performance indicators might be customer satisfaction with specific units and indicators of the financial performance of the various units or the organization as a whole. We need to be aware that it may take some time for changes in individual and group performance level to be translated into unit- and organization-level results. We should not expect results as soon as the system is implemented; however, we should start to see some tangible results at the unit level a few months after the system is in place.

Consider the case of Caterpillar, which designs, develops, engineers, manufactures, markets and sells machinery, engines, financial products, and insurance. Caterpillar is a leading manufacturer of construction and mining equipment, diesel and natural gas engines, industrial gas turbines, and diesel-electric locomotives. In 2017, Caterpillar was ranked #74 on the Fortune 500 list and #264 on the Global Fortune 500 list. In their own words, Caterpillar's "value advantage" is that they "have the people, processes, tools and investments to deliver the quality, reliability and durability customers expect from Caterpillar in each new product introduction." Given this value proposition, Caterpillar has a strategic view of how managers should improve the performance of their people, so they have had a performance management system in place for many years. Caterpillar embarked on an impressive initiative to evaluate their performance management system. Specifically, the goal of this evaluation was to assess the cost/benefit ratio—return on investment (ROI)—of the training sections of the system that targeted managers and included modules about goal setting and coaching, among others. This evaluation included three steps. First, there was an estimated ROI, based on how much performance management training would cost and its expected benefits. This information was used prior to implementing the program to establish the program's business case. Second, there was an ROI forecast, which enabled the program's leaders to better understand how to make full deployment of the initiative successful. Participants in this study completed a questionnaire in which they described the potential financial and nonfinancial effects of the program. Third, an ROI study was conducted three months after the performance management training intervention to learn about financial as well as nontangible returns. This was done via focus groups that documented how training participants had used the knowledge they had acquired and the business impact and financial benefits. Finally, a follow-up study was conducted two months later to confirm the results of the third step. This final study included an online questionnaire completed by the direct reports of the managers who had participated in the program. This final step provided cross-validation data from the perspective of direct reports.

Results were quite impressive. For example, results of the ROI study indicated that 88 percent of respondents believed the program had a positive impact on the organization; 5 percent reported that their personal productivity increased; 28 percent reported that product quality improved; and 33 percent reported that costs were reduced. The overall ROI was calculated as follows: [(Benefits – Costs)/Costs] $\times$ 100. Benefits were annualized, treated as sustainable benefits to the business, and one-time benefits were excluded, and were not treated at face value—rather, they included weighting factors. For example, assume a respondent who reported that his productivity increased 5 hours per week, his estimate of percentage of these hours saved due to the performance management training program was 60 percent, and his confidence in this estimate is 75%. If the hourly rate is estimated at US$65 and we consider 48 weeks per year, then 5 hours $\times$ $65 $\times$ 48 = $15,600. This estimate was revised, taking into account the answers to the follow-up questions (i.e., hours due to performance management and confidence in the estimate). In other words, $15,600 $\times$ 60% $\times$ 75% = $7,020. This resulting dollar figure was added to the total benefits pool. Finally, costs included all those associated with the program, including administration, communication, training design and delivery, evaluation, vendor fees, and so forth. What was the bottom-line? The final calculation indicated an impressive ROI of 194 percent.[30]

Now, let us return to the performance management system at the Washington State Patrol to examine how it has evaluated effectiveness since the system was implemented.[31] The patrol has several measures in place for continual evaluation of the effectiveness of the program. First, before all employees were reviewed using the system, they were surveyed regarding their satisfaction with the new system. This input was then used to further improve the appraisal process. In addition, the patrol used the results of a biyearly citizen's survey conducted by Washington State University. The results of this survey are used to determine whether the state patrol's customers are satisfied with its performance, and the data are also used to adjust and reprioritize performance objectives. In addition, the data are used to measure division-level performance, one indicator of the success of the performance management process. The Washington State Patrol collects other types of data as well. For example, every six months, division managers give presentations regarding performance management to their peers and to several executives. Initially, the meetings focused on efforts to implement the new performance management system and increase quality, but this will change as new issues arise. The presentation is 30–40 minutes long, followed by 20–30 minutes of questions from peers and executives. The feedback from these presentations is used to measure how well the system is being implemented, and feedback on the success of the meetings will be used to make any necessary changes to the system. The Washington State Patrol may also want to consider measuring how many people are participating in the system. The patrol would also benefit from assessing whether the new system is distinguishing high- from low-level performers and from ascertaining the overall cost/benefit ratio of implementing the system.

Box 7-2 describes the process of rolling out the performance management system at BT Global. As you will see, this included a communication plan, training, and ongoing commitment to monitoring and improvement.

The next chapter addresses a critical goal of good performance management systems: Employee development. This includes the creation of personal development plans, the role of one's supervisor, and the use of 360-degree feedback systems.

Box 7-2

Company Spotlight: Performance Management System Rollout at BT Global Services

BT Global Services, a global communication services company, employs more than 17,000 people worldwide, and provides information and communications technology services to 5,500 multinational companies in 180 countries. They provide services in three core areas (a) digital customer (aimed at driving deeper and richer interactions with their end customers), (b) digital business (aimed at increasing business agility and innovation through the move to cloud), and (c) digital employee (aimed at creating a productive and efficient business environment by facilitating employee collaboration across technologies). BT Global Services utilized several steps to effectively roll out a new performance management system, called "Maximizing Performance," designed to bring new consistency to managing and developing employees and to create a high-performance culture. After obtaining support from senior management, the first steps included a series of communications, including a workshop for executives so all employees would receive a clear message about why a new system was being developed, what roles employees would play, and how those roles would contribute to the success of the company. The next step included training line managers, to ensure involvement and commitment, including the important role these managers play in ensuring success. Among other areas covered, training included how to set effective goals with employees, and how to provide coaching and feedback to facilitate development. Roles were reviewed and clarified to ensure employees understood expectations and how their work contributes to the success of their team, business unit, and the company as a whole. For ongoing monitoring of the program, data were collected through employee surveys, face-to-face meetings with line managers, and team meetings. In summary, BT Global Services illustrates an example of an effective rollout of a new performance management system, including communication plan, training, and ongoing commitment to monitoring and improvement.[32]

SUMMARY POINTS

- Four important steps need to be taken before the new or revised and updated performance management system is launched and implemented. These include (1) implementing a communication plan and then (2) an appeals process, which will help gain system acceptance, (3) training programs for raters, which will help minimize unintentional errors in performance ratings, and (4) pilot testing the system, which will allow revisions and changes to be made before the system is actually implemented. Careful attention to these pre-system implementation steps will help improve the integrity and success of the system.
- The main goal of the communication plan is to gain support for the system. A good communication plan addresses the following questions:
  - What is performance management? What are its general goals? How have performance management systems been implemented in other organizations?
  - How does performance management fit with the organizational strategy?
  - What are the tangible benefits of the performance management system for all parties involved?
  - How does the system work? What are the various steps in the process?

- What are the roles and responsibilities of each organizational member?
- How does performance management relate to other initiatives and programs, such as training, promotion, and compensation?

- Including detailed, convincing, and clear answers for each of these questions is likely to help increase support for the system.
- People engage in unconscious cognitive processes in how they take in and process information. Even though a good communication plan may be in place, these biases create misperceptions about the system, and also, resistance to change. First, selective exposure is a tendency to expose our minds only to ideas with which we already agree. Second, selective perception is a tendency to perceive a piece of information as meaning what we would like it to mean even though the information, as intended by the communicator, may mean the exact opposite. Finally, selective retention is a tendency to remember only those pieces of information with which we already agree.
- The negative effects of the unconscious cognitive processes can be minimized by involving employees in system design, considering employees' needs in designing and implementing the system, delivering the communication plan before negative attitudes are established and rumors start circulating, putting information concerning the system in writing, providing facts and consequences and not just facts, using multiple channels of communication to present information about the system, using credible and powerful communicators, and repeating the information frequently. A good communication plan includes as many of these features as possible.
- In addition to a communication plan, the establishment of an appeals process helps gain system acceptance. An appeals process allows employees to understand that if there is a disagreement regarding performance ratings or any resulting decisions, such disagreements can be resolved in an amicable and nonretaliatory way.
- The appeals process begins with an employee filing an appeal with the HR department, which serves as a mediator between the employee and her supervisor. This is a Level 1 appeal. If the appeal is not resolved, then an outside and unbiased arbitrator makes a final and binding resolution. This is a Level 2 appeal. The arbitrator for a Level 2 appeal is usually a panel that includes peers and managers. Finally, the Level 3 appeal involves the participation of a senior level manager, who makes the final decision.
- In rating performance, raters may make unintentional errors, which occur because observing, encoding, storing, and retrieving performance information is a complex cognitive task. Unintentional errors include the following (1) similar to me, (2) contrast, (3) halo, (4) primacy, (5) recency, (6) negativity, (7) first impression, (8) spillover, (9) stereotype, and (10) attribution. Unintentional errors can be minimized by implementing three types of rater training program.
- Rater error training (RET) exposes raters to the different errors and their causes. RET does not guarantee rating accuracy, but becoming aware of what types of errors are likely to occur and the reasons for these errors is a very good first step in minimizing them.

- Frame of reference (FOR) training familiarizes raters with the various performance dimensions to be assessed. The goal is that raters will develop a common FOR in observing and evaluating performance. This type of training is most appropriate when performance measurement focuses on behaviors.

- Behavioral observation (BO) training focuses on how raters observe, store, recall, and use information about performance. For example, this program teaches raters how to use aids such as diaries to standardize performance observation. This type of training is most appropriate when performance measurement focuses on counting and recording how frequently certain behaviors and results take place.

- Pilot testing the system before it is rolled out fully is useful because it allows potential problems and glitches to be discovered and corrective action to be taken before the system is put in place. Pilot testing consists of implementing the entire system, including all of its components, but only with a select group of people. Results are not recorded in employees' records. Instead, the goal is that the people participating in the pilot test provide feedback on any possible problems and on how to improve the system.

- The group participating in the pilot test needs to understand that the test will take time and resources. A representative group should be selected so that conclusions drawn from the group can be generalized for the organization as a whole. The group should not be regarded as an exception in either a positive or negative way.

- As soon as the system has been implemented, there should be a measurement system to evaluate the extent to which it is working the way it should and producing the results that were expected. Such measures include confidential employee surveys assessing perceptions and attitudes about the system and whether there is an upward trend in performance scores over time. Other measures include number of individuals evaluated, quality of performance information gathered, quality of performance discussion meetings, user satisfaction with the system, overall cost/benefit ratio, and unit- and organization-level performance indicators. Taken together, these indicators are a powerful tool that can be used to demonstrate the value of the performance management system.

EXERCISE 7-1   TRAINING RATERS AT BIG QUALITY CARE CENTER

Located near the city of Caesarea, Israel, Big Quality Care Center (BQCC) is a nursing home facility for the elderly, serving about 125 residents. Because of the sheer size and diverse range of occupants served, the Center predominantly relies on highly skilled nursing professionals. Since Caesarea has had a long-term shortage of quality nursing professionals, the Center has some of the state-of-the-art management practices to both retain and maximize the performance of the Center's nurses.

Recently, however, BQCC has received several anonymous complaints from the nursing staff that many ratings seemed inaccurate and inconsistent.

Concerned that the Center may lose many of its quality nurses to competitors if the complaints are left unaddressed, the head of HR has decided to implement an organization-wide rater training program to correct for any true rater inaccuracies and inconsistencies.

Your performance management consulting business is now thriving, and luckily for you, the head of HR has gathered enough trust in you that she has decided to let you design the rater training program. But before hiring you to do so, she wants you to create a five-minute video presentation offering an overview and details of your recommended training program. This video clip will be shown to the company's CEO and the rest of the senior staff. Although you are somewhat nervous and scared, you soon regain your confidence and comfort level when you find out that you had kept a copy of a textbook called "Performance Management."

Using the information in Section 7-3 Training Programs for Minimizing Unintentional Rating Errors, create this five-minute video presentation to include (a) a brief explanation of the nature of your suggested rater training program; (b) anticipated benefits; and (c) its requirements in terms of resources (e.g., time, cost).

EXERCISE 7-2 PROPOSING AN APPEALS PROCESS FOR NURSING HOMES

As a follow-up to Exercise 7-1, your training proposal for Big Quality Care Center (BQCC) was a success. Congratulations! Your proposal has been accepted and the training program, together with the entire performance management system is now in place at BQCC. In fact, BQCC's CEO is so pleased with your work that she has forwarded your name to the American Association of Americans and Canadians in Israel (AACI), which keeps a list of nursing homes in Israel. And now, several nursing homes have reached out to you to solicit your consulting services so they can improve their own performance management systems.

To make your services more scalable, you decided to create online tools and services that you can offer to several nursing homes without the need to have to physically visit each. This is particularly important for you, given that you do not reside in Israel. Although no nursing home other than BQCC has reached out to you yet, BQCC's CEO told you that she heard through the grapevine that this will happen soon. So, you decided to create a five-minute video presentation describing what an appeals process is and how it would work at a nursing home.

You have done your homework about nursing homes and know that in addition to registered and licensed nurses, they typically employ administration staff (HR, accounting, operations), and also, support staff including custodians, maintenance staff, and groundskeepers. Using the information in Section 7-3 Training Programs for Minimizing Unintentional Rating Errors, and in Section 7-2 Appeals Process, create this five-minute video presentation to include (a) a brief explanation of the nature of an appeals process; (b) its anticipated benefits; and (c) its requirements in terms of resources (e.g., time, cost).

Implementing a Performance Management Communication Plan at Accounting, Inc.

Accounting, Inc. is a consulting and accounting firm headquartered in Amsterdam, the Netherlands. Recently, Accounting, Inc. implemented a performance management system. The first step in the implementation of the new system was the development of a set of core competencies that would be used to evaluate most employees, regardless of function or level. In addition, each employee was evaluated using more job-specific performance dimensions.

As the first step in the communication plan, the employees received individual email messages, asking them to define what the core competencies meant to them and to give descriptions and examples of how each of the core competencies played out in their specific positions. Next, the company held meetings, handed out frequently asked questions (FAQs) sheets, and placed posters around the company, detailing how the core competencies were related to the organization's strategic priorities and how performance scores would be related to monetary rewards. In these communications, Accounting, Inc., detailed how the performance system worked, how the raters were chosen, how performance feedback was used, and other details about the system. The information also outlined the benefits employees could expect from the new system as well as employees' responsibilities regarding the system.

Please evaluate Accounting, Inc.'s communication plan. Specifically, does it answer all of the questions that a good communication plan should answer (Hint: see Figure 7-1)? Which questions are left unanswered? How would you provide answers to the unanswered questions (if any)?

Source: Adapted from Brotherton, P. (2003). Meyners pays for performance: Changing a compensation system is a sensitive undertaking. Here's how one firm handled it. *Journal of Accountancy, 196*, 41–46.

Implementing an Appeals Process at Accounting, Inc.

Following up on Case Study 7-1, when the system was implemented, many employees were not happy with the ratings and the type of performance feedback information they received from their supervisors. If you were to design an appeals process to handle these complaints well, what would the appeals process be like? (Hint: Use the appeals process shown in Box 7-1: *University of Lethbridge Performance Management Appeals Process* as a model.)

ENDNOTES

1. Kim, M. Y., & Park, S. M. (2017). Antecedents and outcomes of acceptance of performance appraisal system in Korean non-profit organizations. *Public Management Review, 19*, 479–500.
2. Grote, D. (1996). *The complete guide to performance appraisal*. New York, NY: AMACOM.
3. U.S. Department of Commerce, Human Resources, Senior Executive Service Performance management system. Retrieved January 2, 2018, from http://hr.commerce.gov/s/groups/public/@doc/@cfoasa/@ohrm/documents/content/dev01_006513.pdf
4. Rafferty, A. E., & Jimmieson, N. L. (2017). Subjective perceptions of organizational change and employee resistance to change: Direct and mediated relationships with employee well-being. *British Journal of Management, 28*, 248–264.
5. Kahneman, D. (2011). *Thinking fast and slow*. New York, NY: Farrar, Straus, and Giroux.
6. Morhman, A. M., Resnick-West, S. M., & Lawler, E. E. (1989). *Designing performance appraisal systems* (p. 133). San Francisco, CA: Jossey-Bass.
7. O'Reilly, J. T. (2001). Burying Caesar: Replacement of the veterans appeals process is needed to provide fairness to claimants. *Administrative Law Review, 53*, 223–256.
8. Grote, D. (1996). *The complete guide to performance appraisal* (pp. 263–269). New York, NY: AMACOM.
9. Spears, M. C., & Parker, D. F. (2002). A probit analysis of the impact of training on performance appraisal satisfaction. *American Business Review, 20*, 12–16.
10. Aguinis, H., Joo, H., & Gottfredson, R. K. (2011). Why we hate performance management—And why we should love it. *Business Horizons, 54*, 503–507.
11. Aguinis, H., & Adams, S. K. R. (1998). Social-role versus structural models of gender and influence use in organizations: A strong inference approach. *Group and Organization Management, 23*, 414–446.
12. Heilman, M. E., Wallen, A. S., Fuchs, D., & Tamkins, M. M. (2004). Penalties for success: Reactions to women who succeed at male gender-typed tasks. *Journal of Applied Psychology, 89*, 416–427.
13. Stauffer, J. M., & Buckley, M. R. (2005). The existence and nature of racial bias in supervisory ratings. *Journal of Applied Psychology, 90*, 586–591.
14. Jawahar, I. M. (2005). Do raters consider the influence of situational factors on observed performance when evaluating performance? Evidence from three experiments. *Group & Organization Management, 30*, 6–41.
15. London, M., Mone, E. M., & Scott, J. C. (2004). Performance management and assessment: Methods for improved rater accuracy and employee goal setting. *Human Resource Management, 43*, 319–336.
16. Aguinis, H., Mazurkiewicz, M. D., & Heggestad, E. D. (2009). Using web-based frame-of-reference training to decrease biases in personality-based job analysis: An experimental field study. *Personnel Psychology, 62*, 405–438.
17. Pulakos, E. D. (1986). The development of training programs to increase accuracy with different rating tasks. *Organizational Behavior and Human Decision Processes, 38*, 76–91.
18. Noonan, L. E., & Sulsky, L. M. (2001). Impact of frame-of-reference and behavioral observation training on alternative training effectiveness criteria in a Canadian military sample. *Human Performance, 14*, 3–26.
19. Gorman, C. A., & Rentsch, J. R. (2017). Retention of assessment center rater training: Improving performance schema accuracy using frame-of-reference training. *Journal of Personnel Psychology, 16*, 1–11.
20. Duarte, N. T., Goodson, J. R., & Klich, N. R. (2004). Effects of dyadic quality and duration on performance appraisal. *Academy of Management Journal, 37*, 499–521.
21. Grote, D. (1996). *The complete guide to performance appraisal* (pp. 254–256). New York, NY: AMACOM.
22. Gap Inc. encourages employees to grow, performance and succeed without ratings. Retrieved January 2, 2018 from https://www.e-reward.co.uk/uploads/editor/files/GapInc_Case_Study.pdf
23. Cederblom, D., & Pemerl, D. E. (2002). From performance appraisal to performance management: One agency's experience. *Public Personnel Management, 31*, 131–140.
24. Grote, D. (1996). *The complete guide to performance appraisal* (pp. 260–263). New York, NY: AMACOM.

25. Somers, M. (2017). Government accountability legislation gets house backing, heads to senate. *Federal News Radio*. Retrieved January 2, 2018, from https://federalnewsradio.com/congress/2017/01/government-accountability-legislation-gets-house-backing-heads-senate/

26. Aguinis, H., Davis, G. F., Detert, J. R., Glynn, M. A., Jackson, S. E., Kochan, T., . . . Sutcliffe, K. M. (2016). Using organizational science research to address U.S. federal agencies' management and labor needs. *Behavioral Science & Policy, 2*(2), 67–76.

27. Harper, S., & Vilkinas, T. (2005). Determining the impact of an organisation's performance management system. *Asia Pacific Journal of Human Resources, 43*, 76–97.

28. Fletcher, C. (2008). *Appraisal, feedback, and development: Making performance review work*. New York, NY: Routledge.

29. Dipboye, R. L., & de Pontbriand, R. (1981). Correlates of employee reactions to performance appraisal and appraisal systems. *Journal of Applied Psychology, 66*, 248–251.

30. Goh, F. A., & Anderson, M. C. (2007). Driving business value from performance management at Caterpillar. *Organization Development Journal, 25*(2), 219–226.

31. Cederblom, D., & Pemerl, D. E. (2002). From performance appraisal to performance management: One agency's experience. *Public Personnel Management, 31*, 131–140.

32. Kelly, S. (2004). Maximizing performance at BT Global Services. *Strategic HR Review, 3*, 32–35.

Employee and Leadership Development

chapter

8

Performance Management and Employee Development

*One of the tests of leadership is the ability to recognize
a problem before it becomes an emergency.*

—*Arnold H. Glasow*

Learning Objectives

By the end of this chapter, you will be able to do the following:

1. Design your own personal developmental plan that addresses how you can continually learn and grow in the next year, how you can do better in the future, how you can avoid performance problems faced in the past, and where you are now and where you would like to be in terms of your career path.

2. Formulate a developmental plan so you can improve your own reflective, communicative, and behavioral career competencies.

3. Prepare a developmental plan that includes professional development needs, resources/support needed, and a timeline for meeting each need with the goals of improving performance in current position, sustaining performance in current position, preparing employees for advancement, and enriching the employee's work experience.

4. Produce a development plan that includes a range of activities (e.g., on-the-job training, courses, self-guided studying, mentoring, attending a conference or trade show, mixing with the best, job rotation, getting a degree).

5. Propose a developmental plan that highlights the key role of the supervisor as a guide and facilitator of the developmental process (e.g., explaining what is required of the employee to reach a required performance level, referring to appropriate developmental activities, reviewing and making suggestions about developmental objectives).

6. Implement a multisource (i.e., supervisors, peers, self, direct reports, customers) feedback system with the goal of providing feedback on and improving performance.

7. Implement multisource feedback systems that takes advantage of all of its benefits (e.g., increased awareness of expectations, improved performance, reduced "undiscussables" and defensiveness).

8. Implement multisource feedback systems that minimize potential risks and pitfalls (e.g., could hurt employees' feelings, individuals may feel uncomfortable with the system and believe they will not be rated honestly and treated fairly, is unlikely to work well in organizations that have highly hierarchical cultures that do not support open and honest feedback).

225

Part I of this text described strategic and macro-organizational issues in designing a performance management system. Part II described operational and technical details on how to roll out and implement the system. As is mentioned throughout this book, employee development is a key result of state-of-the-science performance management systems. Accordingly, Part III includes two chapters dealing with developmental issues and pertains to two key stakeholders in the developmental process: (1) the employees of the organization, who are improving their own performance, and (2) the managers (i.e., performance management leaders), who guide and facilitate the process of employee development for their direct reports so that it can successfully occur. Development planning is a joint activity entered into by both the employee and the manager. This chapter addresses how to use a performance management system to help employees develop and improve their performance. Chapter 9 addresses the leadership skills needed by managers so that they can best manage the performance of their employees. Let us begin this chapter by discussing personal developmental plans.

8-1 PERSONAL DEVELOPMENT PLANS

Personal development plans specify courses of action to be taken to improve performance. Also, achieving the goals stated in the development plan allows employees to keep abreast of changes in their field or profession. Such plans highlight an employee's strengths and the areas in need of development, and they provide an action plan to improve in areas of weaknesses and further develop areas of strength.[1] In a nutshell, personal development plans allow employees to answer the following questions:

- How can I continually learn and grow in the next year?
- How can I do better in the future?
- How can I avoid performance problems faced in the past?
- Where am I now and where would I like to be in terms of my career path?

Development plans can be created for every job, ranging from entry level to the executive suite (e.g., CEO, CFO). No matter how high up the position within the organization and how simple or complex the nature of the job in question, there is always room for improvement. Information to be used in designing development plans comes from the appraisal form. Specifically, a development plan can be designed based on each of the performance dimensions evaluated. For example, if the performance dimension "communication" is rated as substandard, this area would be included in the development plan.

Development plans focus on the short term and on specific roles and positions, but also on the knowledge and skills needed for more long-term career aspirations and career development. Specifically, good development plans also focus on developing *career competencies*, including the following three sets of competencies[2]:

- *Reflective career competencies*. Being aware of one's career and combining personal reflections with one's professional career. The two competencies that comprise this dimension are *reflection on motivation*, which refers to reflecting on values, passions, and motivations with regard to one's career; and *reflection on qualities*, which refers to reflection on strengths, shortcomings, and skills with regard to one's career.

- *Communicative career competencies.* Being able to effectively communicate with others to improve one's chances of career success. The two competencies are *networking*, which refers to the awareness of the presence and professional value of one's network, and the ability to expand this network for career-related purposes; and *self-profiling*, which refers to presenting and communicating one's personal knowledge, abilities, and skills to individuals inside and outside the organization.
- *Behavioral career competencies.* Being able to shape one's career by taking action and being proactive. The two specific competencies are *work exploration*, which refers to actively exploring and searching for work-related and career-related opportunities inside and outside the organization, and *career control*, which refers to actively influencing learning processes and work processes related to one's career by setting goals and planning how to reach these goals.

Now, pause for a few minutes and give yourself some time to think about the three aforementioned sets of career competencies. Where do you stand regarding reflective, communicative, and behavioral career competencies? What are your strongest and your weakest competencies? Which ones should you be working on to improve your future career prospects?

In addition to improved short-term performance and career path clarity, the inclusion of development plans, and in more general terms, the identification of employee strengths and weaknesses as part of the performance management system have another important benefit: employees are more likely to be satisfied with the performance management system.[3] For example, a study including 137 employees at a production equipment facility in the southern United States showed that the greater the extent to which employees believed that the system was being used for development purposes, the more satisfied they were with the system. On the contrary, perceptions of the extent to which the system was

Box 8-1

Company Spotlight: Individual Development Plans at General Mills

At General Mills, individual development plans (IDPs) are promoted strongly throughout the company. The Minneapolis, Minnesota-based General Mills is an international foods company. Some of the best-known brands include Annie's Homegrown, Betty Crocker, Yoplait, Colombo, Totino's, Pillsbury, Old El Paso, Häagen-Dazs, Cheerios, Trix, Cocoa Puffs, and Lucky Charms. The formally written IDPs are completed annually, but the expectation is for ongoing conversations with managers and employees, focusing not only on competencies that are well developed and those that are in need of improvement, but also on the employee's career aspirations. The company's IDP sessions promote the process for employees by hosting speakers, offering Web-based learning tools, and holding workshops for employees and managers to get the most out of the process. Some of these sessions are specifically tailored to different kinds of positions within the company with different needs in the development process. Also, the IDP is kept separate from the annual performance appraisal, as the belief is that development planning cannot be sufficiently addressed in the context of appraisal. In summary, General Mills provides an example of a company that has made a strong commitment to the growth and learning of all employees.[4]

used for evaluative purposes did not relate to employee satisfaction with the system. In other words, using the system for evaluative purposes did not relate to employee satisfaction, but using the system for development purposes had a positive relationship with satisfaction. This is precisely the reason why so many companies, such as the The Gap, Ely Lilly, Microsoft, and Accenture, emphasize that their performance management systems have a strong focus on employee development. Box 8-1 describes how development plans, including short- and long-term objectives, are implemented at General Mills.

Finally, another important aspect of personal development plans is that they allow organizations to gather information that can be used for *succession planning* purposes.[5] For example, based on individual career aspirations, an organization is able to identify employees who may be interested and able to serve in leadership positions in the future. Many "high-potential" programs are essentially based on combining employees' current performance and future aspirations with the organization's future talent needs. Thus, development plans serve an important strategic role in helping an organization address future possible talent gaps.

8-1-1 Development Plan Objectives

The overall objective of a development plan is to encourage continuous learning, performance improvement, and personal growth. In addition, development plans have other, more specific objectives:

- *Improve performance in current position.* A good development plan helps employees meet performance standards. Thus, a development plan includes suggested courses of action to address each of the performance dimensions that are deficient. This is an important point, given that surveys have shown that about 25 percent of federal employees and between 11 percent and 16 percent of private sector employees in the United States are not performing up to standards.[6]
- *Sustain performance in current position.* A good development plan provides tools so that employees can continue to meet and exceed expectations regarding their current position. Thus, the plan includes suggestions about how to continue to meet and exceed expectations for each of the performance dimensions included in the appraisal form.
- *Prepare employees for advancement.* A good development plan includes advice and courses of action that should be taken so that employees will be able to take advantage of future opportunities and career advancement. For example, a good plan indicates which new competencies should be learned to help with career advancement.
- *Enrich the employee's work experience.* Even if career opportunities within the organization are not readily available, a good plan provides employees with growth opportunities and opportunities to learn new skills. These opportunities provide employees with intrinsic rewards and a more challenging work experience, even if the new skills learned are not a formal part of their jobs.[7] Such opportunities can make jobs more attractive and serve as a powerful employee retention tool. In addition, the new skills can be useful in case of lateral transfers within the organization.

As an illustration, consider the employee development plan used for staff at Texas A&M University in College Station, Texas. Because the development plan is a formal component of the university's performance management system, the development plan is included within the appraisal form. The appraisal form used by Texas A&M first lists the six objectives of the performance management system:

1. Provide employees with feedback to improve or maintain job performance.
2. Outline areas for employee development.
3. Set standards for the next review period.
4. Recognize job-related accomplishments.
5. Enhance communication and working relationships.
6. Identify job performance deficiencies (any factor "Does Not Meet Expectations") and report to the next level of supervisory responsibility.

Based on objective 2, the employee development plan is an important component of the performance management system. The inclusion of this objective upfront sets the tone for the development process by helping managers understand that this is an important issue.

After the sections in the form in which the manager rates employee performance, the following material is included:

SECTION B: PROFESSIONAL DEVELOPMENT PLAN

Please list professional development activities to be completed and resources needed to support these activities, if applicable

Professional Development Needs	Resources/Support Needed	Time Frame

---

The inclusion of this information after performance ratings allows the manager and employee to focus on developmental areas identified as weaknesses in the performance review process. In this way, the development plans created for employees at Texas A&M are directly related to performance dimensions important for the unit and the overall organization. In addition, including the development plan at the end of the review and after setting annual performance goals allows the employee to determine whether there are areas he or she needs to develop in order to attain the specified goals.

8-1-2 Content of Development Plan

What does a developmental plan look like? Plans should include a description of specific steps to be taken and specific objectives to reach. In other words, what is the new skill or knowledge that will be acquired and how will this occur? This includes information on the resources and strategies that will be used to achieve the objectives. For example, will the employee learn the skill from a coworker through on-the-job training? Will the company reimburse the employee for expenses associated with taking an online course?

The plan's objectives should include not only the end product, such as the new skill to be learned, but also, the completion date and what evidence will be gathered to know whether the new skill has indeed been acquired. For example, in the case of an online course, the objective could state that it will be completed by July 23, 2019, and the employee is expected to receive a grade of B+ or better. Overall, objectives included in the development plans should be practical, specific, time-oriented, linked to a standard, and developed jointly by the supervisor and the employee.

An additional important feature of development plans is that it should keep the needs of both the organization and the employee in mind. As mentioned earlier, state-of-the-science development plans are used *strategically* to connect the organization's future talent needs with an employee's performance and aspirations. The choice of what specific skills or performance areas will be improved is influenced by the needs of the organization, especially when the organization is investing substantial resources in the plan. In addition, the plan created is influenced by the needs of the employee. The supervisor and the employee need to agree on what development or new skills will help enrich the employee's work experience, as well as help accomplish organizational goals now or in the near future.

As an example, let us consider once again the content of the development plan at Texas A&M. First, employees are directed to a website that includes examples of possible developmental activities. This list includes workshops; certifications; local, state, and national conferences; on-the-job training; and other activities. This information presents employees and managers with various options they can use to achieve the developmental objectives. Second, the form includes space so that each professional developmental need is paired with a description of resources or support needed and a time frame for completion. For example, the developmental plan for an administrative assistant in the business school may look like this:

SECTION B: PROFESSIONAL DEVELOPMENT PLAN

Please list professional development activities to be completed and resources needed to support these activities, if applicable

Professional Development Needs	Resources/Support Needed	Time Frame
1. Knowledge of Excel (spreadsheet program)	Reimbursement for online course	Course to be completed by August 1, 2019
2. Customer service skills in dealing with students and faculty	Reimbursement for one-day workshop. Time to receive on-the-job training from administrative assistant in communications department	Workshop to be completed by October 15, 2019. On-the-job training to be completed by November 8, 2019

Overall, the Texas A&M plan includes all of the required components. There is a description of developmental objectives, activities that will be conducted to reach these objectives, and dates of completion. One important piece seems to be missing, however. The plan does not include specifics of how the accomplishment of each objective will be measured. Specifically, how will the supervisor know if the administrative assistant has a good working knowledge of Excel after he has completed the online course? How will the supervisor know if the administrative assistant's customer service skills have improved after he has attended the workshop and has undergone on-the-job training? Excel proficiency could be measured by the administrative assistant's performance in the course or by examining answers to questions about knowledge of Excel that faculty, and others giving Excel assignments to the administrative assistant, answer in filling out appraisal forms. Regarding customer service skills, the accomplishment of the objective might be measured by gathering data from those customers served by the administrative assistant (i.e., faculty and students).

8-1-3 Developmental Activities

Clearly, developmental activities are dependent on an organization's strategic goals and objectives, and also, on resources that may or may not be available. For example, on-the-job training is more likely to take place in small, compared to large organizations, which may have a training and development unit, or have sufficient resources to offer in-house courses, or pay for an employee to take a course at a local university. There are several ways through which employees can reach the objectives stated in their development plans, including:

- *On-the-job training.* Employees are paired with a peer or supervisor who designs a formal on-the-job training course. The design of these "mini-training programs" includes how many hours a day or week training will take place and specific learning objectives.
- *Courses.* Some large organizations, such as McDonald's, Motorola, Capgemini, Ernst & Young, and others, offer in-house courses given at their own corporate universities. Other organizations may provide tuition reimbursement. Given the proliferation of online courses, there is a wide variety of options from which to choose.
- *Self-guided studying.* Employees can read books, watch video presentations, and study other materials on their own. Once again, it is important that an objective be set regarding what will be read and within what time frame, as well as what measure(s) will be used to assess whether learning has taken place.
- *Mentoring.* Many organizations have mentoring programs. In general terms, mentoring is a developmental process that consists of a one-on-one relationship between a senior (mentor) and junior (protégé) employee. For such programs to be successful, it is best to allow the mentor and protégé to choose each other, rather than arbitrarily assigning who will be mentoring whom. In general, mentors serve as role models and teach protégés what it takes to succeed in the organization. In more specific terms, mentors can help protégés gain targeted skills.

- *Attending a conference or trade show.* Another way to acquire required knowledge and skills is to sponsor an employee's attendance at a conference or trade show. It is useful to require that the employee provide a written report and deliver a brief presentation upon returning from the conference. In this way, it is easier to assess what has been learned, and in addition, the knowledge gained can be shared with other organizational members. As is true for most developmental activities, they have to be directly linked to an employee's development plan and also an organization's needs. This principle clearly applies to attending off-site conferences and trade shows, given that this developmental activity is particularly prone to abuse.[8]
- *Mixing with the best.* A developmental activity particularly targeting entrepreneurs and high-level executives involves the "Genius Network," a by-application-only network whose participants pay $100,000 to attend three meetings a year. This network connects high-achieving entrepreneurs, industry innovators, and best-selling authors and their goal is to help them grow their business tenfold.[9]
- *Getting a degree.* Some organizations provide tuition reimbursement benefits for their employees to obtain additional degrees or certifications. For example, the organization can sponsor an employee's MBA program or an employee's taking specialized courses with the goal of earning a certification designation (e.g., Certified Novell Administrator, Professional in Human Resources). In most cases, employees commit to continuing the relationship with their employer for a prespecified amount of time after completing the degree. If the employee leaves the organization before this time frame, she may have to reimburse the organization for the cost of her education. As an example, the firm Boston Consulting Group (BCG) sponsors "BCG MBA Fellows," which is a scholarship program that includes not only a tuition reimbursement, but also individual mentorship by senior BCG consultants. To be eligible for this program, a BCG employee must work for the company for at least two years, and then, be enrolled in a full-time MBA program approved by BCG. This is a developmental activity that serves an important strategic purpose for BCG because it helps build a talent pool needed for its succession planning needs, given that it has more than 80 offices in 48 countries and more than 14,000 employees.
- *Job rotation.* Another way to gain necessary skills is to be assigned to a different job on a temporary basis. This is the model followed in the medical profession in which residents have to rotate across specialty areas for several months (e.g., OB-GYN, psychiatry, pediatrics). For example, residents may be required to rotate across the various emergency medicine services for a 19-month period.
- *Temporary assignments.* A less systematic rotation system includes the opportunity to work on a challenging temporary assignment. This allows employees to gain specific skills within a limited time frame.
- *Membership or leadership role in professional, trade, or nonprofit organizations.* Some employers sponsor membership in professional, trade, or nonprofit organizations. Such an organization distributes publications to its members and holds informal and formal meetings in which employees have an opportunity to learn about best practices and other useful information for

On-the-job training
Courses
Self-guided studying
Mentoring
Attending a conference or trade show
Mixing with the best
Getting a degree
Job rotation
Temporary assignments
Membership or leadership role in professional, trade, or nonprofit organizations

TABLE 8-1
Summary List of Development Activities

their jobs. For example, this could include the Society for Human Resource Management, Chartered Institute of Personnel and Development for Human Resources (HR) Professionals or the Australian Human Resources Institute. Also, presentation, communication, planning, and other skills can be learned while serving in a leadership role in a volunteer organization outside of work (e.g., local charity, church, or synagogue).

Table 8-1 includes a summarized list of developmental activities that may be available to achieve goals included in a development plan. Based on your own preferences and learning style, which of these activities do you believe would be most beneficial to you? Please rank these activities in terms of your preference. Does the organization you work for now, or worked for most recently, offer any of these opportunities? If not, to what extent is this a factor that would motivate you to look for a job elsewhere, where more of these developmental activities would be made available to you?

An example of a development plan is included in Figure 8-1. The development plan can be part of the appraisal form, or it can be included in a separate form. The form included in Figure 8-1 shows that employees have several choices in terms of developmental activities. Note that the form includes space so that information can be inserted regarding what activities will take place when, what the objectives are, and whether the objective has been met or not.

Many of the activities listed above are relevant for employees at all levels. However, some, such as the "mixing with the best" activity, pertain specifically to high-level managers. In fact, the issue of *managerial development* is very important on its own because it is directly related to succession planning—as discussed earlier. For example, employees who aspire to secure managerial positions should evaluate all developmental activities to understand which ones would be most beneficial to achieve this particular career goal.[10]

Consider your future career expectations and developmental needs. Then, fill out the form included in Figure 8-1, assuming your current or future employer will be willing to provide any developmental opportunities of your choosing. What does your plan look like? What did you discover about what you would like to learn in the future? What does this information tell you about your level of aspirations and future prospects for your career advancement?

FIGURE 8-1

Example of a Development Plan Form

Update Date:
Name:
Job Title/Job Code:
Department:
Primary Reviewer:
Education:
Prior Training:
Job History:
Career Goals:
Next 1 year
Next 2 years
Next 3 years
Next 5 years

Developmental Options OJT (on-the-job) Training	Description	Type of Development	When	How Long	Completed Hours (This Quarter)	Comments—Approximate Cost—Other	Objectives/ Evaluation
Classes	Current Quarter						
Conferences							
On-line							
Self-study							
Job rotation	Next Quarter						
Videos							
Books							
Temporary assignment							
Mentorship	Current +2						
Other (specify)							
	Current +3						

8-2 DIRECT SUPERVISOR'S ROLE

The direct supervisor has an important role in the creation and completion of the employee's development plan. Because of the pivotal role of the direct supervisor in the employee development process, it is a good idea for the supervisor to have her own development plan as well. This will help the supervisor understand the process from the employee's perspective, anticipate potential roadblocks and defensive attitudes, and create a plan in a collaborative fashion.[11]

In terms of the specific role of the supervisor, consider the following five functions:

1. explaining what is required of the employee to reach a required performance level
2. referring to appropriate developmental activities
3. reviewing and making suggestions about developmental objectives
4. checking on the employee's progress toward developmental objective achievement
5. offering the opportunity for regular check-ins and reinforcing positive behaviors

Let us discuss each of these functions in turn. First, the supervisor needs to explain what would be required for the employee to achieve the desired performance level, including the steps that an employee must take to improve her performance. This information needs to be provided together with information on the probability of success if the employee completes the suggested steps. A good tool that supervisors can use to accomplish this goal is to use the *feedforward interview* (FFI). The goal of the FFI is to understand the types of behaviors and skills that individuals have that allow them to perform well, and to think about ways to use these same behaviors and skills in other contexts to make further improvements in the future. The FFI includes a meeting between the supervisor and employee and involves the following three steps[12]:

1. *Eliciting a success story.* The supervisor sets the stage as follows: "All of us have both negative and positive experiences at work. I would like to meet with you to discuss some positives aspects only and see how we can learn from those experiences about things that work well." Then, the supervisor can ask, "Could you please tell me a story about an event or experience at work during which you felt at your best, full of life and in flow, and you were content even before the results of your actions were known?" It is important that the story be very specific about an actual incident and not a general statement about "In general, these are the things I do at work. . . ." So, the story must be situated within a specific context. After the supervisor hears the story, she can summarize it for the employee to hear it, and then, the supervisor can ask whether any information is missing or anything else should be added to the story. A follow-up question is, "Would you be happy to experience a similar process again?" If the answer is in the affirmative, then the subsequent questions attempt to go deeper into the details of the story. If the story is associated with mixed feelings and is not completely positive, then a different story must be elicited.

2. *Uncover the underlying success factors.* The second step involves understanding the factors that led to the successful story. For example, the supervisor can ask, "What were some of the things you did or did not do, such as your specific personal strengths and capabilities, that made this success story possible?" and "What were the conditions that made this success story possible?" It is important to uncover both the personal and contextual factors that led to the success story. This step is similar to conducting detective work to try to understand the various factors

that led to success, including the role that the work environment (e.g., technology) and others (e.g., customers, peers) played in the story.

3. *Extrapolating the past into the future.* The third step involves asking questions that will lead to an employee's ability to replicate the conditions that led to success in the past into the future. So, the supervisor can first note that "The conditions you have just described seem to be your personal code for reaching [insert the key achievement in the story such as happiness at work, optimal performance, outstanding leadership, etc.]." Then, follow up with questions such as, "Think about your current actions, priorities, and plans for the near future (e.g., next week, month, or quarter) and tell me how you think you may be able to replicate these conditions to be able to achieve the same level of [insert satisfaction, achievement, performance, etc.] as you did before."

An experiment involving all 25 managers in the sales and customer service units of a business equipment firm in Canada provided evidence regarding the effectiveness of the FFI.[13] The managers and their direct reports were randomly assigned to one of two experimental conditions (a) feedforward interview ($n = 13$ managers, 70 employees), or (2) traditional feedback ($n = 12$ managers, 75 employees). Results showed that compared to traditional feedback, the FFI increased performance four months later. So, the effects of the FFI are relatively enduring. Also, the training required to teach managers how to use the FFI is fairly short. In this particular experiment, it took just two-and-a-half hours to train 13 managers, which helped shift the role of the manager from a judge or critic of an employee's past performance to appreciative inquiry of what an employee will do in the future.

As an outcome of the FFI, there may be resources that the employee may need to achieve his developmental goals. Thus, as a second important function, the supervisor has a primary role in referring to appropriate developmental activities that can assist the employee in achieving her goals. For example, this includes helping the employee select a mentor, appropriate study resources, courses, and so forth.

Third, the supervisor reviews and makes suggestions about the developmental objectives. Specifically, the supervisor helps assure the goals are achievable, specific, and doable (recall our discussion about goals in Chapter 5).

Fourth, the supervisor has primary responsibility for checking on the employee's progress toward achieving the developmental goals. For example, the supervisor can remind the employee of due dates and revise goals, if needed.

Finally, in addition to regular check-ins, the supervisor needs to provide reinforcements so the employee will be motivated to achieve the developmental goals. Reinforcements can be extrinsic and include rewards such as bonuses and additional benefits, but reinforcements can also include the assignment of more challenging and interesting work that takes advantage of the new skills learned.

To be successful in performing the five aforementioned functions, supervisors themselves need to be motivated to support the employees' completion of their developmental objectives. For this to happen, supervisors must be held accountable and rewarded for doing a good job in helping their employees develop.[14] Consider how this is done at KLA-Tencor Corporation, one of the world's top 10 developers and manufacturers of inspection and measurement equipment for the semiconductor and nanoeletronics industries. KLA-Tencor is a global company including 6,000 people in 17 countries, united by a "culture that rewards innovation and recognizes the power of collaboration to deliver breakthroughs." At KLA-Tencor, between 10 percent and 30 percent of supervisors' bonus pay is directly tied to employee development, which is measured in terms of employee training and certification levels. Managers are given at least quarterly updates on the status of their staff development. In addition, employees themselves are rewarded for engaging in developmental activities. In fact, only employees with up-to-date training and certification levels are eligible for bonuses. Thus, employee development is successful at KLA-Tencor because both employees and managers are directly rewarded for employee development. After several years of implementing these practices, employee development has become the norm and is part of the KLA-Tencor's culture.[15] As an additional example specifically regarding the role of supervisors in implementing the development plan, learn how this is done at Diageo, as described in Box 8-2.

In sum, direct supervisors play a key role in the success of the development plan because they are directly involved in the assessment of objective accomplishment and monitor progress toward accomplishing developmental objectives. Also, they must be highly committed to the development of their employees and motivated to help their employees fulfill their career aspirations. To do so, supervisors must be evaluated, in part, based on how well they manage the developmental process for their employees. When these conditions are present, the development plan becomes an integral part of the performance management system, all employees have a plan (including managers from all levels in the organization), all employees are able to access different types of developmental opportunities on an ongoing basis, and alignment between employee and organizational goals is enhanced.[16]

Box 8-2

Company Spotlight: Role of Direct Supervisor in Development at Diageo

Diageo makes and distributes alcoholic beverages that include brands such as Smirnoff (the world's best-selling vodka), Johnnie Walker (the world's best-selling blended Scotch whisky), Baileys (the world's best-selling liqueur), and Guinness (the world's best-selling stout). Also, Diageo owns 34 percent of Moët Hennessy, which owns brands including Moët & Chandon, Veuve Clicquot, and Hennessy. Diageo sells its products in more than 180 countries and has offices in about 80 countries. The company has recognized the value of employee development and expects supervisors to play an important role in the development of their direct reports. Specifically, the company's career development program includes a formal review and goal setting, along with regular meetings to keep development fresh in the minds of employees. The supervisor facilitates the process in several ways. The supervisor helps identify specific development goals that are aligned with the employee's career aspirations. Monthly meetings, referred to as "call overs," are held to review progress toward goals and to adjust goals as necessary. Also, the supervisor helps provide a means for development and reaching goals by ensuring employees receive training, course work, or studying material on relevant topics. Another strategy includes giving assignments outside of one's current position responsibilities, such as leading a project, to test one's skills and practice what the employee has learned in the development process. In summary, Diageo has recognized the critical role that managers should play in the employee development process. This involvement benefits the individual employee's growth and also aids in aligning employee skills and actions with the strategic goals of the organization as a whole.[17]

Next, we address an important tool used for employee development purposes: multisource feedback systems. Although these systems are called using different labels, such as 360-degree systems, multi-rater, multisource, full circle, or 450 feedback, the basic principle is the same: We gather the most useful information about employee's development needs when we use multiple sources of performance information.[18]

....

8-3 MULTISOURCE FEEDBACK SYSTEMS

The multisource feedback system has become a preferred tool for helping employees, particularly those in supervisory roles, improve performance by gathering information on their performance from different sources.[19] As mentioned above, multisource feedback systems are usually called "360-degree" systems because information is gathered from sources all around the employee. Specifically, information on what performance dimensions could be improved is gathered from superiors, peers, customers, and direct reports. This information is usually collected anonymously to minimize rating inflation. Employees also rate themselves on the various performance dimensions and compare self-perceptions with the information provided by others. A gap analysis is conducted to examine the areas for which there are large discrepancies between self-perceptions and the perceptions of others. A multisource feedback system report usually includes information on dimensions for which there is agreement that further development is needed. This information is used to create a development plan, as described earlier in the chapter.

A multisource feedback system is most helpful when it is used for developmental purposes only and not for administrative purposes.[20] This is because people are more likely to be honest if they know the information will be used to help individuals improve and not to punish or to reward them. However, it is possible to implement such systems successfully for administrative purposes after they have been in place for some time—usually, two years or so.[21]

Feedback reports usually include graphs showing the areas in which employees' perceptions differ the most from the perceptions of other sources of performance data. They can also show average scores, across sources of information, so that the areas that need improvement are readily identified. The resulting report is usually made available to the employee and his supervisor so that both have an opportunity to review it before meeting to create a development plan.

A trend adopted by many vendors that offer online multisource feedback systems is to offer a bundle of systems, including multisource feedback together with learning management, compensation, and even recruiting and succession planning.[22] These integrative applications, usually called "talent management" systems, allow organizations to manage data about employees in a systematic and coordinated way.[23] Such integrative software applications allow organizations to create an inventory of their human capital and better understand their strengths and weaknesses at the organizational level. For example, an organization that uses such applications is quickly able to deploy project teams with the appropriate mix of skills and experience after doing a quick search in the database. Another important advantage of these integrative applications is that performance management can be more easily linked to recruiting, compensation, training, and succession planning. In other words, the system can keep track of an employee's developmental needs and how these needs have been addressed (e.g., via training) over time.

As an illustration, consider a system offered by Profiles International, called CheckPoint 360. This system, designed for employees in supervisory roles, includes information on the following competencies:

- Communication (listens to others, processes information, communicates effectively)
- Leadership (instills trust, provides direction, delegates responsibility)
- Adaptability (adjusts to circumstances, thinks creatively)
- Relationships (builds personal relationships, facilitates team success)
- Task management (works efficiently, works competently)
- Production (takes action, achieves results)
- Development of others (cultivates individual talent, motivates successfully)
- Personal development (displays commitment, seeks improvement)

The CheckPoint 360 system includes self-evaluations as well as evaluations provided by the direct supervisor, direct reports, and peers. After performance information has been collected from all these sources, the manager evaluated receives feedback in the form of the graph shown in Figure 8-2. This graph illustrates the discrepancies between self- and others' ratings as well as the scores obtained for each competency. For example, this graph shows that this particular manager has the greatest gap for the competency "development of others." Specifically, the manager assigned a score of about 4.5 to herself, whereas the average score provided by her direct supervisor, direct reports, and peers is only 2.55. The CheckPoint system uses the following scale to rate competencies:

0	**Not Applicable** (not averaged into scores)
1	**Never** demonstrates this
2	**Seldom** demonstrates this
3	**Sometimes** demonstrates this
4	**Usually** demonstrates this
5	**Always** demonstrates this

In this particular illustration, the manager believes that she displays behaviors indicating the competency "development of others" somewhere between "usually" and "always." By contrast, her supervisor (i.e., "boss"), employees, and peers believe that she demonstrates these behaviors somewhere between "seldom" and "sometimes." In other words, the self-rating falls within the favorable zone whereas the ratings provided by others do not.

To explore this gap further, the report provided to the manager also includes more detailed information on the scores provided by each source of information. The Reference Group Comparison chart included in Figure 8-3 shows this information. An examination of the scores provided for the competency "development of others" indicates that all sources, except for the manager herself, agree that work is needed regarding this competency because all scores are between the "seldom" and "sometimes" categories. By contrast, the manager believes she is doing an exceptional job of cultivating individual talent (score of 5) and motivating successfully (score of 4).

FIGURE 8-2
Checkpoint 360-degree
Competency System:
Executive Overview.
© Profiles International, Inc.,
Waco, Texas, USA

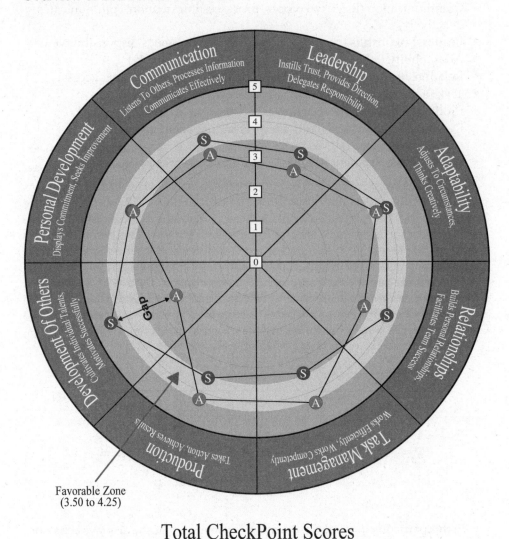

Executive Overview
Overview of Self vs. All Observers

Favorable Zone
(3.50 to 4.25)

Total CheckPoint Scores

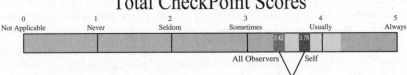

Color Key: **S** Self **A** All Observers (combined scores of Boss, Direct Reports and Peers)
◄—Gap—►: Self perception varies from All Observers by 1 point or more.

Source: Bob Gately, Strategic Business Partner of Profiles International, Inc. 508-634-7748, bob@gatelyconsulting.
com, http://www.gatelyconsulting.com/chkpoint.htm. Courtesy of Profiles International, Inc.

Reference Group Comparison
with Management Alignment of Self and Boss

FIGURE 8-3
Checkpoint 360-degree
Competency System:
Reference Group
Comparison. © Profiles
International, Inc., Waco,
Texas, USA

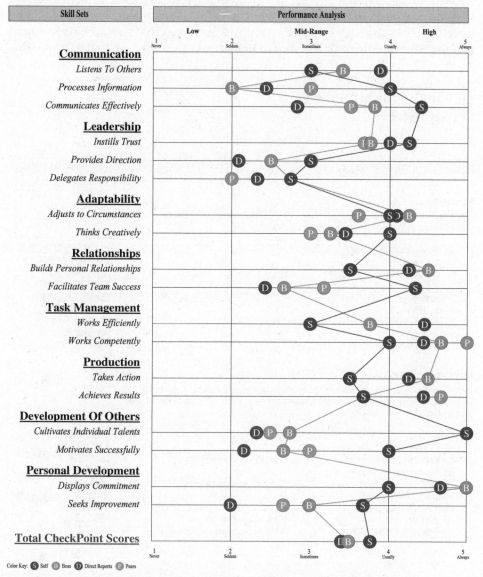

Color Key: **S** Self **B** Boss **D** Direct Reports **P** Peers

Source: Bob Gately, Strategic Business Partner of Profiles International, Inc. 508-634-7748, bob@gatelyconsulting.com, http://www.gatelyconsulting.com/chkpoint.htm. Courtesy of Profiles International, Inc.

It is not sufficient, however, just to provide scores regarding each of the competencies. Becoming aware that there is a problem with a competency is a very good first step, but a good multisource feedback system also provides concrete suggestions about what to do to improve competencies.[24] The CheckPoint system does this by providing what is called a *development summary*. The development summary describes strengths and areas that should be developed further. An example of this is shown in Figure 8-4. According to the graph, this

FIGURE 8-4

Checkpoint 360-degree
Competency System:
Development Summary.
© Profiles International, Inc.,
Waco, Texas, USA

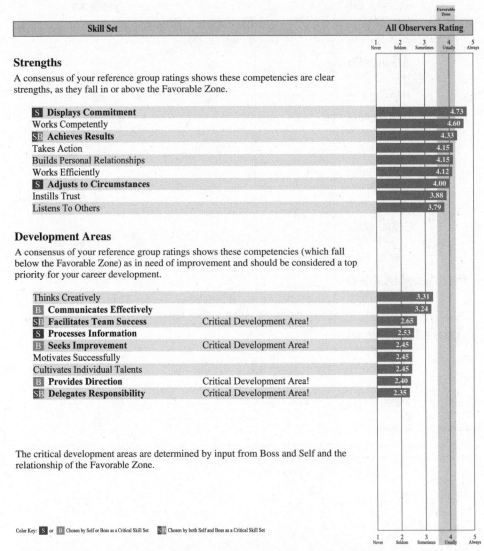

Development Summary
for Darcy Walker

Skill Set		All Observers Rating

Rating scale: 1 Never, 2 Seldom, 3 Sometimes, 4 Usually, 5 Always (Favorable Zone at 4)

Strengths

A consensus of your reference group ratings shows these competencies are clear strengths, as they fall in or above the Favorable Zone.

Skill Set	Rating
S Displays Commitment	4.73
Works Competently	4.60
SB Achieves Results	4.33
Takes Action	4.15
Builds Personal Relationships	4.15
Works Efficiently	4.12
S Adjusts to Circumstances	4.00
Instills Trust	3.88
Listens To Others	3.79

Development Areas

A consensus of your reference group ratings shows these competencies (which fall below the Favorable Zone) as in need of improvement and should be considered a top priority for your career development.

Skill Set	Note	Rating
Thinks Creatively		3.31
B Communicates Effectively		3.24
SB Facilitates Team Success	Critical Development Area!	2.65
S Processes Information		2.53
B Seeks Improvement	Critical Development Area!	2.45
Motivates Successfully		2.45
Cultivates Individual Talents		2.45
B Provides Direction	Critical Development Area!	2.40
SB Delegates Responsibility	Critical Development Area!	2.35

The critical development areas are determined by input from Boss and Self and the relationship of the Favorable Zone.

Color Key: S or B Chosen by Self or Boss as a Critical Skill Set SB Chosen by both Self and Boss as a Critical Skill Set

Source: Bob Gately, Strategic Business Partner of Profiles International, Inc. 508-634-7748, bob@gatelyconsulting .com, http://www.gatelyconsulting.com/chkpoint.htm. Courtesy of Profiles International, Inc.

particular manager has several strengths, but also, some areas that deserve further development. For example, there is a need to work on the "facilitates team success" dimension of the competency "relationships." The report also includes specific suggestions on how to improve this competency, which are shown in Figure 8-5. Specifically, the manager is given tips and advice regarding concrete steps to be taken to improve performance. For example, in terms of learning to collaborate on team decisions, the manager is given advice about how to compromise and reach win-win decisions and how to gain support for decisions.

Suggestions for Improvement
for Darcy Walker

FIGURE 8-5
Checkpoint 360-degree Competency System: Suggestions for Improvement. © Profiles International, Inc., Waco, Texas, USA

The following suggestions will help direct your development efforts:

Facilitates Team Success

Handle Conflict in a Direct and Effective Manner.

- Don't ignore conflict, thinking it will disappear. It won't. And don't expect a conflict-free workplace. Some discord is inevitable and constructively dealing with it will create a more productive work environment.
- Listen carefully to all viewpoints in a disagreement. Define the problem. Then begin the process of resolution.
- Explore multiple options. Then resolve differences with solutions that are acceptable to all involved parties.

Encourage Cooperation in Order to Reap the Benefits of a Strongly Unified Group Effort.

- When recognizing outstanding performance, go beyond the acknowledgment of individual successes. Give equal emphasis to team achievements and effective cooperation among teams.
- Validate the importance of each and every team member's contribution.

Learn to Collaborate on Team Decisions.

- Practice the art of compromise when making decisions, creating win/win situations.
- To gain support for decisions, involve the team in considering alternative approaches. Strive for consensus in order to increase commitment to the final decision.

Establish Team Objectives.

- As much as possible involve the team in formulating goals consistent with, and supportive of, the overall mission of your business. Also solicit input when planning the implementation of the goals.
- Make sure everyone understands the team's goals, as well as their role in attaining the goals.
- Keep everyone apprised of team progress.

Develop Group Dynamics That Bring Out the Best in Everyone.

- Recruit individuals with talents that will complement the skills of other team members.
- Capitalize on each person's strengths and experiences to create a potent team effort.

Source: Bob Gately, Strategic Business Partner of Profiles International, Inc. 508-634-7748, bob@gatelyconsulting.com, http://www.gatelyconsulting.com/chkpoint.htm. Courtesy of Profiles International, Inc.

8-3-1 Benefits of Multisource Feedback Systems

Organizations and individuals can gain several advantages as a consequence of implementing a multisource feedback system. These include the following:

- *Decreased possibility of biases.* Because these systems include information from more than one source, there is a decreased possibility of biases in the identification of employees' weaknesses.
- *Increased awareness of expectations.* Employees become aware of others' expectations about their performance. This includes not only the supervisor's expectations, but also, the expectations of other managers, peers, direct reports, and customers.
- *Increased commitment to improve.* By using multisource feedback systems, information about performance is no longer a private matter. Thus, employees become aware of what others think about their performance, which increases their commitment to improve in the future.
- *Improved self-perceptions of performance.* Employees' distorted views of their own performance are likely to change as a result of the feedback received from other sources. In other words, it is difficult to continue to have distorted views of one's own performance in the presence of overwhelming evidence that these perceptions may not be correct.
- *Improved performance.* Although receiving information about one's performance is not sufficient cause to improve, it is certainly a very important step. Thus, having information on one's performance, if paired with a good development plan, is likely to lead to performance improvement.
- *Reduced "undiscussables" and defensiveness.* Multisource feedback systems provide an excellent opportunity for coworkers, superiors, and direct reports to give information about performance in an anonymous and nonthreatening way. Many supervisors may feel uncomfortable about providing negative feedback and some issues become "undiscussables." But a multisource system makes providing such feedback easier. Also, from the perspective of employees, it is harder to ignore and become defensive regarding the accuracy of performance feedback when it originates from multiple sources.[25]
- *Employees enabled to take control of their careers.* By receiving detailed and constructive feedback on weaknesses and strengths in various areas, employees can gain a realistic assessment of where they should go with their careers.

Table 8-2 includes a summarized list of benefits that organizations can obtain from implementing a multisource feedback system. Consider an organization for which you have worked that has implemented a multisource feedback system. If you cannot think of one, talk to friends or family members and ask them about a system they

TABLE 8-2

Summary List of Benefits Resulting From a Multisource Feedback System

Decreased possibility of biases
Increased awareness of expectations
Increased commitment to improve
Improved self-perceptions of performance
Improved performance
Reduced "undiscussables" and defensiveness
Employees enabled to take control of their careers

have experienced. Then, consider the list of benefits listed in Table 8-2. Which of these were *not* actually realized by the system? Why not?

8-3-2 Risks, Contingencies, and Potential Pitfalls in Implementing Multisource Feedback Systems

We have discussed the many advantages of multisource feedback systems, but we should also consider that there are some risks and potential pitfalls involved.[26] For example, negative feedback can hurt an employee's feelings, particularly if those giving the feedback do not offer their comments in a constructive way. Second, the system is likely to lead to positive results only if individuals feel comfortable with the system and believe they will be rated honestly and treated fairly. User acceptance is an important determinant of the system's success. Third, when very few raters are providing the information, say, two or three, it may be easy for the employee being rated to identify who the raters are. When anonymity is compromised, raters are more likely to distort the information they provide. Fourth, raters may become overloaded with forms to fill out because they need to provide information on so many individuals (peers, superiors, and direct reports). Finally, implementing a multisource feedback system should not be a one-time-only event. The system should be in place and data collected over time on an ongoing basis. The implementation of ongoing multisource feedback systems is sometimes labeled a *720-degree feedback system*, referring to the fact that the collection of multisource data takes place at least twice. In short, administering the system only once will not be as beneficial as administering the system repeatedly.

In addition, we need to be cognizant that multisource feedback systems are not necessarily beneficial for *all* individuals and *all* organizations. For example, individuals who are high on self-efficacy (i.e., they believe they can perform any task) are more likely to improve their performance based on feedback received from peers compared to individuals low on self-efficacy.[27] Also, the effect of receiving feedback from multiple sources is most beneficial for individuals who perceive there is a need to change their behavior, react positively to feedback, believe change is feasible, set appropriate goals to improve their performance, and take concrete actions that lead to performance improvement.[28] On the other hand, individuals who score lower on self-efficacy pay more attention to the feedback received from their line managers. In other words, an employee's confidence in her own performance influences which sources of feedback are most useful to her.

In terms of organizational characteristics, multisource systems work best in organizations that have cultures that support open and honest feedback. Also, these systems work best in organizations that have a participatory, as opposed to authoritarian, leadership style in which giving and receiving feedback is the norm and is regarded as valuable. For example, consider the case of the Patent Office of the United Kingdom. This organization is characterized by a hierarchical structure, typical of many civil service organizations, as opposed to a flat structure, where employees are involved and teamwork is the norm. The implementation of a multisource feedback system did not lead to the anticipated positive results, and there was a mismatch of expectations between what the board members wanted (i.e., better working relations and a culture change) and what the employees wanted (i.e., individual improvement). Moreover, managers did not show a good understanding of the behaviors they were expected to display, and their performance did not show improvement. Overall, the multisource feedback system was not sufficiently linked to other HR systems and policies.[29]

Answering the following questions can give a good indication as to whether implementing a multisource system would be beneficial in a specific organization:

1. Are decisions that are made about rewards and promotion fairly free of favoritism?
2. Are decisions made that take into account the input of people affected by such decisions?
3. Do people from across departments usually cooperate with each other and help each other?
4. Is there little or no fear of speaking up?
5. Do people believe that their peers and direct reports can provide valuable information about their performance?
6. Are employees trusted to get the job done?
7. Do people want to improve their performance?

In short, the successful implementation of a multisource feedback system is heavily dependent on the culture of the organization and the work context.[30] If the answer to most of these questions is "yes," the implementation of a multisource feedback system is likely to be successful and lead to performance improvement.

The risks associated with implementing a multisource system can be illustrated by Watson Wyatt's Human Capital Index (HCI).[31] This is an ongoing study of the effects of HR practices on the stock value of more than 700 publicly traded companies. One particular result was especially alarming. Of the companies surveyed, those that had implemented multisource feedback had lower stock value! Specifically, the companies that used peer reviews had 4.9 percent lower market value than did similar companies that did not implement peer reviews. Furthermore, companies that implemented upward feedback, where employees rated managers, had a 5.7 percent lower stock value than did similar companies that did not implement upward feedback. Does this necessarily mean that implementing multisource feedback systems causes the stock price to decrease? Based on the data collected, there is no definitive answer to this question. It could be that organizations that are not performing well financially decide to implement multisource feedback systems precisely to help improve their performance. Nevertheless, these results highlight the importance of following best practices in implementing multisource feedback systems to avoid any negative consequences of implementing such a system, which we address next.

8-3-3 Characteristics of a Good Multisource Feedback System

Fortunately, there are several things that can be done to maximize the chance that the system will work properly. When systems have the following characteristics, they are most likely to be successful[32]:

- *Anonymity.* In good systems, feedback is anonymous and confidential. When such is the case, raters are more likely to provide honest information regarding performance, particularly when direct reports are providing information about superiors.

- *Observation of employee performance.* Only those with good knowledge and firsthand experience with the person being rated should participate in the process. There is no point in asking for performance feedback from people who are not able to observe performance directly.

- *Feedback interpretation.* Good systems allow the person being rated to discuss the feedback received with those genuinely interested in the employee's development. In most cases, feedback is discussed with the direct supervisor. In other cases, the discussion can involve a representative of the HR department, a superior, or peer to whom the person does not report directly.

- *Follow-up.* The information gathered has little value if there is no follow-up action. Once feedback is received, it is essential that a development plan is created right away.

- *Used for developmental purposes only (at least initially).* When multisource feedback systems are used for administrative purposes such as promotions and compensation, raters are likely to distort the information provided. Make it clear that the purpose of the system is developmental, and developmental only. Initially, the information collected should not be used for making reward allocations or any other administrative decisions. However, the system may be used for administrative purposes after it has been in place for some time— approximately, two years or so.

- *Avoidance of rater fatigue.* Rater fatigue can be avoided if individuals are not asked to rate too many people at the same time. For example, data collection can be staggered so that not all surveys are distributed at the same time.

- *Emphasis on behaviors.* Although systems can include feedback on both behaviors (competencies) and results, it is better to emphasize behaviors. Focusing on behaviors can lead to the identification of concrete actions that the person being rated can take to improve performance.

- *Raters go beyond ratings.* In addition to providing scores on the various dimensions, raters should provide written descriptive feedback that gives detailed and constructive comments on how to improve performance.[33] It is helpful if this information also includes specific examples that help support the ratings and recommendations provided.

- *Raters are trained.* As in the case of providing evaluations for administrative purposes, raters should be trained. Mainly, this includes skills to discriminate good from poor performance and how to provide feedback in a constructive manner.

Table 8-3 includes a summarized list of characteristics of good multisource feedback systems. Given this list, consider the case of AAH Pharmaceuticals, described in Box 8-3. Based on this information, which characteristics are present? Which are absent?

In closing, this chapter referred to the important role of supervisors in the employee development process. But for managers to become true "performance management leaders," they require specific knowledge and skills. This is the topic that we will address in Chapter 9.

TABLE 8-3
Characteristics of a Good
Multisource Feedback
System

Anonymity
Observation of employee performance
Feedback interpretation
Follow-up
Used for developmental purposes only (at least initially)
Avoidance of rater fatigue
Emphasis on behaviors
Raters go beyond ratings
Raters are trained

Box 8-3

Company Spotlight: Multisource Feedback at AAH Pharmaceuticals

AAH Pharmaceuticals (AAH) utilizes a multisource feedback system that includes several characteristics of a good system. The company, which has nine depots around the United Kingdom, including locations in Belfast, Glasgow, and Sussex, is a wholesaler of pharmaceuticals, providing medical products and services in the UK. AAH, with the help of professional consultants, found the multisource feedback process helpful in providing feedback and useful information for development planning. To help ease employee concern, the company clearly outlined for employees that development planning and feedback were the only purposes, and information would not be used for any other purpose. Employees were also given the option of sharing information with supervisors. The system included gathering performance data from several sources through an automated online system of questionnaires, ensuring that information was anonymous and confidential. After the results were obtained, participants attended a one-day meeting about the results away from the office that included one-on-one interpretation and discussion with the consultant to initiate a development plan. Six-month follow-up meetings were held to review progress toward developmental objectives. AAH found the process to be successful with a first group of managers who went through the process and made plans for a broad rollout of the program for more employees to take advantage of developmental opportunities. In summary, the system utilized by AAH provides an example of several of the characteristics of a successful multisource feedback instrument.[34]

SUMMARY POINTS

- Personal developmental plans are a key component of a performance management system because they specify courses of action to be taken to improve performance. A performance management system that lacks information about how to improve performance will not help employees learn skills beyond what they know and use already. In a nutshell, a good development plan allows employees to answer the following four questions: How can I continually learn and grow in the next year? How can I do better in the future? How can I avoid performance problems faced in the past? Where am I now and where would I like to be in terms of my career path?

- Development plans focus on both the short term and the long term. Specifically, development plans address how to improve performance in the current position, how to sustain good levels of performance in the current position, and how to prepare employees for future advancement. In addition, development plans provide employees with growth opportunities so that even if advancement within the organization is not clear, employees are able to enrich their daily work experiences. In terms of the future, good development plans also help employees build three types of career competencies: reflective (i.e., reflection on motivation, reflection on qualities), communication (i.e., networking and self-profiling), and behavioral (i.e., work exploration and career control). A long-term orientation is also important for organizations because it allows them to use development plans strategically and to gather information useful for succession planning.

- Good development plans include a description of the specific steps to be taken and specific developmental objectives. A good plan includes information about (1) developmental objectives, (2) how the new skills or knowledge will be acquired, (3) a time line regarding the acquisition of the new skills or knowledge, and (4) standards and measures that will be used to assess whether the objectives have been achieved. Learning objectives should be designed strategically to take into account both the needs of the individual and those of the organization.

- Developmental objectives can be achieved by one or more of the following activities (1) on-the-job training, (2) courses, (3) self-guided studying, (4) mentoring, (5) attending a conference or trade show, (6) mixing with the best, (7) getting a degree, (8) job rotation, (9) temporary assignments, and (10) membership or leadership role in professional, trade, or nonprofit organizations. Developmental activities for specific objectives are chosen by the employee and the direct supervisor. This choice is guided by taking into account the employee's learning preferences, the developmental objective in question, and the organization's available resources. Many of these activities are suited for all positions, but some are particularly suited for managerial jobs (e.g., mixing with the best).

- The direct supervisor has a key role in helping the employee define the scope of the development plan and in explaining the relationship between the developmental objectives and strategic priorities for the unit and the organization. The direct supervisor also has direct responsibility for checking on the employee's progress toward achieving the developmental objectives and providing resources so that the employee will be able to engage in the appropriate activities (e.g., courses, mentoring). Also, supervisors can help employees uncover the factors that lead to achievement and job satisfaction by conducting feedforward interviews, whose goal is to understand the types of behaviors and skills that individuals have that allow them to perform well and to think about ways to use these same behaviors and skills in other contexts to make further improvements in the future. Supervisors must reinforce an employee's accomplishments toward completing a development plan so that the employee remains motivated. Finally, supervisors themselves must be motivated to perform all these functions in support of their employees' development plans. To do so, supervisors' performance regarding how well they help their employees develop should be measured and rewarded appropriately. In short, the supervisory role includes the following five functions (1) explaining what is required of the employee to reach a required performance level, (2) referring to appropriate developmental activities, (3) reviewing and making suggestions about developmental objectives, (4) checking on the employee's progress toward developmental objective achievement, and (5) offering the opportunity for regular check-ins and reinforcing positive behaviors.

- Multisource feedback systems are tools that help employees build new skills and improve their performance in general by gathering and analyzing performance information from several sources, including peers, superiors, direct reports, and oneself. Performance information gathered from oneself is compared to information gathered by other sources to perform a gap analysis showing discrepancies between how one sees one's own performance in relation to how others see one's performance. These types of systems are also used to identify performance dimensions for which all, or most, performance information sources agree there is little or substantial room for improvement. Accordingly, this information can be used in creating a development plan.

- The implementation of multisource feedback systems can produce many benefits, including (1) decreased possibility of biases, (2) increased awareness of performance expectations, (3) increased commitment to improve, (4) improved self-perceptions of performance, (5) improved performance, (6) reduction of undiscussables and defensiveness, and (7) increased career control on the part of employees.

- In spite of the many advantages associated with implementing multisource feedback systems, there are some risks involved. For example, negative feedback can hurt an employee's feelings; individuals may not be ready to receive such feedback and may therefore not participate willingly; anonymity may be compromised, and therefore, information may be distorted; and raters may be overloaded with forms to fill out. These risks, and the associated failure of the system, are particularly high when the organization does not value participation in decision making; there is little cooperation among employees; there is favoritism; employees do not value the opinion of others (i.e., peers, direct reports); decisions are based on hearsay; and/or employees are not trusted to get the job done.

- There are some characteristics that will enhance the success rate of a multisource feedback system. These features include the following: there is anonymity; raters have firsthand knowledge of the performance of the person being evaluated; feedback is interpreted by a person genuinely interested in the development of the person evaluated; there is follow-up after receiving feedback; the system is used for development purposes only; raters do not become fatigued; there is an emphasis on behaviors, instead of on results; raters provide information beyond performance ratings only; and raters are trained. The presence of these characteristics is likely to lead to the successful design and implementation of the system.

EXERCISE 8-1 MAKING THE CASE FOR A TOP-NOTCH MULTISOURCE FEEDBACK SYSTEM DEMO

You are in charge of selecting a multisource feedback system that will be purchased by the organization for which you work for or have most recently worked for. First, you need to make sure the system has as many of the ideal characteristics as possible as described in this chapter. Second, you need to select a system that will be particularly suitable to your organization's culture and goals, industry context, as well as resource constraints.

As a first step, do a Google search for "360-degree" and "multisource" feedback system demos. For example, one such demo is available at https://www.hr-survey.com/360FeedbackDemos.htm. Second, critically review a few of the demos, taking into account their positive and less positive features. Third, select a good system and prepare a 5–10 minute presentation to be delivered to the rest of the class, describing the reasons you selected the system you did. Keep in mind that you need to describe, at a minimum, what the good features of the system are and why this system is appropriate for your particular organization.

EXERCISE 8-2 OBTAINING MULTISOURCE FEEDBACK ON YOUR OWN PERFORMANCE

The goal in this exercise is to conduct a multisource feedback system regarding your performance in this class. First, create a list of competencies that are related to the performance of a student taking a performance management course (hint: see Figure 8-2). Second, create a rating form including these competencies (hint: see Figure 8-3). Third, fill out the form and also give the same form to at least three other classmates. After you collect the forms, create a list of strengths and development areas (hint: see Figures 8-4 and 8-5). Finally, schedule individual meetings with each of the classmates who filled out the forms to discuss areas in which there was disagreement. What were those areas? What are the reasons for disagreements across raters? Also, what are your strengths? What are your areas in need of development and what specific actions would you take to address each?

Content of a Personal Development Plan at Brainstorm, Inc.

Cathy is a sales manager at Brainstorm, Inc., a computer software training company that sells Microsoft, Novell, Corel, and Open Office training software, located in Lehi, Utah. One of Cathy's responsibilities is to complete annual performance evaluations with all of her direct reports and create individual development plans for these employees, based on their performance evaluations. Recently, Jay, an inside sales representative and Cathy's direct report, finished his first year's performance evaluation with Cathy. Cathy's performance evaluation of Jay's key competencies and key results is as follows:

Performance Appraisal Form

Key Competencies	Supervisor Comments	Score
Sales and Marketing: Demonstrate knowledge of principles and methods for showing, promoting, and selling products or services.	Could be more proficient with greater product knowledge. Needs greater understanding of the benefits of each of the products.	B–
Customer and Personal Service: Knowledge of principles and processes for providing high-quality customer and personal services.	Good verbal and sales skills most of the time. Had a couple occasions when customers felt like they weren't getting enough personal assistance with recently purchased products.	B+
Interpersonal Communication: Talking to others to convey information effectively as well as giving full attention to what other people are saying, taking time to understand the points being made, and asking questions as appropriate.	Very good. Always enthusiastic with customers and quickly develops a good rapport with new customers.	A–
Persuasion and Negotiation: Persuading others to change their minds or behavior. Bringing others together and trying to reconcile differences.	Adequate, but could be more direct and persuasive with customers.	B
Problem Sensitivity and Ethics: The ability to tell when something is wrong or is likely to go wrong, ethically or otherwise. It does not involve solving the problem, only recognizing there is a problem.	Excellent. Shown great ability to anticipate if contract negotiations are taking an unethical or unprofitable turn for the worse.	A

Key Results	Supervisor Comments	Score
Degree to which employee met monthly sales goals ($50,000 in sales revenue a month):	Adequate. Met sales goals 66 percent of the time in the last six months.	B
Degree to which employee met referral goals (10 referrals a month):	Needs improvement. Met referral goals 50 percent of the time in the last six months.	B–
Number of cold calls made monthly (250):	Excellent. Tirelessly exhibits persistence and hard work in reaching out to businesses.	A

Place yourself in Cathy's shoes, and use the above performance evaluation to develop an individual development plan for Jay (Hint: use information included in Section 8-1 Personal Development Plans).

Improving a Personal Development Plan at Brainstorm, Inc.—Part II

Joe, one of the Partners of Brainstorm, Inc., has been looking into development plans as a possible way of increasing the productivity and morale of the company's sales force. To help him in this project, Cathy has adapted a development plan form from a business magazine she has recently seen and asks you for feedback. Since Cathy is unfamiliar with the characteristics of good development plans, she is particularly interested in your critique of a development plan that she developed for a sales representative, Jay. Note: Brainstorm, Inc., may not be able to finance much in the way of outside learning; however, the company could provide some paid time off and may be able to negotiate some better rates for attending classes or conferences, based on various industry memberships.

1. How would you improve and/or change the following form and its content?
2. Because there are only six employees in the company, how would you adapt the form to meet the needs of this small business? Provide an example.

Brainstorm, Inc., Development Plan

Updated: June 28, 2019

Name: Jay

Job Title/Job Code: Sales Representative

Department: Sales

Developmental Options
OJT (On-the-job training)
Courses
Self-guided studying
Mentoring
Attending a conference or trade show
Mixing with the best
Getting a degree
Temporary assignments
Membership or leadership role (professional, trade, non-profit organizations)
Other (specify)

Description
Type of Development
When
How Long
Completed Hours (this Quarter)
Comments—Approximate Cost—Other
Objectives/
Evaluation

Current Quarter

Next Quarter

Current +2

Current +3

(Continued)

Primary Reviewer: Cathy

Education: High school graduate

Prior Training: Bachelor's degree in Sales and Marketing

Job History: 10 years of experience in sales. Two years of experience in software training sales.

Career Goals:

Next 1 year

Next 2 years

Next 3 years

Next 5 years—Become head of sales and lead sales trainer.

ENDNOTES

1. Orlando, J., & Bank, E. (2016). A new approach to performance management at Deloitte. *People & Strategy, 39*(2), 42–44.
2. Akkermans, J., Brenninkmeijer, V., Schaufeli, W. B., & Blonk, R. B. (2015). It's all about CareerSKILLS: Effectiveness of a career development intervention for young employees. *Human Resource Management, 54,* 533–551.
3. Boswell, W. R., & Boudreau, J. W. (2000). Employee satisfaction with performance appraisals and appraisers: The role of perceived appraisal use. *Human Resource Development Quarterly, 11,* 283–299.
4. Ellis, K. (2004). Individual development plans: The building blocks of development. *Training, 41*(December), 20–25.
5. Church, A. H., Rotolo, C. T., Ginther, N. M., & Levine, R. (2015). How are top companies designing and managing their high-potential programs? A follow-up talent management benchmark study. *Consulting Psychology Journal: Practice & Research, 67,* 17–47.
6. Tyler, K. (2004). One bad apple: Before the whole bunch spoils, train managers to deal with poor performance. *HR Magazine, 49*(12), 77–86.
7. Parker, S. K., Morgeson, F. P., & Johns, G. (2017). One hundred years of work design research: Looking back and looking forward. *Journal of Applied Psychology, 102,* 403–420.
8. Watanabe, T. (2016). UC Berkeley chancellor under investigation for alleged misuse of public funds. *Los Angeles Times.* Retrieved January 2, 2018, from http://www.latimes.com/local/education/la-me-ln-berkeley-chancellor-probe-20160712-snap-story.html
9. Harnish, V. (2017). 5 trends to ride in 2017. *Fortune, 175*(4), 32.
10. Dragoni, L., Tesluk, P. E., Russell, J. A., & Oh, I. (2009). Understanding managerial development: Integrating developmental assignments, learning orientation, and access to developmental opportunities in predicting managerial competencies. *Academy of Management Journal, 52,* 731–743.
11. Dunning, D. (2004). TLC at work: Training, leading, coaching all types for star performance. Palo Alto, CA: Davies-Black.
12. Kluger, A. N., & Nir, D. (2010). The feedforward interview. *Human Resource Management Review, 20,* 235–246.
13. Budworth, M., Latham, G. P., & Manroop, L. (2015). Looking forward to performance improvement: A field test of the feedforward interview for performance management. *Human Resource Management, 54,* 45–54.
14. Young, S., Gentry, W., & Braddy, P. (2016). Holding leaders accountable during the 360° feedback process. *Industrial and Organizational Psychology, 9,* 811–813.
15. Ellis, K. (2003). Developing for dollars. *Training, 40*(5), 34–38.
16. Bracken, D. W., & Rose, D. S. (2011). When does 360-degree feedback create behavior change? And how would we know it when it does? *Journal of Business and Psychology, 26,* 183–192.
17. Garretson, C. (2005, January). Diageo distills IS Leaders. *Network World*, 42.
18. Bracken, D., Rose, D., & Church, A. (2016). The evolution and devolution of 360° feedback. *Industrial and Organizational Psychology, 9,* 761–794.

19. Morgeson, F. P., Mumford, T. V., & Campion, M. A. (2005). Coming full circle: Using research and practice to address 27 questions about 360-degree feedback programs. *Consulting Psychology Journal: Practice and Research, 57*, 196–209.

20. Toegel, G., & Conger, J. A. (2003). 360-degree assessment: Time for reinvention. *Academy of Management Learning & Education, 2*, 297–311.

21. Mone, E. M., & London, M. (2010). *Employee engagement through effective performance management*. New York, NY: Routledge.

22. 360 employee feedback from app on Morf Playbook. (2016). *Worldwide Videotex Update, 35*(6), 7–8.

23. Frauenheim, E. (2006). Talent management software is bundling up. *Workforce Management, 85*(19), 35.

24. Luthans, F., & Peterson, S. J. (2003). 360-degree feedback with systematic coaching: Empirical analysis suggests a winning combination. *Human Resource Management, 42*, 243–256.

25. Campion, M. C., Campion, E. D., & Campion, M. A. (2015). Improvements in performance management through the use of 360 feedback. *Industrial and Organizational Psychology, 8*, 85–93.

26. Vukotich, G. (2014). 360° feedback: Ready, fire, aim-Issues with improper implementation. *Performance Improvement, 53*(1), 30–35.

27. Bailey, C., & Austin, M. (2006). 360 degree feedback and developmental outcomes: The role of feedback characteristics, self-efficacy and importance of feedback dimensions to focal managers' current role. *International Journal of Selection and Assessment, 14*, 51–66.

28. Smither, J. W., London, M., & Reilly, R. R. (2005). Does performance improve following multisource feedback? A theoretical model, meta-analysis, and review of empirical findings. *Personnel Psychology, 58*, 33–66.

29. Morgan, A., Cannan, K., & Cullinane, J. (2005). 360° feedback: A critical enquiry. *Personnel Review, 34*, 663–680.

30. Maurer, T. J., Barbeite, F. G., & Mitchell, D. R. (2002). Predictors of attitudes toward a 360-degree feedback system and involvement in post-feedback management development activity. *Journal of Occupational & Organizational Psychology, 75*, 87–107.

31. Pfau, B., & Kay, I. (2002). Does 360-degree feedback negatively affect company performance? *HR Magazine, 47*(6), 54–59.

32. Some of these recommendations are adapted from DeNisi, A. S., & Kluger, A. N. (2000). Feedback effectiveness: Can 360-degree appraisals be improved? *Academy of Management Executive, 14*, 129–139; and McCarthy, A. M., & Garavan, T. N. (2001). 360° feedback process: Performance, improvement and employee career development. *Journal of European Industrial Training, 25*, 5–32.

33. Kabins, A. (2016). Why the qualms with qualitative? Utilizing qualitative methods in 360° feedback. *Industrial and Organizational Psychology, 9*, 806–810.

34. Towner, N. (2004, February). Turning appraisals 360 degrees. *Personnel Today*, 18. Retrieved January 2, 2018, from http://www.personneltoday.com/Articles/2004/02/17/22398/turning-appraisals-360-degrees.html

chapter

9

Performance Management Leadership

The ability to learn is the most important quality a leader can have.

—Sheryl Sandberg

Learning Objectives

By the end of this chapter, you will be able to do the following:

1. Become an effective performance management leader by being a coach who creates a good relationship with direct reports, understands that the employee is the source and director of change, that each employee is unique, and that you, as a performance management leader, are the facilitator of the employee growth process.

2. Prepare a coaching program that (a) abides by the key principles of a good manager–employee relationship, an understanding that the employee is the source and director of change, and that each employee is unique; (b) includes actionable functions such as giving advice, providing guidance, giving support, and promoting employee confidence and competence; and (c) includes specific behaviors such as establishing development objectives, communicating effectively, motivating employees, documenting performance, giving feedback, diagnosing performance problems and performance decline, and developing employees.

3. Assess your own coaching style as a driver, persuader, amiable, or analyzer.

4. Minimize time, situational, and activity constraints that create biases when assessing the extent to which employees have made progress in achieving developmental goals.

5. Give effective praise (i.e., also called "positive feedback") and constructive (i.e., also called "negative") feedback that helps build confidence and self-efficacy, develops employee competence and engagement, minimizes defensiveness, and considers generational and individual differences in feedback preferences and reactions.

6. Implement a disciplinary or termination process if an employee does not overcome performance problems over time.

7. Design and lead formal performance review meetings that serve the purposes of allowing employees to improve their performance, building a good relationship between the supervisor and the employee, and identifying important factors that will motivate star performers to stay in the organization.

8. Lead effective performance review meetings by establishing and maintaining rapport, being empathetic and open-minded, observing verbal and nonverbal cues, minimizing threats, and encouraging employee participation.

257

Chapter 8 addressed issues about employee development. Specifically, Chapter 8 discussed how to use a performance management system to help employees develop and improve their performance, and also address more long-term career goals and aspirations. However, performance management systems are not likely to help employees develop and improve their performance if managers do not guide and facilitate the employee development process. To do so, managers must learn several important skills to become *performance management leaders*. These skills include being able to serve as coaches, to observe and document performance accurately, to give both positive feedback (i.e., praise) and constructive feedback (referred to as "negative" feedback), and to conduct useful performance review discussions—including discussions about employee termination and the retention of star performers. Unfortunately, these skills seem to be in short supply; hence, this chapter addresses each of these topics. Let us begin with the first of these issues: coaching.

9-1 COACHING

Coaching is a collaborative, ongoing process in which the managers interact with their direct reports and take an active role and interest in their performance. In general, coaching involves directing, motivating, and rewarding employee behavior. Coaching is a day-to-day and ongoing function that involves observing performance, complimenting good work, and helping to correct and improve performance when it does not meet expectations and standards. Coaching is also concerned with long-term performance and involves ensuring that the development plan is being achieved. Being a coach thus is similar to serving as a consultant, and for coaching to be successful, a coach must establish a helping relationship.[1] Establishing this helping and trusting relationship is particularly important when the supervisor and direct report do not share similar cultural backgrounds, as is often the case with expatriates or when implementing global performance management systems.[2] In such situations, a helping and trusting relationship allows for what is labeled *cultural transvergence* in performance management, which means that cultural differences are discussed openly, and alternate practices, which enhance individual and team performance, are implemented.

Coaching is a pervasive organizational activity, and since the mid-1990s, there has been an explosion of interest in coaching. Currently, organizations are becoming more aware that the tight pool of talent makes employee development much more attractive and cost-effective than replacement; the massive retirement of baby boomers has forced organizations to think seriously and systematically about succession planning; and at the same time, many managers lack performance management skills and time and often outsource feedback and development of employees to external consultants.[3]

The increased importance given to coaching is certainly justified, given its positive results. For example, consider a study involving sales teams of between 6 and 12 members each and district managers in a U.S. affiliate of a global pharmaceuticals company.[4] Results showed that managerial coaching skills had a significant, direct effect on sales goal attainment. In this particular study, the reason why coaching was effective is that it helped improve team role clarity. In other words, managers who had better coaching skills were able to help sales teams resolve ambiguity in what they should and should not do to reach their sales goals. In addition, coaching is not beneficial to large organizations only. On the contrary, it is particularly important in small and medium-sized enterprises (SMEs) as well. A study conducted in the United Kingdom involving more than 1,200 SME managers over a three-year period revealed that coaching training was seen as a very positive experience. Moreover, for some of the SME managers, it was seen as a "life changing experience."[5] Also, coaching seems to be a worldwide phenomenon. For example, a study involving 324 employee–supervisor pairs from 11 service companies in Taiwan found that coaching has positive effects on both employees' task performance and their proactive career behaviors. In other words, coaching helped employee development regarding their current positions as well as their future career prospects and advancement.[6]

Taken together, the evidence regarding coaching effectiveness is quite convincing. A review and integration of 17 different empirical studies found that employees who received coaching do their jobs better and improve their task-related as well as affective-related skills. As a result, coaching also improves performance measured in terms of results and overall organizational performance as well. These effects were larger when coaching was done by an internal organizational coach (e.g., one's direct supervisor), as compared to an external coach (i.e., external consultant).[7]

Although many theories on coaching exist, there are four guiding principles that provide a good framework for understanding successful coaching[8]:

1. *A good coaching relationship is essential.* For coaching to work, it is imperative that the relationship between the coach and the employee be trusting and collaborative. As noted by Professors Farr and Jacobs, the "collective trust" of all stakeholders in the process is necessary.[9] To achieve this type of relationship, first, the coach must listen in order to understand. In other words, the coach needs to try to walk in the employee's shoes and view the job and organization from the employee's perspective. Second, the coach needs to search for positive aspects of the employee because this is likely to lead to a better understanding and acceptance of the employee. Third, the coach needs to understand that coaching is not something done *to* the employee, but done *with* the employee. Overall, the manager needs to coach with empathy and compassion. Such compassionate coaching will help develop a good relationship with the employee. In addition, there is an important personal benefit for the coach. This type of compassionate coaching has the potential to serve as an antidote to the chronic stress experienced by many managers.[10] Specifically, this type of coaching can ameliorate stress because the experience of compassion elicits responses within the human body that arouse the parasympathetic nervous system (PSNS), which can help mitigate stress.

2. *The employee is the source and director of change.* The coach must understand that the employee is the source of change and self-growth. After all, the purpose of coaching is to change employee behavior and set a direction for what the employee will do better in the future.[11] This type of change will not happen if the employee is not in the driver's

seat. Accordingly, the coach needs to facilitate the employee's setting the agenda, goals, and direction.

3. *The employee is whole and unique.* The coach must understand that each employee is a unique individual with several job-related and job-unrelated identities (e.g., computer network specialist, father, skier) and a unique personal history. The coach must try to create a whole and complete and rich picture of the employee so that employees bring their whole selves to work and are fully engaged.[12] It will be beneficial if the coach has knowledge of the employee's life and can help the employee connect his life and work experiences in meaningful ways.

4. *The coach is the facilitator of the employee's growth.* The coach's main role is one of facilitation. A coach must direct the process and help with the content (e.g., of a developmental plan), but not take control of these issues. The coach needs to maintain an attitude of exploration; help expand the employee's awareness of strengths, resources, and challenges; and facilitate goal setting.

In more actionable terms, coaching involves the following functions[13]:

- Giving *advice* to help employees improve their performance. In other words, coaching involves not only describing *what* needs to be done, but also, *how* things need to be done. Thus, coaching is concerned with both results and behaviors.

- Providing employees with *guidance* so that employees can develop their skills and knowledge appropriately. Coaching involves providing information both about the skills and knowledge that are required to do the work correctly and information about how the employee can acquire these skills and knowledge.

- Providing employees *support* and being there only when needed. Coaching involves being available when the employee needs help, but it also involves not monitoring, controlling, and micromanaging an employee's every move. In the end, coaching is about facilitation. As already mentioned, the responsibility for improving performance ultimately rests on the shoulders of the employee.

- Giving employees *confidence* that will enable them to enhance their performance continuously and to increase their sense of responsibility for managing their own performance. Coaching involves giving positive feedback that allows employees to feel confident about what they do, but it also involves giving feedback on things that can be improved (i.e., constructive feedback).

- Helping employees gain greater *competence* by guiding them toward acquiring knowledge and sharpening the skills that can prepare them for more complex tasks and higher-level positions. Coaching involves a consideration of both short-term and long-term objectives, including how the employee can benefit from acquiring new skills and knowledge that could be useful in future positions and in novel tasks and responsibilities.

Based on this list of the various actionable functions of coaching, it is evident that coaching requires a lot of effort from the managers. But when done right, mangers become performance management leaders and an organization is able to create a "coaching culture," as illustrated in the case of Becton, Dickinson, and Company (BD), described in Box 9-1.

Box 9-1

Company Spotlight: Turning Managers into Performance Management Leaders at Becton, Dickinson, and Company

A coaching culture and leadership development are viewed as competitive strengths at Becton, Dickinson, and Company (BD). The Washington, D.C.-based company manufactures and sells medical supplies, devices, laboratory instruments, antibodies, reagents, and diagnostic products to health-care organizations, clinical laboratories, private industry, and the public. BD provides innovative solutions that help advance medical research and genomics, enhance the diagnosis of infectious diseases and cancer, improve medication management, promote infection prevention, equip surgical and interventional procedures, and support the management of diabetes. The coaching culture at BD includes the following points, as noted by Joseph Toto, who served as the company's director of leadership development and learning for about a decade:

1. We place high expectations on corporate leaders to model coaching as a productive and effective way to improve performance.

2. We expect leaders at all management levels to be coached, as well as to coach the development of others.

3. We establish coaching as a norm. Leaders must view coaching and development as one of the key responsibilities and deliverables in their roles.

Part of the company's training program includes developing skills through peer coaching and building management skills through peer interaction, support, and guidance. The training sessions emphasize several skills, including listening, asking facilitating and open-ended questions, sharing experiences, and challenging assumptions or discussing actions that might not be productive in the view of the coach. Training of managers also involves self-assessment of strengths and weaknesses and identifying behaviors that would assist them in any given circumstance in which they might find themselves as managers in the company. In summary, BD has utilized training programs to turn managers into performance management leaders by developing and reinforcing a coaching culture. This culture is credited with developing performance management leaders who play a critical role in helping people develop and grow within a very challenging context of a constantly changing industry and business environment.[14]

Given the available empirical evidence, coaching helps turn feedback into results. For this to happen, coaches need to engage in the following specific behaviors:

- *Establish development objectives.* The manager works jointly with the employees in creating the development plan and its objectives.
- *Communicate effectively.* The manager maintains regular and clear communication with employees about their performance, including both behaviors and results.
- *Motivate employees.* Managers must reward positive performance. When positive performance is rewarded, employees are motivated to repeat the same level of positive performance in the future.
- *Document performance.* Managers observe employee behaviors and results. Evidence must be gathered regarding instances of good and poor performance.
- *Give feedback.* Managers measure employee performance and progress toward goals. They praise good performance and point out instances of substandard performance. Managers also help employees avoid poor performance in the future.

- *Diagnose performance problems and performance decline.* Managers must listen to employees and gather information to determine whether performance deficiencies and declines in performance are the result of a lack of knowledge and skills, abilities, or motivation or whether they stem from situational and contextual factors beyond the control of the employee. Diagnosing performance problems is important because such a diagnosis dictates whether the course of action should be, for example, providing the employee with resources so she can acquire more knowledge and skills, or addressing contextual issues that may be beyond the control of the employee (e.g., the employee is usually late in delivering the product because he receives the parts too late).

- *Develop employees.* Managers provide financial support and resources for employee development (e.g., funding training, allowing time away from the job for developmental activities) by helping employees plan for the future and by giving challenging assignments that force employees to learn new things.

Not all coaches abide by the guiding principles, fulfill the coaching functions, and engage in the specific coaching behaviors described here. Managers who do so, of course, are highly effective performance management leaders. In fact, some have become legendary. Consider Table 9-1, which summarizes the key coaching principles, functions, and behaviors, and let us examine the case of Jack Welch, who was extremely dedicated to performance management when he was CEO of General Electric (GE).[15] To get involved with his employees, Welch spoke during a class held at a three-week developmental course for GE's high-potential managers. Over the course of his career, he attended more than 750 of these classes, engaging over 15,000 GE managers and executives. During these presentations, he answered hard questions, and he communicated honestly and candidly with his employees. After the class, he invited all the participants to talk with him after the course concluded. In addition to attending these sessions, he held meetings with his top 500 executives every January. Although Welch did not engage in formal coaching, he used the opportunities to communicate his expectations and receive feedback from the various business groups at GE.

Welch also conducted formal performance reviews in which he engaged in several of the behaviors included in Table 9-1, including establishing developmental

TABLE 9-1

Coaching: Guiding Principles, Actionable Functions, and Specific Behaviors

Principles	Functions	Behaviors
1. A good coaching relationship is essential	1. Give advice	1. Establish developmental objectives
2. The employee is the source and director of change	2. Provide guidance	2. Communicate effectively
	3. Provide support	3. Motivate employees
3. The employee is whole and unique	4. Give confidence	4. Document performance
	5. Promote greater competence	5. Give feedback
4. The coach is the facilitator of the employee's growth		6. Diagnose performance problems and performance decline
		7. Develop employees

objectives, motivating employees, documenting performance, giving feedback, and diagnosing performance problems. He set performance targets and monitored them throughout the year. Each year, the operating heads of GE's 12 businesses received individual, two-page, handwritten notes about their performance. Welch attached the previous year's comments to the new reviews with comments in the margin about the progress made by the individual managers toward his goal or the work that he still needed to do to reach the goal. Then, he distributed bonuses and reiterated the goals for the upcoming year. This process cascaded throughout the organization, as other operating heads engaged in the same performance review discussions with their direct reports.

Another example of Welch's coaching behaviors occurred after he had heard customer complaints about a specific product. Welch charged the manager of the division with improving the productivity of that product fourfold. The manager sent Welch detailed weekly reports over the course of the next four years. Welch would send the reports back every three or four weeks, with comments congratulating successes or pointing out areas in which the manager needed to improve. The manager stated that the fact that the CEO took the time to read his reports each week and send back comments motivated him to reach the lofty goal that Welch had set for him.

In addition to this, Jack Welch took the time to recognize hourly workers and managers who impressed him. For example, after one high-ranking leader turned down a promotion and transfer because he did not want his daughter to change schools, Welch sent him a personal note stating that he admired the man for many reasons and he appreciated his decision to put his family first. The employee explained later that this incident proved that Welch cared about him both as a person and as an employee.

In short, Jack Welch was a legendary performance management leader who developed his employees by setting expectations, communicating clearly, documenting and diagnosing performance, motivating and rewarding his employees, and taking an interest in their personal development. In fact, he followed the principles, played the functions, and engaged in virtually all the behaviors listed in Table 9-1.

Now, give yourself some time to reflect on the following issue. How does Jack Welch compare to the CEO of your current company, or to a CEO you have known or heard about? Which of the principles, functions, and behaviors are missing? What would happen in the organization if these missing principles, functions, and behaviors were put in place?

9-2 COACHING STYLES

A manager's personality and behavioral preferences influence his or her coaching style. There are four main coaching styles: driver, persuader, amiable, and analyzer. First, coaches can adopt a driving style in which they tell the employee being coached what to do. Assume that the coach wants to provide guidance regarding how to deal with a customer. In this situation, the preference for a *driver* is to say to the employee, "You must talk to the customer in *this* way." Such coaches are assertive, speak quickly and often firmly, usually talk about tasks and facts, are not very expressive, and expose a narrow range of personal feelings to others. Second, coaches can use a persuading style in which they try to sell what they want the employee to do. Someone who is a *persuader* would try to explain to the employee why it is beneficial for the organization, as well as for the employee himself, to talk to a customer in a specific way. Like drivers, persuaders are assertive, but they tend to use expansive body gestures, talk more about people and relationships, and expose others to a broad range of personal feelings. Third, other coaches may adopt an *amiable* style and want everyone to be happy. Such coaches are likely to be more subjective than objective and direct employees to talk to customers in a certain way because it "feels" like the right thing to do or because the employee feels it is the right way to do it. Such coaches tend not to be very assertive and to speak deliberately and pause often, seldom interrupt others, and make many conditional statements. Finally, coaches may have a preference for analyzing performance in a logical and systematic way, and then, follow rules and procedures when providing a recommendation. To use the same example, such *analyzer* coaches may tell employees to talk to a customer in a specific way "because this is what the manual says." Analyzers, then, are not very assertive, but like drivers, are likely to talk about tasks and facts, rather than personal feelings.

Which of these four styles is best? Are drivers, persuaders, amiable coaches, or analyzers most effective? The answer is that no style is necessarily superior to the others. Performance management leadership involves sometimes providing direction, sometimes persuading employees how to do things a certain way, sometimes showing empathy and creating positive effects, and sometimes paying close attention to established rules and procedures. One thing is for sure, however: an exclusive emphasis on one of these four styles is not likely to help employees develop and grow. Ineffective coaches stick to one style only and cannot adapt to using any of the other styles. On the other hand, adaptive coaches, who are able to adjust their style according to an employee's needs, are most effective. In fact, 56% of participants in a survey of employees who had a coach at work reported that coaching was not helping them because there was a mismatch between coaching style and employee need.[16] In sum, a combination of styles is needed.

9-3 COACHING PROCESS

The coaching process is shown in Figure 9-1. We already discussed the first three stages of the process in previous chapters. The first step involves setting developmental goals. As discussed in Chapter 8, these developmental goals are a key component of the developmental plan. These goals must be reasonable, attainable, and derived from a careful analysis of the areas in which an employee needs to improve. In addition, goals should take into account both short- and long-term career objectives.

The second step in the coaching process is to identify developmental activities and needed resources that will help the employee achieve the developmental goals. As discussed in Chapter 8, these activities can include on-the-job training, courses, self-guided studying, mentoring, attending a conference or trade show, mixing with the best, getting a degree, job rotation, temporary assignments, and membership or leadership role in professional, trade, or nonprofit organizations.

FIGURE 9-1
Overview of Coaching Process

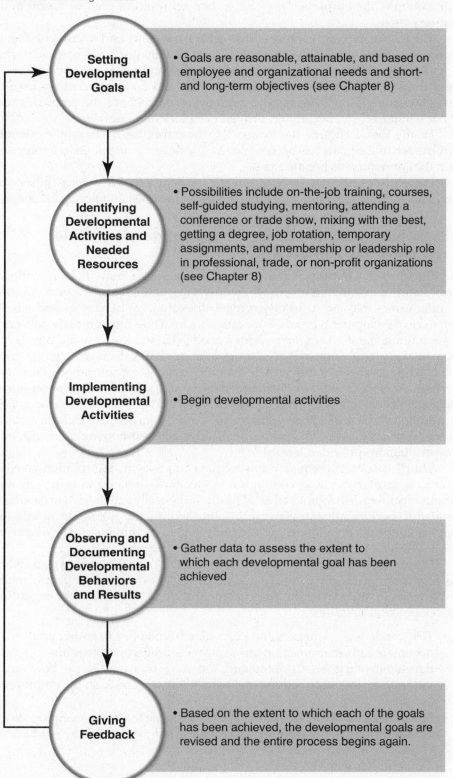

The third step involves implementing the particular developmental activities that will allow the employee to achieve the developmental goals. For example, the employee may begin her job rotation plan or enroll in an online course.

The fourth step in the process is to collect, evaluate, and document data to assess the extent to which each of the developmental goals has been achieved. For example, did the employee complete the developmental activity within the agreed-upon timeline? What are the standards and measures that are used to assess whether the objectives have been achieved and has the employee met these standards (e.g., becoming certified in a particular knowledge domain)?

Finally, the coach provides feedback to the employee. Based on the extent to which each of the goals has been achieved, the developmental goals are revised and the entire process begins again.

Let us discuss the two last stages in the coaching process in detail: observing and documenting developmental behaviors and results, and giving feedback.

9-3-1 Observation and Documentation of Developmental Behaviors and Results

As described in Chapters 6 and 7, respectively, people may make intentional errors and unintentional errors while observing and evaluating performance. Similar errors may occur in observing and evaluating behaviors and results related to developmental goals. For example, a manager might make a halo error by assuming that if an employee does a good job at working toward one developmental goal (e.g., improving her programming skills), she is also doing a good job of working toward a different developmental goal (e.g., improving customer service). As is the case for performance in general, it is important to observe and document behaviors and results specifically related to developmental activities. In addition to data collected by supervisors, other data can also include memos, letters, email messages, handwritten notes, comments, observations, descriptions, and evaluations provided by peers.[17]

The discussion presented in this section complements information given in previous chapters because although it is specifically related to behaviors and results regarding developmental activities, it can be easily generalized to behaviors related to performance in general. In other words, the following discussion applies to the observation of performance in general, not just those displayed while working toward achieving developmental goals.

Observing an employee's progress in achieving developmental goals is not as easy as it may seem. Consider the following constraints that people might experience in attempting to observe an employee's performance regarding developmental activities:

- *Time constraints.* Managers and peers may be too busy to gather and document information about an employee's progress toward his developmental goals. Consequently, too much time may elapse between the assignment of the activity and when there is a check on the employee's progress.
- *Situational constraints.* Managers are often unable to observe employees as they engage in developmental activities, and therefore, may not have

firsthand knowledge about their performance. For example, managers do not observe the extent to which an employee enrolled in an online course is an active participant and contributor or is a passive learner. In this context, it may be appropriate to gather performance data from peers or others who are able to observe performance directly.

- *Activity constraints.* When the developmental activity is highly unstructured, such as an employee reading a book, the manager may have to wait until the activity is completed to assess whether the activity has been beneficial.

How can we address these constraints and make sure that a manager will be able to observe and evaluate an employee's performance regarding developmental activities? The recommendations provided in Chapter 7 regarding the observation and evaluation of performance in general apply here as well. Specifically, a good communication plan should explain the benefits of implementing a development plan effectively. This helps managers accept the plan. Also, managers should be trained so that they minimize errors (i.e., rater error training), share notions of what it means to complete developmental activities successfully (i.e., frame-of-reference training), and observe performance accurately (i.e., behavioral observation training). As an example, Box 9-2 includes a description of how managers are trained at Hallmark.

Finally, we need to understand the forces that motivate managers to invest time and effort, or not, in the development of their employees. Clearly, some managers will be more motivated than others to help their direct reports because they may be "givers" rather than "takers."[18] In other words, there are individual differences in how different people behave toward others. However, in spite of differences in how people tend to behave naturally, it is important that managers see a direct connection between their efforts to develop people around them and outcomes for themselves. In other words,

Box 9-2

Company Spotlight: Turning Managers into Performance Management Leaders at Hallmark

Hallmark sought to improve management communications with employees and initiated a training program that has been well received and viewed as a strategic benefit to the company. U.S.-based Hallmark is a retailer and wholesaler of greeting cards, stationery, flowers, and gifts, with operations in the United States and Great Britain. The company initiated training to help managers become performance management leaders. The training program sought to provide skill development in increasing two-way communication, with a greater frequency of communication and increased interaction of managers with employees. Training sessions included self-assessment, small group role-playing, and viewing video clips to enhance understanding of the role of communication. Engagement training focused on gaining the trust of employees as well as their involvement and ownership in business outcomes. Follow-up resources were also made available for managers to continue to improve their leadership competency. Following the training in this area, managers gave positive feedback, and employee surveys have shown that employee engagement has increased at all levels of the organization.[19]

what does the manager gain if her employee's developmental activities are supervised appropriately? What does the manager gain if she becomes a performance management leader?

The importance of documenting an employee's progress toward the achievement of developmental goals cannot be overemphasized. Similarly, it is critical to document employee performance in general. Why is it so important for performance management leaders to do so? Consider the following reasons:

- *Minimize cognitive load.* Observing and evaluating developmental activities, and performance in general, is a complex cognitive task. Thus, documentation helps prevent memory-related errors.
- *Create trust.* When documentation exists to support evaluations, there is no mystery regarding the outcomes. This, in turn, promotes trust and acceptance of decisions based on the evaluation provided.
- *Plan for the future.* Documenting developmental activities and their outcomes enables discussion about specific facts instead of assumptions and hearsay. A careful examination of these facts permits better planning of developmental activities for the future.
- *Provide legal protection.* Specific laws prohibit discrimination against members of various classes (e.g., sex or religion) in how developmental activities are allocated. For example, it is prohibited to provide male employees with better developmental opportunities than female employees. In addition, some court rulings have determined that employees working under contract may challenge a dismissal. Thus, keeping accurate records of what developmental activities employees have completed and with what degree of success, as well as performance in general, provides a good line of defense in case of litigation based on discrimination or wrongful termination.

The importance of keeping thorough performance documentation and taking actions consistent with this documentation is illustrated by the outcome of several legal cases. In one such case, John E. Cleverly, an employee at Western Electric Co., was discharged after 14 years of good service.[20] Western Electric was found guilty of age discrimination, and Cleverly was awarded back pay because the documentation indicated that Cleverly had been given adequate performance ratings and increases to his salary over a course of 14 years. Upon his discharge, six months before his pension vested, Cleverly was informed that one reason for his discharge was to make room for younger employees. As illustrated by this case, documentation of performance should be taken seriously. In this case, the documentation available indicated the employee had a valid claim. In other cases, documentation could be used to discount charges of discrimination. If Cleverly had alleged age discrimination, but the company could show that his performance was declining over time, then the company could have won the case.

What can performance management leaders do to document performance regarding developmental activities, and performance in general, in a useful and constructive way? Consider the following recommendations[21]:

- *Be specific.* Document specific events and outcomes. Avoid making general statements, such as "He's lazy." Provide specific examples to illustrate your point, for example, "He turns in reports after deadlines at least once a month."
- *Use adjectives and adverbs sparingly.* The use of evaluative adjectives (e.g., good, poor) and adverbs (e.g., speedily, sometimes) may lead to ambiguous interpretations. In addition, it may not be clear whether the level of achievement has been average or outstanding.
- *Balance positives with negatives.* Document instances of both good and poor performance. Do not focus only on the positives or only on the negatives.
- *Focus on job-related information.* Focus on information that is job-related, and specifically, related to the developmental activities and goals at hand.
- *Be comprehensive.* Include information on performance regarding all developmental goals and activities and cover the entire review period as opposed to a shorter time period. Also, document the performance of all employees, not just those who are not achieving their developmental goals.
- *Standardize procedures.* Use the same method and format to document information for all employees.
- *Describe observable behavior and results.* Phrase your notes in behavioral and results terms and avoid statements that would imply subjective judgment or prejudice.

Obviously, not all managers do a good job of documenting performance about the accomplishment of developmental goals or performance in general. Table 9-2 includes a summarized list of recommendations to follow in the documentation process.

Now, consider the recommendations listed in Table 9-2 in evaluating the set of quotes appearing in Table 9-3 taken from actual employee performance evaluations in a large corporation in the United States.[22] We can be sure that the employees at the receiving end of these quotes would not be very happy with them. It also goes without saying that this type of documentation would be extremely detrimental to the performance management system. In fact, this organization would have serious problems beyond the scope of its performance evaluation system.

Now, let us turn to the final important component of the coaching process: giving feedback.

9-3-2 Giving Feedback

Giving feedback to an employee regarding her progress toward achieving goals is a key component of the coaching process.[23] Feedback is information about past

TABLE 9-2

Documenting Developmental Performance Activities and Performance in General: Some Recommendations

Be specific.
Use adjectives and adverbs sparingly.
Balance positives with negatives.
Focus on job-related information.
Be comprehensive.
Standardize procedures.
Describe observable behavior.

TABLE 9-3
Individual Quotes Taken from Actual Employee Performance Evaluations

Since my last report, this employee has reached rock bottom . . . and has started to dig.
I would not allow this employee to breed.
This employee is really not so much of a has-been, but more of a definitely won't be.
Works well when under constant supervision and cornered like a rat in a trap.
He would be out of his depth in a parking lot puddle.
He sets low personal standards and then consistently fails to achieve them.
This employee is depriving a village somewhere of an idiot.
This employee should go far, . . . and the sooner he starts, the better.
He's been working with glue too much.
He would argue with a signpost.
He has a knack for making strangers immediately detest him.
He brings a lot of joy whenever he leaves the room.
If you see two people talking and one looks bored . . . he's the other one.
Donated his brain to science before he was done using it.
Gates are down, the lights are flashing, but the train isn't coming.
If he were any more stupid, he'd have to be watered twice a week.
If you gave him a penny for his thoughts, you'd get change.
If you stand close enough to him, you can hear the ocean.
One neuron short of a synapse.
Some drink from the fountain of knowledge . . . he only gargled.
Takes him 2 hours to watch *60 Minutes*.
The wheel is turning, but the hamster is dead.

performance with the goal of improving future performance. Although "back" is part of feed*back*, giving feedback has both a past and a future component. This is why, when done properly, feedback can be relabeled feed*forward*—as described in Chapter 8 regarding the feedforward interview.

Feedback includes information about both positive and negative aspects of job performance and lets employees know how well they are doing with respect to meeting the established standards.[24] For example, the so-called 2 + 2 performance appraisal model for teachers includes peer teachers who observe each other perform in the classroom, and then, offer two compliments and two suggestions for improvement.[25] Feedback is important in the context of performance regarding development activities and goals. Our discussion of feedback, however, goes beyond that and includes feedback about performance in general. Feedback is not a magic bullet for performance improvement[26]; however, it serves several important purposes:

- *Helps build confidence and self-efficacy*. Praising good performance builds employee confidence regarding future performance. It also lets employees know that their manager cares about them. In addition, praising good performance enhances self-efficacy: An employee's belief that she will succeed in specific situations or accomplish a task.[27] Note that self-efficacy is not the actual probability that the employee will succeed, but an employee's subjective belief that she will. Self-efficacy is critical because if an employee does not believe he has a good chance of improving his performance, he is not likely to even try.

- *Develops competence.* Communicating clearly about what has been done right and how to do the work correctly is valuable information that helps employees become more competent and improve their performance. In addition, communicating clearly about what has not been done right and explaining what to do the next time provides useful information so that past mistakes are not repeated.
- *Enhances engagement.* Receiving feedback and discussing performance issues allow employees to understand their roles in the unit and organization as a whole. This, in turn, helps employees become more engaged in the unit and the organization.

Unfortunately, however, the mere presence of feedback, even if it is delivered correctly, does not necessarily mean that all of these purposes will be fulfilled. For example, a review of 131 studies that examined the effects of feedback on performance concluded that 38% of the feedback programs reviewed had a *negative* effect on performance.[28] In other words, in many cases, the implementation of feedback led to *lower* performance levels. This can happen when, for example, feedback does not include useful information or is not delivered in the right way.

As an alternative perspective and course of action, now consider the possible cost of *not* providing feedback. First, organizations would be depriving employees of a chance to improve their performance. Second, organizations might be stuck with chronic poor performance because employees do not recognize any performance problems and feel justified in continuing to perform at substandard levels. Finally, employees might develop inaccurate perceptions of how their performance is regarded by others.

Given that, overall, feedback systems can be beneficial, what can we do to make the most of them? Consider the following suggestions to enhance the positive effects of feedback[29]:

- *Timeliness.* Feedback should be delivered as close to the performance event as possible. For feedback to be most meaningful, it must be given immediately after the event.
- *Frequency.* Feedback should be provided on an ongoing basis; daily, if possible. If performance improvement is an ongoing activity, then feedback about performance should also be provided on an ongoing basis.
- *Specificity.* Feedback should include specific work behaviors, results, and the situation in which these behaviors and results were observed.[30] Feedback is not about the employee and how the employee "is," but about behaviors and results and situations in which these behaviors and results occurred.
- *Verifiability.* Feedback should include information that is verifiable and accurate. It should not be based on inferences or rumors. Using information that is verifiable leads to more accurate feedback and subsequent acceptance.

- *Consistency.* Feedback should be consistent. In other words, information about specific aspects of performance should not vary unpredictably between overwhelming praise and harsh criticism.
- *Privacy.* Feedback should be given in a place and at a time that prevents any potential embarrassment. This applies to both criticism and praise, because some employees, owing to personality or cultural background, may not wish to be rewarded in public.
- *Consequences.* Feedback should include contextual information that allows the employee to understand the importance and consequences of the behaviors and results in question. For example, if an employee became frustrated and behaved inappropriately with an angry customer and the customer's complaint was not addressed satisfactorily, feedback should explain the impact of these behaviors (e.g., behaving inappropriately) and results for the organization (e.g., the customer's problem was not resolved, the customer was upset, the customer was not likely to give repeat business to the organization).
- *Description first, evaluation second.* Feedback should first focus on describing behaviors and results rather than on evaluating and judging behaviors and results. It is better first to report what has been observed, and once there is agreement about what happened, to evaluate what has been observed. If evaluation takes place first, employees may become defensive and reject the feedback.
- *Performance continuum.* Feedback should describe performance as a continuum, going from less to more in the case of good performance, and from more to less in the case of poor performance. In other words, feedback should include information on how to display good performance behaviors more often and poor performance behaviors less often. Thus, performance is a matter of degree, and even the worst performer is likely to show nuggets of good performance that can be described as a starting point for a discussion on how to improve performance.
- *Pattern identification.* Feedback is most useful if it is about a pattern of poor performance, rather than isolated events or mistakes. Identifying a pattern of poor performance also allows for a better understanding of the causes leading to poor performance.
- *Confidence in the employee.* Good feedback includes a statement that the manager has confidence that the employee will be able to improve her performance. It is important for the employee to hear this from the manager, as this enhances employee self-efficacy. This reinforces the idea that feedback is about performance and not the performer. Note, however, that this should be done only if the manager indeed believes the employee can improve her performance. In the case of a chronic poor performance, this type of information could be used out of context later if the employee is fired.
- *Advice and idea generation.* Feedback can include advice given by the supervisor about how to improve performance. In addition, however, the employee should play an active role in generating ideas about how to improve performance in the future.

Consider the following vignette in which Alexandra, a supervisor, has observed a specific performance event and provides feedback to her direct report. Alexandra is the manager of a small retail store with approximately five employees. With a small staff, Alexandra looks for coaching opportunities on a weekly basis. Alexandra is working with Caleb today, and she has just witnessed him complete a customer sale. Caleb did not follow several steps, however, that should be included at each sale, and because the store is now empty, Alexandra decides it is a perfect opportunity for a coaching session.

ALEXANDRA: Hey, Caleb, that was great the way that you just assisted that customer in finding her correct size in the jeans. Thanks for taking the extra time to help her.

CALEB: Thanks, Alexandra, not a problem.

ALEXANDRA: I would like to go over the sales transaction with you.

CALEB: Sure.

ALEXANDRA: After you helped the woman find her jeans, you promptly brought her over and rang her up. That was a good sale because those jeans were a full-priced item; however, you didn't complete all of the tasks associated with closing a sale. In the training last week, we discussed the importance of adding on additional sales, entering the customer's personal contact information in our system, and letting them know about upcoming sales.

CALEB: Yes, I just remembered us talking about that. When customers seem in a hurry, I feel bad about asking them additional questions.

ALEXANDRA: That's a very valid concern. Can you think of ways to increase the efficiency of adding these few steps into the sales transaction process so that you feel comfortable performing them in the future? I would like to help you do that because increasing the number of items you sell during each transaction could help you win the upcoming sales contests.

CALEB: That would be great. I would really like some new ideas about talking to customers.

ALEXANDRA: No problem; I know that you are a very capable salesperson. You have great customer service skills, and I think that you can improve your sales and possibly win one of the upcoming contests.

Alexandra and Caleb then generate ideas about how to improve Caleb's performance.

In this vignette, Alexandra demonstrated several of the behaviors listed in Table 9-4. She was specific about the behaviors and results, the information was verifiable, and it was timely because the behavior had just occurred. In addition, since Alexandra communicates her expectations on a weekly basis,

TABLE 9-4

Characteristics of Effective Feedback

Timely
Frequent
Specific
Verifiable
Consistent
Private
Consequential
Descriptive first and evaluative second
Related to a performance continuum
Based on identifiable patterns of performance
A confidence builder for employees
A tool for generating advice and ideas

the information she provides is consistent. Finally, she described the behavior first, and then, evaluated its effectiveness; she communicated confidence in Caleb and she offered to help him generate ideas about how to improve his effectiveness. On the other hand, Alexandra left out several important things while coaching Caleb. First, she did not communicate the consequences of his behavior, for example, that his failure to follow the procedures could hurt sales for the entire store. Although the vignette does not describe the idea generation portion of the feedback session, Alexandra did not describe small behaviors that Caleb could use to improve his performance. Finally, Alexandra did not communicate to Caleb whether this behavior was a one-time incident or whether it was a pattern that was affecting his overall work performance.

Overall, if Alexandra continues to look for coaching opportunities with her employees, her relationship with her employees and their performance in the store will continue to improve. To be more effective as a performance management leader, however, she may need to work on communicating the patterns of behavior that result in poor performance and the consequences of continued poor performance. Now, let us discuss the nuts and bolts of how to give two types of feedback: praise and constructive (i.e., "negative").

Giving Praise   Good feedback includes information about both good and poor performance. Although most people are a lot more comfortable giving feedback on good performance than they are on poor performance, some guidelines must be followed when giving praise—also called "positive feedback"—so that the feedback is useful in terms of future performance.

First, praise should be sincere and given only when it is deserved. If praise is given repeatedly and when it is not deserved, employees are not able to see when a change in direction may be needed.[31] Second, praise should be about specific behaviors or results and be given within context so that employees know what they need to repeat in the future. For example, a manager can say the following[32]:

> Naomi, thanks for providing such excellent service to our client. Your efforts helped us renew our contract with them for another two years. It's these types of behaviors and results that our group needs to achieve our goal for this year. And, this is exactly what our company is all about: providing outstanding customer service.

Third, in giving praise, managers should take their time and act pleased, rather than rush through the information, looking embarrassed. Finally, avoid giving praise by referring to the absence of the negative, for example, "not bad" or "better than last time." Instead, praise should emphasize the positives and be phrased, for example, as "I like the way you did that" or "I admire how you did that."[33]

Consider the following vignette, which illustrates how a manager might give praise to her employee.

After the successful completion of a three-month project at a large telecommunications company, Hannah, the manager, wants to congratulate Jacob on a job well done. Hannah calls Jacob into his office one day after the project is completed.

HANNAH: Thanks for stopping by Jacob, and thank you for all of your hard work over the past three months. I know that I might not have congratulated you on every milestone you reached along the way, but I wanted to take the time to congratulate you now. Your organizational skills and ability to interact successfully with multiple departments led to the successful completion of the project on time and within budget.

JACOB: Thanks, Hannah. I have really been putting extra effort into completing this project on time.

HANNAH: It shows, Jacob, and I appreciate all of your hard work and dedication to this team and our department. Thanks again and congratulations on a great end to a long three months.

In this vignette, Hannah delivered praise to Jacob successfully and followed the recommendations provided earlier. She was sincere and made sure not to praise Jacob too often, so that when she did praise him, it was meaningful. She described how Jacob's organizational and project management skills led to the successful completion of the project. Finally, Hannah took her time in delivering the praise and made sure that Jacob took the praise seriously.

Giving Constructive Feedback Constructive feedback includes information that performance has fallen short of accepted standards. This type of feedback is sometimes referred to as "negative feedback," but we use constructive feedback because this label has a more positive and future-oriented connotation.

The goal of providing constructive feedback is to help employees improve their performance in the future; it is not to punish, embarrass, or chastise them. It is important to give constructive feedback when it is warranted because the consequences of not doing so can be detrimental for the organization as a whole. For example, Francie Dalton, founder and president of Columbia, Maryland-based Dalton Alliances, Inc., noted the following:

> In organizations where management imposes no consequences for poor performance, high achievers will leave because they don't want to be where mediocrity is tolerated. But mediocre performers will remain because they know they're safe. The entire organizational culture, along with its reputation in the marketplace, can be affected by poor performers.[34]

In spite of the need to address poor performance, managers are usually not very comfortable providing constructive feedback. Why is this so? Consider the following reasons:

- *Negative reactions and consequences.* Managers may fear that employees will react negatively. Negative reactions can include being defensive and even becoming angry at the information received. In addition, managers may fear that the working relationship, or even friendship, with their direct reports may be affected adversely and that giving constructive feedback can introduce elements of mistrust and annoyance.

- *Negative experiences in the past.* Managers themselves may have received constructive feedback at some point in their careers and have experienced firsthand how feelings can be hurt. Receiving constructive feedback can be painful and upsetting, and managers may not want to put their direct reports in such a situation.
- *Playing "God."* Managers may be reluctant to play the role of an all-knowing, judgmental God. They may feel that giving constructive feedback puts them in that position.
- *Need for irrefutable and conclusive evidence.* Managers may not want to provide constructive feedback until after they have been able to gather irrefutable and conclusive evidence about a performance problem. Because this task may be perceived as too onerous, managers may choose to skip giving constructive feedback altogether.

What happens when managers avoid giving constructive feedback and employees avoid seeking it? A *feedback gap* results, in which managers and employees mutually instigate and reinforce lack of communication, which creates a vacuum of meaningful exchanges about poor performance.[35] A typical consequence of a feedback gap is that in the absence of information to the contrary, the manager gives the employee the message that performance is adequate. When performance problems exist, they are likely to become more intense over time. For example, clients may be so dissatisfied with the service they are receiving that they may eventually choose to close their accounts and work instead with the competition. At that time, it becomes impossible for the manager to overlook the performance problem, and she has no choice but to deliver the feedback. At this stage of the process, however, feedback is delivered too late and often in a punitive fashion. Of course, feedback delivered so late in the process and in a punitive fashion is not likely to be helpful.

Alternatively, constructive feedback is most useful when early coaching has been instrumental in identifying warning signs and the performance problem is still manageable. Constructive feedback is also useful when it clarifies unwanted behaviors and consequences and focuses on behaviors that can be changed. There is no point in providing feedback on issues that are beyond the employee's control because there is not much she can do to improve the situation. In addition, employees are more likely to respond positively to constructive feedback when the manager is perceived as being trustworthy and making a genuine attempt to improve the employee's performance. In other words, the manager needs to be perceived as credible, and also, as instrumental in improving the employee's performance in the future.[36] Finally, constructive feedback is most likely to be accepted when it is given by a source who uses straight talk and not subtle pressure and when it is supported by hard data. The supervisor must control her emotions and stay calm. If managers follow these suggestions, it is more likely that employees will benefit from constructive feedback, even if employees are not particularly open to receiving it.[37] Following these suggestions leads to what has been labeled "actionable feedback," meaning that such feedback will allow employees to respond in constructive ways and will lead to learning and performance improvement.[38]

A final and important issue to consider when giving constructive feedback is to use a *strengths-based approach*.[39] The traditional, also called weaknesses-based approach, involves identifying employee weaknesses (e.g., deficiencies in terms of their job performance, knowledge, and skills); providing negative feedback on what the employees are doing wrong or what the employees did not accomplish; and finally, asking them to improve their behaviors or results by overcoming their weaknesses. In contrast, using a strengths-based approach involves identifying employee strengths in terms of their exceptional job performance and asking them to improve their behaviors or results by making continued or more intensive use of their strengths. The key issue is to highlight how strengths can generate success on the job, as this motivates employees to intensify the use of their strengths to produce even more positive behaviors and results.

How is this done? First, the conversation can start with something like "I want to talk to you about some of the great things that you've been doing lately, as well as areas where you can improve. I'd like this time to be about how I can help you be your very best." The supervisor can request assistance from the employee in identifying strength areas by asking, "In what ways do you feel like you've been standing out?" Then, the last step involves identifying how employee strengths, which are used in some types of behaviors and results, can be used in others.

Generational and Individual Differences Regarding Feedback Reactions and Preferences   Regardless of whether feedback includes praise or constructive comments, an important contemporary issue that we should consider is related to feedback reactions and generational differences regarding feedback preference and reactions.[40] Specifically, socioemotional selectivity theory (SST) suggests that younger individuals, because they are closer to the beginning of their life cycles, anchor the concept of "time" as time since birth, and in their minds, time is mostly open-ended. As a consequence of this particular time orientation, Millennials and Post-Millennials (i.e., Generation Z) tend to have work-related goals that are clearly future-oriented: knowledge acquisition, career planning, and the development of ability and skills that will pay off in the future. In contrast, older workers (e.g., Baby Boomers) anchor the concept of time as time left in their careers and in life in general, and thus, see time as more limited. Consequently, they tend to have work-related goals that are more present-oriented: regulating their emotions to be positive and the pursuit of positive social relationships at work (i.e., "social awareness" goals). Offering support for SST, a recent study found that older workers were more open to feedback regarding social awareness issues, but less open to feedback that can be readily used to improve future performance and achieve desired career goals (i.e., "utility" goals) compared to younger workers. The lesson? Performance management leaders are aware of the needs and feedback orientations and reactions of their employees. Accordingly, they modify the type of feedback so that it is most useful, given individual needs and orientations.

Pause for a moment to consider how open you are to receiving feedback about your performance. What is your personal feedback orientation? How receptive are you to receiving feedback? Are you more interested in social awareness or utility feedback? Given your own age, is your feedback orientation consistent with other members of your generation? To help you ponder on these issues, answer the following questions, which are part of the Feedback Orientation Scale.[41] In answering these questions, use a 5-point scale, ranging from strongly disagree to strongly agree. Then, compare your scores with those of a coworker, classmate, or family member who is a member of a different generation:

Social Awareness:

1. I try to be aware of what other people think of me.
2. Using feedback, I am more aware of what people think of me.
3. Feedback helps me manage the impression I make on others.
4. Feedback lets me know how I am perceived by others.
5. I rely on feedback to help me make a good impression.

Utility:

1. Feedback contributes to my success at work.
2. To develop my skills at work, I rely on feedback.
3. Feedback is critical for improving performance.
4. Feedback from supervisors can help me advance in a company.
5. I find that feedback is critical for reaching my goals.

In addition to generational differences, individuals also differ in what is called *feedback-seeking behavior*.[42] In other words, individuals differ in the amount of effort they devote toward understanding the extent to which they are performing well. Specifically, people differ regarding the extent to which they proactively ask peers, supervisors, and others for feedback, and also, in the extent to which they proactively monitor their own performance themselves. What this means in terms of being a performance management leader is that feedback-giving should be proactive and ongoing. Otherwise, individuals who are higher on the feedback-seeking behavior continuum are more likely to receive feedback compared to those who are lower. This is particularly important for newcomers in the organization because not receiving sufficient feedback early on may mean that they may not be able to meet organizational objectives, and possibly, remain within the organization in the long term.

Making the Tough Calls: Disciplinary Process and Organizational Exit This last section about giving feedback is about making some tough calls. In some cases, an employee may not respond to the feedback provided and may not make any improvements in terms of performance. Giving bad news is never an easy process.[43] But in such cases, there is one intermediate step that can be taken before the employee enters a formal disciplinary process, which involves a verbal warning, a written warning, and may lead to termination. The employee can be given a once-in-a-career *decision-making leave*.[44] This is a "day of contemplation" that is paid and allows the employee to stay home and decide whether working in this organization is what he or she really wants to do. This practice is based on adult learning theory, which holds individuals responsible for their actions. Unlike a formal disciplinary action, the decision-making leave does not affect employee pay. As noted by Tim Field, principal of a consulting firm in Los Angeles, California, "This element of holding people accountable without negatively impacting their personnel file or payroll tends to catch people off guard, because problem employees, like problem children, are often expecting negative attention for their bad behavior." How can the decision to grant an employee a decision-making leave be communicated? Assuming this is a company policy and there is senior management support, you can communicate the leave as follows[45]:

> Hailey, as you know, you and I have met on several occasions to talk about your performance. In spite of these feedback sessions, I see that you are still having some difficulties with important tasks and projects. Consistent with my observations, I have received comments from some of your peers related to some performance deficiencies they have also noticed. I think that issuing a written warning would be counterproductive—I am concerned that it may decrease your motivation and do more harm than good. Instead, what I am going to do is to put you on what we call a "decision-making leave" for a day. This is a type of intervention that has worked very well with other individuals in your same position in the past. I want you to know that this is a once-in-a-career benefit that you should use to your advantage and I decided to do this because I truly believe that you are capable of improving your performance. It works like this. I am going to ask you to not come to the office tomorrow but you will be paid for that day, so you don't have to worry about your paycheck being affected. While you are away from the office tomorrow, I want you to give serious thought about whether you really want to work in this company. You and I will meet when you return to the office the day after tomorrow and I will ask you to tell me whether you'd rather resign and look for work elsewhere. I will understand and will be fully supportive if that is your decision. On the other hand, if when we meet, you tell me you want to keep your job here, then I will give you an additional assignment the day you return to the office. I will ask you to prepare a one-page letter addressed to me, convincing me that you assume full and total responsibility for the performance issues we discussed during our feedback sessions. You will have to provide clear and specific arguments as well as describe a specific set of actions you will take to convince me that you will address the problems. I will keep the letter in a safe place but I am not planning on including it in your personnel file for now. To be clear, however, this letter is a personal commitment from you to me and our agreement is that if you don't stick to the terms of your letter, you will essentially fire yourself. This is a very important moment for you and also for me and it could be a turning point in your career development. Now that I have explained the process, I would like to hear any questions or comments you may have about this "decision-making leave day" that you will be taking tomorrow.

Using a decision-making leave as part of the performance management system can be a powerful tool to give problem employees an opportunity to improve their performance. However, this tool may not lead to the desired outcomes and the employee may have to enter into a disciplinary process. Note that a demotion or transfer may be a more appropriate action when there is evidence that the employee is actually trying to overcome the performance deficiencies, but is not able to do so. However, termination is the appropriate action when performance does not improve and the employee continues to make the same mistakes or fails to meet standards. Also, termination is the appropriate course of action when an employee engages in serious violations of policies, laws, or regulations such as theft, fraud, falsifying documents, and related serious offences.

The disciplinary process should not come as a surprise to the employee or supervisor if there is a good performance management system in place because there are ongoing check-ins and plenty of opportunities for the employee to overcome performance problems and for the supervisor to offer support and feedback so that willing and able employees will be able to do so. However, when a disciplinary process seems to be the only recourse, it is important to follow a set of steps so as not to fall into legal problems. Also, all employees, even those who are terminated, deserve to be treated with respect and dignity. Nevertheless, even if there is a top-notch performance management system in place, there are several pitfalls that must be avoided and specific actions supervisors can take to do so, which are the following[46]:

1. *Pitfall 1: Acceptance of poor performance.* Many supervisors may just want to ignore poor performance, hoping that the problem will go away. Unfortunately, in most cases, the performance problems escalate and become worse over time.

   Suggested course of action: Do not ignore the problem. Addressing it as soon as possible can not only avoid negative consequences for the employee in question, peers, and customers, but also help put the employee back in track in terms of his career objectives.

2. *Pitfall 2: Failure to get the message through.* The poor performing employee may argue that she did not know the problem was serious or that it existed at all.

   Suggested course of action: In the decision-making leave described earlier, make sure to be very specific about the performance problem and the consequences of not addressing it effectively. Make sure you document the action plan and that you have secured the employee's agreement regarding the plan.

3. *Pitfall 3: Performance standards are "unrealistic" or "unfair."* The employee may argue that performance standards and expectations are unrealistic or unfair.

   Suggested course of action: Remind the employee that his performance standards are similar to others holding the same position. Also, remind the employee that performance standards have been developed over time with the participation of the employee in question and share with him documentation regarding past review meetings, including past appraisal forms with the employee signature on them.

4. *Pitfall 4: Negative affective reactions.* The employee may respond emotionally, ranging from tears to shouts and even threats of violence. This, in turn, creates an emotional response on the part of the supervisor.

   Suggested course of action: Do not let emotional reactions derail you from your mission and role as a performance management leader, which is to describe the nature of the problem, what needs to be done, and consequences of not doing so. If the employee is crying, do offer compassion and give him some space to compose himself. You can give the employee some time and resume the meeting a few minutes later or a rescheduling of the meeting at a later time may be a good alternative. If the employee reaction involves a threat or suggest possible violence, call security immediately. If such threats do take place, report them to the human resources (HR) department.

5. *Pitfall 5: Failure to consult HR.* There are hundreds of wrongful termination cases that have cost millions of dollars to organizations that have not followed the appropriate termination procedures.

   Suggested course of action: If you are planning on implementing a disciplinary or termination process, consult with your HR department regarding legal requirements. For the most part, if you have a good performance management system in place, you have all necessary steps in place. However, consulting with HR is a good idea to ensure you are following all appropriate steps.

Avoiding the above pitfalls will minimize the possibility of problems during the formal disciplinary process. If the goals are not reached, there will be a need for a termination meeting. This meeting is, of course, extremely unpleasant for all involved, to say the least. However, it is the right and fair thing to do at this stage. Suggestions for the termination meeting are as follows[47]:

1. *Be respectful.* It is important to treat the terminated employee with respect and dignity. Keep the information about the termination confidential, although it is likely others will learn about it in subsequent days.

2. *Get right to the point.* At this stage, the less said, the better. You can start by saying "There is no easy way to say this . . .," and then, summarize the performance problems, actions taken to try to overcome these problems, outcomes of these actions, and the decision about termination that you have reached.

3. *Let the employee grieve.*[48] It is important to let the employee grieve because it is likely that there will be a sense of loss. Show empathy with phrases such as "I know this is sad for you . . ." and "Go ahead and take a moment . . . when you're ready, we'll continue."

4. *Wish the employee well.* The purpose of the meeting is not to rehash every single reason why you are letting the employee go and every single instance of poor performance. Instead, use the meeting to wish the person well in her next job and endeavors and tell her that she will be missed.

5. *Send the employee to HR.* Let the employee know that she needs to go to HR to receive information on benefits, including vacation pay, and also to receive information on legal rights. If you are working in a small business, seek outside legal counsel regarding the information to give to the terminated employee.

6. *Have the employee leave immediately.* Keeping the terminated employee on-site can lead to gossip and conflict, and disgruntled employees may engage in sabotage.

7. *Have the termination meeting at the end of the day.* It is better to conduct the termination meeting at the end of the day so the employee can leave the office as everyone else and there are fewer people around.

The aforementioned information regarding the disciplinary process and termination may be used as a follow-up to a formal performance review meeting held because of a lack of remedial action on the part of the employee. So, let us discuss performance review meetings next, which may or may not lead to the disciplinary process and termination we just discussed.

9-4 COACHING, DEVELOPMENT, AND PERFORMANCE REVIEW MEETINGS

Performance management leaders often feel uncomfortable in this role because managing performance requires that they judge and coach at the same time.[49] In other words, supervisors serve as *judges* by evaluating performance and allocating rewards. In addition, supervisors serve as *coaches* by helping employees solve performance problems, identify performance weaknesses, and design developmental plans that will be instrumental in future career development. In addition, supervisors feel uncomfortable because they feel they need to convey bad news and employees may react negatively. In other words, there is a concern that managing performance unavoidably leads to negative surprises.

Because performance management leaders play these paradoxical roles, it is usually helpful to separate the various meetings related to performance. Separating the meetings also minimizes the possibility of negative surprises.[50] Moreover, when meetings are separated, it is easier to separate the discussion of rewards from the discussion about future career development. This allows employees to give their full attention to each issue, one at a time.

Chapter 6 noted that performance management systems can involve as many as six formal meetings. Each of these sessions should be seen as a work meeting with specific goal, including the following:

- *System inauguration.* The purpose of this meeting is to discuss how the performance management system works and which requirements and responsibilities rest primarily on the employee and which rest primarily on the supervisor.
- *Self-appraisal.* The purpose of this meeting is to discuss the self-appraisal prepared by the employee.
- *Classical performance review.* The purpose of this meeting is to discuss employee performance, including the perspectives of both the supervisor and the employee.
- *Merit/salary review.* The purpose of this meeting is to discuss what, if any, compensation changes will result as a consequence of the employee's performance during this period.
- *Developmental plan.* The purpose of this meeting is to discuss the employee's developmental needs and what steps will be taken so that performance will be improved during the following period.
- *Objective setting.* The purpose of this meeting is to set performance goals, both behavioral and results-oriented, regarding the following review period.

Although six types of meetings are possible, not all six take place as separate meetings. For example, the self-appraisal, classical performance review, merit/salary review, development plan, and objective setting meetings may all take place during one umbrella meeting, labeled "performance review meeting." As noted above, however, it is better to separate the various types of information discussed so that the employee and supervisor focus on each of the components separately. Note, however, that the conversation about compensation should be related to performance (i.e., employees must understand the direct link between performance and compensation decisions).

Regardless of the specific type of meeting, there are several steps that performance management leaders take before the meeting takes place.[51] Specifically, it is useful to give at least a two-week advance notice to the employee to inform her of the purpose of the meeting and enable her to prepare for it. Also, it is useful to block out sufficient time for the meeting and arrange to meet in a private location without interruptions. Taking these steps sends a clear message that the meeting is important and that, consequently, performance management is important.

As noted above, most organizations merge several meetings into one labeled "performance review meeting." The typical sequence of events for such a meeting is the following[52]:

- *Explain the purpose of the meeting.* The first step includes a description of the purpose of the meeting and the topics to be discussed.
- *Conduct self-appraisal.* The second step includes asking the employee to summarize her accomplishments during the review period. This is more easily accomplished when the employee is given the appraisal form to be used by the supervisor before the meeting. This portion of the meeting allows the employee to provide her perspective regarding performance. The role of the supervisor is to listen to what the employee has to say and to summarize what he hears. This is not an appropriate time for the supervisor to disagree with what the employee says.
- *Share performance data and explain rationale.* Next, the supervisor explains the rating he provided for each performance dimension and explains the reasons that led to each score. It is more effective to start with a discussion of the performance dimensions for which there is agreement between the employee's self-appraisal and the supervisor's appraisal. This is likely to reduce tension and to demonstrate to the employee that there is common ground and that the meeting is not confrontational. Also, it is better to start with a discussion of the performance dimensions for which the scores are highest, and then, move on to the dimensions for which the scores are lower. For areas for which there is disagreement between self- and supervisor ratings, the supervisor must take great care in discussing the reason for his rating and provide specific examples and evidence to support the score given. At this point, there should be an effort to resolve discrepancies and the supervisor should take extra care with sensitive areas. The employee should be provided with the opportunity to explain her viewpoint thoroughly. This is a very useful discussion because it leads to clarifying performance expectations. For dimensions for which the score is low, there should be a discussion of the possible causes for poor performance. For example, are the reasons related to lack of knowledge, lack of motivation, or contextual factors beyond the control of the employee?

- *Discuss development.* After the supervisor and employee have agreed on the scores given to each performance dimension, there should be a discussion about the developmental plan. At this point, the supervisor and the employee should discuss and agree on the developmental steps that will be taken to improve performance in the future.
- *Ask employee to summarize.* Next, the employee should summarize, in her own words, the main conclusions of the meeting: which performance dimensions are satisfactory, which need improvement, and how improvement will be achieved. This is an important component of the meeting because it gives the supervisor an opportunity to determine whether he and the employee are in accord.
- *Discuss rewards.* The next step during the meeting includes discussing the relationship between performance and any reward allocation. The supervisor should explain the rules used to allocate rewards and how the employee would be able to reach higher reward levels as a consequence of future performance improvement.
- *Schedule follow-up meeting.* Before the meeting is over, it is important to schedule the next performance-related formal meeting. It is important that the employee understand that there will be a formal follow-up and that performance management is not just about meeting with the supervisor once a year. Usually, the next meeting will take place just a few weeks later to review whether the developmental plan is being implemented effectively.
- *Discuss approval and appeals process.* Finally, the supervisor asks the employee to sign the form to attest that the evaluation has been discussed with him. This is also an opportunity for the employee to add any comments or additional information he would like to see included on the form. In addition, if disagreements about ratings have not been resolved, the supervisor should remind the employee of the appeals process.
- *Conduct final recap.* Finally, the supervisor should use the "past-present-future model." In other words, the supervisor summarizes what happened during the review period in terms of performance levels in the various dimensions, reviews how rewards will change based on this level of performance, and sums up what the employee will need to do in the next year to maintain and enhance performance.

Performance review discussions serve very important purposes. First, these discussions allow employees to improve their performance by identifying performance problems and solutions for overcoming them. Second, they help build a good relationship between the supervisor and the employee because the supervisor shows that she cares about the employee's ongoing growth and development and that she is willing to invest resources, including time, in helping the employee improve. Third, good performance management leaders use review discussions as *stay interviews*.[53] Stay interviews focus on finding out what makes employees stay in the organization and help managers create strategies to enhance employee engagements and retain star performers. As part of the stay interview, managers can ask questions such as (a) Have you ever thought about leaving our team? (b) How can I best support you? (c) What do you want to learn here? (d) What can you learn here that will make you feel good when you go home every day? Although stay interviews will not ensure that a star employee will never move, they can be very useful in identifying the factors that matter most to a firm's or team's most impactful contributors.

Unfortunately, these purposes are not always realized because employees may be defensive and many supervisors do not know how to deal with this attitude because they lack the necessary skills to conduct an effective performance review. How can we tell when an employee is being defensive? Typically, there are two patterns of behavior that indicate defensiveness.[54] First, employees may engage in a *fight response.* This includes blaming others for performance deficiencies, staring mutely at the supervisor, and other, more aggressive responses, such as raising her voice or even pounding the desk. Second, employees may engage in a *flight response.* This includes looking away, turning away, speaking softly, continually changing the subject, or quickly agreeing with what the supervisor is saying without basing the agreement on a thoughtful and thorough discussion about the issues at stake. When employees have a fight-or-flight response during the performance review discussion, it is unlikely that the meeting will lead to improved performance in the future. What can supervisors do to prevent defensive responses? Consider the following suggestions:

- *Establish and maintain rapport.* It is important that the meeting take place in a good climate. As noted earlier, this can be achieved by choosing a meeting place that is private and by preventing interruptions from taking place. Also, the supervisor should emphasize two-way communication and put the employee at ease as quickly as possible. This can be done by sitting next to the employee as opposed to across a desk, by saying his name, by thanking him for coming, and by beginning with small talk to reduce the initial tension. When good rapport is established, both the supervisor and the employee are at ease, relaxed, and comfortable. They can have a friendly conversation and neither is afraid to speak freely. Both are open-minded and can express disagreement without offending. On the other hand, when there is no good rapport, both participants may be nervous and anxious. The conversation is cold and formal and both may fear to speak openly. The supervisor and employee are likely to interrupt each other frequently and challenge what the other is saying.

- *Be empathetic.* It is important for the supervisor to put herself in the shoes of the employee. The supervisor needs to make an effort to understand why the employee has performed at a certain level during the review period. This includes not making attributions that any employee success was caused by outside forces (e.g., a good economy) or that employee failures were caused by inside forces (e.g., employee incompetence).

- *Be open-minded.* If the employee presents an alternative and different point of view, be open-minded and discuss them directly and openly. There is a possibility that the employee may provide information that is relevant and of which you are not aware. If this is the case, ask for specific evidence.[55]

- *Observe verbal and nonverbal cues.* The supervisor should be able to read verbal and nonverbal signals from the employee to determine whether further clarification is necessary. The supervisor should be attentive to the employee's emotions and react accordingly. For example, if the employee becomes defensive, the supervisor should stop talking and allow the employee to express her point of view regarding the issue being discussed.

- *Minimize threats.* The performance review meeting should be framed as a meeting that will benefit the employee, not punish him.
- *Encourage participation.* The employee needs to have her own conversational space to speak and express her views. The supervisor should not dominate the meeting; rather, she should listen without interrupting and avoid confrontation and argument.

In spite of these suggestions, defensiveness may be unavoidable in some situations. In such situations, supervisors need to recognize that employee defensiveness is inevitable, and they need to allow it. Rather than ignoring the defensive attitude, supervisors need to deal with the situation head on. First, it is important to let the employee vent and to acknowledge the employee's feelings. To do this, the supervisor may want to pause to accept the employee's feelings. Then, the supervisor may want to ask the employee for additional information and clarification. If the situation is reaching a point where communication becomes impossible, the supervisor may want to suggest suspending the meeting until a later time.[56] For example, the supervisor may say,

> I understand that you are angry, and that you believe you have been treated unfairly. It's important that I understand your perspective, but it's difficult for me to absorb the information when you are so upset. This is an important matter. Let's take a break, and get back together at 3:00 P.M. to continue our discussion.

To be sure, if the relationship between the supervisor and the employee is not good, the performance review meeting is likely to expose these issues in a blatant and often painful way.

Consider the following vignette. Hannah is the manager at a large accounting firm, and Sofia is one of the employees on her team. She chooses a conference room with privacy away from the other offices.

HANNAH:	Hi, Sofia. I wanted to meet with you today to discuss your performance appraisal for this quarter. At any time, please offer your input and ask questions if you have any.
SOFIA:	OK.
HANNAH:	You did meet two important objectives that we set this quarter: sales and customer service. Thanks for your hard work.
SOFIA:	No problem.
HANNAH:	You did miss three of the other objectives.
SOFIA:	What? I worked as hard as I could! It wasn't *my* fault that the other people on the team did not carry their weight.
HANNAH:	Sofia, I am not here to blame anyone or to attack you. I want to generate some ideas on what we can do to ensure that you meet your objectives and receive your bonus next quarter.

SOFIA:	*SITTING BACK WITH CROSSED ARMS:* I told you I worked as hard as I could.
HANNAH:	I know that you worked hard, Sofia, and I know how hard it is to balance all of the objectives that we have in our department. When I first started, I had a hard time meeting all of the objectives as well.
SOFIA:	It is hard and I try my best.
HANNAH:	Sofia, can you think of anything that we can work on together that would help you meet the last three objectives? Is there any additional training or resources that you need?
SOFIA:	I am having a hard time prioritizing all of my daily tasks. There is a class offered online on prioritizing, but I feel I am too busy to take it.
HANNAH:	That is good that you think the class will help. Take the class online, which will not disrupt your work schedule, and I will go to all of your meetings and follow up with clients as needed.
SOFIA:	Thanks, Hannah. I really appreciate your help.

How did Hannah do in dealing with Sofia's defensiveness? Overall, she did a good job. Hannah was empathetic, she picked up on Sofia's nonverbal behavior, she had Sofia offer her input, she held the meeting in a comfortable, private location, and she emphasized that the meeting was to work on future performance and not to punish Sofia. In the end, she was able to address Sofia's defensiveness and turned a meeting that could have gone very poorly into a productive exchange of information and ideas.

In closing, this third section in the book addressed employee development (Chapter 8) and skills that managers need to acquire and things they need to do to become performance management leaders (Chapter 9). The next section will address additional important issues in all performance management systems. Specifically, Chapter 10 will address the relation between performance management and rewards and performance management and the law, and Chapter 11 will discuss team performance management.

SUMMARY POINTS

- To become performance management leaders, managers must acquire several important skills. Managers need to serve as coaches, to observe and document performance accurately, to give both positive and constructive feedback, and to conduct performance review meetings—including meetings that address disciplinary and termination issues.

- Coaching is a collaborative and ongoing process in which the manager directs, motivates, and rewards employee behavior. Successful coaching involves a good manager–employee relationship, an understanding that the employee is the source and director of change, and that each employee is unique.

- Effective coaching involves giving advice about performance expectations and how to perform well, giving employees guidance so they know how to improve their performance, providing employees with support without being controlling, and enhancing employees' confidence and competence. Coaching must be based on a helping and trusting relationship. This is particularly important when the supervisor and the direct report do not share similar cultural backgrounds.

- Performance management leaders need to engage in a complex set of behaviors to perform the various coaching functions. These include the following: establish developmental objectives, communicate effectively, motivate employees, document performance, give feedback, diagnose performance problems, and help employees improve their performance.

- Managers' personalities and behavioral preferences influence their coaching style. Some managers prefer to be drivers and just tell employees what to do. Others prefer to be persuaders and try to sell what they want the employees to do. Yet others adopt an amiable style in which feelings take precedence and urge the employee to do what feels right or what the employee feels is the right way to do things. Finally, others prefer to be analyzers and have a tendency to follow rules and procedures in recommending how to perform. None of these four styles is necessarily better than the others in all conditions. The best performance management leaders are able to change their styles and adapt to the needs of the employees.

- The coaching process is ongoing and cyclical, and it includes the following five components: (1) setting developmental goals, (2) identifying the activities needed to achieve the developmental goals as well as securing resources that will allow employees to engage in activities to achieve their developmental goals, (3) implementing developmental activities (e.g., enrolling the employee in an online course), (4) observing and documenting developmental behaviors (e.g., checking on the progress of the employee toward the attainment of developmental goals), and (5) giving feedback (e.g., providing information to the employee that will help him adjust his current developmental goals and guide his future goals).

- Observing and documenting developmental behaviors and results and performance in general is not as easy as it may seem. Time constraints can play a role when managers are too busy to gather performance information. Situational constraints may prevent managers from observing the employee directly. Finally, activity constraints may be a factor; when developmental activities are unstructured, such as reading a book, the manager may have to wait until the activity is completed to assess whether any new skills and knowledge have been acquired.

- Observation and documentation of performance can be improved in several ways. These issues, which were described in detail in Chapter 7, include implementing a good communication plan and establishing training programs that help managers minimize rater errors (i.e., rater error training); share notions of what it means to complete developmental activities successfully (i.e., frame-of-reference training); and observe performance more accurately (i.e., behavioral observation training).

- Documenting an employee's progress toward achieving developmental goals and improving performance in general has several important benefits. These include the reduction of the manager's cognitive load, the enhancement of trust between the employee and the manager, the collection of important input to be used in planning developmental activities in the future, and the development of a good line of defense in case of litigation.

- For performance documentation to be most useful, it must be specific, use adjectives and adverbs sparingly, balance positives with negatives, focus on job-related information, be comprehensive, be standardized across employees, and be stated in behavioral and results terms rather than subjective judgments.

- Feedback about performance in general, and about developmental activities in particular, serves several important purposes. These include building employee confidence and self-efficacy, developing employee competence, and enhancing employee engagement with the unit and the organization as a whole.

- The mere presence of feedback does not mean that there will be positive effects on future performance. For feedback to be most useful, it must be timely, frequent, specific, verifiable, consistent over time and across employees, given in private, and tied closely to consequences (e.g., rewards); address description first, and evaluation second; discuss performance in terms of a continuum and not in terms of dichotomies (i.e., in terms of more and less and not in terms or all versus nothing or present versus absent); address patterns of behavior and events and not isolated errors or mistakes; include a statement that the manager has confidence in the employee; and include the active participation of the employee in generating ideas about how to improve performance in the future.

- When giving praise (i.e., "positive feedback"), it is important to be sincere and to give it only when it is deserved. Also, praise should be about specific behaviors or results and be given within context so that employees know what they need to repeat in the future. In addition, in giving praise, managers should take their time and act pleased, rather than rush through the information looking embarrassed. Finally, avoid giving praise by referring to the absence of the negative—for example, "not bad" or "better than last time."

- In general, managers do not feel comfortable about giving constructive (i.e., "negative") feedback. They may fear that employees will react negatively because they themselves have been given constructive feedback in the past in a way that was not helpful and do not want to put their employees in the same situation, because they do not like playing God, or because they think they need to collect an onerous amount of information and evidence before giving constructive feedback. When constructive feedback is warranted, however, and managers refuse to give it, poor performers may get the message that their performance is not that bad. Eventually, the situation may escalate to the point that the manager has no choice but to give feedback; the situation then becomes punitive, and feedback is not likely to be useful. For constructive feedback to be useful, it must be given early when the performance problem is still manageable.

- Performance management leaders play the paradoxical roles of judge and coach at the same time. These roles are most evident during the performance review meetings, which can include as many as six separate formal meetings: system inauguration, self-appraisal, classical performance review, merit/salary review, developmental plan, and objective setting. In most organizations, these meetings are merged into one or two meetings. It is most effective to separate the meetings so that employees can focus on one issue at a time (e.g., supervisor's view on the employee's performance, rewards allocation, developmental plan).
- In giving feedback, it is important to consider generational and individual differences and preferences and reactions. In general, Millennials and Post-Millennials (i.e., Generation Z) tend to have work-related goals that are more future-oriented (i.e., "utility" goals) compared to Baby Boomers. In contrast, older workers tend to have work-related goals that are more present-oriented (i.e., "social awareness"): regulating their emotions to be positive and the pursuit of positive social relationships at work. Also, individuals differ in the extent to which they proactively seek feedback about their performance (i.e., feedback-seeking behavior). Good performance management leaders are aware of the need to provide feedback to all employees to make sure nobody falls through the cracks.
- In some cases, an employee may be unwilling or unable to overcome performance problems. When that happens, there is a need to implement a formal disciplinary process, including a verbal warning, followed by a written warning, and eventually, if needed, termination. When implementing a disciplinary process, supervisors must be aware of several pitfalls including the acceptance of poor performance, failing to get the message through, arguments that performance standards are unfair or unrealistic, employee and supervisor emotional reactions, and the failure to consult with HR.
- The termination meeting creates important challenges and is extremely unpleasant for both the employee and supervisor. For termination meetings to be more effective and less painful, supervisors must (1) be respectful, (2) get right to the point, (3) let the employee grieve, (4) wish the employee well, (5) send the employee to HR (or offer information, based on the advice of outside counsel), (6) have the employee leave immediately, and (7) conduct the termination meeting at the end of the day. Overall, all employees deserve to be treated with dignity and respect, even those who are being terminated.
- When all the performance review meetings are merged into one, the components of such a meeting include the following (1) explanation of the purpose of the meeting, (2) self-appraisal, (3) discussion of the supervisor's performance ratings and rationale and resolution of discrepancies with self-appraisal, (4) developmental discussion, (5) employee summary, (6) rewards discussion, (7) setting up follow-up meeting, (8) approval and appeals process discussion, and (9) final recap.
- Performance management leaders also use the performance review meetings to conduct "stay interviews," which involve gathering information on what makes employees stay in the organization and help managers create strategies to enhance employee engagements and retain

star performers. As part of the stay interview, managers can ask questions such as (a) Have you ever thought about leaving our team? (b) How can I best support you? (c) What do you want to learn here? (d) What can you learn here that will make you feel good when you go home every day?

- In meeting with the supervisor to discuss performance issues, employees may become defensive. Defensiveness is indicated by a fight-or-flight response. The supervisor can minimize defensiveness by (1) establishing and maintaining rapport, (2) being empathetic, (3) observing verbal and nonverbal cues, (4) minimizing threats, and (5) encouraging employee participation. When defensiveness becomes unavoidable, the employee's attitude must be recognized and allowed expression. If the situation becomes intolerable, the meeting may be interrupted and rescheduled for a later time.

EXERCISE 9-1 WHAT IS YOUR COACHING STYLE?

Below are 15 rows of four words each. From each row, select and circle two words out of the four that best describe the way you see yourself. If all four words sound like you, select the two that are most like you. If none of the four sounds like you, select the two that are closest to the way you are. Then, total the number of words selected under each respective column.

	A	B	C	D
1	All-business	Bold	Personable	Deliberate
2	Organized listening	Telling	Courteous	Listening
3	Industrious	Independent	Companionable	Cooperative
4	No-nonsense	Decisive	Talkative	Reflective
5	Serious	Determined	Warm	Careful
6	To-the-point	Risk-taker	Amiable	Moderate
7	Practical	Aggressive	Empathetic	Nonassertive
8	Self-controlled	Authoritative	Shows emotions	Thorough
9	Goal-directed	Assertive	Friendly	Patient
10	Methodical	Unhesitating	Sincere	Prudent
11	Businesslike	Definite	Sociable	Precise
12	Diligent	Firm	Demonstrative	Particular
13	Systematic	Strong-minded	Sense of humor	Thinking
14	Formal	Confident	Expressive	Hesitative
15	Persevering	Forceful	Trusting	Restrained
Total				

After you have totaled the number of words circled under each respective column, plot those numbers on their respective axes of the grid on the following page. For example, if you circled six words in column A, mark the A axis next to the 6. Complete the same procedures for columns B, C, and D. Then extend the

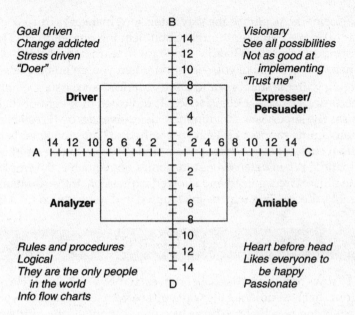

marks into each respective quadrant to create a rectangle. For example, consider the example of circling nine words from the A list, eight from the B list, seven from the C list, and eight from the D list. The rectangle would be the following:

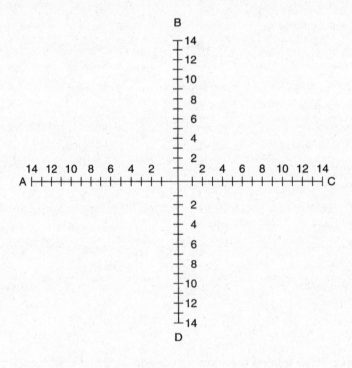

In this particular example, the area covered by the rectangle shows that this person is predominantly a driver and an analyzer, but can also be a persuader and amiable. Now, create your own rectangle using your scores:

What is your coaching style? Is there a dominance of one style over the other three, as indicated by an area predominantly covering one of the quadrants and not the others? If there is, what can you do to start using the other styles as well?

Source: Coaching Guides. Available online at http://www.specialolympicswisconsin.org/wp-content/uploads/2015/08/coach_philo_course.pdf. Retrieved on January 2, 2018. Used with the kind permission of Special Olympics, Inc.

EXERCISE 9-2 DEALING WITH DEFENSIVENESS

Spencer, Jeff's manager, needs to talk to Jeff about his poor performance over the previous quarter. Jeff enters the room and sits across the desk from Spencer.

JEFF: Spencer, you wanted to talk to me?

SPENCER: Yes, Jeff, thanks for coming by. I wanted to talk about your performance last quarter. (*Spencer's phone rings and he answers it. Five minutes later, Jeff is still waiting for Spencer. Jeff finally gets frustrated and Spencer notices Jeff looks at his watch several times.*) Sorry for the interruption, Jeff, I know it is frustrating to be kept waiting.

JEFF: I am very busy. Can we get on with this?

SPENCER: Yes, absolutely. As you know you had some problems meeting all of your goals last quarter.

JEFF: Now, wait a second, I met the most important goal.

SPENCER: Yes, you did, but you missed the other four.

JEFF: Just by a little and it wasn't my fault.

SPENCER: Jeff, you need to accept responsibility for your own performance and not push blame onto others. You need to meet your goals this coming quarter or I will have to take more serious action.

JEFF: One bad quarter and you threaten to fire me? I can't believe this!

SPENCER: Just meet all of your goals and I won't have to take that action.

Now, you will play the role of Spencer and one of your classmates will play the role of Jeff—who is behaving defensively. Conduct the entire meeting from scratch. Your goal is to address Jeff's defensiveness more effectively. (Hint: use material from Section 9-4 Coaching, Development, and Performance Review Meetings in this chapter.)

Was Robert Eaton a Good Performance Management Leader?

Robert Eaton was CEO and chairman of Chrysler from 1993 to 1998, replacing Lee Iacocca, who retired after serving in this capacity since 1978. Eaton then served as cochairman of the newly merged DaimlerChrysler organization from 1998 to 2000. In fact, Eaton was responsible for the sale of Chrysler Corporation to Daimler-Benz, thereby creating DaimlerChrysler. With 362,100 employees, DaimlerChrysler had achieved revenues of €136.4 billion in 2003. DaimlerChrysler's passenger car brands included Maybach, Mercedes-Benz, Chrysler, Jeep, Dodge, and Smart. Commercial vehicle brands included Mercedes-Benz, Freightliner, Sterling, Western Star, and Setra.

From the beginning of his tenure as CEO, Eaton communicated with the people under him. He immediately shared his plans for the future with his top four executives, and upon the advice of his colleague, Bob Lutz, decided to look around the company before making any hasty decisions concerning the state of affairs at Chrysler. Eaton and Lutz ascertained that Chrysler was employing the right staff and that they did not need to hire new people; they just had to lead them in a different manner, in a more participative style.

Eaton listened to everyone in the organization, including executives, suppliers, and assembly-line workers, to determine how to help the company succeed. Eaton also encouraged the employees at Chrysler to talk with one another. The atmosphere of collaboration and open-door communication between Eaton and Lutz (the two men sat across the hall from one another and never closed their doors) permeated the entire organization. Eaton and Lutz's walk-around management style indicated to employees that they were committed to and engaged in the organization. Furthermore, Eaton and Lutz held meetings with their executive team on a regular basis to exchange ideas and information from all areas of the organization.

Eaton even reorganized the manner in which Chrysler designed cars, based on a study, previously disregarded by Iacocca, that indicated that Chrysler needed to be more flexible and its executives needed to be in constant communication with the product design team. One employee was quoted as saying,

> Bob Eaton does not shoot the messenger when he hears something he doesn't like or understand. He knows that not every idea is right. But Bob is off-the-wall himself. . . . He'll say something, and we'll tell him that it's a crazy idea. . . . He may not change his mind in the end, but he'll spend the time explaining to you what is behind his thought processes. Do you know what kind of confidence that inspires?

This type of open communication at the top proved extremely successful, as summed up by one designer: "It's a system that recognizes talent early and rewards it, and that creates a sense of enthusiasm for your work, and a sense of mission."

Another program that Eaton describes as empowering employees at Chrysler includes requiring all employees, including executives, to participate in the process of building a new vehicle. Eaton explains that this shows all of the employees in the plant that executives are concerned about the proper functioning of new cars, and it gives executives the opportunity to understand and solve problems at the factory level. Eaton states, "When we're done with our discussions, these guys know where we want to go and how we want to get there, and they go back and put the action plans together to do that. This goes for every single thing we do." He concludes,

> Clearly at a company there has to be a shared vision, but we try to teach people to be a leader in their own area, to know where the company wants to go, to know how that affects their area, to benchmark the best in the world and then set goals and programs to go after it. We also encourage

people not only to go after the business plan objectives, but to have stretch goals. And a stretch goal by definition is a fifty-percent increase. . . . If we go after fifty percent, something dramatic has to happen. You have to go outside of the box.

Based on the above description, please evaluate Bob Eaton's performance management leadership skills using the accompanying table. If a certain principle, function, or behavior is missing, please provide recommendations about what he could have done more effectively.

Principles	Present? (Y/N)	Comments/Recommendations
A good coaching relationship is essential		
The employee is the source and director of change		
The employee is whole and unique		
The coach is the facilitator of the employee's growth		

Functions	Present? (Y/N)	Comments/Recommendations
Give advice		
Provide guidance		
Give support		
Give confidence		
Promote greater competence		

Behaviors	Present? (Y/N)	Comments/Recommendations
Establish developmental objectives		
Communicate effectively		
Motivate employees		
Document performance		
Give feedback		
Diagnose performance problems and performance decline		
Develop employees		

Source: This case is loosely based on information provided by Puris, M. (1999). *Comeback: How seven straight-shooting CEOs turned around troubled companies* (pp. 80–118). New York, NY: Times Books, specifically Chap. 4, "Robert Eaton and Robert Lutz; The Copilots."

CASE STUDY 9-2

Performance Management Leadership at Henry's Commercial Sales and Leasing

Henry is the owner of a small real estate agency that handles the sale and leasing of commercial property. He has two real estate agents working in the office, along with himself. He also has two customer service representatives (CSRs), each of whom has a real estate license, and one receptionist who has worked for the company for about three months.

Henry has recently decided that he needs another customer service representative. He has noticed that the receptionist, Tara, is very smart, seems to learn quickly, and is very good in dealing with clients. He has decided to promote Tara to CSR and hire a new receptionist. In order to familiarize Tara with her new duties, Henry has assigned Martin, the senior CSR in the company, to be her direct supervisor and coach her.

1. In the context of the material in this chapter, provide a critical analysis of the decisions that Henry has made in assigning Martin to this role.

2. Provide a detailed discussion of Martin's new role as a performance management leader.

Three months into Tara's training program, she seems constantly upset and has expressed concerns that she is not able to learn the information and feels she may be "in over her head." Henry knows that Tara is capable of the work required and is confident that she will be a very good CSR, so he talks to her about what she feels is going wrong. Some of Tara's comments include information that Martin is very abrupt with her, and rather than explaining why certain procedures are required and why certain procedures are given certain circumstances, he simply directs her to do certain things.

3. Critically assess Martin's coaching style.

4. Discuss possible solutions to help Tara become an effective CSR. What should Martin be doing to help her?

ENDNOTES

1. Schein, E. H. (2006). Coaching and consultation revisited: Are they the same? In M. Goldsmith & L. S. Lyons (Eds.), *Coaching for leadership: The practice of leadership coaching from the world's greatest coaches* (2nd ed., pp. 17–25). San Francisco, CA: John Wiley.

2. Vance, C. M. (2006). Strategic upstream and downstream considerations for effective global performance management. *International Journal of Cross Cultural Management, 6*, 37–56.

3. Bono, J. E., Purvanova, R. K., Towler, A. J., & Peterson, D. B. (2009). A survey of executive coaching practices. *Personnel Psychology, 62*, 361–404.

4. Dahling, J. J., Taylor, S. R., Chau, S. L., & Dwight, S. A. (2016). Does coaching matter? A multilevel model linking managerial coaching skill and frequency to sales goal attainment. *Personnel Psychology, 69*, 863–894.

5. Gray, D. E., Ekinci, Y., & Goregaokar, H. (2011). Coaching SME managers: Business development or personal therapy? A mixed methods study. *International Journal of Human Resource Management, 22*, 863–882.

6. Huang, J., & Hsieh, H. (2015). Supervisors as good coaches: Influences of coaching on employees' in-role behaviors and proactive career behaviors. *International Journal of Human Resource Management, 26*, 42–58.

7. Jones, R. J., Woods, S. A., & Guillaume, Y. F. (2016). The effectiveness of workplace coaching: A meta-analysis of learning and performance outcomes from coaching. *Journal of Occupational and Organizational Psychology, 89*, 249–277.

8. Stober, D. R. (2006). Coaching from the humanistic perspective. In D. R. Stober & A. M. Grant (Eds.), *Evidence based coaching handbook: Putting best practices to work for your clients* (pp. 17–50). Hoboken, NJ: John Wiley.

9. Farr, J. L., & Jacobs, R. (2006). Trust us: New perspectives on performance appraisal. In W. Bennett, C. E. Lance, & D. J. Woehr (Eds.), *Performance measurement: Current perspectives and future challenges* (pp. 321–337). Mahwah, NJ: Lawrence Erlbaum.

10. Boyatzis, R. E., Smith, M. L., & Blaize, N. (2006). Developing sustainable leaders through coaching and compassion. *Academy of Management Learning and Education, 5*, 8–24.

11. Peterson, D. B. (2006). People are complex and the world is messy: A behavior-based approach to executive coaching. In D. R. Stober & A. M. Grant (Eds.), *Evidence based coaching handbook: Putting best practices to work for your clients* (pp. 51–76). Hoboken, NJ: John Wiley.

12. Aguinis, H., & Glavas, A. (2017). On corporate social responsibility, sensemaking, and the search for meaningfulness through work. *Journal of Management.* doi:10.1177/0149206317691575

13. Hunt, J. M., & Weintraub, J. R. (2002). *The coaching manager: Developing top talent in business.* Thousand Oaks, CA: Sage.

14. Toto, J. (2006, April). Untapped world of peer coaching. *T&D, 60,* 69–70.

15. Byne, J. A. (1998, June 8). How Jack Welch runs GE. *Business Week.* Retrieved January 2, 2018, from http://www.businessweek.com/1998/23/b3581001.htm

16. Bacon, T. R., & Spear, K. I. (2003). *Adaptive coaching: The art and practice of a client-centered approach to performance improvement.* Palo Alto, CA: Davies-Black.

17. Foster, P. (2002). Performance documentation. *Business Communication Quarterly, 65,* 108–114.

18. Grant, A. (2013). *Give and take.* New York, NY: Penguin.

19. Fletcher, N., & Rodenbough, D. (2006, June/July). Coaching Hallmark's managers to value communication. *Strategic Communication Management, 10,* 26–29.

20. *Cleverly v. Western Electric Co.,* 594 F.2d 638 (8th Cir. 1979).

21. Walther, F., & Taylor, S. (1988). An active feedback program can spark performance. In A. D. Timpe (Ed.), *Performance: The art & science of business management* (pp. 293–299). New York, NY: Facts on File Publications.

22. These quotes have circulated worldwide on the Internet. See, for example, http://blogannath.blogspot.com/2010/03/humorous-look-at-employee-performance.html. Retrieved January 2, 2018.

23. Blake Jelley, R., & Goffin, R. D. (2001). Can performance-feedback accuracy be improved? Effects of rater priming and rating-scale format on rating accuracy. *Journal of Applied Psychology, 86,* 134–144.

24. Becker, T. E., & Klimoski, R. J. (1989). A field study of the relationship between the organizational feedback environment and performance. *Personnel Psychology, 42,* 343–358.

25. Allen, D. W., & LeBlanc, A. C. (2005). *Collaborative peer coaching that improves instruction: The 2 + 2 performance appraisal model.* Thousand Oaks, CA: Corwin.

26. Silverman, S. B., Pogson, C. E., & Cober, A. B. (2005). When employees at work don't get it: A model for enhancing individual employee change in response to performance feedback. *Academy of Management Executive, 19,* 135–147.

27. Bandura, A. (2012). On the functional properties of perceived self-efficacy revisited. *Journal of Management, 38,* 9–44.

28. Kluger, A. N., & DeNisi, A. S. (1996). The effects of feedback interventions on performance: Historical review, a meta-analysis, and a preliminary feedback intervention theory. *Psychological Bulletin, 119,* 254–284.

29. London, M. (2003). *Job feedback: Giving, seeking, and using feedback for performance improvement* (2nd ed.). Mahwah, NJ: Lawrence Erlbaum.

30. Goodman, J. S., Wood, R. E., & Hendrickx, M. (2004). Feedback specificity, exploration, and learning. *Journal of Applied Psychology, 89,* 248–262.

31. Audia, P. G., Locke, E. A., & Smith, K. G. (2000). The paradox of success: An archival and a laboratory study of strategic persistence following a radical environmental change. *Academy of Management Journal, 43,* 837–853.

32. Nelson, B. (1996). Providing a context for recognition. *Executive Edge Newsletter, 27*(11), 6.

33. Watkins, T. (2004). Have a heart. *New Zealand Management, 51*(2), 46–48.

34. Tyler, K. (2004). One bad apple: Before the whole bunch spoils, train managers to deal with poor performance. *HR Magazine, 49*(12), 79.

35. Moss, S. E., & Sanchez, J. I. (2004). Are your employees avoiding you? Managerial strategies for closing the feedback gap. *Academy of Management Executive, 18,* 32–44.

36. Kinicki, A. J., Prussia, G. E., Wu, B. J., & McKee-Ryan, F. M. (2004). A covariance structure analysis of employees' response to performance feedback. *Journal of Applied Psychology, 89,* 1057–1069.

37. Audia, P. G., & Locke, E. A. (2003). Benefiting from negative feedback. *Human Resource Management Review, 13,* 631–646.

38. Cannon, M. D., & Witherspoon, R. (2005). Actionable feedback: Unlocking the power of learning and performance improvement. *Academy of Management Executive, 19,* 120–134.

39. Aguinis, H., Gottfredson, R. K., & Joo, H. (2012). Delivering effective performance feedback: The strengths-based approach. *Business Horizons, 55,* 105–111.

40. Mo, W., Burlacu, G., Truxillo, D., James, K., & Xiang, Y. (2015). Age differences in feedback reactions: The roles of employee feedback orientation on social awareness and utility. *Journal of Applied Psychology, 100,* 1296–1308.

41. Linderbaum, B. A., & Levy, P. E. (2010). The development and validation of the feedback orientation scale (FOS). *Journal of Management, 36,* 1372–1405.

42. Ashford, S. J., De Stobbeleir, K., & Nujella, M. (2016). To seek or not to seek: Is that the only question? Recent developments in feedback-seeking literature. *Annual Review of Organizational Psychology and Organizational Behavior, 3,* 213–239.

43. Bies, R. J. (2013). The delivery of bad news in organizations: A framework for analysis. *Journal of Management, 39,* 136–162.

44. Falcone, P. (2007). Days of contemplation. *HR Magazine, 52*(2), 107–111.

45. Based on Falcone, "Days of contemplation."

46. Stone, F. M. (2007). *Coaching, counseling, & mentoring* (2nd ed.). New York, NY: American Management Association.

47. Ibid.

48. Folz, C. (2016). Bad news bearer. *HR Magazine, 61*(7), 18.

49. McGregor, D. (1957). An uneasy look at performance appraisal. *Harvard Business Review, 35*(3), 89–94.

50. Falcone, P. (2007). *Productive performance appraisals* (2nd ed.). New York, NY: American Management Association.

51. Meinecke, A. L., Lehmann-Willenbrock, N., & Kauffeld, S. (2017). What happens during annual appraisal interviews? How leader-follower interactions unfold and impact interview outcomes. *Journal of Applied Psychology, 102,* 1054–1074.

52. Adapted from Kirkpatrick, D. L. (1982). *How to improve performance through appraisal and coaching* (pp. 55–57). New York, NY: AMACOM.

53. Tyler, K. (2011). Who will stay and who will go? To retain star employees, train managers to conduct stay interviews. *HR Magazine, December,* 101–103.

54. Grote, D. (2002). *The performance appraisal question and answer book* (pp. 131–132). New York, NY: AMACOM.

55. Mone, E. M., & London, M. (2010). *Employee engagement through effective performance management.* New York, NY: Routledge.

56. Society for Human Resource Management. (2015). *Managing difficult employees and disruptive behaviors.* Retrieved January 2, 2018, from https://www.shrm.org/resourcesandtools/tools-and-samples/toolkits/pages/managingdifficultemployeesa.aspx

part four

Reward Systems, Legal Issues, and Team Performance Management

10

Performance Management, Rewards, and the Law

You have to get rewarded in the soul and the wallet. The money isn't enough, but a plaque isn't enough either . . . you have to give both.

—Jack Welch

Learning Objectives

By the end of this chapter, you will be able to do the following:

1. Design a rewards system that includes returns with varying degrees of dependence on the performance management system, including base pay, cost-of-living adjustments, short-term incentives, long-term incentives, income protection, work-life focus, allowances, and relational (i.e., intangible) returns.

2. Create traditional (i.e., based mostly on position and seniority) and contingent (i.e., based mostly on performance) pay plans.

3. Prepare contingent pay plans that improve employee motivation and performance and minimize potential pitfalls, such as not rewarding meaningful behaviors and results, not offering meaningful rewards, and not holding managers accountable for performance management.

4. Propose a contingent pay plan that takes into account key success factors such as the organization's culture, strategic business objectives, and the right balance between individual and collective incentives.

5. Set up pay plans with the understanding that pay is an important motivator, but to improve performance management effectiveness, there is a need to define and measure performance first, and then, allocate rewards; use only rewards that are available; make sure all employees are eligible; and make rewards visible, contingent, timely, and reversible.

6. Turn recognition and other nonfinancial incentives into meaningful rewards.

7. Create a performance management system that considers key six legal principles: employment at will, negligence, defamation, misrepresentation, adverse impact, and illegal discrimination.

8. Develop a performance management system that does not violate laws regarding discrimination based on race, sex, religion, age, disability status, and sexual orientation and is legally sound.

As you will recall based on material in Chapter 1, one of the six purposes of a performance management system is to make administrative decisions about employees. Decisions about rewards (what used to be labeled "compensation and benefits") are the most meaningful consequences of a performance management system for many employees. Clearly, most people are interested in their personal growth and development. But pay is often at the top of the list in terms of people's needs—although they may rarely admit it openly.[1] In addition, from the perspective of organizations, compensation shapes the culture because it sends a very clear message about what behaviors and results are more and less valued. Accordingly, this chapter provides a detailed discussion of the basic ingredients of reward systems, different types of pay plans (i.e., traditional and contingent), reasons for introducing contingent pay plans and possible pitfalls of those plans, and what pay can and cannot do in terms of motivating employees to perform better.

You will also recall that Chapter 1 referred to the documentation purpose of performance management systems, including the documentation of important administrative decisions. We have also referred to issues about justice and fairness throughout the book. For the most part, our discuss thus far has been about how the performance management system is perceived, which is clearly an important factor influencing reactions, and acceptance and involvement, on the part of all organizational members. In addition, however, there are legal requirements that organizations have to meet when implementing performance management. So, this chapter addresses legal issues regarding performance management which, again, are related to the documentation and administrative purposes.

Let us highlight an important caveat: The topics of compensation and legal issues require their own books. So, this chapter only offers an overview of these topics, with a particular emphasis on their relation with performance management. Let us begin by defining reward systems.

10-1 DEFINITION OF REWARD SYSTEMS

Until a few years ago, the terms "compensation" and "compensation and benefits" were used commonly. But more recently, these terms have been replaced with "rewards" and "total rewards." A reward system is the set of mechanisms for distributing both tangible and intangible returns as part of an employment relationship.

An employee's *tangible returns* include cash compensation (i.e., base pay, cost-of-living and merit pay, short-term incentives, and long-term incentives) and benefits (i.e., income protection, work–life focus, tuition reimbursement, and allowances). In addition, employees also receive intangible or *relational returns*, which include recognition and status, employment security, challenging work, and learning opportunities.

Not all types of returns are directly related to performance management systems. This is the case because not all types of returns are allocated based on performance. For example, some allocations are based on seniority, as opposed to performance. The various types of returns are defined next.[2]

10-1-1 Base Pay

Base pay is given to employees in exchange for work performed. The base pay, which usually includes a range of values, focuses on the position and duties performed, rather than an individual's contribution. Thus, the base pay is usually the same for all employees performing similar duties and ignores differences across employees. However, differences within the base pay range may exist, based on such variables as experience. In some countries (e.g., United States), there is a difference between wage and salary. Salary is base cash compensation received by employees who are exempt from regulations of the Fair Labor Standards Act, and in most cases, cannot receive overtime pay. Employees in most professional and managerial jobs (also called salaried employees) are exempt employees. On the other hand, nonexempt employees receive their pay calculated on an hourly wage.

10-1-2 Cost-of-Living Adjustments and Contingent Pay

Cost-of-living adjustments (COLA) imply the same percentage increase for all employees, regardless of their individual performance. COLA are given to combat the effects of inflation in an attempt to preserve the employees' buying power. For example, in 2017, in the United States, organizations that implemented a COLA used a 3 percent pay increase. In 1980, this same percentage was 14.3 percent, whereas in 2013, it was only 1.5 percent. Year-by-year COLA percentages can be obtained from such agencies as the Social Security Administration in the United States (http://www.ssa.gov/OACT/COLA/colaseries.html).

Contingent pay, sometimes referred to as *merit pay*, is given as an addition to the base pay, based on past performance. As we will describe later in more detail, contingent pay means that the amount of additional compensation depends on an employee's level of performance. So, for example, the top 20 percent of employees in the performance score distribution may receive a 10 percent annual increase, whereas employees in the middle 70 percent of the distribution may receive a 4 percent increase, and employees in the bottom 10 percent may receive no increase at all.

10-1-3 Short-Term Incentives

Similar to contingent pay, short-term incentives are allocated based on past performance. However, incentives are not added to the base pay and are only temporary pay adjustments based on the review period (e.g., quarterly or annual). Incentives are one-time payments, and are sometimes referred to as *variable pay*.

A second difference between incentives and contingent pay is that incentives are known in advance. For example, a salesperson in a pharmaceutical company knows that if she meets her sales quota, she will receive a US$6,000 bonus at the end of the quarter. She also knows that if she exceeds her sales quota by 10 percent, her bonus will be US$12,000. By contrast, in the case of contingent pay, in most cases, the specific value of the reward is not known in advance. As a concrete example, see Box 10-1 describing short-term incentives for physicians.

10-1-4 Long-Term Incentives

Whereas short-term incentives usually involve an attempt to motivate performance in the short term (i.e., quarter, year) and involve cash bonuses or specific prizes (e.g., two extra days off), long-term incentives attempt to influence future performance over a longer period of time. Typically, they involve stock ownership or options to buy stocks at a preestablished and profitable price. The rationale for long-term incentives is that employees will be personally invested in the organization's success, and this investment is expected to translate into a sustained high level of performance.

Box 10-1

Company Spotlight: Short-Term Incentives for Physicians in Colorado

Short-term incentives were used in a reward program in Colorado Springs, Colorado. Eight health care providers and three insurance companies teamed up with the nonprofit Colorado Business Group on Health to pay physicians cash awards per patient for providing diabetes care that results in positive outcomes for patients. Doctors in the program received the additional pay as an incentive without an increase in base salary. The program required doctors to work closely with patients and focus on preventative medicine, including education, goal setting, and follow-up meetings. Physical indicators, such as blood pressure, blood sugar, and cholesterol, are measured against goals to determine whether successful outcomes are being achieved. The goals of the program were to provide better disease control for the patient and to cut down on expensive future treatments, such as emergency room visits and inpatient stays in the hospital. Additional savings were expected through reduced medical claims and health insurance premiums paid by employers. In summary, the health providers and insurers used short-term incentives as part of the performance management systems with the goal of motivating physicians to focus on treatments that will enhance the overall health and well-being of the patient in an ongoing manner.[3]

Both short-term and long-term incentives are quite popular. For example, surveys involving several hundred HR practitioners across the public, private, and voluntary sectors by the Chartered Institute of Personnel and Development conducted over the past few years showed that between 50 percent and 65 percent of their organizations offer performance-based rewards.[4] As we will discuss later in this chapter, some organizations such as Google are taking this idea to the limit and offer what we may call "big pay for big performance."

10-1-5 Income Protection

Income protection programs serve as a backup to employees' salaries in the event that an employee is sick, disabled, or is no longer able to work. Some countries mandate income protection programs by law. For example, Canadian organizations pay into a fund that provides income protection in the case of a disability. Take, for instance, the University of Alberta, which offers a monthly income of 70 percent of salary to employees who become severely disabled. In the United States, employers pay 50 percent of an employee's total contribution to Social Security so that income is protected for family members in case of an employee's death or a disability that prevents the employee from doing substantial work for one year and for an employee when he or she reaches retirement age. For example, a 40-year-old employee earning an annual salary of US$90,000, and expected to continue to earn that salary until retirement age, would receive about US$1,739 a month if he retired at age 62 (in 2039), about US$2,509 a month if he retired at age 67 (in 2044), and about US$3,133 if he retired at age 70 (in 2047)—all of these in 2017 dollars without calculating inflation.

Other types of benefits under the income protection rubric include medical insurance, pension plans, and savings plans. These are optional benefits provided by organizations, but they are becoming increasingly important and often guide an applicant's decision to accept a job offer.

10-1-6 Work–Life Focus

Benefits related to work–life focus include programs that help employees achieve a better balance between work and nonwork activities. These include time away from work (e.g., vacation time), services to meet specific needs (e.g., counseling, financial planning), time off for volunteering, and flexible work schedules (e.g., telecommuting, nonpaid time off). For example, Sun Microsystems actively promotes an equal balance between work and home life and closes its Broomfield, Colorado, campus from late December through early January every year. This benefit (i.e., vacation time for all employees in addition to individual yearly vacation time) is part of Sun's culture. Sun believes in a work hard–play hard attitude, as is evidenced by CEO Scott McNealy's motto: "Kick butt and have fun."[5]

Many Silicon Valley companies, including Google, Apple, Asana, and Facebook, have become famous for offering these types of benefits, which also include free on-site gourmet cafeterias serving anything from Indian food to fresh fruit smoothies, auto insurance, free dry cleaning, concerts and "beer bashes," on-site yoga classes, and "concierge" services that help employees plan vacations and even buy tickets for sporting events.[6,7] But does this mean that Google and other Silicon Valley companies are overly generous with their employees? Maybe not. This is a strategic and well thought-out reward policy because, as noted by Center for Effective Organizations Gerry Ledford, "An employee who never has to leave the workplace to eat, shower, exercise, run errands, or sleep is an employee who can work extraordinarily long hours—and expected to do so."[8] Also, a benefit of these policies is that some programs are designed specifically to attract and retain Millennials, who typically place greater importance on work–life balance, compared to Baby Boomers.[9] For example, Pricewaterhouse Coopers makes annual contributions toward employees' student loan repayment and IBM, GE, and Accenture help nursing mothers by providing materials and funds to ship breast milk home when they are traveling on a work-related assignment.

10-1-7 Allowances

Benefits in some countries and organizations include allowances covering housing and transportation. These kinds of allowances are typical for expatriate personnel and are also popular for high-level managers throughout the world. In South Africa, for example, it is common for a transportation allowance to include one of the following choices:

- The employer provides a car and the employee has the right to use it both privately and for business.
- The employer provides a car allowance, more correctly referred to as a *travel allowance*, which means reimbursing the employee for the business use of the employee's personal car.

Other allowances can include smartphones and their monthly charges, club and gym fees, discount loans, and mortgage subsidies.[10] Although these allowances are clearly a benefit for employees, as mentioned earlier, some of them directly or indirectly also produce a benefit for the employer. For example, smartphones means that employees are reachable via phone, text, and email 24/7. Similarly, if employees take advantage of a gym fee allowance, they are likely to stay healthier, which in turn, may lead to less health-related expenses for the organization.

10-1-8 Relational (Intangible) Returns

Relational returns are intangible in nature. They include recognition and status, employment security, challenging work, opportunities to learn, and opportunities to form personal relationships at work (including friendships and romances).[11] For example, Sun Microsystems allows employees to enroll in SunU, which is Sun's own online education tool. SunU encapsulates a mix of traditional classroom courses with online classes that can be accessed anywhere in the world at any time. Sun offers its employees enormous scope for development and career progression, and there is a commitment to ensuring that all employees are given the opportunity to develop professionally. The new knowledge and skills acquired by employees can help them not only to further their careers within Sun, but also, to take this knowledge with them if they seek employment elsewhere. Thus, some types of relational returns can be long-lasting.

Table 10-1 includes a list of the various returns, together with their degree of dependency on the performance management system. As an example, cost-of-living adjustment has a low degree of dependency on the performance management system, meaning that the system has no impact on this type of return. In other words, all employees receive this type of return, regardless of past performance. On the other end, short-term incentives have a high degree of dependency, meaning that the performance management system dictates who receives these incentives and who does not. Long-term incentives (e.g., profit sharing and stock options, which we discuss later in this chapter) also have a high degree of dependency; although this type of incentive is not specifically tied to individual performance, it does depend on performance measured at the team, unit, or even organizational levels. Between the high and low end, we find some returns with a moderate degree of dependency on the performance management system, such as base pay, a type of return that may or may not be influenced by the system.

Think about the performance management system of your current employer, the system used by your most recent employer, or the system in place at an organization where someone you know is employed at present. Based on Table 10-1, try to think about the various types of tangible and intangible returns allocated in this organization. To what extent is each of these returns dependent on the organization's performance management system? Does the organization

TABLE 10-1

Returns and Their Degree of Dependency on the Performance Management System

Return	Degree of Dependency
Cost-of-living adjustment	Low
Income protection	Low
Work–life focus	Moderate
Allowances	Moderate
Relational returns	Moderate
Base pay	Moderate
Contingent pay	High
Short-term incentives	High
Long-term incentives	High

emphasize returns that are related to performance or not? What does this tell you about the culture of this organization?

10-2 TRADITIONAL AND CONTINGENT PAY PLANS

A "traditional" approach in implementing reward systems is to reward employees for the positions they fill as indicated by their job descriptions and not necessarily by how they do their work. In other words, employees are rewarded for filling a specific slot in the organizational hierarchy. In such traditional pay systems, one's job directly determines pay and indirectly determines benefits and incentives received. Typically, there is a pay range that determines minimum, midpoint, and maximum rates for each job. For example, a university may have five ranks for professors who have just been hired, with the following base pay:

1. Instructor (pay range: US$50,000–US$65,000)
2. Senior instructor (pay range: US$60,000–US$75,000)
3. Assistant professor (pay range: US$80,000–US$110,000)
4. Associate professor (pay range: US$105,000–US$125,000)
5. Professor (pay range: US$120,000–US$160,000)

As noted above, in a traditional reward system, each of these positions would have a minimum, midpoint, and the maximum base salary. For assistant professors, the minimum is US$80,000 per year, the midpoint is US$95,000, and the maximum is US$110,000. Salary increases at the end of the year would be determined by seniority or by a percentage of one's base salary (and the same percentage would be used for all workers). Rewards would not be based on teaching quality, as indicated by student teaching ratings, or research productivity, as indicated by the number and quality of publications. If an assistant professor's base salary is US$110,000, she cannot realize an increase in her salary unless she is promoted to associate professor because US$110,000 is the maximum possible salary for this job title. In short, in traditional reward systems, the type of position and seniority are the determinants of salary and salary increases, not performance. In such reward systems, there is a very weak or no relationship between performance management and rewards.

This type of system is quite pervasive in numerous organizations, particularly outside of North America. South Korea is one country where systems based on seniority are still quite pervasive.[12] In Korea, as is the case in other collectivistic cultures (e.g., China), employees tend to avoid confrontation for fear of losing face.[13] Thus, supervisors may be reluctant to give employees unsatisfactory performance ratings or ratings based on individual performance because this would single out individuals. Instead, systems that measure and reward team performance may be more appropriate in collectivistic cultures. It is possible, however, to move away from more traditional systems based mainly on seniority by establishing clear links between performance management and other functions such as training, as described in Chapter 1. When such links have been clearly established, employees are more likely to see the benefits of the performance management system and believe that the system is fair.

Contingent pay (CP), also called *pay for performance*, means that individuals are rewarded based on how well they perform on the job. Thus, employees receive increases in pay based wholly or partly on job performance. These increases can either be added to an employee's base salary or can be a one-time bonus. Originally, CP plans were used only for top management. Gradually, the use of CP plans extended to sales jobs. Currently, CP plans are more pervasive. For example, in 2001, about 70 percent of workers in the United States have been employed by organizations implementing some type of variable play plan, and many of these organizations tie variable pay (e.g., bonus, commission, cash award, lump sum) directly to performance. A remarkable change in the past two decades has been a steady decrease in base pay and an increase in different types of variable pay.[14] In other words, rewards are increasingly influenced by performance, which highlights the increased importance of having a good performance management system that yields useful and fair information for making decisions about the allocation of rewards.

Let us return to the example of salaries for university professors. When a CP plan is implemented, pay raises are determined in part or wholly based on performance. For example, two assistant professors may be hired at the same time at the same base salary level (e.g., US$80,000). If one of them outperforms the other, year after year for several years, then eventually, the better performing assistant professor may make $117,000, which may be a higher level of pay than many associate professors make. This is because every year, this assistant professor receives a substantial salary increase, part of which may be added to the base salary, based on her outstanding teaching and research performance. On the other hand, the other assistant professor may still be making the same amount, or close to the same amount, he was making when he was first hired. Under a traditional pay plan, an assistant professor would not receive a higher salary than most associate professors. Under such a plan, the assistant professor would have to be promoted to associate professor before she could receive a salary of US$110,000, which is outside the traditional range for assistant professors.

10-3 REASONS FOR INTRODUCING CONTINGENT PAY PLANS

Why are organizations embracing CP plans? One reason is given by results of a survey of Fortune 500 companies, which showed that performance management systems are more effective when results are directly tied to the reward system.[15] When the performance management system has a direct relationship with the reward system, performance measurement and performance improvement are taken more seriously. In other words, CP plans force organizations to define effective performance more clearly and to determine what factors are likely to lead to effective performance. When a CP plan is implemented, organizations need to make clear what is expected of employees, what specific behaviors or results will be rewarded, and how employees can achieve these behaviors or results. This, in and of itself, serves as an important communication tool because supervisors and employees are better able to understand what really matters.

Also, high-achieving performers are attracted to organizations that reward high-level performance, and high-level performers are typically in favor of CP plans.[16] This tendency is called the *sorting effect*: star performers are likely to be attracted to and remain with organizations that have implemented CP plans.[17] An organization's ability to retain its star performers is obviously crucial if it wants to win the talent war and have a people-based competitive advantage.[18] For example, a study conducted at a glass installation company found that productivity improved by 44 percent when the compensation system was changed from salaries to individual incentives.[19] A closer look at the data indicated that about 50 percent of the productivity improvement was due to the current employees being more productive, whereas the other 50 percent improvement was due to less productive employees quitting and the organization's ability to attract and recruit more productive workers. In short, CP plans can serve as a good tool to recruit and retain star performers as a result of the sorting effect, which in turn, can lead to greater productivity.

Hicks Waldron, former CEO of cosmetics giant Avon, in an eloquent statement, explained why CP plans are so popular: "It took me 30 years to figure out that people don't do what you ask them to do; they do what you pay them to do." How about organizations that are struggling financially? Can they still implement CP plans? Can they afford to give performance-based rewards to their employees? The answer is Yes to both questions. Making sure that top performers are rewarded appropriately can help keep them motivated and prevent them from leaving the organization in difficult times. It is these top performers who are the organization's hope for recovery in the future. In fact, giving rewards to poor performers means that these rewards are taken away from high-level performers.[20]

Overall, CP plans enhance employee motivation to accomplish goals that match organizational needs.[21] More specifically, CP plans have the potential to help change people's behaviors and improve performance. For example, assume an organization is trying hard to improve customer satisfaction. Some units in this organization decide to implement a CP plan that awards cash to employees who improve their customer satisfaction ratings. By contrast, other units continue with a traditional pay plan, in which there is no clear tie between performance levels and rewards. Who do you think will perform better—employees under the CP plan or those under the traditional plan? Well, if all other things are equal, it is likely that employees under the CP plan will improve the service they offer to customers.[22] In fact, a review of several studies concluded that using individual pay incentives increased productivity by an average of 30 percent.[23] Similarly, another study, which was based on 21 fast food franchises, showed a 30 percent increase in average profits and a 19 percent decrease in the drive-through times as a result of the implementation of a CP plan.[24] These figures, of course, are averages, and productivity and profits do not necessarily improve by 30 percent in every case. Recall our discussion in Chapter 4 regarding the determinants of performance. An employee's performance is determined by the joint effects of abilities and other traits, knowledge and skills, and context. CP plans address just one aspect of the "knowledge and skills" category: malleable or "state" (versus trait) motivation. In other words, CP plans can influence whether employees are likely to choose to expend effort (e.g., "I will go to work today") and their level of effort (e.g., "I will put in my best effort at work" versus "I will not try very hard"). But the fact that employees are trying hard to provide good customer service does not mean that they will necessarily succeed. They still need abilities and other traits, as well as a context conducive to high performance (e.g., sufficient resources do the job well). If they do not know how to please customers, then they won't be able to satisfy them, no matter how hard they try.

CP plans can help improve the motivation of employees when each of the following conditions is present[25]:

1. Employees see a clear link between their efforts and the resulting performance (expectancy).
2. Employees see a clear link between their performance level and the rewards received (instrumentality).
3. Employees value the rewards available (valence).

There is a multiplicative relationship among these three determinants of motivation so that:

$$\text{Motivation} = \text{Expectancy} \times \text{Instrumentality} \times \text{Valence}$$

If the expectancy, instrumentality, or valence conditions are not met, the CP plan is not likely to improve performance. For example, consider the situation in which the instrumentality condition is not present. Employees may value the rewards available and may want to get them (valence). They may also see that if they exert sufficient effort, they will be able to achieve the desired performance level (expectancy). They believe, however, that the rewards received are not necessarily related to their performance level (i.e., no instrumentality). In this situation, employees are not likely to choose to exert effort because this will not get them the desired rewards.

Let us be clear: CP plans and pay, in general, should not be regarded as the Holy Grail of employee performance. First, pay can affect only the state motivation aspect of performance. Pay may not solve the problem if poor performance results from a lack of knowledge as opposed to lack of motivation. Thus, we should be aware that pay is not necessarily the perfect solution and that giving people more money will not automatically solve performance problems. Even when an excellent CP plan is in place, the best possible result is that there will be an increase in state motivation—but not necessarily in abilities and other traits (including trait motivation). Recall our discussion in Chapter 4 regarding state versus trait motivation. Trait motivation is considered a fairly stable personality trait called "achievement motivation," and it is a facet of conscientiousness.

10-4 POSSIBLE PROBLEMS ASSOCIATED WITH CONTINGENT PAY PLANS

In spite of the overall positive impact of CP plans, we should be aware that not all CP plans work as intended. In fact, several recent corporate scandals are directly related to the implementation of CP plans. Consider the case of Wells Fargo, where retail bank employees had specific rewards associated with specific performance targets, such as selling eight banking products per household. Wells Fargo's retail banking unit is critical because it has about 40 million customers. What did this type of CP plan unwittingly motivate Wells Fargo employees to do? Many employees secretly opened phony bank and credit accounts without customers' knowledge![26] Specifically, bank employees opened over 2.1 million deposit accounts that may not have been authorized. From the employees' perspective, the CP plan was quite straightforward. To receive rewards associated with the CP plan, employees knew what to do exactly: They moved funds from customers' existing accounts into newly created ones, such as credit card accounts (often without their knowledge). Then, customers were charged for insufficient funds or overdraft fees due to lack of funds in their original accounts, which resulted in monetary rewards for employees. About 14,000 of those accounts incurred over US$400,000 in fees, including annual fees, interest charges, and overdraft protection fees. What was the result for Wells Fargo? It faced the largest penalty since the Consumer Financial Protection Bureau was founded in 2011. The bank agreed to pay US$185 million in fines, along with US$5 million to refund customers. The company's latest estimate of the total cost of litigation losses is about US$2 billion. Also, Wells Fargo had perennially been ranked as one of *Fortune*'s most admired companies and it had been ranked #25 in 2016. But, not surprisingly, it did not even make the list in 2017. Also, Harris Poll's 2017 survey of corporate reputation showed that it plunged to the 99th place among the "most visible companies," above only Takata, the company whose defective airbags have been linked to 11 deaths. The scope of the Wells Fargo scandal is truly shocking, but it demonstrates the motivational power of CP plans—even to motivate people to do things clearly not in the interest of customers, the organization, or themselves. In fact, 5,300 Wells Fargo employees have been fired due to this scandal. But the blame should not be put entirely on employees because the performance management system played a critical role. At Wells Fargo, branch managers were told that they "would end up working for McDonald's" if they missed sales quotas.[27]

In general, why is it that CP plans may not succeed and may, in cases such as Wells Fargo, produce results that are so opposite to what they intend to do? Consider the following reasons[28]:

- *A poor performance management system is in place.* What happens when a CP plan is paired with a poorly designed, poorly implemented performance management system, one that includes biased ratings and the measurement of unrelated performance dimensions? This situation may lead some employees to challenge the CP plan legally. Also, rewarding behaviors and results that are not job-related is likely to cause good performers to leave the organization. Finally, those who stay are not likely to be motivated to perform well.

- *There is the folly of rewarding A while hoping for B.*[29] What happens when the system rewards results and behaviors that are not those that will help the organization succeed, such as in the example of Wells Fargo? Employees are likely to engage in counterproductive behaviors when this is what will earn them the desired rewards. One example is the hope that executives will focus on long-term growth and environmental responsibility when, in fact, they are rewarded based on quarterly earnings. Given this situation, what are these executives likely to do? Will they think in the long term, or quarter by quarter? A second example is an organization that would like its employees to be more entrepreneurial and innovative, but it does not reward employees who think creatively. What are employees likely to do? Will they be innovative and risk not getting rewards, or will they continue to do things the old way? A third example is an organization that would like employees to focus on teamwork and a one-for-all spirit, but it rewards employees based on individual results. This happens in many professional sports teams. What are professional athletes likely to do? Will they pass the ball, or will they try to score themselves as often as possible to improve their own individual statistics?

- *Rewards are not considered significant.* What happens when a CP plan includes pay increases, and other rewards, that are so small that they do not differentiate between outstanding and poor performers? For example, what happens when the top performers receive a 5 percent pay increase and an average performer receives a 3 percent or 4 percent pay increase? In this context, rewards are not viewed as performance-based rewards, and they do not make an impact. The message sent to employees is that performance is not something worth being rewarded. For rewards to be meaningful, they need to be significant in the eyes of the employees. Usually, an increase of approximately 12 to 15 percent of one's salary is regarded as a meaningful reward and would motivate people to do things they would not do otherwise.

- *Managers are not accountable.* What happens when managers are not accountable regarding how they handle the performance and the performance evaluation of their employees? They are likely to inflate ratings so that employees receive what the manager thinks are appropriate rewards. Similarly, employees may set goals that are easily attainable so that performance ratings will lead to the highest possible level of reward. In other words, when managers are not held accountable, rewards may become the driver for the performance evaluation, instead of the performance evaluation being the driver for the rewards.

- *There exists extrinsic motivation at the expense of intrinsic motivation.*[30] What happens when there is so much, almost exclusive, emphasis on rewards? Employees who have jobs that require a great deal of absorption and personal investment may start to lose interest in their jobs, which in turn, can decrease motivation. In some cases, the extrinsic value of doing one's job (i.e., rewards) can supersede the intrinsic value (i.e., doing the work because it is interesting and challenging). Sole emphasis on rewards can lead to ignoring the fact that employee motivation can be achieved not only by providing rewards, but also by creating a more challenging, more interesting work environment in which employees have control over what they do and how they do it. Both intrinsic and extrinsic motivation influence performance.

- *Rewards for executives are disproportionately large, compared to rewards for everyone else.* In many organizations, executive rewards are disproportionately large, compared to the rewards received by everyone else in the organization. In 1980, the average U.S. CEO made 42 times the average worker's salary; this multiple was 107 in 1990; and it increased to 525 in the year 2000.[31] Moreover, between 1970 and 2008, the average compensation for CEOs increased from US$850,000 to US$10.5 million, which represents a 1,135 percent increase that is more than twice the 568 percent increase in average wages calculated using the National Average Wage Index.[32] Such a large difference, particularly when the performance of the organization is not stellar, can lead to serious morale problems. CEOs should be compensated according to their performance, and an important indicator of CEO performance is overall firm performance (e.g., stock price in the case of publicly traded organizations).[33]

Table 10-2 summarizes typical reasons for the failure of CP plans. Consider two examples of situations in which CP plans failed because of one or more of the reasons listed in this table. First, consider what happened at Green Giant, which is part of the General Mills global food conglomerate, which includes such brands as Betty Crocker, Wheaties, and Bisquick. Green Giant implemented a bonus plan that rewarded employees for removing insects from vegetables. What was the result regarding performance? Initially, managers were pleased because employees were finding and removing a substantially higher number of insects. The initial enthusiasm disappeared, however, when managers found out that employees were bringing insects from home, putting them into vegetables, and removing them to get the bonus! A second example comes from the automotive division of Sears, a leading retailer of apparel, home, and automotive products and services, with annual revenues of more than US$40 billion. Sears Auto Center's CP plan rewarded employees on the basis of parts and services sold to customers who brought cars in for repair. In California, a disproportionate number of Sears auto centers were making repairs. The California Consumer Affairs Commission conducted an 18-month investigation, during which it sent some of its members to the auto centers posing as customers. What did they find? Sears employees were "finding" a lot of problems and making a lot of unnecessary repairs. Half of Sears' 72 auto-service centers in California were routinely overcharging customers for repairs, and Sears mechanics billed the undercover agents for work that was never done on 34 of 38 undercover operations.[34]

Let us go back to the Wells Fargo Scandal described earlier. Since 2017, Wells Fargo implemented a new CP plan that "eliminates sales goals, measures performance based on customer experience and adds more oversight and risk."[35] Other banks that offer brokerage services are making a similar decision. For example, Merrill Lynch, which has US$2 trillion in assets and has been acquired by Bank of America, announced that it will abandon the industry's traditional CP model based on charging clients for each transaction, and instead, would charge a fee based on a percentage of a portfolio's assets.[36] From what you learned in this chapter, and considering the failure factors listed in Table 10-2, what is the appropriateness of this new way of approaching contingent pay at these brokerage firms?

TABLE 10-2

Reasons Why Contingent Pay Plans Fail

A poor performance management system is in place.
There is the folly of rewarding A while hoping for B.
Rewards are not considered significant
Managers are not accountable.
There exists an extrinsic motivation at the expense of intrinsic motivation.
Rewards for executives are disproportionately large, compared to rewards for everyone else.

10-5 SELECTING A CONTINGENT PAY PLAN

Assuming an organization wishes to implement a CP plan, what should the plan look like? Based on the discussion of different forms of compensation earlier in this chapter, what considerations should be taken into account in choosing, for example, among offering employees group incentives, profit sharing, or individual sales commissions? What is the appropriate mix of incentives at the organization, team, and individual levels?

A critical issue to consider is that of organizational culture. An organization's culture is defined by its unwritten rules and procedures. For example, is the organization fundamentally built around individual performance, or is teamwork the norm? Is the organization one in which high-level performers are regarded as role models who should be emulated, or are they viewed as a threat to upper management? Are we happy with the current culture, or do we wish to change it? CP plans are powerful tools that help solidify the current culture, and they can also be used to create a new type of culture. There should be a careful consideration of the culture of the organization before a specific type of CP plan is selected.

Consider the types of systems that can be implemented in cultures that we can label traditional versus involvement cultures. Traditional cultures are characterized by top-down decision making, vertical communication, and clearly defined jobs. What type of plan should be implemented in organizations with this type of culture? An effective choice would be a plan that rewards specific and observable measures of performance, where that performance is clearly defined and directly linked to pay. Examples of such CP systems are the following:

- *Individual incentives:* (1). *Piece rate.* Employees are paid based on the number of units produced or repaired. This system is usually implemented in manufacturing environments. In service organizations, this could involve the number of calls made or the number of clients, or potential clients, contacted. This system is usually implemented in call centers. (2) *Sales commissions.* Employees are paid based on a percentage of sales. This system is usually implemented in car dealerships.
- *Group incentives.* Employees are paid based on extra group production based on result-oriented measures (e.g., sales volume for the group). This system is implemented frequently in the retail industry.

An involvement culture is different from a traditional culture. Organizations with involvement cultures are characterized by shared decision making, lateral communications, and loosely defined roles. Examples of systems that work well in organizations with involvement cultures are the following:

- *Individual incentives: Skill-based pay.* Employees are paid based on whether they acquire new knowledge and skills that are beneficial to the organization. This type of system is usually implemented in knowledge-based organizations such as software development companies. A Compensation Programs and Practices survey conducted by WorldatWork showed that about 70 percent of private sector firms used skill acquisition as a yardstick for employees' base pay increase.
- *Group, unit, and organizational incentives: Profit sharing.* Employees are paid based on the performance of a group (e.g., team, unit, or entire organization) and on whether the group has exceeded a specific financial goal. This type of system is implemented in many large law firms.

In addition to the organization's culture, an important consideration in selecting a CP plan is the organization's strategic direction. Strategy is not only a key element in designing the performance management system, it is also a key element in designing a CP plan. Table 10-3 includes a selected list of strategic objectives and CP plans that are most conducive to achieving each objective.

Based on Table 10-3, if employee development is a key strategic priority, rewards should emphasize new skills acquired. If customer service is a priority,

Strategic Business Objective	CP Plan
Employee development	Skill-based pay
Customer service	Competency-based pay
	Gain sharing
Productivity: Individual	Piece rate
	Sales commissions
Productivity: Group	Gain sharing
	Group incentives
Teamwork	Team sales commissions
	Gain sharing
	Competency-based pay
Overall profit	Executive pay
	Profit or stock sharing

TABLE 10-3
Plans Recommended for Various Strategic Business Objectives

then rewards should emphasize competencies related to customer service and gain sharing. Gain sharing links individual and group pay to an organization's overall profitability: the greater the organization's overall profit, the greater the rewards given to individuals and teams in the organization. In this case, gain sharing would be based on whether customer service ratings improve during the review period. If the major goal of the CP plan is to increase the organization's overall profit, choices include executive pay and profit or stock sharing. Executive pay includes cash bonuses that are given in response to successful organizational performance. Usually, however, executive pay includes company stock to ensure that executives' activities are consistent with the shareholders' interests and to encourage executives to tend to the long-term performance of the organization. This is also called profit sharing, although profit sharing is usually short-term and focused on organizational goals while stock sharing and executive pay are more long-term.

Stock sharing has caught media attention in recent years. In this type of plan, stock is distributed as a reward, or executives are given the option to buy company stock at a reduced rate per share. Unfortunately, this type of CP plan has led many executives to attempt to maximize their personal wealth by inflating the price of their personal stock, often through fraudulent means, and selling their stock before the public is aware of the situation. This happened at Enron and WorldCom, where thousands of investors lost their retirement funds. This is an example of the folly of rewarding A while hoping for B, described in the previous section.

Consider the example of Google, described in Box 10-2. Some argue that Google can only do this because they have so much money. But this is not accurate. Google, like all other companies, has a limited amount of money to be allocated to employee compensation—albeit the total pool may be larger than other companies. As noted by Google's former VP for People Operations Laszlo Bock, "The only way to stay within budget is to give smaller rewards to the poorer performers, or even

Box 10-2

Company Spotlight: Big Pay for Big Performance at Google

At Google, contingent pay has, for many years, been a part of the company's approach to compensation. Google has long ago realized that the best people are increasingly discoverable and mobile. Just a few years ago, performance information on individual employees was very difficult to come by. But social media websites such as LinkedIn make this information quite obvious. Many companies use systems labeled "internal equity," which involves restricting pay so that top performers are not paid much more than average performers. In contrast, Google's approach emphasizes "fairness" over "equality." Specifically, Google's definition of fairness is not to pay everyone the same, but that pay is commensurate with contribution. Thus, given our discussion of star performers and the non-normal distribution of performance in Chapter 5, at Google, there are situations where "two people doing the same work can have a hundred times difference in their impact and in their rewards. For example, there have been situations where one person received a stock award of US$10,000 and another working in the same area received US$1,000,000 . . . the range for rewards at almost any level can easily vary by 300 to 500 percent . . . we have many cases where people at more junior levels make far more than average performers at more senior levels. It's a natural result of having greater impact, and a compensation system that recognizes that impact."[37]

the average ones. That won't feel good initially, but take comfort in knowing that you've now given your best people a reason to stay with you, and everyone else a reason to aim higher." Google's policy works because it is based on empirical evidence. A review of 146 studies involving more than 30,000 people showed that when rewards are distributed equitably (i.e., based on performance), performance improves compared to a distribution based on the principle of equality (i.e., similar salaries for people in similar positions).[38]

10-6 PUTTING PAY IN CONTEXT

Is pay the main motivating factor driving people? For most of the twentieth century, the belief was that people go to work to collect a paycheck and money was the main, or even the sole, motivator. In the twenty-first century, however, we now recognize that pay is not everything. For most people, money is an important motivator because it supplies many things from fulfilling basic needs (e.g., food and shelter) to providing higher education for one's children and a means for retirement.[39] People seek more than just a paycheck, however, when they go to work. People want to work in an environment of trust and respect, where they can have fun and develop relationships with others, and do meaningful and interesting work. People also want to balance their work and home lives, and this is particularly salient for Millennials. For example, a survey by the online job-searching site CareerBuilder.com showed that 42 percent of working fathers say they are willing to see a reduction in their pay if this means having a better balance between work and home.[40] In addition, people look for learning and developmental opportunities that may lead to better career opportunities in the future. Thus, managers must realize that pay is just one element in a set of management practices that can either improve or reduce employee commitment and satisfaction, teamwork, and performance. It is true that people do work for money and an organization's pay level and pay structure affect productivity.[41] On the other hand, people also seek meaning in their lives and need leisure time to pursue nonwork interests. Organizations that believe that money is all that motivates people are basically bribing their employees and will eventually pay a high price in a lack of employee loyalty and commitment.[42]

When we think about rewards, then, we should think in broader terms than just pay. We can define a reward as something that increases the frequency of an employee action. In other words, when an employee is given a reward, we expect to increase the chances that specific results and behaviors will be repeated or that the employee will engage in new behaviors and produce better results. If pay raises are not producing this result, because they are not meaningful or are given arbitrarily, then they should not be viewed as rewards. What can organizations do to ensure that actions intended to be rewards are actually regarded as rewards? What can we do to make rewards work? Consider the following recommendations[43]:

- *Define and measure performance first, then allocate rewards.* Before rewards are allocated, there must be a good performance management system in place that (1) defines performance and performance expectations, and (2) measures performance well. In many cases, organizations believe that they have a rewards problem when in fact, the problem is with the definition and measurement of performance.

- *Use only rewards that are available.* If the organization does not have financial rewards available, then employee expectations should be adjusted accordingly, and the focus should be on intangible rewards. It makes no sense to discuss pay raises as an important component of a CP plan if existing budget constraints mean meager raises.

- *Make sure that all employees are eligible.* In many organizations, top executives receive benefits such as profit sharing, stock options, executive life and liability insurance, invitations to meetings in attractive locations, and permission to fly first-class. Are these benefits truly rewards as we have defined them here? Do these incentives enhance motivation? In general, they seem to do so because they motivate lower-level employees to strive to become executives; however, what would happen if these types of incentives were extended to the lower ranks of an organization? What if nonexecutive members of organizations were also eligible for such rewards based on their performance level? By making more employees eligible for the potential reward, there is a greater chance that more employees will strive to become top performers.

- *Make rewards visible.* Rewards should be visible to those who receive them. Rewards should also be visible to others, together with information about what needs to happen for an employee to receive the reward in the future. This recommendation applies to both tangible (most financial) and intangible (mostly nonfinancial) rewards. Nonfinancial rewards, in particular, are usually more effective if they are made public. An exception to the visibility recommendation is that some individuals may prefer a nonvisible reward allocation to avoid being singled out for attention or to prevent the disruption of group harmony.

- *Make rewards contingent.* Rewards should be tied to performance directly and exclusively. Imagine that an outsider is asked to guess the salary levels for various employees in an organization. Assume that she can ask the following questions: *What* do people do (e.g., administrative assistant, mailroom clerk, VP for HR)? *How long* have they done it? *How well* have they done it? If information based on the "How well?" question is not the most useful in guessing what salaries are, then the organization is not making rewards contingent on performance. Unfortunately, this is the case in many organizations in which what people do and how long they have done it are far better predictors of their salaries than how well they perform. As an illustration, in many countries around the world, including Eritrea in Africa, all employees receive one month's extra salary as a noncontingent reward each year.[44] In other words, employees receive pay for a "13th month." When rewards are not contingent on performance, organizations can alienate their best workers, precisely those who make the greatest contributions and can easily find employment elsewhere.
- *Make rewards timely.* Rewards should be given soon after the occurrence of the result or behavior being rewarded. Experimental psychologists know that if a mouse in a cage pulls a lever and a lump of sugar appears 10 months later (on the mouse's anniversary date), no learning will take place. This is why many organizations implement on-the-spot rewards.[45] For example, at Lake Federal Bank in Hamburg, Indiana, the president has an annual budget that he can use to give relatively small, spur-of-the-moment gifts to employees who are performing well. These spot bonuses do not have to be cash awards. They can be theater tickets, a prime parking space, or anything else that targets an employee's specific needs. How does he know what type of reward to give? The answer is simple: he gets to know his employees and watches what they do and how they spend their time when they have a chance to choose. If this does not work, he can simply ask them.
- *Make rewards reversible.* Increasing an employee's base pay creates an annuity for the employee's tenure with the organization. If mistakes are made in the allocation of increases in base salary (especially upward), they are usually irreversible and can be very costly over time. This is why variable pay, which is not added to an employee's base salary, has become an attractive option for many organizations. Variable pay is consistent with the recommendations that rewards be contingent and reversible. If high-quality performance occurs again, then the employee receives the additional compensation again. If high-quality performance does not occur, then the additional compensation is not given.

10-6-1 Turning Recognition and Other Relational Incentives into Rewards

Similar to financial incentives, praise and recognition for a job well done, without a monetary value attached, can be a powerful reward *if* such praise and recognition enhance the chances that specific results and behaviors will be repeated. Similarly, praise and recognition should not be considered rewards if they do not motivate employees to perform well in the future. Unfortunately, many organizations underestimate the impact of nonfinancial (i.e., intangible, relational) rewards, including the following:

- Formal commendations and awards
- Favorable mention in company publications
- Private, informal recognition for jobs well done
- Public recognition, including praise, certificate of accomplishment, and letters of appreciation
- Status indicators, such as a new and enhanced job title, larger work area, improved office decoration (e.g., prints, flowers), promotion, ability to supervise more people, and newer or more equipment
- Time, such as taking a longer break, leaving work earlier, and getting time off with or without pay
- A more challenging work environment, responsibility, and freedom
- Sabbaticals (i.e., paid time off work to devote to job-related growth and development activities, such as learning new skills or traveling abroad)

Because so many organizations underestimate the value and impact of nonfinancial rewards, they use the phrase "rewards *and* recognition" to mean that rewards are financial and meaningful, whereas recognition is nonfinancial and not as meaningful. As noted above, we must put pay in context and understand that pay is important, but people go to work for other reasons as well. One advantage of nonfinancial rewards is that they are typically allocated following the recommendations provided here for making rewards work in general. That is, nonfinancial rewards are usually available (there is an unlimited supply of recognition); all employees are usually eligible; and nonfinancial rewards are visible and contingent, usually timely, and certainly reversible. But do they work? Fortunately, the answer is yes. For example, think about the following professions and what they have in common: teachers, soldiers, sailors, police officers, nurses, and volunteer workers in not-for-profit organizations. They all involve nonfinancial rewards, including challenge, responsibility, and interesting and meaningful work.[46] The financial rewards for doing these jobs are not very high or nonexistent. In spite of this, people in these professions tend to be highly motivated to do their jobs well.

To understand the power of nonfinancial rewards more concretely, consider the example of the SAS Institute, the world's leader in business analytics software. This company is legendary for having one of the lowest turnover rates in the software industry. Does SAS pay higher salaries than its competitors? Not really. What do SAS employees say about their organization? They say that they do not leave for other, perhaps more lucrative, jobs because SAS offers opportunities to work with the most up-to-date equipment, jobs have variety, other employees are congenial and smart, and the organization cares about its employees and appreciates their work.[47] In fact, a 2017 survey of tens of thousands of Millennials conducted by Great Place to Work placed SAS as #2 on the list of best workplaces. Millennials at SAS say that there is a "sense of community" and that "management fully believe Millennials are the future of the company."[48]

In sum, the concept of a reward is broader than just pay. Of course, money allows people to do great many things, and people do incredible things to get

TABLE 10-4
Recommendations for Making Rewards Work

Define and measure performance first, and then allocate rewards.
Use only rewards that are available.
Make sure all employees are eligible.
Make rewards visible.
Make rewards contingent.
Make rewards timely.
Make rewards reversible.
Use recognition and other nonfinancial rewards.

Box 10-3

Company Spotlight: Financial and Nonfinancial Rewards at Graniterock

Graniterock utilizes a number of strategies to recognize and reward performance. Graniterock provides materials to the construction industry, including products such as asphalt, concrete, and building materials. The U.S.-based company employs 750 people and its core purpose is to "provide a place where inspired People can do their best work—building great projects, producing quality materials, and developing enduring customer relationships." The company utilizes both financial and nonfinancial incentives. Employees earn bonus pay of as much as US$1,000 for specific performance achievements that require an effort that go "above and beyond" normal job expectations. Several nonfinancial incentives are also utilized, such as sending a letter from the president along with cash rewards. The company holds regular events called "recognition days," where employees give presentations before the CEO, executive management, and coworkers about improvements they have made on the job. This gives employees the chance to receive credit in a highly visible manner, directly from others in the company. As part of an emphasis on improvement, employees continually seek out better ways of handling processes, and about one-third of all company processes are changed each year as a result. The company publishes stories about special efforts in a weekly newsletter. Supervisors also utilize rewards on a day-to-day and less formal basis, such as providing lunch to a group of employees who are putting forth a strong effort on a large job pouring concrete. In summary, Graniterock utilizes both financial and nonfinancial rewards to motivate employees and to reinforce a culture that values constant improvement and innovation in the workplace.[49]

more and more of it. For rewards to be effective, however, they must motivate employees to become, or continue to be, excellent performers. Pay can do this if it is allocated based on the recommendations listed in Table 10-4. We should not forget that people go to work for reasons other than money. If an organization is trying to solve performance problems by focusing on money only, one result is expected for sure: the organization will spend a lot of money. It is not always clear that anything will change unless rewards are given, taking into account the recommendations listed in Table 10-4.

Consider the case of Graniterock, described in Box 10-3. This particular company uses both financial and nonfinancial rewards. Consider this company in the context of recommendations in Table 10-4. Also, think about your current job or the last job you had. How were rewards allocated? Which of the eight recommendations listed in Table 10-4 were followed in the process of allocating rewards? Based on this, how effective were the rewards that were given? Did they help improve employee motivation and performance?

10-7 PERFORMANCE MANAGEMENT AND THE LAW[50]

Although we have not discussed legal issues explicitly, several chapters have touched upon how to design and implement performance management systems to be fair and acceptable. Usually, performance management systems that are fair and acceptable to employees are also legally sound. A basic principle that guides the design of a fair system is that procedures are standardized and that the same procedures are used with all employees. In other words, when the rules and procedures are known by everyone and they are applied in the same way to everyone, the system is likely to be regarded as a fair one. This is also the basic principle that underlies the implementation of performance management systems that are legally sound.

Legislation and court cases in the United States, Canada, the United Kingdom, and many other countries around the world indicate that discriminatory effects of a performance management system can be minimized by applying this "golden rule": *treat everyone in exactly the same way, regardless of sex, ethnicity, and other demographic characteristics that are unrelated to job performance.* This golden rule also applies to international employers—multinational organizations that implement their performance management systems across countries around the world.

Given its increasing global importance and economic power, it is interesting to consider how recent legislation is affecting performance management and reward systems in firms in China. The Chinese government has recognized that performance management systems can contribute to firm productivity and also to the competitiveness of China in the global arena. Thus, the Chinese government is accelerating economic reforms related to performance management, such as giving employers more rights to terminate employees. These changes have led to what can be considered very innovative performance management practices in many Chinese companies. For example, software developers Ufida, Shanda, and Natease are adopting practices that are quite consistent with those used by U.S. firms. Ufida uses performance information to determine as much as 25 percent of annual salaries, and Shanda has a company-wide performance management system with clearly specified standards: employees are evaluated twice a year, there is a multisource feedback system, and bonuses are awarded based on performance ratings.[51]

In spite of an increased global awareness regarding legal issues regarding performance management, the golden rule is not applied as often as it should be. As a consequence, there has been a 100 percent increase in the number of employment discrimination cases filed in the United States from 1995 to 2005, and many of these cases have involved issues around the design and implementation of the performance management system.[52] In 2016, the United States Equal Employment Opportunity Commission received 91,503 charges claiming discrimination based on race, age, national origin, religion, color, retaliation, disability, equal pay, and GINA (discrimination against employees based on genetic information).[53] For an organization to minimize legal exposure regarding performance management, it is important to follow the specific principles described next.

10-8 SOME LEGAL PRINCIPLES AFFECTING PERFORMANCE MANAGEMENT

There are six important concepts that often come into play in the case of litigation related to the implementation of a performance management system: employment at will, negligence, defamation, misrepresentation, adverse impact, and illegal discrimination.

- *Employment at will.* In employment at will, the employer or employee can end the employment relationship at any time. This type of employment relationship gives employers considerable latitude in determining whether, when, and how to measure and reward performance. Thus, an employer could potentially end the employment relationship without documenting any performance problems. There are two exceptions regarding an organization's ability to terminate an employee under these circumstances. First, there may be an implied contract derived from conversations with others in the organization or from information found in the company's documentation (e.g., employee handbook) indicating that employees would be terminated for just cause only. Second, decisions about terminating an employee should consider a potential violation of public policy. A case decided by the United States District Court for the District of Minnesota illustrates that employment-at-will does not mean that employers can terminate employees without proper cause.[54] Charles Freiberg filed a suit against Sprint/Nextel for wrongfully termination based on incorrect performance evaluations by his supervisor although the company had an employment-at-will provision in its "Employment Guide and Code of Conduct." In the case of Mr. Freiberg, his supervisor cautioned him that his performance was inadequate, but the supervisor used a different method of measuring performance than the one used company-wide. Specifically, some of Mr. Freiberg's peers had received similar ratings from the supervisor, but were not cautioned for low performance. Also, the supervisor scheduled Charles' weekly check-in performance review meetings during regularly scheduled training meetings, which prevented Mr. Freiberg from receiving developmental feedback regarding his performance. What did Mr. Freiberg do? He reported his supervisor's actions to the company's ethics hotline. But although he completed a corrective action plan, he was subsequently fired by his supervisor. Because of its employment-at-will provision, Sprint/Nextel argued the dismissal was appropriate. But the company's request for dismissing the suit was denied because the supervisor used different measures of performance, and the court ruled in favor of Mr. Freiberg.
- *Negligence.* Many organizations outline a performance management system in their employee manual, employment contract, or other documents. When the system is described in such documents and not implemented as described, legal problems can arise. For example, there may be a description of how frequently appraisals take place, or how frequently supervisors and employees are to meet formally to discuss performance issues. If an employee receives what she believes is an unfair performance evaluation and the system has not been implemented as was

expected, she may be able to challenge the system, based on negligence on the part of the organization. Consider the 2015 case of Gwendolyn Damiano, who was a principal in the Scranton, Pennsylvania, school district.[55] She was dismissed by the school district due to "unsatisfactory performance." Ms. Damiano claimed that there was negligence in her dismissal because the decision did not properly take into account the performance standards outlined by the district. In its defense, the school district claimed that Ms. Damiano's performance was below par with regard to teacher evaluations and student discipline. For example, the district argued that she had left standardized tests in her office without locking them in a cabinet. Also, regarding teacher evaluations, the district argued that she did not observe teachers' performance for the required number of times per year. However, the court found that the performance management system did not clearly specify a method for conducting such teacher evaluations, nor the number of evaluations to be conducted. In addition, the court also noted that the district did not implement its own policies regarding student disciplinary procedures consistently. Accordingly, the court ruled that the district had been negligent in the manner in which it used its performance management system, and therefore, Ms. Damiano should be reinstated to her position of principal—with full back pay.

- *Defamation.* Defamation is the disclosure of untrue, unfavorable performance information that damages an employee's reputation. An employee can argue that the organization defamed her if the employer states false and libelous information during the course of the performance evaluation, or negligently or intentionally communicates these statements to a third party, such as a potential future employer, thus subjecting the employee to harm or loss of reputation. Note that the definition of defamation includes the disclosure of *untrue* information. Defamation can take place when an employee is evaluated based on behaviors that are irrelevant and not job-related, when an evaluator does not include information that would explain or justify poor performance, or when an evaluator revises a prior evaluation in an attempt to justify subsequent adverse action taken against the employee. Defamation does not exist when information regarding poor performance is clearly documented. As an example, consider the case of Susan Reese, who filed a suit against Barton Healthcare Systems, alleging that the company committed defamation against her by using unrelated information, such as the fact that Ms. Reese taught dancing on the weekends, as factors that were included in her performance evaluation.[56] The court decided that the appraisal forms used in the performance management process by Barton Healthcare systems (e.g., Disciplinary Notices) did rely on unrelated information. Moreover, the court found that the company used disparaging language in referring to Ms. Reese (e.g., "pole dancer").

- *Misrepresentation.* Whereas defamation is about disclosing untrue unfavorable information, misrepresentation is about disclosing untrue *favorable* performance and this information causes risk or harm to others. When a past employer provides a glowing recommendation for a former employee who was actually terminated because of poor performance, that employer is guilty of misrepresentation. As an example, consider a case decided by the Supreme Court of California.[57] Randi W., a 13-year-old female student enrolled in a middle school, accused her school vice-principal, Robert Gadams, of sexual molestation. Gadams had received glowing letters of recommendation from other school districts (i.e., his former employers), who had recommended him without reservation. For example, one letter of recommendation stated, "I wouldn't hesitate to recommend [the vice-principal] for any position!" However, the former employers knew that Gadams had performance problems that included hugging female students and making sexual overtures to them. In fact, he had been pressured to resign because of such behavior. The Supreme Court of California ruled that employers can be held liable for negligent misrepresentation or fraud when an employer fails to use reasonable care in recommending former employees without disclosing material information that has a bearing on their performance.

- *Adverse impact.* Adverse impact, also called *unintentional discrimination*, occurs when the performance management system has an unintentional impact on members of a protected class, such as sex or race.[58] Contrary to a common misconception that "class" refers to ethnic minorities or women only, adverse impact also happens when, for example, men receive consistently lower performance ratings than women. In other words, a protected class is a group of people with a common characteristic who are legally protected from discrimination on the basis of that characteristic. So, if a group of white men consistently receive lower performance scores, then there is adverse impact because these individuals share the same characteristic (male) of a class that is protected (i.e., sex). As an example where adverse impact exists against women, consider the position of firefighter, and more specifically, the performance dimension of physical strength. If members of a protected class receive consistently lower performance ratings, then the employer must be able to demonstrate that the performance dimension measured is an important part of the job. In this case, the fire department should demonstrate that physical strength is a key KSA for the job of firefighter, and based on the argument of business necessity, an appropriate measure should be included as part of the performance evaluation and every employee should be evaluated in the same fashion. As a precautionary measure, data should be gathered on an ongoing basis regarding performance scores obtained by members of various groups, broken down by the categories indicated by the law (e.g., sex, ethnicity). A periodic review of these data can help detect the presence of adverse impact, and the organization can take corrective action if necessary.[59]

- *Illegal discrimination.* Illegal discrimination, also called *disparate treatment*, means that raters assign scores differentially to various employees, based on factors that are not performance related, such as race, nationality, color, or ethnic and national origin. As a consequence of such ratings, some employees receive more training, feedback, or rewards, than others. Illegal discrimination is usually referred to as disparate treatment because employees claim they were intentionally treated differently because of their sex, race, ethnicity, national origin, age, disability status, or other status protected under the law. For example, consider the case of Michael Chapman, who filed suit against the supermarket

Safeway for illegal age discrimination.[60] Mr. Chapman had received positive performance reviews and promotions during his more than 30 years with the supermarket. Then, after a labor dispute between the union representing store employees (including managers) and Safeway, Mr. Chapman's performance evaluations were considerably lower, he was subject to previously undisclosed performance standards, and the company began selectively applying performance standards. The court determined that Safeway had engaged in illegal discrimination based on age to try and "force out" long-serving and older employees and replace them with younger staff, whom they could pay less, by arbitrarily applying performance management standards.

The majority of legal cases involving performance management systems involve a claim of disparate treatment. What can an employee do if, for example, she feels she was given unfairly low performance scores and skipped over for promotion because she is a woman? To make such a claim, an employee can present direct evidence of discrimination, such as a supervisor making sexist comments that may have influenced the performance management process. Alternatively, she needs to provide evidence regarding the following issues:

- She is a member of a protected class.
- She suffered an adverse employment decision as a result of a performance evaluation (i.e., was skipped over for promotion).
- She should not have been skipped over for promotion because her performance level deserved the promotion.
- The promotion was not given to anyone, or it was given to an employee who is not a member of the same protected class (i.e., another woman).

If an employee provides this kind of evidence, the employer must articulate a legitimate and nondiscriminatory reason for not having given the promotion to this female employee. Usually, this involves a reason that is clearly performance related. This is the point at which employers benefit from having designed and implemented a system that is used consistently with all employees (again, our "golden rule"). Such a system is legally defensible, and any decisions that resulted from the system, such as promotion decisions, are also defensible.

Here is an important caveat: We must distinguish *illegal* discrimination from *legal* discrimination. A good performance management system is able to discriminate among employees based on their level of performance, and this is legal discrimination. In fact, a system that does not do this is not very useful. But a good performance management system does not discriminate illegally. Illegal discrimination is based on variables that should not usually be related to performance, such as sex, national origin, ethnicity, and sexual orientation.

10-9 LAWS AFFECTING PERFORMANCE MANAGEMENT

In the past few decades, several countries have passed laws prohibiting discrimination based on several factors, such as race, color, religion, sex (including pregnancy, gender identity, and sexual orientation), national origin, age (40 or older), disability, or genetic information. For example, the following laws have been passed in the United States and are enforced by the United States Equal Employment Opportunity Commission:

- *Equal Pay Act of 1963.* Prohibits sex discrimination in the payment of wages.
- *Title VII of the Civil Rights Act of 1964 (as amended by the Equal Employment Opportunity Act of 1972).* Prohibits discrimination on the basis of race, color, religion, sex, or national origin.
- *Age Discrimination in Employment Act of 1967 (as amended in 1986).* Prohibits discrimination on the basis of age.
- *The Pregnancy Discrimination Act of 1978.* Makes it illegal to discriminate against a woman because of pregnancy, childbirth, or a medical condition related to pregnancy or childbirth.
- *Americans with Disabilities Act (ADA) of 1990.* Makes it illegal to discriminate against people with disabilities.
- *Sections 102 and 103 of the Civil Rights Act of 1991.* Among other things, this law amends Title VII and the ADA to permit jury trials and compensatory and punitive damage awards in intentional discrimination cases.
- *Genetic Information Nondiscrimination Act of 2008 (GINA).* Makes it illegal to discriminate against employees because of genetic information, which includes information about an individual's genetic tests and the genetic tests of an individual's family members, as well as information about any disease, disorder, or condition of an individual's family members.

Similar laws exist in numerous countries around the world, including Canada, Australia, Germany, and Spain, among many others. In fact, a study comparing laws and regulations across 22 countries found that the majority of countries have laws similar to the ones listed above for the United States.[61] For example, in Canada, there is the Canadian Human Rights Code of 1985, Section 15 of the Charter of Rights and Freedoms (1982), Federal Employment Equity Act (2004), Federal Contractors Program, and Pay equity legislation (federal and some provinces). In Australia, there is The Crimes Act (1914), Racial Discrimination Act (1975), Sex Discrimination Act (1984), Human Rights and Equal Opportunity Commission Act (1986), Disability Discrimination Act (1992), Workplace Relations Act (1996), Equal Opportunity for Women in the Workplace Act (1999), and Age Discrimination Act (2004). In Germany, there is the *Allgemeines Gleichbehandlungsgesetz*: General Equal Opportunity Law (last modified in April 2013), which covers all stages of the employment relationship, including definition of payment, performance appraisal, promotion, and dismissal. As a final example, Spain has the Spanish Constitution (1978), Law of Worker's Statute (1980 and 2005), Organic Law for Effective Equality between Women and Men (2007), and the Law of Basic Statute of Public Employee (2005).

Taken together, these laws aim at forcing organizations to implement performance management systems that are applied consistently to all employees, regardless of demographic characteristics. Although these laws are not enforced to the same degree throughout the world, their collective goal is that performance management systems focus on measuring performance by assessing job-related factors and not personal, individual characteristics that are unrelated to job performance.

When you think about it, designing a system that is legally defensible is not a difficult goal to achieve, and it is a natural consequence of following the

- Performance dimensions (including behaviors and results) and standards are clearly defined and explained to the employee, are job-related, and are within the control of the employee.

- Procedures are standardized and uniform for all employees within a job group.

- The system is formally explained and communicated to all employees.

- Employees are given timely information on performance deficiencies and opportunities to correct them.

- Employees are given a voice in the review process and are treated with courtesy and civility throughout the process.

- The performance management system includes a formal appeals process.

- Performance information is gathered from multiple, diverse, and unbiased raters.

- Supervisors and other raters are provided with formal training and information on how to manage the performance of their employees.

- The system includes thorough and consistent documentation, including specific examples of performance based on firsthand knowledge.

- The system includes procedures to detect potentially discriminatory effects or biases and abuses in the system.

TABLE 10-5
Characteristics of Legally Sound Performance Management Systems

Source: Adapted from Exhibits 2.2 and 2.3 in Malos, S. B. (1998). Current legal issues in performance appraisal. In J. W. Smither (Ed.), *Performance appraisal: State of the art in practice* (pp. 49–94). San Francisco, CA: Jossey-Bass.

best-practice recommendations offered in this book. To summarize some of the key issues that have been discussed throughout the book, Table 10-5 lists key recommendations on how to implement a legally sound performance management system. You will see that this table summarizes many of the practices about system design and implementation that we discussed throughout the book.

One question that is particularly pertinent to organizations that operate across borders is the extent to which laws from the company's headquarters apply to performance management systems in the subsidiaries. In the specific case of applying U.S. laws, there are four questions that we need to ask[62]:

1. What is the work geographic location?
2. What is the employer status (e.g., U.S.-based firm or not)?
3. What is the employee status (e.g., U.S. citizenship status)?
4. Are there international law defenses (i.e., international treaties)?

For example, we may assume that U.S. laws apply to non-U.S. firms working in the United States. But U.S. employment discrimination laws do *not* apply to jobs located inside the United States when the employer is a foreign entity exempted by a treaty. As a second example, U.S. employment discrimination laws also do *not* apply to jobs located outside the United States when the employer is a foreign entity, even though the employee is a U.S. citizen. As a third scenario, U.S. laws apply to jobs located outside the United States when the employer is a U.S. entity and the employee is a U.S. citizen, if compliance with U.S. laws would not violate foreign laws.

Two researchers from the United States reviewed 295 different U.S. circuit court decisions regarding litigation involving performance management systems.[63] The goal of their study was to understand the factors carrying the most weight in the decisions reached by the court. They investigated various features of the performance management systems that were challenged in court, including many of the characteristics listed in Table 10-5. What was their conclusion? They found that systems that emphasized the measurement of job-related performance dimensions, provided written instructions to raters, and allowed employees to review appraisal results were more likely to withstand legal challenge. Overall, these researchers concluded that the employees' perceptions of whether the system was fair and whether they were given due process were the most salient issues considered by the courts. This conclusion reinforces the recommendation offered throughout this book: it is important to allow employees to participate in the design and implementation of the system because employee participation leads to the design of systems viewed as fair. Fairness and lawfulness do not necessarily go hand in hand. But systems that are fair are less likely to be challenged on legal grounds.

SUMMARY POINTS

- A reward system is the set of mechanisms for distributing both tangible and intangible returns as part of an employment relationship. Tangible returns include cash compensation (i.e., base pay, cost-of-living and merit pay, short-term incentives, and long-term incentives) and benefits (i.e., income protection, work–life focus, tuition reimbursement, and allowances). Intangible returns, also called relational returns, include recognition and status, employment security, challenging work, and learning opportunities. Not all types of returns are directly related to performance management systems. This is the case because not all types of returns are allocated based on past performance.

- Traditional pay plans do not have a link with the performance management system. Instead, pay and other rewards are allocated based on position and seniority. By contrast, contingent pay plans, also called pay for performance plans, allocate rewards wholly or partly based on job performance. When rewards given in the context of contingent pay plans are not added to an employee's base pay, they are called variable pay.

- Contingent pay plans are increasingly popular because when they are in place, performance measurement and performance improvement are taken more seriously. Specifically, these plans force organizations to define effective performance and to determine what factors are likely to lead to effective performance. In addition, these plans can serve as a good tool to recruit and retain top performers because they are attracted to organizations that reward high-level performance.

- Contingent pay plans also enhance employee motivation to accomplish goals that match organizational needs. But, for contingent pay plans to affect motivation positively, there needs to be a clear link between employee effort and employee performance (expectancy) and between employee performance and the rewards received (instrumentality), and employees need to value the rewards available (valence).

- Contingent pay plans often fail for several reasons. First, they may be tied to a poor performance management system in which the performance dimensions measured are not relevant to organizational success. Second, the system may be rewarding behaviors and results that are counter to the needs of the organization, such as rewarding executives for short-term results as opposed to long-term growth and environmental responsibility. Third, employees may not view the rewards as valuable, for example, when the difference between the rewards received by the best and the average performers is not really meaningful. Fourth, managers may not be accountable for the system and implement it ineffectively. Fifth, the focus may be only on extrinsic rewards, such as pay and other tangible compensation, instead of also on intrinsic rewards, such as a challenging and interesting work environment in which employees have control over what they do and how they do it. Finally, rewards for executives are disproportionately large compared to the rewards for everyone else.

- There are many choices in the design of a contingent pay plan. It is important that the plan be congruent with the culture of the organization. People in organizations that have a traditional or an involvement culture are likely to feel more comfortable with different types of plans and include rewards at the individual or collective (e.g., group, unit, entire organization) level. For example, organizations with a traditional culture involving top-down decision making and clearly defined jobs are likely to find that a system including piece rate, sales commissions, and group incentives works well. On the other hand, organizations with an involvement culture, including shared decision making and loosely defined jobs, would benefit most from a system that includes profit sharing and skill-based pay. In addition to an organization's culture, the strategic business objectives may determine which type of system would work best. For example, if an organization prioritizes customer service, then competency-based pay would work well, whereas an organization prioritizing teamwork would benefit most from a plan including team sales commissions and gain sharing. In sum, decisions about how rewards are allocated and what types of rewards are given must be made based on the organization's culture and strategic business objectives.

- Pay is a critical, but not the only factor that motivates people. People want more out of a job than a paycheck. People seek an environment based on trust and respect, where they can have fun and develop relationships with others, and engage in meaningful and interesting work. Reward systems that focus on pay and other monetary rewards exclusively at the expense of nonfinancial rewards are basically bribing their employees, and eventually, will pay a high price in a lack of employee loyalty and commitment. Rewards systems must go beyond pay and consider as rewards anything that increases the chances that specific behaviors and results will be repeated, or that employees will engage in desirable behaviors and produce desirable results in the future.

- Several recommendations must be followed for rewards to work as intended. First, performance must be defined clearly and measured well before rewards are allocated. Second, if financial rewards are not available, employee expectations should be adjusted accordingly and the focus should be on nonfinancial rewards only. Third, all employees must be potentially eligible to receive the rewards. Fourth, rewards must be visible. Fifth, rewards must be contingent on performance and received only if the desired behaviors are displayed and the desired results are produced. Sixth, rewards must be timely and given soon after the result or behavior being rewarded has taken place. Seventh, rewards must be reversible so that employees do not feel a sense of entitlement and continue to be motivated by the desire to obtain the reward again in the future. Finally, rewards should be both tangible (i.e., mostly financial) and nontangible (mostly nonfinancial).

- Many organizations use nonfinancial incentives, such as formal commendations and awards, favorable mention in company publications, private and public recognition for jobs well done (including certificates of accomplishment and letters of appreciation), status indicators (e.g., a new and enhanced job title, larger work area, improved office decoration), the ability to supervise more people, newer or more equipment, time (e.g., ability to take longer breaks, leaving work earlier, and getting time off with or without pay), a more challenging work environment involving more responsibility and freedom, and sabbaticals (i.e., paid time off work to devote to job-related growth and development activities, such as learning new skills or traveling abroad to job-related activities). But for these activities to become rewards that are valued and lead to positive results (e.g., enhance performance and employee well-being), they have to be meaningful and abide by similar principles as those for tangible rewards such as being timely, relevant, reversible, and so forth.

- One or more of six legal principles are usually involved in cases of litigation regarding performance management systems. First, employment at will implies that the employer can end the relationship at any time and gives employers latitude in determining whether, when, and how to measure and reward performance. Even in employment at will relationships, however, organizations benefit from having a well-designed, well-implemented performance management system to guide decisions because other principles, such as implied contract and violation of public policy, may take precedence over employment at will. Second, employers can be accused of negligence if they do not follow the performance management practices outlined in training manuals, employee handbooks, or other company documents. Third, employers can be accused of defamation if they make false statements during the course of the performance evaluation, negligently or intentionally communicate these statements to a third party such as a potential future employer, and thus, subject employees to harm or loss of reputation. Employers can be accused of misrepresentation if they disclose untrue, favorable performance information that causes risk or harm to others. Fourth, employers can be accused of adverse impact, also called unintentional discrimination, if the performance management system has an unintentional impact on members of a protected class (i.e., groups based on race, sex, or national origin) and they receive consistently lower performance evaluations than members of other groups (e.g., women vs. men, whites vs. Latinos/as). Finally, employers can be accused of illegal discrimination, also called disparate treatment, when evaluators assign scores differentially to various employees based on factors that are not performance-related, such as race, nationality, color, or ethnic and national origin.

- In the context of performance management, an employee alleging illegal discrimination needs to show that he or she is a member of a protected class, suffered an adverse employment decision as a result of a performance evaluation, should not have suffered this adverse impact because he or she performed adequately, and any rewards he or she deserved (e.g., promotion) were not given to anyone or were not given to an employee who is not a member of the same protected class (e.g., religious minority, ethnic minority, women). On the other hand, if an organization receives a legal challenge, it needs to provide evidence that the decision made was based on a legitimate and nondiscriminatory reason that was clearly performance-related. In contrast to *illegal* discrimination, *legal* discrimination, an essential characteristic of a good performance management system, differentiates among employees based on performance-related factors.

- Several countries, such as the United States, Canada, Australia, Germany, and Spain have passed laws prohibiting discrimination based on race, sex, religion, age, and disability status. Although the enforcement of these laws is uneven across countries, these laws have as their goal that organizations implement performance management systems that are applied consistently to all employees, regardless of demographic or other personal characteristics that are not job related.

- Designing and implementing a performance management system that is legally sound is not as difficult as it may seem. Overall, the goal is to follow the "golden rule:" treat everyone in exactly the same way, regardless of sex, ethnicity, and other demographic characteristics that are unrelated to job performance. This involves creating a system following the best-practice recommendations described throughout this text. Specifically, performance dimensions (including behaviors and results) and standards should be clearly defined and explained, job related, and within the control of the employee. Procedures should be standardized, used uniformly, and communicated to all employees. Employees should be given timely information on performance deficiencies and opportunities to correct them. Employees should be given a voice in the review process and treated with courtesy and civility throughout the process. The system should include a formal appeals process, and performance information should be gathered from multiple, diverse, and unbiased raters. Supervisors should be provided with formal training and the system should include consistent and thorough documentation as well as procedures to detect potentially discriminatory effects or biases and abuses. Overall, employees' perceptions that the system is fair go a long way in terms of minimizing legal challenges.

EXERCISE 10-1   PROPOSING A CONTINGENT PAY PLAN FOR SOM ARCHITECTURAL FIRM

SOM (Sanchez, Oliver, & Meirovich) is a large commercial architectural firm that specializes in the design of small- to medium-sized structures, such as churches, private schools, and business offices. The company employs commercial architects and engineers with various levels of education, credentials, and experience. The current performance management system utilizes a traditional pay system that uses seniority for the basis of pay ranges and increases. The company currently has three ranks for architects and engineers. Each of these pay ranges determines minimum, midpoint, and maximum rates. The following outlines the three ranks:

1. Entry-level architect/engineer (base pay range: US$55,000–US$70,000)
2. Junior architect/engineer (base pay range: US$65,000–US$95,000)
3. Senior architect/engineer (base pay range: US$75,000–US$120,000)

Seniority and a percentage of the base salary determine salary increases at the end of the year, and the same percentage is used for all employees. Rewards are not based on the quality of work performed, new design innovations, productivity, or customer satisfaction. Therefore, if a junior architect/engineer reaches a base salary of US$95,000, the employee cannot realize a salary increase unless he or she is promoted to a senior architect/engineer position because the maximum salary for a junior architect/engineer is US$95,000.

You own your own total rewards consulting firm and SOM has invited you to propose the implementation of a contingent pay (CP) plan. Please prepare a 10-minute presentation to be delivered to the president of the company describing the potential benefits of your plan, how you are planning on avoiding possible problems with the CP plan, the particular features and rewards included in your plan and which business objectives will be served by each, and which specific nonfinancial rewards will be included and why. Make sure your presentation is tailored to this specific industry and firm in particular.

EXERCISE 10-2   PERFORMANCE MANAGEMENT MOCK TRIAL

This exercise involves conducting a "mock trial" involving performance management that will include applying the legal principles described in this chapter. The instructor will serve as the judge overseeing proceedings. There will be two teams of attorneys: One representing the plaintiff (employee), and another representing the company (defendant). Other students in the class will serve the role of members of the jury.

Background:

In February 2013, Chloe Smith, was hired by WeinsTech, a technology company, as its senior vice president of sales. Chloe was the only female executive in the company. A veteran with more than 10 years of experience in the technology sales industry, Chloe was recruited by the company's CEO, Aarav Gupta, and reported directly to him. In July 2018, due to family circumstances, Chloe, 45, decided to look for jobs at other companies. She asked Aarav for a letter of recommendation and he agreed.

Given her experience and skills, Chloe was very confident that she would find another job quickly. However, as the months went by, none of her leads materialized into a job offer. As Chloe understood it, the prime reason was the recommendation Aarav (her ex-boss) gave. It said that while she had performed well initially, she had seemed unwilling to support the company's values. Furthermore, the recommendation noted that although Chloe helped boost the company's sales in the first few years, she lacked the perseverance and attitude to continue to drive sales as years went by. In January 2019, Chloe sued WeinsTech for negligence, defamation, and discrimination.

Supporting Information

WeinsTech's company values are: Risk taking, proactiveness, ownership, high-impact, and results focus. The company prides itself in creating a culture where top performers are rewarded (monetary rewards and promotions), regardless of their position in the company. WeinsTech's performance review document includes 10 performance dimensions. For each dimension, both the employee and the supervisor rate performance on a three-point scale: "must improve," "meets requirements," and "exceeds requirements." The form also includes space for comments explaining the rating given. In addition, the form includes five sections to be filled out by both the employee and the supervisor: "strengths," "weaknesses," "challenges to overcome," "future goals," and "overall comments." For the first three years of her employment, Chloe received a rating of "exceeds requirements" on most of the dimensions. Her first two reviews did not have any notes in the "challenges to overcome" section. However, her last two reviews were less positive and listed a number of items in the "weaknesses" and "challenges to overcome" sections. Chloe's own comments on these last two reviews noted that declining performance can be attributed to the general slowdown in the industry, while Aarav noted that Chloe should do better.

Plaintiff's Claims

Chloe Smith claims that:

1. During the course of Chloe's employment with WeinsTech, Chloe consistently averaged "meets requirements" or "exceeds requirements."

2. To the extent that Chloe received negative comments, WeinsTech was using it as a pretext for sex discrimination. In her second performance review (2013), Chloe's review indicated that she had met or exceeded expectations across the board. Under the "Overall comments" section, however, Aarav had noted that Chloe sometimes demonstrated poor attitude. The review noted: "Chloe often seems frustrated or at least comes across that way. She sometimes seems to be too emotional. It would be great if Chloe engaged more with her employees in a more outgoing and friendly manner."

3. Chloe only received a "must improve" rating in the area of "Supporting a culture that aligns with the company's goals and values." Chloe argues

that she emphasized teamwork as the current company's culture resulted in inter-office competition, rivalry, or pitting employees against each other.

4. Chloe claims that she wanted to fire an employee who was accused of sexual harassment by another female employee, but WeinsTech decided to only give him a "strong warning" as the employee in question was a top performer. The employee in question is accused of having made inappropriate comments to another female employee during a company social event.

5. Chloe claims that she received lower performance ratings in the later years of her employment (2015–2018) because she was not a member of the "old boys' club" so typical in the high-tech industry. Chloe alleges that her performance was not evaluated in the same manner as that of her male colleagues, who often seemed to receive "brownie points" for attending parties with Aarav, which, as a married mother of two, she seldom did.

Defendant's Claim

WeinsTech contends that:

1. Under Chloe's leadership, WeinsTech's sales performance had declined in the last six quarters. Throughout her time with the company, sales improved in the first ten quarters (little over two years), stagnated, and then decreased in the last six quarters.

2. Chloe's attitude caused many of her top performers to feel estranged from her and the rest of the team. She was unable to engage with the employees in a positive manner, leading to decreased morale and a decline in sales during the latter period of her tenure.

3. The section on performance management in the company's employee handbook clearly states that adherence to company values is a key requirement and major consideration during the performance management process. As such, a failure to comply with company values is reflected in her performance evaluation.

4. Chloe's desire to fire an employee was not due to his behavior but because he had submitted a complaint about her management style to the HR department. The employee in question claims that Chloe seemed to thwart efforts to obtain the best possible results, rather than encourage high performance. The employee also submitted a complaint that Chloe developed a reputation as an aggressive person who would take offense at the slightest provocation. Finally, because this was a first offense for the employee, HR decided to warn the employee and give him a second chance.

5. The "parties" that Chloe refers to were, in fact, company-sponsored social events aimed at building morale and a sense of community within the company. Furthermore, attendance or non-attendance at these events was not a factor in making performance evaluations. All employees were invited, and had the option of attending or not attending the event.

Plaintiff's Team (Chloe's Attorneys)

Your task is to convince the jury and the judge that WeinsTech indeed violated the law and demonstrated negligence, defamation, and discrimination.

A successful and convincing argument is one that is strictly fact-based, and provides evidence to support your claims. Your ability to present evidence that Chloe was a top performer that deserved a better recommendation than the one Aarav gave will determine your success. To present strong evidence in your favor, you need to analyze the performance management process, and the performance review that Chloe received to identify where WeinsTech (a) violated laws (e.g., created a performance management system that adversely affected Chloe's recommendation), (b) acted in ways that support your claims, and (c) demonstrate that Chloe's performance deserved a better recommendation letter from Aarav.

Defendant's Team (WeinsTech's Attorneys)

Your task is to convince the jury and the judge that WeinsTech did not violate any laws. A successful and convincing argument is one that is strictly fact-based, and provides evidence to support your defense. Your ability to present evidence that Aarav gave what he believed was an honest and truthful recommendation based on a performance management that did not violate any laws will determine your success. To present strong evidence in your favor, you need to analyze the performance management process, and the performance review to demonstrate that WeinsTech (a) did not violate any laws (e.g., created a performance management system that was legal, and fair to all employees), (b) did not act in ways that support Chloe's claims, and (c) demonstrate that Aarav gave a recommendation letter that he perceived to be truthful and honest, one that Chloe deserved, rather than misrepresent the facts.

Jurors

As members of the jury, your task is to reach a final verdict on whether the defendant (WeinsTech) is guilty or not guilty. As members of the jury, you need to suspend all prior judgment regarding the case. You need to make your final determination based solely on the facts as presented by the plaintiff (Chloe) and the defendant (WeinsTech). In other words, even if you have a preconceived judgment that one party is guilty, *your final determination should be based on the evidence and arguments presented by the teams of attorneys*. It is essential to take notes on what the attorneys present. You will use these notes to form your own opinion, and possibly, also to convince other members of the jury why your verdict is correct.

Procedural Steps

1. Opening Statement:
   Select one team member from each team of attorneys (plaintiff/ defendant) to present the opening statement to the judge and jury. The plaintiff's attorney goes first, and the defendant's attorney follows. The opening statement should:

   a. Be brief (one to two minutes)

   b. State why they believe their argument is correct

   c. Outline what evidence they will present during the trial (Hint: *Make sure to mention the legal principles at stake in the case*)

2. Evidence:

Next, the plaintiff's and defendant's attorneys present evidence to build their argument. Again, the plaintiff's side goes first. Once the plaintiff's attorneys have presented all their evidence, the defendant presents their case. Each side can present no more than five pieces of evidence.

a. Evidence presented might include, for example: performance evaluations; relevant sections of the employee handbook, and so forth. (Hint: *The arguments and evidence should focus exclusively on whether it can be proved that the company has violated any of the legal principles outlined in Section 10-8 Some Legal Principles Affecting Performance Management*)

3. Judge Instructions:

The judge then instructs the jury to consider the arguments presented by both sides. Jurors are asked to consider whether either side has proved, beyond a reasonable doubt, whether the lawsuit has merit. Jurors are also asked to pay attention only to the evidence that pertains to the *legal principles* of the case, and disregard any other evidence, arguments, or claims.

4. Closing Statement:

Select one team member from each team of attorneys to present the closing statement to the judge and jury. The plaintiff's attorney goes first, and the defendant's attorney follow. The closing statement should:

a. Be brief (one to two minutes)

b. State why they believe the other side failed to prove their case

c. Request for summary judgment (plaintiff) or dismissal (defendant) (Hint: *Make sure to mention the legal principles at stake in the case*)

5. Jury Deliberation:

The legal teams, plaintiff, and defendant are then asked to stand at the front of the classroom. They may not participate or interrupt the jury deliberation.

a. Each juror is asked to line up on one side of the classroom, based on whether they believe the plaintiff or defendant was correct. Those who believe neither side was convincing are asked to stand in the middle of the classroom.

b. Each side (defendant is guilty or not guilty) has two minutes to present an argument why they are correct to the opposing and undecided jurors. Jurors then receive an additional minute to make their final decision.

c. The votes are tallied by the judge and the side with the highest count is declared the winner. If both sides receive equal votes, the case is declared a mistrial and a date is set for a new trial.

Contingency Pay Plan at Altenergy LLC

Jack, Tom, and Ed are all former employees of Accenture and have just started their own energy consulting company called Altenergy. For the past six months, Jack, Tom, and Ed have been the only consultants in the company. They have now picked up enough business that they want to add five new consultants in order to have three different consulting teams. Because Altenergy LLC has such a unique niche in the consulting market and is a recent start-up, Jack, Tom, and Ed feel that it is necessary that they hire consultants with (a) experience with dealing with alternative energy sources, (b) connections to a variety of alternative energy companies, and (c) sales experience since these new consultants will be responsible for finding and obtaining new clients. Based upon past experience with Accenture, Jack, Tom, and Ed know that it will be very difficult not only to attract consultants with this kind of experience, but also to retain them. In order to combat these concerns, Jack, Tom, and Ed feel that if they can implement a proper contingency pay plan they will be able to recruit and retain consultants with the necessary experience.

Based upon this information, and your knowledge of various contingency pay systems, how would you recommend that Altenergy LLC structure a contingency pay plan for these new consultants? Please explain why you gave the recommendation that you did and why you did not recommend the other contingency pay systems possible. As a way to get started on this case study, consider the table below (Table 10-3 from Section 10-5 Selecting a Contingent Pay Plan of the text), and imagine that you have 100 "weight" points that you can assign to different strategic business objectives. For example, if you think that Altenergy should place a pretty heavy emphasis on the strategic business objective of providing excellent customer service, then you might assign 35 weight points to competency-based pay and 15 weight points to gain sharing. Then, 35 percent of the total compensation will come from competency-based pay, and 15 percent of the total compensation will come from gain sharing for each employee.

Strategic Business Objective	CP Plan
Employee development	Skill-based pay
Customer service	Competency-based pay
	Gain sharing
Productivity: Individual	Piece rate
	Sales commissions
Productivity: Group	Gain sharing
	Group incentives
Teamwork	Team sales commissions
	Gain sharing
	Competency-based pay
Overall profit	Executive pay
	Profit or stock sharing

TABLE 10-3
Plans Recommended for Various Strategic Business Objectives

CASE STUDY 10-2

Possible Illegal Discrimination at Tractors, Inc.

Tractors, Inc., is a family-owned heavy equipment (e.g., excavators, tractors, paving equipment) company that has been in business for more than 25 years. Over the past several years, the company has experienced rapid growth, increasing from 100 employees to 500 employees. Tractors, Inc., is beginning to realize that it needs to change or enhance its current performance management system. The company still uses the performance management system it implemented more than 10 years ago.

The current performance management system consists of the following documented process:

- Performance reviews are to be conducted on a yearly basis (at the time of the employee's anniversary date with the company). One month prior to the employee's anniversary date, the supervisor/manager is to complete the standard performance appraisal form and pay increase form (if applicable), which should then be reviewed by the supervisor's manager prior to the supervisor's meeting with the employee. There are no set guidelines about how to complete the form or rate the employee's actual job performance—this is left to the reviewing supervisor's discretion.
- Once approvals have been secured, the supervisor schedules a formal meeting with the employee to discuss the appraisal.
- During the meeting, the manager reviews the ratings with the employee, including any comments that the manager may have made, discusses opportunities for improvement and development, and informs the employee about his or her change in pay (if applicable). At that time, the employee is given the opportunity to add any comments and sign the form for official submittal to the human resources department. The company's unwritten policy is that employees are not permitted to keep a copy of their performance review; however, they can go to the human resources department at any time to request

permission to review their past performance appraisals. Employee performance reviews are kept on file in the human resources department during the employee's tenure at the organization.

In recent months, the company has received several complaints from female employees regarding the performance management system. Examples include:

- The employee does not have the opportunity to provide input into her performance evaluation prior to the actual meeting.
- Managers do not complete performance reviews in a timely manner. For instance, several employees have complained that they received their review three to six months after their actual anniversary date.
- Two female employees have complained that they were passed up for promotions for reasons other than performance issues. One employee cited the example of her rating in the "attendance" category as follows: "Overall Sue's attendance is acceptable and she works the hours necessary to complete her job; however, if she were to make better arrangements for handling her children's after-school activities, she would be available to work longer hours." Sue felt that because she is a single mother, men in her department with less experience and job knowledge are promoted because they either do not have families or have stay-at-home wives to take care of their children.

Consider Tractors, Inc.'s performance management system in light of what we have discussed as an ideal system and how a company can ensure that its system is legally sound. As the new human resources manager, you have been asked to identify those areas of the current performance management system that could face a legal challenge. Please develop a one-page summary, identifying the potentially illegal aspects of the current system and your suggestions for making the current system more legally sound.

ENDNOTES

1. Rynes, S. L., Gerhart, B., & Minette, M. A. (2004). The importance of pay in employee motivation: Discrepancies between what people say and what they do. *Human Resource Management, 43*, 381–394.

2. The following discussion is based in large part on Chapter 1 from Milcovich G. T., Newman J. M., & Gerhart, B. (2013). *Compensation management* (11th ed.). New York, NY: McGraw-Hill.

3. Kelley, D. (2006, April 25). Doctors test pay-for-performance program. *The Gazette*, Colorado Springs, CO.

4. Fordham, L. (2015). 49% offer performance-related reward. *Employee Benefits*, 3.

5. *Why choose Sun?*. Retrieved January 2, 2018, from http://au.sun.com/employment/student/whysun.html

6. Milligan, S. (2016). The royal treatment. *HR Magazine, 61*(7), 30–35.

7. Bradford, L. (2016). 13 tech companies that Offer cool work perks. *Forbes*. Retrieved January 2, 2018, from https://www.forbes.com/sites/laurencebradford/2016/07/27/13-tech-companies-that-offer-insanely-cool-perks/#35c9d9a879d1

8. Ledford, G. E. (2014). The changing landscape of employee rewards: Observations and prescriptions. *Organizational Dynamics, 43*, 168–179.

9. Ng, E. S., & Parry, E. (2016). Multigenerational research in human resource management. *Research in Personnel and Human Resources Management, 34*, 1–41.

10. Shields, J. (2007). *Managing employee performance and reward*. New York, NY: Cambridge University Press.

11. Pierce, C. A., Aguinis, H., & Adams, S. K. R. (2000). Effects of a dissolved workplace romance and rater characteristics on responses to a sexual harassment accusation. *Academy of Management Journal, 43*, 869–880.

12. Chang, E., & Hahn, J. (2006). Does pay-for-performance enhance perceived distributive justice for collectivistic employees? *Personnel Review, 35*, 397–412.

13. Aguinis, H., & Roth, H. A. (2005). Teaching in China: Culture-based challenges. In I. Alon & J. R. McIntyre (Eds.), *Business and management education in China: Transition, pedagogy, and training* (pp. 141–164). Hackensack, NJ: World Scientific Publishing.

14. Ledford, G. E. (2014). The changing landscape of employee rewards: Observations and prescriptions. *Organizational Dynamics, 43*, 168–179.

15. Lawler III, E. E. (2003). Reward practices and performance management system effectiveness. *Organizational Dynamics, 32*, 396–404.

16. Trevor, C. O., Gerhart, S. L., & Boudreau, J. W. (1997). Voluntary turnover and job performance: Curvilinearity and the moderating influences of salary growth and promotions. *Journal of Applied Psychology, 82*, 44–61.

17. Rynes, S. L., Gerhart, B., & Parks, L. (2005). Personnel psychology: Performance evaluation and pay for performance. *Annual Review of Psychology, 56*, 571–600.

18. Sturman, M. C., Trevor, C. O., Boudreau, J. W., & Gerhart, B. (2003). Is it worth it to win the talent war? Evaluating the utility of performance-based pay. *Personnel Psychology, 56*, 997–1035.

19. Lazear, E. P. (1986). Salaries and piece rates. *Journal of Business, 59*, 405–431.

20. Wells, S. J. (2005). No results, no raise. *HR Magazine, 50*(5), 76–80.

21. Aguinis, H., Joo, H., & Gottfredson, R. K. (2013). What monetary rewards can and cannot do: How to show employees the money. *Business Horizons, 56*, 241–249.

22. Heneman, R. L. (2002). *Strategic reward management: Design, implementation, and evaluation*. Greenwich, CT: Information Age.

23. Locke, E. A., Feren, D. B., McCaleb, V. M., Shaw, K. N., & Denny, A. T. (1980). The relative effectiveness of four methods of motivating employee performance. In K. D. Duncan, M. M. Gruenberg, & D. Wallis (Eds.), *Changes in working life* (pp. 363–388). New York, NY: Wiley.

24. Peterson, S. J., & Luthans, F. (2006). The impact of financial and nonfinancial incentives on business-unit outcomes over time. *Journal of Applied Psychology, 91*, 156–165.

25. Vroom, V. H. (1995). *Work and motivation*. San Francisco, CA: Jossey-Bass.

26. Egan. M. (2016). 5,300 Wells Fargo employees fired over 2 million phony accounts. *CNN Money*. Retrieved January 2, 2018, from http://money.cnn.com/2016/09/08/investing/wells-fargo-created-phony-accounts-bank-fees/index.html

27. Colvin, G. (2017). Can Wells Fargo get well? *Fortune, 175*(8), 138–146.

28. Adapted from Grote, D. (1996). *The complete guide to performance appraisal* (Chap. 14). New York, NY: AMACOM.

29. Kerr, S. (1975). On the folly of rewarding A while hoping for B. *Academy of Management Journal, 18*, 769–783.

30. Cerasoli, C. P., Nicklin, J. M., & Ford, M. T. (2014). Intrinsic motivation and extrinsic incentives jointly predict performance: A 40-year meta-analysis. *Psychological Bulletin, 140*, 980–1008.

31. Gabaix, X., Landier, A., & Sauvagnat, J. (2014). CEO pay and firm size: An update after the crisis. *The Economic Journal, 124*, F40–F59.

32. Faulkender, M., Kadyrzhanova, D., Prabhala, N., & Senbet, L. (2010). Executive compensation: An overview of research on corporate practices and proposed reforms. *Journal of Applied Corporate Finance, 22*, 107–118.

33. Aguinis, H., Martin, G. P., Gomez-Mejia, L. R., O'Boyle, E. H., & Joo, H. (in press). The two sides of CEO pay injustice: A power law conceptualization of CEO over and underpayment. *Management Research, Journal of the Iberoamerican Academy of Management, 16*, 3–30. Also see: Aguinis, H., Gomez-Mejia, L. R., Martin, G. P., & Joo, H. (in press). CEO pay is indeed decoupled from CEO performance: Charting a path for the future. *Management Research, Journal of the Iberoamerican Academy of Management, 16*, 117–136.

34. "Systematic Looting:" In an undercover sting, Sears' auto-repair service gets nailed. (1992, June 22) *Time*. Retrieved January 2, 2018, from http://www.time.com/time/magazine/article/0,9171,975793,00.html

35. Glazer, E. (2017, January 7–8). Wells revamps pay after scandal. *Wall Street Journal*, B1–B2.

36. Wursthorn, M. (2017, January 7–8). Brokerages tack to the adviser model. *Wall Street Journal*, B7.

37. Bock, L. (2015). *Work rules! Insights from inside Google that will transform how you live and lead.* New York, NY: Twelve.

38. Garbers, Y., & Konradt, U. (2014). The effect of financial incentives on performance: A quantitative review of individual and team-based financial incentives. *Journal of Occupational and Organizational Psychology, 87*, 102–137.

39. Rynes, S. L., Gerhart, B., & Minette, K. A. (2004). The importance of pay in employee motivation: Discrepancies between what people say and what they do. *Human Resource Management, 43*, 381–394.

40. Singletary, M. (2004, June 20). Divorced fathers need to be more than cash machines. *The Denver Post, 1*, K13.

41. Brown, M. P., Sturman, M. C., & Simmering, M. J. (2003). Compensation policy and organizational performance: The efficiency, operational, and financial implications of pay levels and pay structure. *Academy of Management Journal, 46*, 752–762.

42. Pfeffer, J. (1998). Six dangerous myths about pay. *Harvard Business Review, 76*(3), 109–111.

43. These recommendations are adapted from Kerr, S. (1999). Organizational rewards: Practical, cost neutral alternatives that you may know, but don't practice. *Organizational Dynamics, 28*, 61–70.

44. Ghebregiorgis, F., & Karsten, L. (2006). Human resource management practices in Eritrea: Challenges and prospects. *Employee Relations, 28*, 144–163.

45. Taylor, C. (2004). On-the-spot incentives. *HR Magazine, 49*(5), 80–84.

46. Aguinis, H., & Glavas, A. (2017). On corporate social responsibility, sensemaking, and the search for meaningfulness through work. *Journal of Management.* doi:10.1177/0149206317691575

47. Pfeffer, J. (1998). Six dangerous myths about pay. *Harvard Business Review, 76*(3), 109–111.

48. Austin, C. (2017). The 10 best workplaces for Millenials. *Fortune, 176*(2), 20.

49. Henneman, T. (2005). Graniterock reinforces innovation. *Workforce Management, 84*(10), 46–48.

50. This section relies heavily on Posthuma, R. A., Roehling, M. V., & Campion, M. A. (2006). Applying US employment discrimination laws to international employers: Advice for scientists and practitioners. *Personnel Psychology, 59*, 705–739; Malos, S. B. (1998). Current legal issues in performance appraisal. In J. W. Smither (Ed.), *Performance appraisal: State of the art in practice* (pp. 49–94). San Francisco, CA: Jossey-Bass.

51. Tsang, D. (2007). Leadership, national cultural and performance management in the Chinese software industry. *International Journal of Productivity and Performance Management, 56*, 270–284.

52. Latham, G. P., Almost, J., Mann, S., & Moore, C. (2005). New developments in performance management. *Organizational Dynamics, 34*, 77–87.

53. U.S. Equal Employment Opportunity Commission. Charge statistics (charges filed with EEOC) FY 1997 through FY 2016. Retrieved January 2, 2018, from https://www.eeoc.gov/eeoc/statistics/enforcement/charges.cfm

54. Freiberg v. Nextel W. Servs. LLC, CIV. NO. 13-361(MJD/JSM), United States District Court for the District of Minnesota, 2013 U.S. Dist. LEXIS 172665, November 18, 2013, Decided, November 18, 2013, Filed, Adopted by, Motion granted by, in part, Motion denied by, in part Freiberg v. Nextel West Servs. LLC, 2013 U.S. Dist. LEXIS 172523 (D. Minn., Dec. 3, 2013)

55. Scranton Sch. Dist. v. Damiano, No. 1369 C.D. 2014, Commonwealth Court of Pennsylvania, 2015 Pa. Commw. Unpub. LEXIS 389, May 5, 2015, Argued, June 5, 2015, Decided, June 5, 2015.

56. Reese v. Barton Healthcare Sys., NO. CIV. S-08-1703 FCD GGH, United States Disctrict Court of the Eastern District of California, 606 F. Supp. 2d 1254; 2008 U.S. Dist. LEXIS 108598; 21 Am. Disabilities Cas. (BNA) 1125, December 15, 2008, Decided, Summary judgment denied by, Motion to strike denied by Reese v. Barton Healthcare Sys., 2010 U.S. Dist. LEXIS 19501 (E.D. Cal., Mar. 2, 2010)

57. *Randi W. v. Muroc Joint Unified School District*, 14 Cal. 4th 1066, 60 Cal.Rptr.2d 263 (1997).

58. Aguinis, H., & Smith, M. A. (2007). Understanding the impact of test validity and bias on selection errors and adverse impact in human resource selection. *Personnel Psychology, 60*, 165–199.

59. Outtz, J. L. (Ed.). (2014). *Adverse impact: Implications for organizational staffing and high stakes selection*. New York, NY: Taylor & Francis.

60. Chapman v. Safeway Inc., No. B218227, Court of Appeal of California, Second Appelate District, Division Six, 2010 Cal. App. Unpub. LEXIS 3824, May 24, 2010, Filed.

61. Myors, B., Lievens, F., Schollaert, E., Van Hoye, G., Cronshaw, S. F., Mladinic, A., . . . Sackett, P. R. (2008). International perspectives on the legal environment for selection. *Industrial and Organizational Psychology: Perspectives on Science and Practice, 1*, 206–246.

62. Posthuma, R. A., Roehling, M. V., & Campion, M. A. (2006). Applying US employment discrimination laws to international employers: Advice for scientists and practitioners. *Personnel Psychology, 59*, 705–739.

63. Werner, J. M., & Bolino, M. C. (1997). Explaining U.S. courts of appeals decisions involving performance appraisal: Accuracy, fairness, and validation. *Personnel Psychology, 50*, 1–24.

11

Team Performance Management

*Great things in business are never done by one person.
They're done by a team of people.*

—Steve Jobs

Learning Objectives

By the end of this chapter, you will be able to do the following:

1. Include a formal team performance management component in the performance management system.

2. Design a performance management system that is congruent with the types of existing teams, including work or service teams, project teams, and network teams.

3. Prepare a performance management system for virtual teams.

4. Set up team performance management following the following six principles: make sure teams are really teams, make the necessary investment to measure, define measurement goals clearly, use a multi-method approach to measurement, focus on process as well as outcomes, and measure long-term changes.

5. Propose a performance management system that addresses team-related challenges, such as how to assess relative individual contribution, how to balance individual and team performance, and how to identify individual and team measures of performance.

6. Roll out a team performance management system that includes the components of a state-of-the-science system: prerequisites (e.g., team charters), performance planning (i.e., results and behaviors), performance execution (e.g., how to turn a B-player team into a winning team), performance assessment (e.g., individual contributions to team performance, performance of the team as a whole), and performance review (i.e., meetings with individual team members and the team as a whole).

7. Set up team-based rewards directly linked to the performance management system.

8. Formulate an effective team-based contingent-pay reward system.

11-1 DEFINITION AND IMPORTANCE OF TEAMS

Thus far, this book has focused mainly on the performance of employees working individually and not in teams. Although the book has referred to individual and team performance, the emphasis until this point has been on individual performance. The discussion of team performance is important and deserves its own chapter, given the increasing pervasiveness of teams in organizations worldwide. It is virtually impossible to think of an organization that does not organize its functions, at least in part, based on teams.

Team-based organization design is often seen as a way to keep pace with the challenges of a fluid and unpredictable world. Several surveys conducted by Deloitte and other consulting firms show that more than 90 percent of companies believe that redesigning organizations by including a team component is of critical importance to achieve goals such as decentralizing authority, improving communication, and creating more customer-centric organizations.[1] And this is not an industry-based phenomenon. It is happening everywhere: IT, consulting, health care, and the military.[2] For example, the U.S. military's hierarchical command and control structure hindered operational success during the early stages of the Iraq war. Consequently, retired U.S. Army General Stanley McChrystal, who served as Commander of U.S. Forces in Afghanistan, decentralized authority to empowered teams. In his view, a team-based approach led to greater dynamism and flexibility and enabled officers to quickly move from their administrative positions to mission-oriented projects for a set purpose, knowing that they would once again have a home to return to within the larger organizational structure after the mission was completed. This type of organization structure, which consisted of a "network of teams" is now becoming popular in nonmilitary organizations in all industries.[3] Given the pervasiveness of teams in organizations, it is only natural that so many undergraduate and graduate level courses include team assignments.[4] The goal of these assignment is to prepare students for future jobs that, in all likelihood, will include a team component.

A team is in place when *two or more people who have different roles or responsibilities interact dynamically and interdependently and share a common and valued goal, objective, or mission.*[5] Examples of teams range from a group of top managers working together face-to-face on an ongoing basis with the goal of achieving corporate goals to a group of programmers in India and the United States writing code that eventually will be put together as one app. Teams do not have to be permanent, and team members do not have to be in the same geographical location. In fact, team members do not need to have ever met in person to be members of the same team. As long as they work together, need each other, and share common goals, they are considered to be members of the same team. Numerous organizations are structured around teams, including teams called autonomous work groups, process teams, self-managing work teams, or cross-functional teams. When autonomous work groups are in place, members have the authority to manage their own tasks and interpersonal processes as they carry out their work.

Why are teams so popular? First, businesses are facing increased pressures and global competition. Using teams is one way to address these challenges because teams can include members from different parts of the world. Second, due to rapid changes in the environment, organizations need to be prepared to adapt and change quickly. Using teams provides greater flexibility because individuals can be rotated in and out of teams, based on particular needs. Third, products and services are becoming very complex, requiring many people contributing their diverse talents to the same project. Teams are able to respond more quickly and more effectively to changes than can individuals working alone. Finally, many organizations have gone through downsizing and restructuring, which has led them to become flatter and has reduced the number of hierarchical levels. A team-based structure is more congruent to these changes compared to traditional hierarchical structures.

Although many organizations choose to structure themselves around autonomous work teams, and teams in general, team-based organizations do not necessarily outperform organizations that are not structured around teams.[6] In other words, team performance does not always fulfill its promise; therefore, it is important for performance management systems to go beyond focusing on individual performance and, following the definition of performance management, to also aim at identifying, measuring, and developing the performance of *teams* and aligning their performance with the strategic goals of the organization. Specifically, the system should target not only (1) individual performance, but also (2) an individual's contribution to the performance of his or her team(s) and (3) the performance of teams as a whole. An organization that includes any type of team would therefore benefit from managing the performance of both individuals *and* teams.[7]

Including team performance as part of a performance management system is an extension of a system that has focused on individual performance only. The general principles that we have discussed in this book thus far still apply. For example, we are still trying to design and implement the best possible system. Specifically, the system should be congruent with strategy (i.e., there is a clear link among team and organizational goals), congruent with context (i.e., the system is consistent with norms based on the culture of the organization and the region and country in which the organization is located), thorough (i.e., all teams are evaluated, they include all relevant performance dimensions), practical (i.e., they do not require excessive time and resources), meaningful (i.e., they have important consequences), specific (i.e., they provide a concrete team improvement agenda), able to identify effective and ineffective performance (i.e., they help distinguish teams at different performance levels), reliable (i.e., the measurement of performance is consistent), valid (i.e., the measures of performance are not contaminated or deficient), acceptable and fair (i.e., people participating in the system believe the processes and outcomes are just), inclusive (i.e., they include input from multiple sources on an ongoing basis), open (i.e., they are transparent and there are no secrets), correctable (i.e., they include mechanisms so that errors can be corrected), standardized (i.e., performance is evaluated consistently across teams and time), and ethical (i.e., they comply with ethical standards) (see Section 1-5 Characteristics of an Ideal Performance Management System in Chapter 1).

In addition, a system that includes team performance should also consider the possible dangers of a poorly implemented system, such as lowered self-esteem (i.e., self-esteem may be lowered if feedback is provided in an inappropriate and inaccurate way), increased turnover (i.e., if the process is not seen as fair, employees may become upset and leave the organization), damaged relationships (i.e., as a consequence of a deficient system, the relationship among the individuals involved may be damaged, often permanently), decreased motivation to perform (i.e., motivation may be lowered for many reasons, including the feeling that superior performance is not translated into meaningful tangible or intangible rewards), employee burnout and job dissatisfaction (i.e., when the performance assessment instrument is not seen as valid and the system is not perceived as fair, employees are likely to feel increased levels of job burnout and job dissatisfaction), use of misleading information (i.e., if a standardized system is not in place, there are multiple opportunities for fabricating information about an employee's performance), wasted time and money (i.e., performance management systems cost money and quite a bit of time and these resources are wasted when systems are poorly designed and implemented), emerging biases (i.e., personal values, biases, and relationships are likely to replace organizational standards), unclear ratings system (i.e., because of poor communication, teams may not know how their ratings are generated and how the ratings are translated into rewards), varying and unfair standards and ratings (i.e., both standards and individual ratings may vary across teams and also be unfair), unjustified demands on team leaders and team members' resources (i.e., poorly implemented systems do not provide the benefits provided by well-implemented systems, yet they take up people's time), and increased risk of litigation (i.e., expensive lawsuits may be filed by individuals who feel they have been appraised unfairly) (see Section 1-4 When Performance Management Breaks Down: Dangers of Poorly Implemented Systems in Chapter 1). Team performance, of course, adds a layer of complexity to any performance management system, but the fundamental principles that guide the design and implementation of the system discussed throughout this book remain the same.

It is important to note that some conditions are necessary for team performance management to lead to improved team performance; for example[8]:

- The processes involved in the performance of the team are relatively unconstrained by other requirements of the task or the organization. For example, the organization should not constrain the amount of effort and skill that the team members can invest in a particular team-based project. An example of a constraint may be individual and team goals that compete against each other.
- The team is designed well and the organizational context supports team performance. In other words, there are elements in the organization that support team performance (e.g., reward systems, training systems, resources are made available to the team, the team has an opportunity to perform).
- Performance feedback focuses on team processes that are under the control of team members. There is no point in providing feedback on aspects of performance that are beyond the control of the team.

11-2 TYPES OF TEAMS AND IMPLICATIONS FOR TEAM PERFORMANCE MANAGEMENT

Teams can be classified based on the complexity of the task (from routine to non-routine tasks) and membership configuration (from static to dynamic).[9] Routine tasks are well defined; there are few deviations in how the work is done; and

Box 11-1

Company Spotlight: Expatriate Teams at an Aerospace Company

The globalization of business has led many organizations to move from a traditional individual expatriate assignment (i.e., sending an individual manager overseas) to a team-based assignment, whereby several individuals are assigned—together—to a foreign location. Service firms rely on this strategy frequently because it is difficult to separate service "production" from service consumption. In other words, the nature of many services is such that it is needed for an entire team to work closely with a client to understand their needs. This was precisely the situation faced by a multinational aerospace firm based in North America. A total of 17 expatriate teams originating from seven different countries from around the globe were assigned to the aerospace company's location to work

together on the design of a new product. What types of challenges do such teams face in terms of implementing performance management? Moreover, what additional challenges exist when such expatriate teams include members who themselves are from different countries? The most important challenge is that each team will have to perform based on standards and expectations of their home country. However, expatriate teams must be concerned with three different stakeholders: the local client, the home company, and the other on-site teams. Thus, it is important that performance be measured in relationship to these three stakeholders groups. In other words, performance management of expatriate teams must include a multi-stakeholder perspective.[10]

outcomes are easily assessed after the task has been completed. By contrast, nonroutine tasks are not defined well; there are no clear specifications about how to do the work; and outcomes are usually very long-term and difficult to assess. Membership configuration includes how long the team is expected to work together and the stability of its membership. For example, there can be product development teams, task forces, and committees. Also, teams could be created for a specific project or to assist a particular client, as in the example included in Box 11-1 of an aerospace company that sent teams of expatriates originating from seven different places around the world to the same location to work on common project. Figure 11-1 illustrates the three main types of teams based on task complexity and membership configuration dimensions.

FIGURE 11-1

Types of Teams Based on Membership Configuration and Task Complexity Dimensions

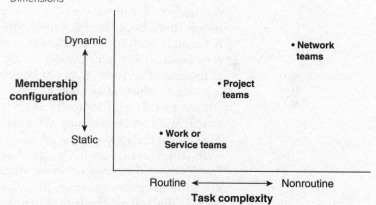

Source: Adapted from Scott, S. G., & Einstein, W. O. (2001). Strategic performance appraisal in team-based organizations: One size does not fit all. *Academy of Management Executive, 15*, 107–116, Fig. 1. p. 110.

- *Work or service teams.* These intact teams are engaged in routine tasks, including manufacturing or service tasks. An example is a group of people working at the assembly line in a car manufacturing plant, such as Toyota or Saab. The work or service team includes people who have worked together for some time and know each other well. Most members share a similar set of skills.

- *Project teams.* These teams are assembled for a specific purpose and are expected to disband as soon as their specific tasks have been completed. The tasks are outside the core production or service of the organization, and are therefore not as routine as those of work or service teams. Examples are the team that developed IBM's first personal computer and the team that developed the original Taurus/Sable at Ford. Project teams include members from different functional areas who may not know each others' specialties, and therefore, are highly dependent on one another's high level of specific knowledge and usually sophisticated skill sets.

- *Network teams.* These teams include members who are not constrained by time or space and members who are not limited by organizational boundaries. Usually, team members are geographically dispersed and stay in touch via telecommunications technology such as email, Skype and Facetime, and of course, telephone. Their work is extremely nonroutine. Network teams usually include a combination of temporary and full-time workers, customers, vendors, and even consultants. One example is the group of Russian and U.S. astronauts and scientists who communicated and worked together during months of training using telecommunications technology, from their respective countries, before some of them actually worked face-to-face in the Mir space station.

Team performance management must consider the type of team in question before performance measures are put in place. Different performance measurement methods are particularly appropriate, depending on the type of team being evaluated. Work and service teams can clearly benefit from peer ratings because members observe one another's performance on a daily basis. In addition, because team members have similar responsibilities, everyone is familiar with the competencies needed to do the job. Project teams do not stay together for long periods of time, and therefore, the measure of results at the end of a project may not benefit the team's development since the team is likely to disband as soon as the project is finished. Instead, measurements should be taken periodically as the team works on the project so that corrective action can be taken as necessary before the project has been completed. This is precisely the type of measurement system Hewlett-Packard uses with its project teams in charge of product development. Network teams are transitory and engage in unique tasks on an as-needed basis. It is difficult to measure specific outcomes. Instead, performance management of network teams emphasizes the future instead of the past, and focuses on developing individual competencies, such as the team members' capacity to innovate, adapt, be flexible, and solve problems.

11-2-1 Virtual Teams

In a 1974 television interview, science fiction author Arthur C. Clarke predicted what the world would look like at the beginning of the twenty-first century. One of his many extraordinarily accurate predictions was about a "a console . . . in a compact form . . . with a screen . . . through which he can talk" that people would have in their homes or offices: "Any businessman [sic], any executive, could live almost anywhere on Earth and still do his business through a device like this and this is a wonderful thing."[11]

Regardless of the particular type of team, the reality of today's organizations, which are immersed in a global and highly competitive environment, dictates that many teams are virtual in nature. In other words, armed with laptops and smartphones, team members can do their work from anywhere and at any time. Virtual teams have become very popular, as shown by results of a Career Builders survey involving 1,700 knowledge workers—79 percent reported working always or frequently as part of virtual teams.[12] And results of a 2014 survey of business leaders at the Global Leadership Summit indicated that about 60 percent of them predict that more than half of their entire workforce will work remotely by 2020.

From an organization's practical and resource-based standpoint, it seems that the use of virtual teams has many benefits. First, virtual teams allow organizations to save money on travel expenses. Second, from the employee point of view, personal and professional disruptions due to travel are minimized. Third, virtual teams also include individuals who live locally, but telecommute—an important benefit for employees with various personal and family needs who may want to minimize commuting time. Moreover, this type of work arrangement seems very attractive to Millennials.[13] And it also allows organizations to reduce the size of their brick-and-mortar offices, which can lead to substantial savings, particularly in highly populated urban areas with high leasing cost.

However, managing the performance of virtual teams also has its own unique challenges.[14] For example, many virtual teams, precisely because of a lack of face-to-face interactions, sometimes become "invisible" in organizations, and therefore, may lack clear performance standards and even an identity as a team. Feeling that one is member of the team and trusting other team members are important determinants of team performance, but these factors may not be present in virtual teams. Also, only about 20 percent of organizations offer training on how employees can improve their performance within the context of virtual teams. In addition, although team members may communicate using Skype and other videoconferencing technology, they usually communicate less frequently compared to members of nonvirtual teams. And, this lower degree of communication often makes it difficult for team members to understand what is going on in the group. This is a particularly challenging issue when there is a team conflict that needs to be addressed or a controversial decision, such as charting a particular course of action that needs to be made.[15]

Fortunately, as described later in this chapter, a state-of-the-science performance management system can address the aforementioned challenges posed by virtual teams.[16] For example, creating team charters (similar to job descriptions, but for teams rather than individuals) and regular check-ins help members feel that they are connected, which leads to improved cooperation and conflict management tactics. Also, team performance review meetings provide structure and increase team effectiveness. In addition, team developmental activities including intercultural skills, teamwork, and technology usage also lead to improved team performance.

The reality of work today is that virtual teams are here to stay. This highlights the importance of implementing performance management systems that include a team component. Not doing so is likely to result in more negative than positive outcomes resulting from the work of virtual teams. For an example of how MySQL attempts to reap the benefits and minimize potential pitfalls associated with virtual teams, see Box 11-2.

Box 11-2

Company Spotlight: Managing the Performance of Virtual Teams at MySQL

MySQL, (pronounced "My S-Q-L"), based in Cupertino, California, produces and develops database servers, software, and related tools. MySQL is the world's most popular open source database. The company employs more than 300 people spread across 25 countries, and 70 percent of the employees work from home. Employees in some cases have never met anyone they work with in person. This work arrangement requires a different approach to managing team performance, as compared to the traditional office where face-to-face meetings and contact are the norm. Technology enables a different approach to performance management. The company utilizes an Internet Relay Chat, which employees sign onto regularly to hold real-time meetings. Also, a software system called Worklog was developed by the company specifically to allow employees to mark off tasks when they have been accomplished. The company's method for evaluation and feedback are also adapted for virtual teams. Output and results produced are the focus of measuring productivity. There is not a strict chain of command in the MySQL work environment. Colleagues often seek out advice or ask questions of coworkers electronically, and all employees help manage individual and team performance by evaluating one another. Performance is also evaluated based on required weekly reports of accomplishments and by keeping track of employee involvement through conference calls and frequency of electronic communications, such as chat sessions and emails. In summary, MySQL has adapted to a virtual work environment by utilizing technology that enables some unique strategies to be used for managing the performance of individuals and teams.[17]

11-3 PURPOSES AND CHALLENGES OF TEAM PERFORMANCE MANAGEMENT

Regardless of the extent to which a performance management system is concerned with individual performance, team performance, or both, the goals of the system are the same as those discussed in Chapter 1: strategic, administrative, informational, developmental, organizational maintenance, and documentation. In the specific case of a system concerned with team performance, one additional goal is to make all team members accountable and to motivate them to have a stake in team performance.

Many organizations have become more team-based, but they have not changed their performance management systems to accommodate this new organizational reality, which presents a unique challenge. If the organization is based on teams, but performance is still measured and rewarded at the individual level, team performance will suffer. In fact, some of the existing individual rewards may motivate people to *not* contribute to team performance, and instead, to focus on individual performance only. In general, organizations that choose to include a team component in their performance management system must ask the following questions:

- *How do we assess relative individual contribution?* How do we know the extent to which particular individuals have contributed to team results? How much has one member contributed in relation to the other members? Are there any slackers or free riders on the team? Is everyone contributing to the same extent, or are some members covering up for the lack of contribution of others?

- *How do we balance individual and team performance?* How can we motivate team members so that they support a collective mission and collective goals? In addition, how do we motivate team members to be accountable and responsible individually? In other words, how do we achieve a good balance between measuring and rewarding individual performance in relation to team performance?

- *How do we identify individual and team measures of performance?* How can we identify measures of performance that indicate individual performance versus measures of performance that indicate team performance? Where does individual performance end and team performance begin? Finally, based on these measures, how do we allocate rewards to individuals versus teams?

A study including structured interviews with 102 working adults in Hong Kong and another 96 working adults in the Pearl River Delta (i.e., cities of Chung-shan, Quang-zhou, and Zhu-hai) suggested that, indeed, organizations are faced with these challenging questions.[18] For example, interview results indicated that about 38 percent of individuals participated in systems based on individual performance only, whereas about 34 percent participated in systems that included both individual and team components, and about 25 percent of respondents participated in systems that included a team component only. The remainder of this chapter discusses how to include a team component in a performance management system. In doing so, we consider how organizations can address each of these questions.

11-4 INCLUDING TEAM PERFORMANCE IN THE PERFORMANCE MANAGEMENT SYSTEM

Although the questions posed in the previous section may seem difficult to address, designing a performance management system that includes team performance is not difficult if we follow the following six team performance management principles[19]:

1. *Make sure your team is really a team.* As noted earlier, there are different types of teams. Before a team component is introduced in the performance management system, we need to make sure the organization has actual teams.

2. *Invest in performance management analytics.* Measuring team performance, as is the case with measuring individual performance, takes time and effort. The organization must be ready to make this investment for the measures to yield useful data.

3. *Define measurement goals clearly.* Defining how the data will be used (e.g., administrative versus developmental purposes, or both) is a decision that must be made before measures of team performance are designed. As is the case with individual-level analytics discussed throughout the book, there are different variables that must be taken into account in relationship to the measures' purpose (e.g., what will be the sources of data, how data will be collected, and so forth).

4. *Use a multimethod and multisource approach to measurement.* The measurement of team performance is complex. Thus, multiple methods and sources of data are often necessary.

5. *Focus on process as well as results.* Behavioral and process-oriented measures as well as results and outcomes are as useful for team performance management systems as for individuals. Thus, serious consideration must be given to how both types of measures will be used within the context of managing team performance. In other words, we should measure the results that teams produce, but also how they achieve those results.

6. *Measure long-term changes.* Although short-term processes and results are easier to measure, it is important to also consider long-term measures of performance. Team performance must be sampled over a variety of contexts and also over time.

Recall the basic components of the performance management process as shown in Figure 11-2. You may recall that this same figure appears in Chapter 2. Now, let us consider each of the components of the process when we design a system that includes team performance and let us incorporate the aforementioned six team performance management principles into the various steps in the process.

FIGURE 11-2
Performance Management
Process

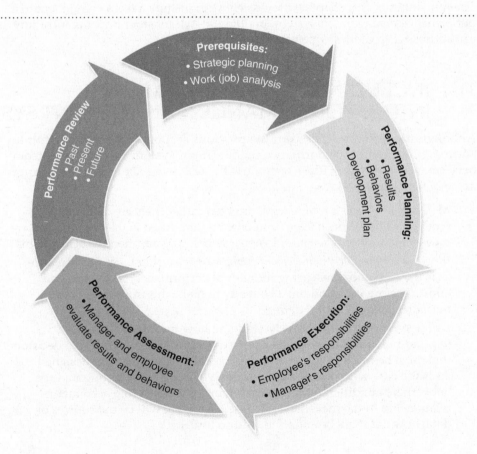

11-4-1 Prerequisites

The first component of the performance management process involves two prerequisites. First, there is a need to have good knowledge of the organization's mission. This prerequisite is present regardless of whether there is an emphasis on team performance. This knowledge, combined with knowledge regarding the mission of the team's unit, allows employees and teams to make contributions that will have a positive impact on the unit and organization as a whole. Second, there is a need to have good knowledge of the job in question. In the case of individual jobs, a job analysis is conducted to determine the key components of a particular job: what tasks need to be done, how they are to be done, and what knowledge, skills, and abilities (KSAs) are needed to do them. Similarly, if we have good information about what a *team* is supposed to do and how, then it is easier to establish criteria and measures for team success.

You will recall our discussion in Chapter 2 regarding job descriptions, which summarize the job duties, needed KSAs, and working conditions for a particular position. In the case of teams, job descriptions take the form of what is called *team charters*. Much like job descriptions, team charters can be very detailed and refer to the team activities. However, team charters differ from job descriptions in that they also include information on within-team processes such as communication.[20] Overall, team charters can include the following components[21]:

1. *Strategic alignment:* how does the team's work support and relate to unit and organizational goals?
2. *Team purpose:* what is the team's reason for being?
3. *Team objectives, goals, and priorities:* what are the team's primary objectives and how are they prioritized?
4. *Key stakeholders:* who are the key stakeholders that have an interest in the team's work?
5. *Team customers:* who are the team's internal and external customers?
6. *Team leader and sponsor:* who is the team leader and who is its champion (i.e., a team supporter who is not a member of the team and has decision-making power in the organization)?
7. *Team member roles and responsibilities:* who are the team members and what are their respective roles and responsibilities?
8. *Team member time commitments:* what time commitments are expected of all team members?
9. *Team communication plan:* what are the communication rules for the team? How often will they communicate and what forms will communication take?
10. *Team ground rules:* what rules will the team adopt about interactions among team members such as how to conduct meetings?
11. *In/out of scope elements:* what tasks and functions are in scope for the team and which ones are out of scope?
12. *Key deliverables:* what are the team's key deliverables or tangible work products?
13. *Performance analytics:* how will we measure team success?

In addition to considering the team's charter, we still need to identify KSAs that will allow individuals to make a positive contribution to the team. These include not only KSAs related directly to the task at hand, such as a programmer who needs to have knowledge of a particular programming language, which are usually included in each employee's job description. Rather, these are KSAs that are especially conducive to team performance. Examples include the following[22,23]:

- *Communication.* Giving and receiving constructive feedback, listening, and sharing information and ideas.
- *Decision making.* Helping the team make decisions.
- *Collaboration.* Dealing with conflict effectively, committing to the team and its goals, valuing the diversity and experience of other team members, and sharing accountability.
- *Team leadership.* Taking on the role of team leader, including knowing how to extract the best out of the team.
- *Self-control.* Keeping emotions under control and not displaying negative reactions even when faced with opposition or even hostility from others.

You will probably recognize these KSAs because they are closely related to our discussion in Chapter 4 of what we labeled contextual performance, prosocial behaviors, or organizational citizenship behaviors. Contextual and task performance must be considered separately because they are not necessarily parallel. An employee can be highly proficient at her task, but be an underperformer regarding contextual performance. In other words, an employee can be an excellent performer when working individually, but a substandard performer when working with others.

Consider how the prerequisites component in Figure 11-2 is implemented at the University of California at San Diego (UCSD). This university, as are many others around the world, is structured around academic and administrative units called departments. Each of these departments can be considered a team. In terms of the prerequisites component, individual departments at UCSD develop a mission statement that is clearly related to the overall university's mission. This process allows each member of the team to become knowledgeable regarding the university's overall mission. After the department's mission has been established, individual job descriptions are discussed and directly linked to both the mission of the university and the mission of the department. Job descriptions include KSAs needed for both individual and department performance.

11-4-2 Performance Planning

The second component of the performance management process involves performance planning. Performance planning includes the consideration of results and behavior. In addition, performance planning involves the creation of a developmental plan. Each of these issues needs to be considered at the team level: results expected of the team, behaviors and process expected, and developmental objectives to be achieved by the team and its members. A discussion of results must include key team accountabilities, specific objectives for each key accountability (i.e., goals to be reached), and performance standards (i.e., what constitutes acceptable and unacceptable levels of performance). A discussion of behaviors needs to include competencies (i.e., clusters of KSAs). Finally, the developmental plan includes a description of areas that need improving and goals to be achieved in each area. The plan includes not only goals for the team as a whole, but also developmental objectives for individual performance that will benefit team performance. For example, the team may have as its goal improvement of its internal decision-making processes, and some team members may have the individual goal to improve listening skills, which would help to improve the team's decision-making processes.

Consider the following recommendations regarding how to facilitate and accelerate team learning and development[24]:

1. *Facilitate adaptive learning.* As part of the team developmental plan, team members can be encouraged to try new behaviors. Also, as the team completes work or a specific project, changes that were made in processes can be reviewed in detail to understand what worked and what did not.
2. *Facilitate generative learning.* Teams can be given information regarding best practices implemented by other teams in the same organization or even in other organizations. Teams can be given time to practice new skills until they become habitual.
3. *Facilitate transformative learning.* Teams can be encouraged to experiment with new ways of working together, including a discussion of feelings of uncertainty when facing change. Members from other teams can be invited to participate in discussions about performance or even to work as team members temporarily as a way of importing innovation and change into the team.

Consider how the planning component of the performance management system is played out at Duke University in Durham, North Carolina.[25] Duke considers planning to be the foundation of its performance management system, which creates the groundwork for what the supervisor and the team expect of the individual throughout the performance year. The process at Duke consists of two parts (1) understanding the behaviors that will be expected, and (2) defining the job results expected.

11-4-3 Performance Execution

The third component of the performance management process involves performance execution. Autonomous teams are solely responsible for performance execution; however, when a team has a supervisor or team leader, then both the team and the supervisor share responsibilities for performance execution. For example, team members need to be committed to goal achievement and should take a proactive role in seeking feedback from one another as well as from the team leader (if there is one). The burden is on the team to communicate openly and regularly with its supervisor. Also, team members are responsible for being prepared for the performance review by conducting regular and realistic peer assessments and check-ins. In this way, team members have solid information regarding their performance as perceived by other team members before they meet the team leader. The team leader also has important responsibilities, including observing and documenting team performance and the relative contribution of the team members, updating the team on any changes in the goals of the organization, and providing resources and reinforcement so that team members will be motivated to succeed.

Building and leading high-performing teams requires specific KSAs. First, trust is a critical issue in most organizational contexts.[26] But trust is especially important in virtual teams.[27] Specifically, team members have to trust their leaders, but also their peers, and the entire organization, to be most effective.

Second, team leaders also need to help establish a motivating vision and goals for the team. Third, they need to be able to provide helpful feedback to the entire team, as well as individual team members (as described in the Section 11-4-5 Performance Review later in this chapter).[28]

What can team leaders do to turn "B players" into a winning team?[29] In 2004, Greece, which was an underdog by a long shot, won the European Championship, which is one of the most competitive soccer tournaments in the world. Greece was considered a peripheral team composed of mostly unknown players. But they defeated favorites France and Portugal and lifted the trophy. This victory made Greece the first team to defeat both the holder (France) and the host (Portugal) in the same tournament. The odds that Greece would win had been estimated at 1 out of 150! But, they won. Why? The following four factors were key:

- *Vision.* The first success factor needed to turn B players into an A team is vision, which is the performance planning component of the performance management system. There needs to be a good idea of future goals. In addition, there should be a clear strategy on how to achieve them. In other words, what are the specific results and behaviors expected of team members and the team as a whole?
- *Performance analytics.* The second success factor is performance analytics, which is the performance assessment component of the performance management system. Team leaders can make better decisions if they have accurate and fair performance data—from multiple sources.
- *Feedback.* The third success factor is feedback, which is an essential ingredient of the performance review component of the performance management system. In the context of team performance management, this involves information on individuals, but also information on the team as a whole.
- *Morale.* Finally, turning B players into a winning team requires the collective engagement of the entire team. When all the components of a state-of-the-science performance management system are in place, the natural result is that team members share common goals, are motivated to achieve those common goals, and have the necessary resources to do so. When team members feel that they are part of something bigger than each individual, they work together and are able to achieve great things. This means that cooperation is valued more than competition, and the team—as a whole—is on a journey of continuous improvement. To be able to enhance a team's morale, it is important for team members to also see that the leader is committed to the team, and not just using the team as a springboard of his next career move.

The German coach Otto Rehhagel, who led the 2004 Greek team, helped his team achieve such an amazing and unexpected victory following the aforementioned principles. For example, Rehhagel was able to create a common vision and improve morale—what in the sports world is known as "team spirit." As a result, the Greek team turned from a "dead-end squad nobody wanted to play for into a must-be-there-at-all-costs team." The government of Greece was so immensely pleased that he was given the "Greek of the Year" award after the team won the championship, the first time ever that a foreigner won this award.

Related to team performance execution, team performance management can be fun. For example, consider the case of Whataburger, a San Antonio, Texas-based fast food chain of about 800 restaurants that serves hamburgers, chicken, and other meals in the southern United States and in Mexico. The company holds an event called the "Whataburger games" twice per year, during which managers, cooks, dishwashers, servers, and busboys compete in events testing their team skills against others in the company. The top prize winners receive US$5,000 in cash. The company believes that many benefits result from holding the games twice per year. According to management, the goals of the games are to emphasize operating procedures, to improve skills, to enhance teamwork, to reduce turnover, and to enhance the overall performance of the restaurants. The finals of the competition are held in conjunction with the managers' convention, where winners are formally recognized before corporate owners and executives, along with peers and management in a ceremony awarding medals and cash prizes. In summary, the leadership at Whataburger has identified a friendly and fun competition as part of the overall performance management system that aims to contribute to improved team performance and the success of the company.[30]

11-4-4 Performance Assessment

The fourth component of the performance management process is performance assessment. All team members must evaluate one another's performance as well as the overall performance of the team. Peer evaluations are a key component of the assessment stage because they lead to higher levels of workload sharing, cooperation, and performance.[31] Also, team coordination and feedback improve when peers monitor the performance of all other members in the team. This, in turn, leads to the recognition of errors and to taking subsequent actions to correct these errors quickly.[32] Peer evaluations can also include team members nominating someone else as the review period's most valuable performer (MVP). In addition, the team leader evaluates the performance of each team member as well as the team as a whole. Finally, members from other teams may also evaluate the performance of the team.[33] This would apply only if members of other teams have firsthand experience with the performance of the team in question.

Involvement of each team member in the performance assessment process increases the members' ownership and commitment to the system. Self-appraisals also provide important information to be discussed during the performance review. In the absence of self-appraisals, it is often not clear to team leaders whether the team and its members have a real understanding of what is expected of them.

Similar to situations in which peers evaluate others regarding individual performance outside of team contexts, the assessment phase is prone to biases. A study including 34 teams of about four members each found that team members were more lenient in rating one another when they had previously received positive peer feedback, and they were more severe in rating one another when they had previously received negative peer feedback.[34] Thus, it seems that receiving a positive rating from a peer leads to positive feelings, and receiving a negative rating from a peer leads to negative feelings, which translate into giving peers more positive and negative ratings, respectively. Accordingly, the model for rater motivation discussed in Chapter 6, as well as the training programs conducted to minimize rating biases as discussed in Chapter 7 are just as applicable to team performance management systems.

In short, three types of performance need to be assessed (1) individual performance based on task performance, which refers to the specific activities required by one's individual job, such as a programmer's ability to write quality code; (2) individual performance based on contextual performance, which refers to specific activities that contribute to team performance, such as team members cooperating with each other; and (3) team performance as a whole. Although the saying goes, "There is no 'I' in team," this just isn't so because teams consist of individuals with their individual motivation, needs, and talents. The system should include a good combination of both "me" and "we" considerations.[35]

How can we assess the "we" side of performance? As in the case of measures of individual performance, measures of team performance should include both results and behaviors. Team performance as a whole can be measured using the following four performance dimensions[36]:

1. *Effectiveness.* This is the degree to which results satisfy team customers and stakeholders, including both internal and external customers. Results could be the same as those that are measured to evaluate individual performance. Specifically, these can include measures of quality, quantity, cost, and time.

2. *Efficiency.* This is the degree to which internal team processes support the achievement of results, team growth, and team member satisfaction. This can include measures of communication, coordination, collaboration, and decision making.

3. *Learning and growth.* This is the degree to which the team is able to learn new skills and improve performance over time. Specific measures can include innovation, documented learning, best practices, and process improvements.

4. *Team member satisfaction.* This is the degree to which team members are satisfied with their team membership. Specific measures can include team members' perceptions regarding the extent to which teamwork contributes to their growth and personal well-being.

In total, there should not be more than about 15 measures of overall team performance[37]; otherwise, team members may spend too much time collecting information and monitoring their activities and insufficient time actually working on their assigned tasks. In addition, when the team has a meeting to assess its own overall performance, it is helpful to include a person from outside the team as part of the performance discussion. This helps team members to be as objective as possible when they evaluate their performance.

11-4-5 Performance Review

The fifth component of the performance management process is the performance review, which takes place when the team members meet with the team leader or manager. In organizations that are structured around autonomous teams, there may not be a supervisor or manager. In that case, a team leader or representative would meet with a performance review board, which includes representatives from all teams.

At least two meetings are needed. First, the team leader meets with all members of the team together. The focus of this meeting is to discuss the overall team performance, including results achieved by the team as a whole. Information for this meeting comes from team members evaluating their collective performance, other teams evaluating the team in question, and the supervisor's evaluation. Second, the team leader meets each team member individually. The focus of this meeting is to discuss how the individual's behaviors contributed to team performance. Information for this meeting comes from individuals evaluating their own performance, peer ratings of the individual's performance, and the supervisor's evaluation. Recall our discussion in Chapter 9 regarding giving praise and constructive feedback (including the use of a strengths-based approach to giving feedback).

Both meetings emphasize the past, the present, and the future. The past involves a discussion of performance during the review period. The present involves any changes in compensation, depending on results obtained. The future involves a discussion about goals and developmental plans the team and its members will be expected to achieve during the next review period. Are there specific KSAs that would be important for a particular team member to develop further in the future? In the particular case of virtual teams, a study involving more than 400 professionals, recruited through social networks or human resource representatives who distributed the link in their organization, identified the following two KSAs that are related to virtual team member performance[38]:

- *Leading and deciding*: making clear decisions, taking responsibility, motivating other team members, acting on own initiative, working autonomously, and setting clear goals for other team members.
- *Analyzing and interpreting*: using communication media effectively, communicating in writing understandably and in a structured way, working in a solution-oriented way, analyzing data effectively, effectively learning to use new technologies, gaining an understanding of others' tasks, working effectively with computers and digital media, and showing analytical skills.

Now, pause for a moment to reflect on the two aforementioned competencies. Which of the behaviors involved in each of the competencies are your strengths? Which your weaknesses? Given the inevitability of virtual teams in your career progression, what steps could you take to improve your proficiency regarding each of your weaknesses?

In short, including team performance as a part of the performance management system includes the same five components as when a system included individual performance only. An important difference is that in addition to individual performance, the system includes individual performance as it affects the functioning of the team, as well as the performance of the team as a whole. As an additional example of team performance management in an organization that is global and includes thousands of teams, most of them virtual, see Box 11-3 describing Wikipedia.

Box 11-3

Company Spotlight: Managing Performance of Volunteer and Virtual Teams at Wikipedia

Wikipedia is a free online encyclopedia that any Internet user can edit. The encyclopedia is available in several languages and has over 40 million articles in 293 languages. Wikipedia is run by the Wikimedia Foundation, a nonprofit organization with only 300 employees; however, the website has approximately 31.7 million registered user accounts across all language editions, of which around 270,000 are "active" (made at least one edit every month). The organization has tackled the question of how to manage the performance of this large, virtual, and volunteer community. Several steps are taken to maintain the website in a way that allows readers to contribute and make edits. First, volunteers monitor one another. If an entry is made on a given page that a volunteer previously worked on, volunteers are immediately alerted so that they can review the new entry. Edits are also traced directly and openly to the person who made the edit. Others can correct errors, and the software allows simple reversals of any errors to be made. Any discussion between volunteers is also easily retrievable, so others can read about any disagreement or questions. Second, Wikipedia has policies that request all users to treat one another in a civil manner, and it is possible to be banished from making entries on the site. Volunteers are encouraged to work out disagreements. If that fails, an established escalation and dispute-resolution process can be enacted, which includes a process of appeals with arbitration or mediation. In summary, Wikipedia provides an example of how an organization utilizes policies and procedures to manage the performance of a virtual, volunteer workforce.[39]

11-5 REWARDING TEAM PERFORMANCE

Teams are a pervasive fact of organizational life. Because of this, organizations that implement performance management systems that include team performance must redesign their rewards system to reward team performance. As an illustration, teams of workers in the production line at Motorola's plant in Tianjin, China, receive additional compensation if they keep the percentage of errors under a prespecified threshold. In a second example, a recent study investigated the effects of implementing a pay-for-performance system at the team level with top management teams at a global information technology company.[40] The teams included seven or eight members. Each of the teams had team-level performance goals, which were specific but differed from team to team. Rewards were allocated based on organizational performance goals (25 percent), team-level goals (50 percent), and individual-level goals (25 percent). Similarly, at Apple and Google, team performance assessment and rewards are part of the formal review process.[41]

Organizations can reward team performance in ways similar to those in which they reward individual performance. For example, consider the case of Phelps Dodge Mining Company. The company implemented a team-based reward system involving more than 4,200 employees in six locations throughout North America. The company moved from being unionized to being nonunionized, and a key strategic objective was to help employees move away from working for an hourly wage to understanding how to work as a salaried workforce. To accomplish this goal, team performance was measured and rewarded accordingly. For example, a team goal in a truck maintenance shop was to shorten the time that trucks were off-line for maintenance. Goals were set through the active participation of all team members, and employees are given additional compensation, depending on whether they accomplish team-based goals.

An organization can have a variable pay system in which an individual is eligible for a bonus if her team achieves specific results. This reward would be in addition to any performance-based rewards allocated according to individual performance (either task performance or contextual performance). The amount of the bonus could also be controlled by the team: teams that are able to generate savings that result from controlling cost and improving efficiency may see some of this money come back in the form of bonuses. In this case, the rewards are called *self-funded*. In other cases, the bonus can come from a company-wide pool that varies each year, based on overall organizational performance.

Team-based rewards are effective if they are implemented following similar principles as those used for individual rewards discussed in Chapter 10 (see Table 10-4). For example, all teams should be eligible, and rewards should be visible, contingent, and reversible. Do these team-based reward systems work? In one study, team performance-based pay motivated teams to spend 22 percent more time on the task at hand, which led to improved performance.[42]

There are several success factors specifically related to team rewards. First, a study consisting of a review of 30 separate investigations concluded that team rewards are more potent in smaller, compared to larger, teams.[43] The reason? In smaller teams, it is easier for everyone to see everyone else's effort, motivation, and performance. Second, studies have provided evidence in support of team-based contingent pay plans. But similar to the case of individual rewards, in implementing team rewards, we need to be aware of the factors that make rewards fail (see Table 10-2). For example, rewards given to team members based on the extent to which they cooperate with each other are likely to enhance accuracy, but not necessarily speed.[44] If the goal of the reward is to motivate employees to work faster, giving rewards for cooperation may be yet another example of the "folly of rewarding A while hoping for B."

SUMMARY POINTS

- A team is in place when two or more people interact dynamically and interdependently and share a common and valued goal, objective, or mission. Individuals can be members of the same team even if they work in different geographic locations. Teams are pervasive in today's organizations, and it would be difficult to find an organization in which some type of work is not done by teams.
- Teams have become popular because businesses are facing increased pressures, including global competition, and the use of teams is a way to improve products and services and to increase productivity. Also, many organizations have gone through downsizing and restructuring, which has led them to become flatter and has reduced the number of hierarchical levels. Using teams provides greater flexibility for these organizations. Third, products and services are becoming very complex, requiring many

people contributing their diverse talents to the same project. In most cases, no one individual can surpass the combined talent of an entire group. Finally, rapidly changing business environments are also responsible for the popularity of teams because teams are able to respond more quickly and more effectively to changes than can individuals working alone.

- Because teams are so pervasive, it is important that the performance management system focus not only on individuals, but also on teams. Organizations should take proactive steps to make sure that teams perform well, that their performance improves on an ongoing basis, and that individuals are active and motivated contributors to their teams. So, performance management should include individual performance, an individual's contribution to the performance of his or her teams, and the performance of teams as a whole.

- There are three conditions that are necessary for team performance management to lead to improved team performance. First, the processes involved in the performance of the team are relatively unconstrained by other requirements of the task or the organization. Second, the team is designed well and the organizational context supports team performance. Third, performance feedback focuses on team processes that are under the control of team members.

- There are three basic types of teams, based on the tasks they perform (from routine to nonroutine) and based on membership configuration (from static to dynamic): work or service teams, project teams, and network teams. Also, these teams can be virtual (i.e., members do not interact in person, but through technology). A good performance management system should include measures of team performance that are congruent with the types of teams under consideration.

- A performance management system that includes a team component needs to focus on three types of performance (1) individual performance, (2) individual performance that contributes to team performance, and (3) team performance. All three are necessary for a system to be successful.

- We must consider six basic principles in including a team component in a performance management system: make sure teams are really teams, make the investment to measure, define measurement goals clearly, use a multi-method approach to measurement, focus on process as well as outcomes, and measure long-term changes.

- Including a team component in the performance management system has some unique challenges. The system needs to achieve a good balance between individual and team performance measurement and rewards. In other words, it is not sufficient to measure and reward overall team performance. There also needs to be a way to measure and reward the contribution that each individual makes to the team. In this way, individuals are held accountable for contributing to team performance.

- The performance management process of a system including a team performance component is similar to the process of a system including individual performance only. The components of the process include (1) prerequisites (e.g., knowledge of the organization's mission, team charters—serving a similar purpose as individual job descriptions),

(2) performance planning (e.g., consideration of results, behaviors, and a developmental plan), (3) performance execution (e.g., role of team leaders, how to turn a team of B-players into a winning team), (4) performance assessment (e.g., evaluations from other team members, assessing the "we" side of performance), and (5) performance review (e.g., feedback about individual contributions to team performance, feedback on the performance of the team as a whole). Although the inclusion of a team component adds a layer of complexity to the process, the fundamental principles guiding the design and implementation of the system discussed throughout this book remain the same.

- If the performance management system includes the measurement of individuals' contribution to team performance and overall team performance, it also needs to reward these types of performance. The principles guiding the allocation of rewards in systems including a team component are similar to those guiding the allocation of rewards in systems including individual performance only. For example, rewards should be visible, contingent, and reversible. Also, similar pitfalls that take place in the allocation of individual rewards should be avoided, such as the "folly of rewarding A while hoping for B."

EXERCISE 11-1   TEAM PERFORMANCE MANAGEMENT AT BOSE

Bose Corporation is an organization that specializes in audio equipment that meets virtually any audio challenge. Bose Corporation's audio technologies can be found in home stereos, stadiums, the Sistine Chapel, and even the U.S. space program. Bose Corporation was founded in 1964 and is headquartered in Framingham, Massachusetts, but has employees around the globe.

Many Bose employees work in a variety of teams. Three different types of teams within Bose are work teams, project teams, and network teams. The work teams are responsible for the production of audio equipment. These teams are long-term and are typically focused on producing a certain type of audio equipment. Project teams are responsible for the research and development of innovative audio equipment. Typically, these teams are focused on the development of a specific type of equipment (e.g., new home entertainment speakers). Network teams arise in instances where team members are spread across the globe. A specific example of a network team within Bose is a team that is designing a new audio system for Ferrari. Within this team, there are members located at Bose's headquarters, at Ferrari's plant location in Italy, and at one of Bose's production factories in Japan. The members at these various locations rarely meet face-to-face, but communicate frequently using technology.

Recently, Bose's executive team has been interested in implementing a new team-based performance management system for these different teams. They know of your expertise in performance management and they have asked you to help them. You have explained to them the five key components of a proper performance management system, but now, Bose's executive team is specifically interested in knowing how they may have to be expanded so the system can be used effectively across their three different types of teams. The reason why the executive team is interested in this is that they would like to establish a main performance management framework that can work across the different types of teams.

Please prepare a 10-minute video presentation specifying how you suggest expanding the performance management system to accommodate the three types of teams. Make sure the proposed system refers to each of the components (i.e., prerequisites, performance planning, performance execution, performance assessment, and performance review). Also, make sure your recommendations comply with as many of the ideal characteristics as possible (e.g., congruent with strategy, congruent with context, thorough, practical) and avoids potential pitfalls (e.g., lowered self-esteem, increased turnover, damaged relationships).

EXERCISE 11-2 TEAM PERFORMANCE REVIEW

The goal of this exercise is to learn how to successfully conduct a team performance review. For this exercise, the instructor will divide the class into separate teams and appoint a "leader" for each team.

Team Leaders:

You are the leader of a team at Carrefour, a large department store. The store is divided into teams based on the product types they sell, such as housewares, sporting goods, women's clothing, and cosmetics. Rewards for performance are distributed in the form of individual monetary bonuses at the end of the year, and are calculated using an average of the percent of team and individual sales targets achieved. So, for example, if the sporting goods department achieves 80 percent of its target, and an individual achieves 50 percent of his target, the bonus for this person will be calculated based on average target achievement of 65 percent. In addition, you as the team leader have the ability to increase or decrease the bonus for a particular employee by up to 10 percent, based on their performance evaluations (which include self, peer, customer, and supervisor evaluations).

You are now going to conduct the team performance review meeting. This meeting, which lasts 15–20 minutes, is used to discuss overall team performance and give the team an opportunity to ask questions. Overall, the team achieved 70 percent of its team sales target. However, some team members significantly outperformed relative to their individual sales target, while others were well below the desired level.

1. Deliver an opening statement that outlines the goal and format of the meeting.

2. Reiterate the criteria used to evaluate overall performance and determine bonuses.

3. Provide information on how the team performed relative to its overall sales target.

4. Answer team member questions about the performance management and reward allocation processes.

5. Your goal, as you provide feedback, is to address the concerns of top performers and average/low performers in a satisfactory manner, where all members accept that the review was fair.

(Hint: It is important that this meeting focuses specifically on the results achieved by the team as a whole, and not highlight (positively or negatively) any specific individual. In addition, see Section 9-4 Coaching, Development, and Performance Review Meetings in Chapter 9 for additional information on key considerations to keep in mind when conducting performance review meetings).

Team Members:

You are a member of one of the departments at Carrefour. It is now time for the annual performance review meeting and distribution of monetary bonuses. As described above, rewards for performance at Carrefour are calculated using a mix of team- and individual-performance data, and also include a percentage allocated at the manager's discretion. Some of you have done very well this year, and have generated considerably more sales revenue than your individual target. Others however have fallen well short of their target.

1. To perform this exercise, as a team, you will need to assign members who will play the role of either an excellent performer or an average performer. Decide on the performance achieved by each team member with regard to their individual sales targets. At a minimum, two employees should have exceeded their target by 10 percent to 15 percent, while another two should have achieved 50 percent to 70 percent of their goal. Overall, the team should include employees with varying levels of performance.

2. After the leader provides information on the team's performance, respond with follow-up questions and comments consistent with your level of performance. For example:

   a. High performers (those who exceeded their sales goal) might talk about how the feedback and rewards are unfair because they are being penalized for others' poor performance. For example, a top performer may say, "It is not fair that our team bonus won't be as good because of the poor performance of others on the team."

   b. Average/Low performers (those who met or fell short of their sales goal) may opine that their contributions are being overlooked. They might mention that the situation is unfair because they undertook important functions, such as training, team-building, and boundary-spanning, which are not adequately factored into the bonus reward system.

   c. Yet other employees might mention that they did not receive adequate information and coaching about their performance throughout the year. Therefore, the system is unfair because they did not have opportunities to improve their performance.

Team Performance Management at American Electric and Gas

American Electric and Gas (AE&G) is a large public utility organization offering electricity and gas. The company's performance management system reflects the focus placed on results, the need for creativity and imagination, and the need for continuous improvement. Under its current framework, the system links individual performance with that of the team or department, as well as the organization. Therefore,

- Department business plan goals link to the business plan and business priorities.
- Performance goals and measures grow out of a department's business plan.
- Employee performance measures align with those of the organization.
- The department, teams, and individuals are rewarded and recognized on the basis of these measures.

The organization's team structure consists primarily of *work or service teams*, which align with the company's departments. Because of the close relationship with local government entities, however, the organization also utilizes *network teams* that focus on government regulatory needs as they relate to public service providers and *project teams* that are assembled on an as-needed basis to work on various projects that come from the *network teams*.

The elements of the current performance management system are as follows:

Organizational performance. Organizational performance measurement is a continuous process conducted to assess the department's performance—efficiency, effectiveness, and client satisfaction—in relation to the vision and business plan. The steps in the process include:

1. *Business plan goals and strategies.* Identify the desired outcomes that the organization is seeking to achieve and outline how the goals will be realized.

2. *Human resources department plan.* Outline the key strategies the department will undertake to address identified human resources (HR) issues to meet its business plan, within the context of the vision, values, government business plan, and the HR plan.

3. *Performance measures.* Identify specific criteria that will be used to monitor progress toward the goals.

4. *Targets.* Describe specific performance levels that will be used to achieve the desired outcome.

5. *Learning supports.* Identify practices, policies, and initiatives that provide incentive and encouragement to employees to develop new skills, knowledge, and abilities.

Employee performance. Employee performance can be enhanced through a continuous and interactive process to help departments and teams achieve business goals and to help employees continually improve. The steps in the process include:

1. *Performance plans.* Link employee performance to that of the organization and identify and set measures for desired outcomes.

2. *Orientation.* Provide information for employees regarding their new job and the organization to enhance understanding and effectiveness.

3. *Learning and developmental plans.* Identify competency development required for employees to carry out the performance plan.

4. *Performance coaching.* Provide ongoing performance feedback and assistance to employees from managers, supervisors, and other key individuals.

5. *Performance assessment.* Provide a summary of feedback received throughout the

performance period, analyze what employees have achieved relative to the desired outcomes set out in their performance and learning plans, and handle the subject of performance pay increases.

AE&G's current performance recognition (pay) plan supports and reinforces the desired performance for both the organization and the employee as follows:

- *Performance pay.* This compensation for employees links pay with individual performance. It consists of a market-driven base pay and a market-driven increase system that provides the ability to address cost-of-living increases and a bonus based on achievement of department, individual, and team goals.
- *Special programs.* The company also has two recognition programs for outstanding performance: (1) Award of Excellence, which can be applied for and awarded to team leaders, and (2) Executive Excellence Recognition, which is a unique program that

recognizes teams that achieve measurable enhancements in the service they provide. Each of these programs requires an application process, and the award is determined by a committee.

Consider the performance management process (see Figure 11-2) as it is applied in implementing team-based systems. Then, please answer the following questions:

1. How is AE&G implementing each of the components of the performance management process?
2. Consider how AE&G assesses performance. Which aspects of the measurement system are appropriate and which are not, given its goal of enhancing team performance?
3. What additions or revisions should be made to each of the components of the performance management process to make the system more effective from a team performance point of view?

CASE STUDY 11-2

Team-Based Rewards for the State of Georgia

The state of Georgia's Department of Human Resources (DHR) updated its performance management system. The performance management process is used for all employees who are to receive performance evaluations. The following outlines the critical features of this system:

- *Manager training.* Prior to utilizing the system, all managers receive training in how the system works and how to implement each phase of the system.
- *Performance planning.* This is the first step of the performance management system process and is used to create the employee's performance plan. Developing a performance plan involves identifying job and

individual responsibilities and performance expectations. It is the primary responsibility of the manager to develop this plan using input from the employee that he or she may want included in the performance plan.

- *Performance coaching.* Coaching is the key supervisory activity during a performance period. It involves ongoing communication, both formal and informal, that motivates employees by letting them know where they stand in meeting expectations and carrying out responsibilities. The three steps to performance coaching are (1) observing performance; (2) providing regular performance feedback, based on information gathered through personal observation, team input, and input from the employee; and (3) documenting performance.

- *Performance evaluation.* This phase culminates with a meeting of the evaluating supervisor and the employee to rate performance and discuss appropriate salary increases and developmental planning for the employee.
- *Performance development.* Supervisors should discuss performance development with each employee. A developmental plan *must* be developed for each employee who is rated "does not meet expectations" or "needs improvement" in the area of Employment Terms and Conditions. The structured approach of the developmental plan has three objectives (1) to enhance employee strengths, (2) to decrease employee areas that need improvements, and (3) to meet organizational and team needs.
- *Salary increase.* Salary increases are awarded annually to each eligible employee. To be eligible for a performance-based salary increase, employees must:
  - Receive an overall rating for Job and Individual Responsibilities of at least "met expectations."
  - Receive an overall rating for Terms and Conditions of Employment of at least "needs improvement."
  - Salary increases for each evaluation period for employees who "met or exceeded expectations" are restricted to the following guidelines:
    - An overall rating of "met expectations" will receive a standard increase, based on the amount identified for the evaluation period.

- An overall rating of "exceeded expectations" will receive a standard increase as noted above, along with a lump sum identified for the evaluation period.
- Each year, a specified amount of money is set aside for salary increases. Because funds are limited, the salary increase amounts may be reduced if the department exceeds the allocated funds. If the salary increase amounts must be reduced, the reduction percentage will be the same for all employees.
- Unless otherwise authorized, employees at or above pay grade are not eligible for a performance-based salary increase, and employees who are near the pay grade maximum will be granted an increase to the pay grade maximum only.

The performance management and reward system, as currently in place, focuses mainly on individual performance. But given the changing nature of work that is now team-based in many different units and departments, there is a need to revise the system so that it can accommodate team-based rewards. Please answer the following questions:

1. How would you revise the system to include team-based rewards?
2. What are some of the anticipated challenges in including a team-based reward component, given the nature of the organization and its customers?
3. Given the effectiveness of contingent pay plans for teams, what are your recommendations on how to implement this type of system in this particular organization?

Source: This case is based, in part, on information available online at http://team.georgia.gov/performance/ Retrieval date: January, 2, 2018.

ENDNOTES

1. McDowell, T., Agarwal, D., Miller, D., Okamoto, T., & Page, T. (2016). *Organizational design: The rise of teams.* Deloitte University Press. Retrieved January 2, 2018, from https://dupress.deloitte.com/dup-us-en/focus/human-capital-trends/2016/organizational-models-network-of-teams.html
2. Mjelde, F. V., Smith, K., Lunde, P., & Espevik, R. (2016). Military teams—A demand for resilience. *Work, 54*(2), 283–294.

3. McChrystal, S. (2015). *Team of teams: New rules of engagement for a complex world*. New York, NY: Penguin.

4. Boni, A. A., Weingart, L. R., & Evenson, S. (2009). Innovation in an academic setting: Designing and leading a business through market-focused, interdisciplinary teams. *Academy of Management Learning and Education, 8*, 407–417.

5. Mathieu, J. E., Hollenbeck, J. R., van Knippenberg, D., & Ilgen, D. R. (2017). A century of work teams in the Journal of Applied Psychology. *Journal of Applied Psychology, 102*, 452–467.

6. D'Innocenzo, L., Mathieu, J. E., & Kukenberger, M. R. (2016). A meta-analysis of different forms of shared leadership–team performance relations. *Journal of Management, 42*, 1964–1991.

7. Aguinis, H., Gottfredson, R. K., & Joo, H. (2013). Avoiding a "me" versus "we" dilemma: Using performance management to turn teams into a source of competitive advantage. *Business Horizons, 56*, 503–512.

8. Hackman, J. R., & Wageman, R. (2005). A theory of team coaching. *Academy of Management Review, 30*, 269–287.

9. Scott, S. G., & Einstein, W. O. (2001). Strategic performance appraisal in team-based organizations: One size does not fit all. *Academy of Management Executive, 15*, 107–116.

10. O'Sullivan, A., & O'Sullivan, S. L. (2008). The performance challenges of expatriate supplier teams: A multi-firm case study. *International Journal of Human Resource Management, 19*, 999–1017.

11. One day, a computer will fit on a desk (1974). Retrieved January 2, 2018, from https://www.youtube.com/watch?v=sTdWQAKzESA

12. Pathak, M. (2015). Managing virtual teams. *Human Capital, 19*(2), 52–53.

13. Bertisen, M. (2016). Employers need to step up tech and IT to attract Millennials. *Grocer, 22*. Retrieved January 2, 2018, from https://www.thegrocer.co.uk/home/topics/technology-and-supply-chain/employers-need-to-step-up-tech-and-it-to-attract-millenials/536383.article

14. McCafferty, D. (2016). Top challenges of managing a virtual team. *CIO Insight, 1*. Retrieved January 2, 2018, from https://www.cioinsight.com/it-management/careers/slideshows/top-challenges-of-managing-a-virtual-team.html

15. Hill, N. S., & Bartol, K. M. (2016). Empowering leadership and effective collaboration in geographically dispersed teams. *Personnel Psychology, 69*, 159–198.

16. Gilson, L. L., Maynard, M. T., Jones Young, N. C., Vartiainen, M., & Hakonen, M. (2015). Virtual teams research: 10 years, 10 themes, and 10 opportunities. *Journal of Management, 41*, 1313–1337.

17. Hyatt, J. (2006). The soul of a new team. *Fortune, 135*(11), 134–143.

18. Cheng, K. H. C., & Cascio, W. F. (2009). Performance-appraisal beliefs of Chinese employees in Hong Kong and the Pearl River Delta. *International Journal of Selection and Assessment, 17*, 329–333.

19. Salas, E., Burke, C. S., & Fowlkes, J. E. (2006). Measuring team performance "in the wild": Challenges and tips. In W. Bennett, C. E. Lance, & D. J. Woehr (Eds.), *Performance measurement: Current perspectives and future challenges* (pp. 245–272). Mahwah, NJ: Lawrence Erlbaum.

20. Pilette, P. C. (2017). Team charters: Mapping clearer communication. *Nursing Management, 48*(5), 52–55.

21. Brownlee, D. (2012). Team charter. *Leadership Excellence Essentials, 29*(10), 15.

22. Reilly, R. R., & McGourty, J. (1998). Performance appraisal in team settings. In J. W. Smither (Ed.), *Performance appraisal: State of the art in practice* (pp. 245–277). San Francisco, CA: Jossey-Bass.

23. Rousseau, V., Aubé, C., & Savoie, A. (2006). Teamwork behaviors: A review and an integration of frameworks. *Small Group Research, 37*, 540–570.

24. London, M., & Sessa, V. I. (2007). How groups learn, continuously. *Human Resource Management, 46*, 651–669.

25. Duke University Health System. *Duke HR performance management process*. Retrieved January 2, 2018, from https://hr.duke.edu/managers/performance-management/duhs/about-performance

26. Connelly, B. L., Ketchen, D. J., Crook, T. R., Combs, J. G., & Aguinis, H. (2015). Competence- and integrity-based trust in interorganizational relationships: Which matters most? *Journal of Management, 44*(3), 919–945. doi:10.1177/0149206315596813

27. Ford, R. C., Piccolo, R. F., & Ford, L. R. (2017). Strategies for building effective virtual teams: Trust is key. *Business Horizons, 60*, 25–34.

28. Matthews, R., & McLees, J. (2015). Building effective projects teams and teamwork. *Journal of Information Technology & Economic Development, 6*(2), 20–30.

29. Chamorro-Premuzic, T. (2015). How to manage a team of B players. *Harvard Business Review Digital Articles,* 2–4.

30. Berta, D. (2004, June 28). Restaurant companies boost employee morale with contests, games. *Nation's Restaurant News,* 6. Retrieved January 2, 2018, from http://www.nrn.com/

31. Erez, A., Lepine, J. A., & Elms, H. (2002). Effects of rotated leadership and peer evaluation on the functioning of effectiveness of self-managed teams: A quasi-experiment. *Personnel Psychology, 55*, 929–948.

32. Marks, M. A., & Panzer, F. J. (2004). The influence of team monitoring on team processes and performance. *Human Performance, 17*, 25–41.

33. Breugst, N., Patzelt, H., Shepherd, D. A., & Aguinis, H. (2012). Relationship conflict improves team performance assessment accuracy: Evidence from a multilevel study. *Academy of Management Learning and Education, 11*, 187–206.

34. Taggar, S., & Brown, T. C. (2006). Interpersonal affect and peer rating bias in teams. *Small Group Research, 37*, 86–111.

35. Brumback, G. B. (2003). Blending "we/me" in performance management. *Team Performance Management: An International Journal, 9*, 167–173.

36. MacBryde, J., & Mendibil, K. (2003). Designing performance measurement systems for teams: Theory and practice. *Management Decision, 41*, 722–733.

37. Meyer, C. (1994). How the right measures help teams excel. *Harvard Business Review, 72*, 95–101.

38. Krumm, S., Kanthak, J., Hartmann, K., & Hertel, G. (2016). What does it take to be a virtual team player? The knowledge, skills, abilities, and other characteristics required in virtual teams. *Human Performance, 29*, 123–142.

39. Hyatt, J. (2006). The soul of a new team. *Fortune, 135*(11), 134–143.

40. van Vijfeijken, H., Kleingeld, A., van Tuijl, H., Algera, J. A., & Thierry, H. (2006). Interdependence and fit in team performance management. *Personnel Review, 35*, 98–117.

41. Gallo, A. (2013). How to reward your stellar team. *Harvard Business Review.* Retrieved January 2, 2018, from https://hbr.org/2013/08/how-to-reward-your-stellar-tea

42. Super, J. F., Li, P., Ishqaidef, G., & Guthrie, J. P. (2016). Group rewards, group composition and information sharing: A motivated information processing perspective. *Organizational Behavior and Human Decision Processes, 13*, 431–444.

43. Garbers, Y., & Konradt, U. (2014). The effect of financial incentives on performance: A quantitative review of individual and team-based financial incentives. *Journal of Occupational and Organizational Psychology, 87*, 102–137.

44. Beersma, B., Hollenbeck, J. R., Humphrey, S. E., Moon, H., Conlon, D. E., & Ilgen, D. R. (2003). Cooperation, competition, and team performance: Toward a contingency approach. *Academy of Management Journal, 46*, 572–590.

NAME AND COMPANY INDEX

SUBJECT INDEX